Jeffrey Aven

Sams **Teach Yourself**

Apache Spark™

in **24 Hours**

  800 East 96th Street, Indianapolis, Indiana, 46240 USA

Sams Teach Yourself Apache Spark™ in 24 Hours

ISBN-13: 978-0-672-33851-9

ISBN-10: 0-672-33851-3

Library of Congress Control Number: 2016946659

Printed in the United States of America

1   16

Trademarks

All terms mentioned in this book that are known to be trademarks or service marks have been appropriately capitalized. Sams Publishing cannot attest to the accuracy of this information. Use of a term in this book should not be regarded as affecting the validity of any trademark or service mark.

Warning and Disclaimer

Every effort has been made to make this book as complete and as accurate as possible, but no warranty or fitness is implied. The information provided is on an "as is" basis. The author and the publisher shall have neither liability nor responsibility to any person or entity with respect to any loss or damages arising from the information contained in this book.

Special Sales

For information about buying this title in bulk quantities, or for special sales opportunities (which may include electronic versions; custom cover designs; and content particular to your business, training goals, marketing focus, or branding interests), please contact our corporate sales department at corpsales@pearsoned.com or (800) 382-3419.

For government sales inquiries, please contact

governmentsales@pearsoned.com.

For questions about sales outside the U.S., please contact

intlcs@pearsoned.com.

Editor in Chief
Greg Wiegand

Acquisitions Editor
Trina McDonald

Development Editor
Chris Zahn

Technical Editor
Cody Koeninger

Managing Editor
Sandra Schroeder

Project Editor
Lori Lyons

Project Manager
Ellora Sengupta

Copy Editor
Linda Morris

Indexer
Cheryl Lenser

Proofreader
Sudhakaran

Editorial Assistant
Olivia Basegio

Cover Designer
Chuti Prasertsith

Compositor
codeMantra

Contents at a Glance

Table of Contents

Preface

This book assumes nothing, unlike many big data (Spark and Hadoop) books before it, which are often shrouded in complexity and assume years of prior experience. I don't assume that you are a seasoned software engineer with years of experience in Java, I don't assume that you are an experienced big data practitioner with extensive experience in Hadoop and other related open source software projects, and I don't assume that you are an experienced data scientist.

By the same token, you will not find this book patronizing or an insult to your intelligence either. The only prerequisite to this book is that you are "comfortable" with Python. Spark includes several application programming interfaces (APIs). The Python API was selected as the basis for this book as it is an intuitive, interpreted language that is widely known and easily learned by those who haven't used it.

This book could have easily been titled *Sams Teach Yourself Big Data Using Spark* because this is what I attempt to do, taking it from the beginning. I will introduce you to Hadoop, MapReduce, cloud computing, SQL, NoSQL, real-time stream processing, machine learning, and more, covering all topics in the context of how they pertain to Spark. I focus on core Spark concepts such as the Resilient Distributed Dataset (RDD), interacting with Spark using the shell, implementing common processing patterns, practical data engineering/analysis approaches using Spark, and much more.

I was first introduced to Spark in early 2013, which seems like a short time ago but is a lifetime ago in the context of the Hadoop ecosystem. Prior to this, I had been a Hadoop consultant and instructor for several years. Before writing this book, I had implemented and used Spark in several projects ranging in scale from small to medium business to enterprise implementations. Even having substantial exposure to Spark, researching and writing this book was a learning journey for myself, taking me further into areas of Spark that I had not yet appreciated. I would like to take you on this journey as well as you read this book.

Spark and Hadoop are subject areas I have dedicated myself to and that I am passionate about. The making of this book has been hard work but has truly been a labor of love. I hope this book launches your career as a big data practitioner and inspires you to do amazing things with Spark.

Why Should I Learn Spark?

Spark is one of the most prominent big data processing platforms in use today and is one of the most popular big data open source projects ever. Spark has risen from its roots in academia to Silicon Valley start-ups to proliferation within traditional businesses such as banking, retail, and telecommunications. Whether you are a data analyst, data engineer, data scientist, or data steward, learning Spark will help you to advance your career or embark on a new career in the booming area of big data.

How This Book Is Organized

This book starts by establishing some of the basic concepts behind Spark and Hadoop, which are covered in Part I, "Getting Started with Apache Spark." I also cover deployment of Spark both locally and in the cloud in Part I.

Part II, "Programming with Apache Spark," is focused on programming with Spark, which includes an introduction to functional programming with both Python and Scala as well as a detailed introduction to the Spark core API.

Part III, "Extensions to Spark," covers extensions to Spark, which include Spark SQL, Spark Streaming, machine learning, and graph processing with Spark. Other areas such as NoSQL systems (such as Cassandra and HBase) and messaging systems (such as Kafka) are covered here as well.

I wrap things up in Part IV, "Managing Spark," by discussing Spark management, administration, monitoring, and logging as well as securing Spark.

Data Used in the Exercises

Data for the Try It Yourself exercises can be downloaded from the book's Amazon Web Services (AWS) S3 bucket (if you are not familiar with AWS, don't worry—I cover this topic in the book as well). When running the exercises, you can use the data directly from the S3 bucket or you can download the data locally first (examples of both methods are shown). If you choose to download the data first, you can do so from the book's download page at http://sty-spark.s3-website-us-east-1.amazonaws.com/.

Conventions Used in This Book

Each hour begins with "What You'll Learn in This Hour," which provides a list of bullet points highlighting the topics covered in that hour. Each hour concludes with a "Summary" page summarizing the main points covered in the hour as well as "Q&A" and "Quiz" sections to help you consolidate your learning from that hour.

Key topics being introduced for the first time are typically *italicized* by convention. Most hours also include programming examples in numbered code listings. Where functions, commands, classes, or objects are referred to in text, they appear in `monospace` type.

Other asides in this book include the following:

NOTE

Content not integral to the subject matter but worth noting or being aware of.

TIP

TIP Subtitle

A hint or tip relating to the current topic that could be useful.

CAUTION

Caution Subtitle

Something related to the current topic that could lead to issues if not addressed.

▼ TRY IT YOURSELF

Exercise Title

An exercise related to the current topic including a step-by-step guide and descriptions of expected outputs.

About the Author

Jeffrey Aven is a big data consultant and instructor based in Melbourne, Australia. Jeff has an extensive background in data management and several years of experience consulting and teaching in the areas or Hadoop, HBase, Spark, and other big data ecosystem technologies. Jeff has won accolades as a big data instructor and is also an accomplished consultant who has been involved in several high-profile, enterprise-scale big data implementations across different industries in the region.

Dedication

This book is dedicated to my wife and three children. I have been burning the candle at both ends during the writing of this book and I appreciate your patience and understanding...

Acknowledgments

Special thanks to Cody Koeninger and Chris Zahn for their input and feedback as editors. Also thanks to Trina McDonald and all of the team at Pearson for keeping me in line during the writing of this book!

We Want to Hear from You

As the reader of this book, *you* are our most important critic and commentator. We value your opinion and want to know what we're doing right, what we could do better, what areas you'd like to see us publish in, and any other words of wisdom you're willing to pass our way.

We welcome your comments. You can email or write to let us know what you did or didn't like about this book—as well as what we can do to make our books better.

Please note that we cannot help you with technical problems related to the topic of this book.

When you write, please be sure to include this book's title and author as well as your name and email address. We will carefully review your comments and share them with the author and editors who worked on the book.

E-mail: feedback@samspublishing.com

Mail: Sams Publishing
ATTN: Reader Feedback
800 East 96th Street
Indianapolis, IN 46240 USA

Reader Services

Visit our website and register this book at informit.com/register for convenient access to any updates, downloads, or errata that might be available for this book.

HOUR 1
Introducing Apache Spark

What You'll Learn in This Hour:

▶ What Spark is
▶ The advantages of using Spark
▶ Ways in which Spark is being used today
▶ How to interact with Spark

At the time of this writing, Spark is currently the most active open source project under the Apache Software Foundation (ASF) framework and one of the most active open source big data projects ever.

With so much interest in Spark from the analytics, data processing, and data science communities, it's important to know exactly what Spark is, what purpose it serves, and what the advantages of using Spark are. This hour covers just that.

What Is Spark?

Apache Spark is an open source distributed data processing project that was started in 2009 by Matei Zaharia at the University of California, Berkeley RAD Lab. Spark was originally open sourced under the BSD (Berkeley Software Distribution) licensing scheme and was later open sourced under the ASF (Apache Software Foundation) framework ultimately graduating to become an ASF Top-Level Project in 2014. The Spark project has more than 400 individual contributors and committers from companies such as Facebook, Yahoo!, Intel, Netflix, Databricks, and others.

NOTE

The Apache Software Foundation (ASF) is a non-profit organization founded in 1999 to provide an open source software structure and framework for developers to contribute to projects, encouraging collaboration and community involvement and protecting volunteers from litigation. ASF is premised upon the concept of meritocracy, meaning projects are governed by merit.

Contributors are developers who contribute code or documentation to projects. They are also typically active on mailing lists and support forums and provide patches to address defects, suggestions, and criticism.

Committers are developers who are given (by merit) access to commit code to the main repository for the project. They have signed a Contributor License Agreement (CLA) and have an `apache.org` email address. Committers act as a committee to make decisions about the project.

Spark is written in Scala, which is built on top of the Java Virtual Machine (JVM) and Java runtime. This makes Spark a cross-platform application capable of running on Windows as well as Linux.

Spark and Hadoop

Spark and Hadoop, although separate projects, are closely related to each other as critical components of the big data landscape. I will discuss Hadoop in greater detail in **Hour 2, "Understanding Hadoop."** The chronologies of Hadoop and Spark are summarized in Figure 1.1.

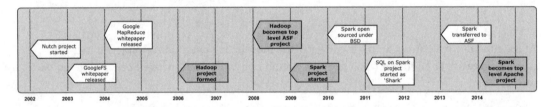

FIGURE 1.1
Chronology of Hadoop and Spark.

Spark is seen by many to be the future of data processing in Hadoop.

Spark as an Abstraction

Spark enables developers to create complex, multi-stage data processing routines, providing a high-level API and fault tolerant framework that allows programmers to focus on logic rather than infrastructure or environmental issues, such as hardware failure.

Spark Is Fast, Efficient, and Scalable

Spark was founded as an alternative to using traditional MapReduce on Hadoop, which was deemed to be unsuited for interactive queries or real time, low latency applications. A major disadvantage of Hadoop's MapReduce implementation was its persistence of intermediate data to disk between the Map and Reduce processing phases.

Spark implements a distributed, fault tolerant, in-memory structure called a Resilient Distributed Dataset (RDD). Spark maximizes the use of memory across multiple machines, improving overall performance by orders of magnitude. Spark's reuse of these in-memory structures makes it well suited for iterative, machine learning operations, as well as interactive queries.

What Sort of Applications Use Spark?

Spark supports a wide range of applications, including the following:

- ▶ Extract-transform-load (ETL) operations
- ▶ Predictive analytics and machine learning
- ▶ Data access operations (such as SQL queries and visualizations)
- ▶ Text mining and text processing
- ▶ Real-time event processing
- ▶ Graph applications
- ▶ Pattern recognition
- ▶ Recommendation engines

As of the time of this writing, more than 500 organizations are known to be using Spark in production, with some organizations running Spark on hundreds to thousands of cluster nodes against petabytes of data.

NOTE

The Powered by Spark web page lists some of the major customers using applications built on Spark: https://cwiki.apache.org/confluence/display/SPARK/Powered+By+Spark.

Spark's speed and versatility have been further complemented by the numerous extensions now included with Spark (including Spark SQL, Spark Streaming, and SparkR, to name a few—all to be discussed in more detail later in this book).

It is now more a matter of what Spark *can't* do rather than what you *can* do with Spark, and if what you want to do involves data, chances are you can use a Spark approach. Spark's usefulness is only limited by your imagination.

Programming Interfaces to Spark

As mentioned previously, Spark itself is written in Scala. It runs in Java virtual machines (JVMs). Spark provides native support for programming interfaces including the following:

- ▶ Scala
- ▶ Python (using Python's functional programming operators)
- ▶ Java
- ▶ SQL
- ▶ R

Additionally, Spark includes extended support for Clojure and other languages.

In Listing 1.1, Listing 1.2, and Listing 1.3, I show some examples of Spark programming using some of the various interfaces. Don't worry if it looks a bit odd at first. I will cover the basics of functional programming and the Spark API in much more detail when we discuss programming with Spark.

LISTING 1.1   Word Count in Spark Using Python

```
text_file = sc.textFile("hdfs://mycluster/data/warandpeace.txt")

counts = text_file.flatMap(lambda line: line.split())
  .map(lambda word: (word, 1))
  .reduceByKey(lambda a, b: a+b)
  .map(lambda (a, b): (b, a))

counts.saveAsTextFile("hdfs://mycluster/output")
```

Python used in Spark is referred to as *PySpark*. In Listing 1.1, you may have noticed the *lambda* operator. This indicates the declaration and use of an anonymous function. I will discuss anonymous functions and functional programming in **Hour 9, "Functional Programming with Python,"** but by the end of the book, you will be perfectly comfortable with the PySpark and functional Python programming dialect.

LISTING 1.2   Word Count in Spark Using Scala

```
val textFile = sc.textFile("hdfs://mycluster/data/warandpeace.txt")

val counts = textFile.flatMap(line => line.split(" "))
  .map(word => (word, 1))
  .reduceByKey(_ + _)

counts.saveAsTextFile("hdfs://mycluster/output")
```

LISTING 1.3   Word Count in Spark Using Java 7

```
JavaRDD<String> textFile = sc.textFile("hdfs://mycluster/data/warandpeace.txt");
;
JavaRDD<String> words = textFile.flatMap(new FlatMapFunction<String, String>() {
;
public Iterable<String> call(String s) { return Arrays.asList(s.split(" ")); }
;
});
;
```

```
JavaPairRDD<String, Integer> pairs = words.mapToPair(new PairFunction<String,
String, Integer>() {
;
public Tuple2<String, Integer> call(String s) { return new Tuple2<String,
Integer>(s, 1); }
;
});
;
JavaPairRDD<String, Integer> counts = pairs.reduceByKey(new Function2<Integer,
Integer, Integer>() {
;
public Integer call(Integer a, Integer b) { return a + b; }<br />
});

counts.saveAsTextFile("hdfs://mycluster/output");
```

NOTE

Java 8 introduces support for functional programming and the `lambda` operator (`->`), making Spark programming in Java much more readable and succinct.

I will run most of the exercises and examples, beyond the introduction and specific hours dedicated to Scala and R, using Python (PySpark). I have chosen Python as the primary programming language for this book because it is well known, intuitive, and does not require compilation or packaging. That means we can focus more on the Spark API, which is largely the same regardless of the language in which it is implemented.

Ways to Use Spark

Spark programs can be run interactively or submitted as batch jobs, including *mini-batch* and *micro-batch* jobs.

Interactive Use

Interactive programming shells are available in Python and Scala. The *PySpark* and *Scala* shells are shown in Figures 1.2 and 1.3, respectively.

FIGURE 1.2
The PySpark shell.

FIGURE 1.3
The Spark Scala shell.

When you launch these interactive shells, by default, you will see quite a few *INFO* messages. In the cases shown these have been suppressed for brevity. I show you how to do this in **Hour 3, "Installing Spark."**

Interactive R and SQL shells are also included with Spark as well.

Non-interactive Use

Non-interactive applications can be submitted using the `spark-submit` command, as shown in Listing 1.4.

LISTING 1.4   **Non-interactive Spark Job Submission**

```
$SPARK_HOME/bin/spark-submit \S
--class org.apache.spark.examples.SparkPi \
--master yarn-cluster \
--num-executors 4 \
--driver-memory 10g \
--executor-memory 10g \
--executor-cores 1 \
lib/spark-examples*.jar 10
```

Input/Output Types

Although in the majority of cases, Spark is used to process data in Hadoop, Spark can be used with a multitude of other source and target systems, including the following:

- ▶ Local or network file systems

- ▶ Object storage (such as Amazon S3 or Ceph)

- ▶ Relational database systems

- ▶ NoSQL stores (including Apache Cassandra, HBase, and others)

- ▶ Messaging systems (such as Kafka)

Summary

Spark is a versatile, scalable, high-performance data processing platform. Spark's runtime resiliency, fault tolerance, and clean programming abstraction make it a reliable, efficient solution that can provide significant productivity benefits as well.

The lineages of the Hadoop and Spark projects are closely aligned, and even though Spark is not dependent upon Hadoop, Spark is considered to be a "first class citizen" in the Hadoop ecosystem.

In fact, many sources in the Hadoop community envisage Spark supplanting MapReduce as the preferred runtime processing framework for data in the Hadoop Distributed File System (HDFS).

In this hour, you learned about the origins of Spark and why it was created, as well as how Spark relates to the wider Hadoop and big data movements. I have also covered how to interact with Spark and some of the many ways Spark is in use by organizations today.

Q&A

Q. How do Spark and Hadoop interact with one another?

A. The HDFS can be a source of input data for a Spark program as well as being a target for output data from a process. Hadoop's scheduling subsystem can be used to schedule resources for Spark as well.

Q. Why is Spark so much faster than disk-based MapReduce?

A. Spark uses in-memory structures (Resilient Distributed Datasets, or RDDs) parallelized across worker nodes in the cluster to distribute processing and minimize the writing of intermediate or transient data to disk, making it up to 100 times faster than an equivalent disk-based MapReduce application.

Q. What is different about using the interactive shell as compared to submitting applications using `spark-submit`?

A. The interactive shells in Scala and Python are used primarily for discovery and development, whereas production jobs are typically run using `spark-submit`, which has more control over the execution of the program.

Workshop

The workshop contains quiz questions and exercises to help you solidify your understanding of the material covered. Try to answer all questions before looking at the "Answers" section that follows.

Quiz

1. **True or false:** The Spark API provides a clean abstraction for programmers, enabling them to concentrate simply on data processing and not have to concern themselves with external issues.

2. `spark-submit` is used to invoke what type of Spark application?

    A. Interactive

    B. Non-interactive

3. List the programming languages that are natively supported by Spark.

4. **True or false:** Spark does not allow you to write output to a local filesystem.

Answers

1. **True.**

2. **B.** `spark-submit` is used to submit non-interactive background or batch processes.

3. **Scala**, **Python**, **Java**, and **R** are supported natively by Spark.

4. **False.** Spark can write output to local or network filesystems, HDFS, S3, and multiple other targets.

HOUR 2
Understanding Hadoop

What You'll Learn in This Hour:

▶ Background on big data and Hadoop
▶ The basics of the Hadoop Distributed File System (HDFS)
▶ An overview of YARN, Hadoop's resource scheduler
▶ How Spark is used with Hadoop

Big data and Hadoop are inexorably linked together. Hadoop as a data storage and processing platform was a major reason and driver for the creation of Spark, and thus Hadoop and Spark are closely linked to each other. Hadoop continues to be a key platform in use with Spark, and the Hadoop and Spark communities continue to work together as pillars of the big data ecosystem.

This hour introduces the concepts behind Hadoop and discusses how Spark is used with Hadoop, both as a source of data and as a resource scheduling framework.

Because Hadoop is a broad topic to which I could devote an entire book, this is a reasonably conceptually rich and intense hour. If you're familiar with Hadoop already, feel free to skip this hour. If you're not familiar with Hadoop or would like to understand it further, this hour gives you a great start!

Hadoop and a Brief History of Big Data

The set of storage and processing methodologies commonly known as "big data" emanated from the search engine providers in the early 2000s, principally Google and Yahoo!.

The search engine providers were the first group of users faced with Internet scale problems, mainly how to store and index all of the documents in the Internet universe. This seemed an insurmountable challenge at the time, even though the entire body of content in the Internet was a fraction of what it is today.

Yahoo! and Google independently set about to develop a set of capabilities to meet this challenge. In 2003, Google released a whitepaper called "The Google File System." Subsequently, in 2004, Google released another whitepaper called "MapReduce: Simplified Data Processing on Large Clusters." At the same time, at Yahoo!, Doug Cutting (who is generally known as the initial creator of Hadoop) was working on a web indexing project called Nutch.

The Google whitepapers inspired Doug Cutting to take the work he had done to date on the Nutch project and incorporate the storage and processing principles outlined in these whitepapers. The resultant product is what is known today as Hadoop.

Around the same time as the birth of the Hadoop project, several other technology innovations were afoot. These included

- ▶ The rapid expansion of ecommerce
- ▶ The birth and rapid growth of the mobile Internet
- ▶ Blogs and user-driven web content
- ▶ Social media

These innovations cumulatively led to what is now known as the *data deluge*. This accelerated the expansion of the big data movement and led to the emergence of Spark, open source messaging systems, and NoSQL platforms, all of which I will discuss in much more detail later in this book.

But it all started with Hadoop.

Hadoop Explained

Hadoop is a data storage and processing platform, based upon a central concept: data locality. *Data locality* refers to the processing of data where it resides by bringing the computation to the data, rather than the typical pattern of requesting data from its location (for example, a database management system) and sending this data to a remote processing system or host.

With Internet scale data—"big data"—it is no longer efficient (or even possible, in some cases) to move the large volumes of data required for processing across the network at compute time.

Hadoop is schemaless with respect to its write operations (it is what's called a *schema-on-read* system). This means that it can store and process a wide range of data, from unstructured text documents, to semi-structured JSON (JavaScript Object Notation) or XML documents, to well-structured extracts from relational database systems.

Because the schema is not interpreted during write operations to Hadoop, there are no indexes, statistics, or other constructs typically employed by database systems to optimize query operations and filter or reduce the amount of data returned to a client. This further necessitates the requirement for data locality.

Hadoop has two core components: *Hadoop Distributed File System (HDFS)* and *YARN* (which stands for Yet Another Resource Negotiator). HDFS is Hadoop's storage subsystem, whereas YARN can be thought of as Hadoop's process scheduling subsystem.

Each component is independent of one another and can operate in its own cluster; for example, a HDFS cluster and a YARN cluster can operate independently. However, when they are co-located with one another, the combination of both systems is considered to be a Hadoop cluster.

NOTE

A *cluster* is a collection of systems that work together to perform functions, such as computational or processing functions. Individual servers within a cluster are referred to as *nodes*.

Any other projects that interact or integrate with Hadoop in some way—for instance, data ingestion projects such as Flume or Sqoop, or data analysis tools such as Pig or Hive—are called Hadoop "ecosystem" projects. In many ways, you could consider Spark an ecosystem project, although this can be disputed because Spark does not require Hadoop to run.

I will focus on what you need to know about the Hadoop core components, HDFS and YARN, in the next sections.

Introducing HDFS

Firstly, lets provide an overview of HDFS before we detail the HDFS architecture.

HDFS Overview

The Hadoop Distributed Filesystem (HDFS) is Hadoop's storage platform. Although Hadoop can interact with multiple different filesystems, HDFS is Hadoop's primary input data source and target for data processing operations.

As discussed in the introduction to this hour, Hadoop was originally developed as a platform to support the requirements of search engine providers such as Yahoo!. HDFS was inspired by the GoogleFS whitepaper released in 2003, in which Google outlined how they were storing the large amount of data captured by their web crawlers.

There are several key design principles behind HDFS, which in turn underpinned Google's early distributed filesystem implementation (GoogleFS). These principles require that the filesystem...

- ▶ is scalable (economically)
- ▶ is fault tolerant
- ▶ uses commodity hardware
- ▶ supports high concurrency
- ▶ favors high sustained bandwidth over low latency random access

HDFS Architecture

The HDFS architecture consists of several key areas. First I will discuss HDFS files, blocks, and replication. Then I will introduce the NameNode and the DataNodes. Finally, I will cover off how to interact with HDFS.

HDFS Files, Blocks, and Replication

HDFS is a virtual filesystem, meaning that it appears to a client as if it is one system, but the underlying data is located in multiple different locations. HDFS is deployed on top of native filesystems such as the ext3, ext4, and xfs filesystems available in Linux or the Windows NTFS filesystem.

One of the most important properties of HDFS is it's immutability. *Immutability* refers to the inability to update data after it is committed to the filesystem. HDFS is often referred to as a *WORM* (Write Once Read Many) filesystem.

Files in HDFS consist of *blocks*. HDFS blocks default to 128MB in size, although this is configurable by the client or the server. Files are split into blocks upon ingestion into HDFS.

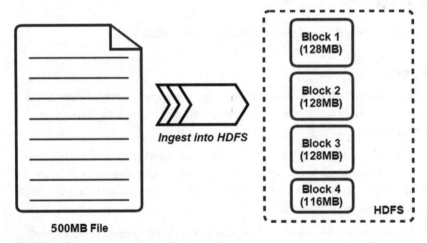

500MB File

Ingest into HDFS

Block 1 (128MB)

Block 2 (128MB)

Block 3 (128MB)

Block 4 (116MB)

HDFS

FIGURE 2.1
HDFS blocks.

As shown in Figure 2.1, when a 500MB file is ingested into HDFS, it is split indiscriminately on 128MB boundaries (meaning that at this stage, no assumptions are made about the file's format or definition of a record). As the file in this case is not evenly divisible by 128MB, which is often the case, the last block (Block 4) contains the remaining contents of the file. This is still considered to be a HDFS block, no different than any other block in the filesystem, except this block contains less data than the other three blocks in this case.

In the HDFS filesystem, the file is logically presented to users as a 500MB file.

NOTE

If you are familiar with local filesystem programming, you will note that HDFS block sizes are significantly larger than operating system filesystem block sizes (which tend to be in the KB range). This is intentional as HDFS blocks are actually files themselves that reside on slave node filesystems.

Blocks Are Distributed

If a cluster contains more than one node, blocks are distributed among slave nodes in the cluster upon ingest. This enables *shared nothing*—distributed, parallel processing of data. Figure 2.2 shows an example ingested into a three-node cluster.

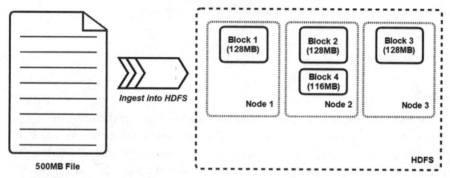

FIGURE 2.2
File ingestion into a multinode cluster.

Blocks Are Replicated

Blocks are replicated according to a preconfigured *replication factor*. In a fully distributed cluster environment (with three or more nodes), this configuration value is typically set to 3. Block replication happens upon ingest, as does the splitting of files into blocks.

Block replication serves two key purposes:

▶ Increased opportunities for data locality

▶ Fault tolerance

The replication process happens between nodes (DataNodes) on the cluster during ingestion as shown in Figure 2.3.

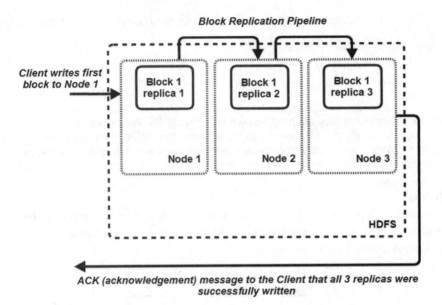

FIGURE 2.3
The HDFS block replication pipeline.

The NameNode

The *NameNode* is the HDFS master node process, which governs the distributed filesystem. The NameNode's most important function is management of the filesystem's *metadata*. The HDFS Metadata is the filesystem catalog, which contains all of the directory and file objects and their related properties and attributes (such as object ACLs—Access Control Lists—which define what users or groups have access to certain objects).

The metadata is stored in resident memory on the NameNode instance to efficiently service client queries related to the filesystem. There are also disk images of the metadata including a snapshot and a journaling function to ensure durability and crash consistency (not dissimilar to a relational database).

Most importantly, the NameNode's in-memory representation of the metadata includes the block locations of the blocks, which comprise files in HDFS. This is the only stateful representation of the relationship between files and blocks in HDFS.

The NameNode services queries from clients (which could be users querying the filesystem, or a Spark application wishing to write output files to a directory in HDFS).

CAUTION

Data Does Not Go Through the NameNode

It is a common misconception that data goes into HDFS via the NameNode. This is not the case as it would create a bottleneck. Instead, the client interacts with the NameNode to get directives on which cluster node(s) to communicate with to get or put blocks that pertain to the file the client is trying to read or write.

There are several other NameNode-related HDFS concepts, such as high availability, rack aware-ness, checkpointing, snapshotting, and federation, as well as other NameNode-related services including the *SecondaryNameNode* and the *StandbyNameNode*. Because this hour is only meant to be a simple introduction to Hadoop, I won't cover these topics. Many resources are available to help you learn more about Hadoop if you are interested.

The DataNodes

The **DataNodes** are the nodes of the cluster on which HDFS blocks are stored and managed. DataNodes are responsible for

- ▶ participating in the block replication pipeline (see Figure 2.3)

- ▶ managing local volumes and storage

- ▶ providing *block reports* to the NameNode

Block reports are regular messages sent from the DataNode to the NameNode to provide the NameNode with an inventory of blocks stored on the DataNode. This inventory is then used to populate and maintain the NameNode's metadata discussed previously.

Checksums are calculated upon ingestion into HDFS and are kept with the blocks. The DataNode recalculates and compares these checksums periodically and reports mismatches to the NameNode. Because HDFS is an immutable filesystem (where objects are not updatable after they are written to the filesystem), the checksums should never change for the lifetime of the block. If they do differ from the initial checksums, it's evidence of block corruption, which will be handled by HDFS.

CAUTION

DataNodes Are Not Aware of HDFS Files and Directories

DataNodes store and manage physical HDFS blocks only, without having any knowledge of how these blocks are related to files and directories in the HDFS filesystem. This relationship is held *only* in the NameNode's metadata. A common misconception is that because DataNode's store all of the data in a HDFS filesystem, they can be used to reconstruct the filesystem if the NameNode's metadata was lost. This is not the case.

Interacting with HDFS

HDFS provides multiple interfaces to read, write, interrogate, and manage the filesystem, including

▶ The filesystem shell (`hadoop fs` or `hdfs dfs`)

▶ The Hadoop FileSystem Java API

▶ RESTful proxy interfaces such as HttpFS and WebHDFS

There are many other ways to access HDFS as well. For simplicity, I will demonstrate using the filesystem shell in the examples that follow.

Hadoop's filesystem is based on the POSIX (*Portable Operating System Interface*) standard, using POSIX conventions found in Unix and Linux for representations of files and directories.

The Hadoop filesystem shell uses verbs similar to the FTP commands, so you will notice some semantic similarities if you are familiar with the FTP syntax.

Examples of some common simple file or directory operations are shown next.

Uploading (or Ingesting) a File

To put a local file named `warandpeace.txt` in the current local directory into an existing directory in HDFS called `/data/books`, you would execute the following:

```
hadoop fs -put warandpeace.txt /data/books/
```

Synonymous commands include

```
hadoop fs -copyFromLocal warandpeace.txt /data/books
```

and

```
hdfs dfs -put warandpeace.txt /data/books
```

NOTE

Hadoop has no concept of *current directory*. Every filesystem command starts from a relative path of the user's home directory in HDFS: `/user/<username>`. In the preceding example, I have used an absolute path to specify the destination location for the file in HDFS. If a user `javen` were to specify `hadoopfs -put warandpeace.txt`, the file would be created as `/user/javen/warandpeace.txt`.

Downloading a File

Many applications cannot interact directly with HDFS, so often you will need to retrieve a file from HDFS into a local or network filesystem to use the file with one of these applications.

As an example, suppose you need to retrieve a file called `report.csv` from `/data/reports` in HDFS into the user's current directory on his or her local filesystem. It could be done as follows:

```
hadoop fs -get /data/reports/report.csv.
```

As with the uploading example, there are similar, synonymous commands to perform other actions such as downloading a file. For the sake of brevity, I won't list these.

Listing a Directory's Contents

To list the contents of `/data/reports`, you would simply execute

```
hadoop fs -ls /data/reports
```

Deleting Objects in HDFS

To delete `report.csv` from `/data/reports` in HDFS, you would execute

```
hadoop fs -rm /data/reports/report.csv
```

To delete the entire `/data/reports` directory, you would execute

```
hadoop fs -rm -r /data/reports
```

CAUTION

Ensure the Trash Setting Is Enabled

HDFS has the concept of a Trash folder or Recycling Bin. This is configured by a parameter set either on the client or the server called `fs.trash.interval`, which is set in the configuration file `hdfs-site.xml`. This parameter is the amount of time (in minutes) to keep a deleted object in a hidden `Trash` directory before it is permanently removed from the filesystem. The default is 0, meaning all deletes are immediate and irreversible, so ensure your administrator has set this to a non-zero value before performing a delete.

Introducing YARN

To introduce YARN, I first need to answer the question "What is YARN?" and then I can discuss running an application in Hadoop using YARN.

What Is YARN?

YARN schedules and orchestrates applications and tasks in Hadoop. When tasks to be run require data from HDFS, YARN will attempt to schedule these tasks on the node where the data resides (applying the concept of data locality discussed previously).

YARN is the second-generation processing platform for Hadoop, the first of which was called MapReduce v1 or *MR1*. MR1 was a purpose-built scheduling platform for Hadoop MapReduce workloads (I discuss the MapReduce processing approach in detail in **Hour 7, "Understanding Map Reduce Concepts"**). MR1 was effective at scheduling Map and Reduce tasks and coordinating the interaction between these processes, ensuring that data locality is achieved wherever possible.

Although MapReduce as a cluster framework was very adept at scheduling MapReduce programs written in Java or programming abstractions such as Apache Pig or Apache Hive, it had three major shortcomings:

▶ It was not intended to schedule and manage non-MapReduce programs

▶ Its practical upper limit to scalability

▶ Its inflexibility for leveraging underutilized processing assets

On the first point, there is an ever-expanding requirement to manage other types of application workloads in addition to MapReduce. This includes applications such as Spark, Impala and Tez (common SQL-on-Hadoop projects), Apache Giraph, and many others.

YARN provides an application-agnostic framework to schedule applications, jobs, and tasks on a Hadoop cluster.

On the second point, although the initial MapReduce framework was known to have supported clusters of up to 4000 or more nodes, the limits of its scalability were starting to be encroached. With the effects of Moore's Law and the economics of processing power (and the further amplification of the data deluge), it was only a matter of time before MapReduce was no longer capable of delivering the processing capabilities required.

To the last point, the MR1 framework had strict definitions of processing *slots* that were designated for either Map or Reduce operations. These definitions led to inflexibility and under utilization of resources.

YARN addresses the deficiencies of MR1, which enables it to provide a scheduling backbone for running Spark in a distributed environment.

Running an Application on YARN

YARN is designed to distribute an application's workload across multiple worker daemons or processes called *NodeManagers*. NodeManagers are the workers or agents responsible for carrying out *tasks*, the complete set of which comprise an *application*. A YARN daemon called the *ResourceManager* is responsible for assigning an *ApplicationsMaster*, a delegate process for managing the execution and status of an application. In addition, the *ResourceManager* (a YARN *master* node process) keeps track of available resources on the NodeManagers (CPU cores and memory). Compute and memory resources are presented to applications to perform task attempts in processing units called *containers*.

NOTE

In Hadoop or YARN terminology, an *application* (or *job*) is a complete set of *tasks*, which are individual units of work, such as Map tasks. Each task will have at least one *task attempt*. A task may be attempted more than once due to task failure or a phenomena known as speculative execution. *Speculative execution* occurs when a parallel processing task is running slowly relative to other concurrent tasks. In this case, a separate task is started on another NodeManager and the results of the first successfully completed task are used.

The ApplicationsMaster determines container requirements for the application and negotiates these resources with the ResourceManager, hence the name Yet Another Resource Negotiator, or YARN.

The process is detailed in Figure 2.4.

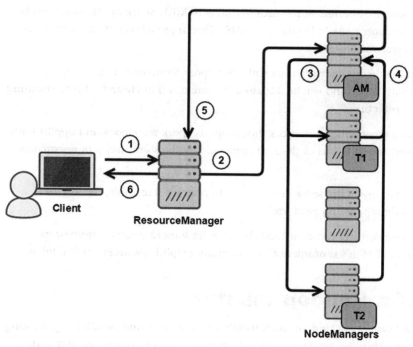

FIGURE 2.4
YARN application submission, scheduling, and execution.

The process pictured in Figure 2.4 is described here:

1. A client submits an application to the ResourceManager.

2. The ResourceManager allocates an ApplicationsMaster process on a NodeManager with sufficient capacity to be assigned this role.

3. The ApplicationsMaster negotiates task containers on NodeManagers (this can include the NodeManager on which the ApplicationsMaster is running as well), and dispatches processing to the NodeManagers hosting the task containers for the application.

4. The NodeManagers report their task attempt status and progress to the ApplicationsMaster.

5. The ApplicationsMaster in turn reports progress and the status of the application to the ResourceManager.

6. The ResourceManager reports application progress, status, and results to the client.

Other Resource Managers

I have already mentioned one alternative resource manager in MR1. Spark applications can be run using MapReduce through *Spark In MapReduce (SIMR)*. This approach is not as common as other Spark scheduling systems however.

Spark has its own built-in scheduling framework called the Spark Standalone Scheduler. This framework is included with Spark and will be discussed in more detail in **Hour 4, "Understanding the Spark Runtime Architecture."**

Mesos is another resource scheduling framework that supports Spark workloads and applications. Mesos started as a project called Nexus at the same time and by the same group of researchers who created Spark.

Mesos and YARN shared many of the same design goals to produce a scalable, flexible, and extensible next-generation scheduling platform.

For the purposes of this book, I will focus on YARN because it's a more common framework found in Hadoop clusters. If Mesos is of interest to you, many helpful resources are available.

Anatomy of a Hadoop Cluster

The HDFS and YARN subsystems of Hadoop work together to distribute and parallelize processing and to maximize the opportunities for data locality. Now that I've given a functional overview of each subsystem in the preceding sections, I will describe a fully functional Hadoop cluster with both HDFS and YARN processes.

As discussed, data is dispersed and replicated amongst DataNodes upon ingestion into HDFS. These DataNodes are co-located with NodeManager processes on cluster slave nodes, enabling Hadoop to bring the computation to the data. Multiple replicas of HDFS blocks make it possible for the MapReduce process to reallocate failed tasks to other NodeManagers with the same block(s).

Figure 2.5 describes the service layout on a typical Hadoop cluster.

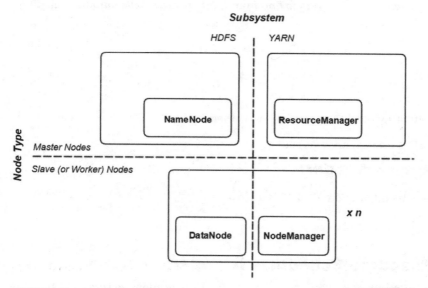

FIGURE 2.5
The anatomy of a Hadoop cluster.

For brevity, I've omitted services such as the StandbyNameNode, SecondaryNameNode, or other processes or daemons involved with Hadoop.

Nodes in a cluster are classified as *master nodes* or *slave nodes*. Master nodes are responsible for coordinating and orchestrating the functions of slave nodes. For instance, in the HDFS core subsystem, the NameNode master node process manages the filesystem metadata and the DataNode slave node process(es) manage the storage and retrieval of the actual blocks for client operations.

In a fully distributed environment, there are typically multiple slave nodes performing similar processing operations on different data in a shared nothing environment.

How Spark Works with Hadoop

In this section, you learn about the specific ways in which Spark works with Hadoop.

HDFS as a Data Source for Spark

Spark can be deployed as a processing framework for data in Hadoop (typically in HDFS). Spark has built-in support for reading and writing to and from HDFS in various file formats, including

- Text

- Sequence

- Parquet

with extended support for Avro, ORCFile formats, and others.

Reading a file from HDFS using Spark is as easy as

```
textfile = sc.textFile("hdfs://mycluster/data/file.txt")
```

Writing data from a Spark application to HDFS is as easy as

```
myRDD.saveAsTextFile("hdfs://mycluster/data/output.txt")
```

YARN as a Resource Scheduler for Spark

YARN is one of the most common process schedulers for Spark applications. Because YARN is usually colocated with HDFS on Hadoop clusters, YARN is a convenient platform for managing Spark applications.

Also, as YARN governs available compute resources across distributed nodes in a Hadoop cluster, it is able to schedule Spark processing stages to run in parallel wherever possible. Furthermore, where HDFS is used as the input source for a Spark application, YARN will schedule map tasks to take full advantage of data locality, thereby minimizing the amount of data that needs to be transferred across the network during the critical initial stages of processing.

Summary

Hadoop is the most prolific big data platform to date and is now an accepted part of many enterprise environments both in on-premise form and in the cloud.

Hadoop is premised on the concept of data locality, whereby processes are dispatched to where the data to be processed resides. This is the concept of bringing the computation to the data.

Two other concepts integral to Hadoop are shared nothing and schema-on-read. *Shared nothing* refers to tasks running independently, especially during the Map processing stage, so that nodes do not need to share state or synchronize with other nodes during key processing phases. *Schema-on-read* refers to the property of accepting data in any format, which is only described when it is processed, making Hadoop a schemaless platform capable of true multistructured data storage and processing.

Hadoop is the platform most commonly used with Spark, both as a source of data and as a resource scheduler.

Spark has built-in support for reading and writing files to and from HDFS, supporting many of the common Hadoop file formats and compression codecs. In addition, Spark integrates with Hive (which provides a SQL-like programming interface to Hadoop) and HCatalog (which provides relational database-like table definitions and schemas to filesystem objects in HDFS).

Spark provides native support to run applications on YARN, meaning that Spark workloads can coexist with and be managed alongside other workloads on a Hadoop cluster.

Q&A

Q. What does the term *data locality* refer to?

A. Data locality is the concept of processing data locally wherever possible. This concept is central to Hadoop, a platform that intentionally attempts to minimize the amount of data transferred across the network by bringing the processing to the data instead of the reverse.

Q. What are the main drivers behind block replication in HDFS?

A. Block replication in HDFS serves two primary purposes: to create as many opportunities for data locality as possible, and to provide built-in data redundancy and fault tolerance.

Q. What were the primary reasons behind the development of YARN as a process management framework for Hadoop?

A. Major factors that led to the development of YARN included the requirement to schedule and manage non-MapReduce applications, as well as increasing scalability and achieving more effective resource utilization across the cluster.

Workshop

The workshop contains quiz questions and exercises to help you solidify your understanding of the material covered. Try to answer all questions before looking at the "Answers" section that follows.

Quiz

1. Which of the following systems or data structures is typically *not* an example of a schema-on-read source?

    A. Hadoop

    B. A table in an Oracle database

    C. A NoSQL database such as Apache HBase

2. **True or false:** HDFS blocks can be updated.

3. The YARN process that monitors the status of an application is called

    A. The ResourceManager

    B. The NodeManager

    C. The ApplicationsMaster

Answers

1. **B.** Typically, tables in a relational database system such as Oracle have a well defined schema that is imposed upon write, sometimes referred to as a schema-on-write structure rather than a schema-on-read structure.

2. **False.** HDFS is an immutable filesystem, meaning data can not be updated after it is written to HDFS.

3. **C.** The ApplicationsMaster is the delegate process that is responsible for negotiating containers to run task attempts for the application as well as monitoring the progress and status of these tasks, the complete set of which define a YARN application.

HOUR 3
Installing Spark

What You'll Learn in This Hour:

▶ What the different Spark deployment modes are

▶ How to install Spark in Standalone mode

▶ How to install and use Spark on YARN

Now that you've gotten through the heavy stuff in the last two hours, you can dive headfirst into Spark and get your hands dirty, so to speak.

This hour covers the basics about how Spark is deployed and how to install Spark. I will also cover how to deploy Spark on Hadoop using the Hadoop scheduler, YARN, discussed in Hour 2.

By the end of this hour, you'll be up and running with an installation of Spark that you will use in subsequent hours.

Spark Deployment Modes

There are three primary deployment modes for Spark:

▶ Spark Standalone

▶ Spark on YARN (Hadoop)

▶ Spark on Mesos

Spark Standalone refers to the built-in or "standalone" scheduler. The term can be confusing because you can have a single machine or a multinode fully distributed cluster both running in Spark Standalone mode. The term "standalone" simply means it does not need an external scheduler.

With Spark Standalone, you can get up an running quickly with few dependencies or environmental considerations. Spark Standalone includes everything you need to get started.

Spark on YARN and Spark on Mesos are deployment modes that use the resource schedulers YARN and Mesos respectively. In each case, you would need to establish a working YARN or Mesos cluster prior to installing and configuring Spark. In the case of Spark on YARN, this typically involves deploying Spark to an existing Hadoop cluster.

I will cover Spark Standalone and Spark on YARN installation examples in this hour because these are the most common deployment modes in use today.

Preparing to Install Spark

Spark is a cross-platform application that can be deployed on

- ▶ Linux (all distributions)
- ▶ Windows
- ▶ Mac OS X

Although there are no specific hardware requirements, general Spark instance hardware recommendations are

- ▶ 8 GB or more memory
- ▶ Eight or more CPU cores
- ▶ 10 gigabit or greater network speed
- ▶ Four or more disks in *JBOD* configuration (JBOD stands for "Just a Bunch of Disks," referring to independent hard disks not in a RAID—or Redundant Array of Independent Disks—configuration)

Spark is written in Scala with programming interfaces in Python (PySpark) and Scala. The following are software prerequisites for installing and running Spark:

- ▶ Java
- ▶ Python (if you intend to use PySpark)

If you wish to use Spark with R (as I will discuss in **Hour 15, "Getting Started with Spark and R"**), you will need to install R as well. Git, Maven, or SBT may be useful as well if you intend on building Spark from source or compiling Spark programs.

If you are deploying Spark on YARN or Mesos, of course, you need to have a functioning YARN or Mesos cluster before deploying and configuring Spark to work with these platforms.

I will cover installing Spark in Standalone mode on a single machine on each type of platform, including satisfying all of the dependencies and prerequisites.

Installing Spark in Standalone Mode

In this section I will cover deploying Spark in Standalone mode on a single machine using various platforms. Feel free to choose the platform that is most relevant to you to install Spark on.

Getting Spark

In the installation steps for Linux and Mac OS X, I will use pre-built releases of Spark. You could also download the source code for Spark and build it yourself for your target platform using the build instructions provided on the official Spark website. I will use the latest Spark binary release in my examples. In either case, your first step, regardless of the intended installation platform, is to download either the release or source from: **http://spark.apache.org/downloads.html**

This page will allow you to download the latest release of Spark. In this example, the latest release is 1.5.2, your release will likely be greater than this (e.g. 1.6.x or 2.x.x).

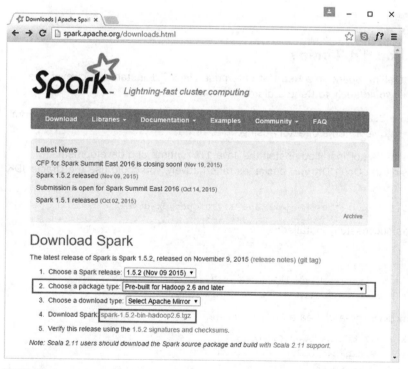

FIGURE 3.1
The Apache Spark downloads page.

NOTE

The Spark releases do not actually include Hadoop as the names may imply. They simply include libraries to integrate with the Hadoop clusters and distributions listed. Many of the Hadoop classes are required regardless of whether you are using Hadoop. I will use the `spark-1.5.2-bin-hadoop2.6.tgz` package for this installation.

CAUTION

Using the "Without Hadoop" Builds

You may be tempted to download the "without Hadoop" or `spark-x.x.x-bin-without-hadoop.tgz` options if you are installing in Standalone mode and not using Hadoop.

The nomenclature can be confusing, but this build is expecting many of the required classes that are implemented in Hadoop to be present on the system. Select this option only if you have Hadoop installed on the system already. Otherwise, as I have done in my case, use one of the `spark-x.x.x-bin-hadoopx.x` builds.

▼ TRY IT YOURSELF

Install Spark on Red Hat/Centos

In this example, I'm installing Spark on a Red Hat Enterprise Linux 7.1 instance. However, the same installation steps would apply to Centos distributions as well.

1. As shown in Figure 3.1, download the `spark-1.5.2-bin-hadoop2.6.tgz` package from your local mirror into your home directory using `wget` or `curl`.

2. If Java 1.7 or higher is not installed, install the Java 1.7 runtime and development environments using the OpenJDK `yum` packages (alternatively, you could use the Oracle JDK instead):

```
sudo yum install java-1.7.0-openjdk java-1.7.0-openjdk-devel
```

3. Confirm Java was successfully installed:

```
$ java -version
java version "1.7.0_91"
OpenJDK Runtime Environment (rhel-2.6.2.3.el7-x86_64 u91-b00)
OpenJDK 64-Bit Server VM (build 24.91-b01, mixed mode)
```

4. Extract the Spark package and create SPARK_HOME:

```
tar -xzf spark-1.5.2-bin-hadoop2.6.tgz
sudo mv spark-1.5.2-bin-hadoop2.6 /opt/spark
export SPARK_HOME=/opt/spark
export PATH=$SPARK_HOME/bin:$PATH
```

The SPARK_HOME environment variable could also be set using the .bashrc file or similar user or system profile scripts. You need to do this if you wish to persist the SPARK_HOME variable beyond the current session.

5. Open the PySpark shell by running the pyspark command from any directory (as you've added the Spark bin directory to the PATH). If Spark has been successfully installed, you should see the following output (with informational logging messages omitted for brevity):

```
Welcome to
      ____              __
     / __/__  ___ _____/ /__
    _\ \/ _ \/ _ `/ __/  '_/
   /__ / .__/\_,_/_/ /_/\_\   version 1.5.2
      /_/

Using Python version 2.7.5 (default, Feb 11 2014 07:46:25)
SparkContext available as sc, HiveContext available as sqlContext.
>>>
```

6. You should see a similar result by running the spark-shell command from any directory.

7. Run the included Pi Estimator example by executing the following command:

```
spark-submit --class org.apache.spark.examples.SparkPi \
--master local \
$SPARK_HOME/lib/spark-examples*.jar 10
```

8. If the installation was successful, you should see something similar to the following result (omitting the informational log messages). Note, this is an estimator program, so the actual result may vary:

```
Pi is roughly 3.140576
```

NOTE
_____
Most of the popular Linux distributions include Python 2.x with the python binary in the system path, so you normally don't need to explicitly install Python; in fact, the yum program itself is implemented in Python.

You may also have wondered why you did not have to install Scala as a prerequisite. The Scala binaries are included in the assembly when you build or download a pre-built release of Spark.
_____

▼ TRY IT YOURSELF

Install Spark on Ubuntu/Debian Linux

In this example, I'm installing Spark on an Ubuntu 14.04 LTS Linux distribution.

As with the Red Hat example, Python 2. 7 is already installed with the operating system, so we do not need to install Python.

1. As shown in Figure 3.1, download the `spark-1.5.2-bin-hadoop2.6.tgz` package from your local mirror into your home directory using `wget` or `curl`.

2. If Java 1.7 or higher is not installed, install the Java 1.7 runtime and development environments using Ubuntu's APT (Advanced Packaging Tool). Alternatively, you could use the Oracle JDK instead:

```
sudo apt-get update
sudo apt-get install openjdk-7-jre
sudo apt-get install openjdk-7-jdk
```

3. Confirm Java was successfully installed:

```
$ java -version
java version "1.7.0_91"
OpenJDK Runtime Environment (IcedTea 2.6.3) (7u91-2.6.3-0ubuntu0.14.04.1)
OpenJDK 64-Bit Server VM (build 24.91-b01, mixed mode)
```

4. Extract the Spark package and create `SPARK_HOME`:

```
tar -xzf spark-1.5.2-bin-hadoop2.6.tgz
sudo mv spark-1.5.2-bin-hadoop2.6 /opt/spark
export SPARK_HOME=/opt/spark
export PATH=$SPARK_HOME/bin:$PATH
```

The `SPARK_HOME` environment variable could also be set using the `.bashrc` file or similar user or system profile scripts. You will need to do this if you wish to persist the `SPARK_HOME` variable beyond the current session.

5. Open the `PySpark` shell by running the `pyspark` command from any directory. If Spark has been successfully installed, you should see the following output:

```
Welcome to
```

```
      version 1.5.2

Using Python version 2.7.6 (default, Mar 22 2014 22:59:56)
SparkContext available as sc, HiveContext available as sqlContext.
>>>
```

6. You should see a similar result by running the `spark-shell` command from any directory.

7. Run the included Pi Estimator example by executing the following command:

```
spark-submit --class org.apache.spark.examples.SparkPi \
--master local \
$SPARK_HOME/lib/spark-examples*.jar 10
```

8. If the installation was successful, you should see something similar to the following result (omitting the informational log messages). Note, this is an estimator program, so the actual result may vary:

```
Pi is roughly 3.140576
```

TRY IT YOURSELF

Install Spark on Mac OS X

In this example, I install Spark on OS X Mavericks (10.9.5).

Mavericks includes installed versions of Python (2.7.5) and Java (1.8), so I don't need to install them.

1. As shown in Figure 3.1, download the `spark-1.5.2-bin-hadoop2.6.tgz` package from your local mirror into your home directory using curl.

2. Extract the Spark package and create `SPARK_HOME`:

```
tar -xzf spark-1.5.2-bin-hadoop2.6.tgz
sudo mv spark-1.5.2-bin-hadoop2.6 /opt/spark
export SPARK_HOME=/opt/spark
export PATH=$SPARK_HOME/bin:$PATH
```

3. Open the `PySpark` shell by running the `pyspark` command in the Terminal from any directory. If Spark has been successfully installed, you should see the following output:

```
Welcome to

      ____              __
     / __/__  ___ _____/ /__
    _\ \/ _ \/ _ `/ __/  '_/
   /__ / .__/\_,_/_/ /_/\_\   version 1.5.2
      /_/
Using Python version 2.7.5 (default, Feb 11 2014 07:46:25)
SparkContext available as sc, HiveContext available as sqlContext.
>>>
```

The `SPARK_HOME` environment variable could also be set using the `.profile` file or similar user or system profile scripts.

4. You should see a similar result by running the `spark-shell` command in the terminal from any directory.

5. Run the included Pi Estimator example by executing the following command:

```
spark-submit --class org.apache.spark.examples.SparkPi \
--master local \
$SPARK_HOME/lib/spark-examples*.jar 10
```

6. If the installation was successful, you should see something similar to the following result (omitting the informational log messages). Note, this is an estimator program, so the actual result may vary:

```
Pi is roughly 3.140576
```

▼ TRY IT YOURSELF

Install Spark on Microsoft Windows

Installing Spark on Windows can be more involved than installing it on Linux or Mac OS X because many of the dependencies (such as Python and Java) need to be addressed first.

This example uses a Windows Server 2012, the server version of Windows 8.

1. You will need a decompression utility capable of extracting `.tar.gz` and `.gz` archives because Windows does not have native support for these archives. 7-zip is a suitable program for this. You can obtain it from http://7-zip.org/download.html.

2. As shown in Figure 3.1, download the `spark-1.5.2-bin-hadoop2.6.tgz` package from your local mirror and extract the contents of this archive to a new directory called `C:\Spark`.

3. Install Java using the Oracle JDK Version 1.7, which you can obtain from the Oracle website. In this example, I download and install the `jdk-7u79-windows-x64.exe` package.

4. Disable IPv6 for Java applications by running the following command as an administrator from the Windows command prompt :

```
setx /M _JAVA_OPTIONS "-Djava.net.preferIPv4Stack=true"
```

5. Python is not included with Windows, so you will need to download and install it. You can obtain a Windows installer for Python from https://www.python.org/getit/. I use Python 2.7.10 in this example. Install Python into `C:\Python27`.

6. Download the Hadoop common binaries necessary to run Spark compiled for Windows x64 from `hadoop-common-bin`. Extract these files to a new directory called `C:\Hadoop`.

7. Set an environment variable at the machine level for HADOOP_HOME by running the following command as an administrator from the Windows command prompt:

```
setx /M HADOOP_HOME C:\Hadoop
```

8. Update the system path by running the following command as an administrator from the Windows command prompt:

```
setx /M path "%path%;C:\Python27;%PROGRAMFILES%\Java\jdk1.7.0_79\bin;C:\Hadoop"
```

9. Make a temporary directory, C:\tmp\hive, to enable the HiveContext in Spark. Set permission to this file using the winutils.exe program included with the Hadoop common binaries by running the following commands as an administrator from the Windows command prompt:

```
mkdir C:\tmp\hive
C:\Hadoop\bin\winutils.exe chmod 777 /tmp/hive
```

10. Test the Spark interactive shell in Python by running the following command:

```
C:\Spark\bin\pyspark
```

You should see the output shown in Figure 3.2.

FIGURE 3.2
The PySpark shell in Windows.

11. You should get a similar result by running the following command to open an interactive Scala shell:

```
C:\Spark\bin\spark-shell
```

12. Run the included Pi Estimator example by executing the following command:

```
C:\Spark\bin\spark-submit --class org.apache.spark.examples.SparkPi --master local C:\Spark\lib\spark-examples*.jar 10
```

13. If the installation was successful, you should see something similar to the following result shown in Figure 3.3. Note, this is an estimator program, so the actual result may vary:

```
                 Administrator: C:\Windows\system32\cmd.exe
172 ms on localhost (9/10)
15/11/29 09:29:43 INFO TaskSetManager: Finished task 3.0 in stage 0.0 (TID 3) in
141 ms on localhost (10/10)
15/11/29 09:29:43 INFO DAGScheduler: ResultStage 0 (reduce at SparkPi.scala:36)
finished in 1.672 s
15/11/29 09:29:43 INFO TaskSchedulerImpl: Removed TaskSet 0.0, whose tasks have
all completed, from pool
15/11/29 09:29:43 INFO DAGScheduler: Job 0 finished: reduce at SparkPi.scala:36,
took 2.186269 s
Pi is roughly 3.140576
15/11/29 09:29:44 INFO SparkUI: Stopped Spark web UI at http://172.31.9.69:4040
15/11/29 09:29:44 INFO DAGScheduler: Stopping DAGScheduler
15/11/29 09:29:44 INFO MapOutputTrackerMasterEndpoint: MapOutputTrackerMasterEnd
point stopped!
15/11/29 09:29:44 INFO MemoryStore: MemoryStore cleared
15/11/29 09:29:44 INFO BlockManager: BlockManager stopped
15/11/29 09:29:44 INFO BlockManagerMaster: BlockManagerMaster stopped
15/11/29 09:29:44 INFO SparkContext: Successfully stopped SparkContext
15/11/29 09:29:44 INFO OutputCommitCoordinator$OutputCommitCoordinatorEndpoint:
OutputCommitCoordinator stopped!
15/11/29 09:29:44 INFO ShutdownHookManager: Shutdown hook called
15/11/29 09:29:44 INFO ShutdownHookManager: Deleting directory C:\Users\Administ
rator\AppData\Local\Temp\2\spark-ee480710-b603-4ecc-a471-7a73dcda45fe

C:\Users\Administrator>
```

FIGURE 3.3
The results of the SparkPi example program in Windows.

Installing a Multi-node Spark Standalone Cluster

Using the steps outlined in this section for your preferred target platform, you will have installed a single node Spark Standalone cluster. I will discuss Spark's cluster architecture in more detail in **Hour 4, "Understanding the Spark Runtime Architecture."** However, to create a multi-node cluster from a single node system, you would need to do the following:

▶ Ensure all cluster nodes can resolve hostnames of other cluster members and are routable to one another (typically, nodes are on the same private subnet).

▶ Enable passwordless SSH (Secure Shell) for the Spark master to the Spark slaves (this step is only required to enable remote login for the slave daemon startup and shutdown actions).

▶ Configure the `spark-defaults.conf` file on all nodes with the URL of the Spark master node.

▶ Configure the `spark-env.sh` file on all nodes with the hostname or IP address of the Spark master node.

▶ Run the `start-master.sh` script from the `sbin` directory on the Spark master node.

▶ Run the `start-slave.sh` script from the `sbin` directory on all of the Spark slave nodes.

▶ Check the Spark master UI. You should see each slave node in the `Workers` section.

▶ Run a test Spark job.

Configuring and Testing a Multinode Spark Cluster

Take your single node Spark system and create a basic two-node Spark cluster with a master node and a worker node.

In this example, I use two Linux instances with Spark installed in the same relative paths: one with a hostname of `sparkmaster`, and the other with a hostname of `sparkslave`.

1. Ensure that each node can resolve the other. The `ping` command can be used for this. For example, from `sparkmaster`:

```
ping sparkslave
```

2. Ensure the firewall rules of network ACLs will allow traffic on multiple ports between cluster instances because cluster nodes will communicate using various TCP ports (normally not a concern if all cluster nodes are on the same subnet).

3. Create and configure the `spark-defaults.conf` file on all nodes. Run the following commands on the `sparkmaster` and `sparkslave` hosts:

```
cd $SPARK_HOME/conf
sudo cp spark-defaults.conf.template spark-defaults.conf
sudo sed -i "\$aspark.master\tspark://sparkmaster:7077" spark-defaults.conf
```

4. Create and configure the `spark-env.sh` file on all nodes. Complete the following tasks on the `sparkmaster` and `sparkslave` hosts:

```
cd $SPARK_HOME/conf
sudo cp spark-env.sh.template spark-env.sh
sudo sed -i "\$aSPARK_MASTER_IP=sparkmaster" spark-env.sh
```

5. On the `sparkmaster` host, run the following command:

```
sudo $SPARK_HOME/sbin/start-master.sh
```

6. On the `sparkslave` host, run the following command:

```
sudo $SPARK_HOME/sbin/start-slave.sh spark://sparkmaster:7077
```

7. Check the Spark master web user interface (UI) at http://sparkmaster:8080/.

8. Check the Spark worker web UI at http://sparkslave:8081/.

9. Run the built-in Pi Estimator example from the terminal of either node:

```
spark-submit --class org.apache.spark.examples.SparkPi \
--master spark://sparkmaster:7077 \
--driver-memory 512m \
--executor-memory 512m \
--executor-cores 1 \
$SPARK_HOME/lib/spark-examples*.jar 10
```

10. If the application completes successfully, you should see something like the following (omitting informational log messages). Note, this is an estimator program, so the actual result may vary:

```
Pi is roughly 3.140576
```

This is a simple example. If it was a production cluster, I would set up passwordless SSH to enable the `start-all.sh` and `stop-all.sh` shell scripts. I would also consider modifying additional configuration parameters for optimization.

CAUTION

Spark Master Is a Single Point of Failure in Standalone Mode

Without implementing *High Availability (HA)*, the Spark Master node is a *single point of failure (SPOF)* for the Spark cluster. This means that if the Spark Master node goes down, the Spark cluster would stop functioning, all currently submitted or running applications would fail, and no new applications could be submitted.

High Availability can be configured using *Apache Zookeeper,* a highly reliable distributed coordination service. You can also configure HA using the filesystem instead of Zookeeper; however, this is not recommended for production systems.

Exploring the Spark Install

Now that you have Spark up and running, let's take a closer look at the install and its various components.

If you followed the instructions in the previous section, "Installing Spark in Standalone Mode," you should be able to browse the contents of $SPARK_HOME.

In Table 3.1, I describe each subdirectory of the Spark installation.

TABLE 3.1 Spark Installation Subdirectories

Directory	Description
bin	Contains all of the commands/scripts to run Spark applications interactively through shell programs such as `pyspark`, `spark-shell`, `spark-sql` and `sparkR`, or in batch mode using `spark-submit`.
conf	Contains templates for Spark configuration files, which can be used to set Spark environment variables (`spark-env.sh`) or set default master, slave, or client configuration parameters (`spark-defaults.conf`). There are also configuration templates to control logging (`log4j.properties`), metrics collection (`metrics.properties`), as well as a template for the `slaves` file, which controls which slave nodes can join the Spark cluster.

Directory	Description
ec2	Contains scripts to deploy Spark nodes and clusters on Amazon Web Services (AWS) Elastic Compute Cloud (EC2). I will cover deploying Spark in EC2 in **Hour 5, "Deploying Spark in the Cloud."**
lib	Contains the main assemblies for Spark including the main library (spark-assembly-x.x.x-hadoopx.x.x.jar) and included example programs (spark-examples-x.x.x-hadoopx.x.x.jar), of which we have already run one, SparkPi, to verify the installation in the previous section.
licenses	Includes license files covering other included projects such as Scala and JQuery. These files are for legal compliance purposes only and are not required to run Spark.
python	Contains all of the Python libraries required to run PySpark. You will generally not need to access these files directly.
sbin	Contains administrative scripts to start and stop master and slave services (locally or remotely) as well as start processes related to YARN and Mesos. I used the start-master.sh and start-slave.sh scripts when I covered how to install a multi-node cluster in the previous section.
data	Contains sample data sets used for testing mllib (which we will discuss in more detail in **Hour 16, "Machine Learning with Spark"**).
examples	Contains the source code for all of the examples included in lib/spark-examples-x.x.x-hadoopx.x.x.jar. Example programs are included in Java, Python, R, and Scala. You can also find the latest code for the included examples at https://github.com/apache/spark/tree/master/examples.
R	Contains the SparkR package and associated libraries and documentation. I will discuss SparkR in **Hour 15, "Getting Started with Spark and R"**

Deploying Spark on Hadoop

As discussed previously, deploying Spark with Hadoop is a popular option for many users because Spark can read from and write to the data in Hadoop (in HDFS) and can leverage Hadoop's process scheduling subsystem, YARN.

Using a Management Console or Interface

If you are using a commercial distribution of Hadoop such as Cloudera or Hortonworks, you can often deploy Spark using the management console provided with each respective platform: for example, Cloudera Manager for Cloudera or Ambari for Hortonworks.

If you are using the management facilities of a commercial distribution, the version of Spark deployed may lag the latest stable Apache release because Hadoop vendors typically update their software stacks with their respective major and minor release schedules.

Installing Manually

Installing Spark on a YARN cluster manually (that is, not using a management interface such as Cloudera Manager or Ambari) is quite straightforward to do.

▼ TRY IT YOURSELF

Installing Spark on Hadoop Manually

1. Follow the steps outlined for your target platform (for example, Red Hat Linux, Windows, and so on) in the earlier section "Installing Spark in Standalone Mode."

2. Ensure that the system you are installing on is a Hadoop client with configuration files pointing to a Hadoop cluster. You can do this as shown:

```
hadoop fs -ls
```

   This lists the contents of your user directory in HDFS. You could instead use the path in HDFS where your input data resides, such as

```
hadoop fs -ls /path/to/my/data
```

   If you see an error such as hadoop: command not found, you need to make sure a correctly configured Hadoop client is installed on the system before continuing.

3. Set either the HADOOP_CONF_DIR or YARN_CONF_DIR environment variable as shown:

```
export HADOOP_CONF_DIR=/etc/hadoop/conf
# or
export YARN_CONF_DIR=/etc/hadoop/conf
```

   As with SPARK_HOME, these variables could be set using the .bashrc or similar profile script sourced automatically.

4. Execute the following command to test Spark on YARN:

```
spark-submit --class org.apache.spark.examples.SparkPi \
--master yarn-cluster \
$SPARK_HOME/lib/spark-examples*.jar 10
```

5. If you have access to the YARN Resource Manager UI, you can see the Spark job running in YARN as shown in Figure 3.4:

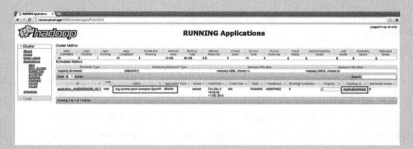

FIGURE 3.4
The YARN ResourceManager UI showing the Spark application running.

6. Clicking the **ApplicationsMaster** link in the **ResourceManager UI** will redirect you to the Spark UI for the application:

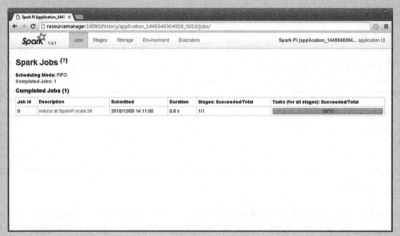

FIGURE 3.5
The Spark UI.

Submitting Spark applications using YARN can be done in two submission modes: `yarn-cluster` or `yarn-client`.

Using the `yarn-cluster` option, the Spark Driver and Spark Context, ApplicationsMaster, and all executors run on YARN NodeManagers. These are all concepts we will explore in detail in **Hour 4, "Understanding the Spark Runtime Architecture."** The `yarn-cluster` submission mode is intended for production or non interactive/batch Spark applications. You cannot use `yarn-cluster` as an option for any of the interactive Spark shells. For instance, running the following command:

```
spark-shell --master yarn-cluster
```

will result in this error:

```
Error: Cluster deploy mode is not applicable to Spark shells.
```

Using the `yarn-client` option, the Spark Driver runs on the client (the host where you ran the Spark application). All of the tasks and the ApplicationsMaster run on the YARN NodeManagers however unlike `yarn-cluster` mode, the Driver does not run on the ApplicationsMaster. The `yarn-client` submission mode is intended to run interactive applications such as pyspark or `spark-shell`.

CAUTION

Running Incompatible Workloads Alongside Spark May Cause Issues

Spark is a memory-intensive processing engine. Using Spark on YARN will allocate containers, associated CPU, and memory resources to applications such as Spark as required. If you have other memory-intensive workloads, such as Impala, Presto, or HAWQ running on the cluster, you need to ensure that these workloads can coexist with Spark and that neither compromises the other. Generally, this can be accomplished through application, YARN cluster, scheduler, or application queue configuration and, in extreme cases, operating system cgroups (on Linux, for instance).

Summary

In this hour, I have covered the different deployment modes for Spark: Spark Standalone, Spark on Mesos, and Spark on YARN.

Spark Standalone refers to the built-in process scheduler it uses as opposed to using a preexisting external scheduler such as Mesos or YARN. A Spark Standalone cluster could have any number of nodes, so the term "Standalone" could be a misnomer if taken out of context. I have showed you how to install Spark both in Standalone mode (as a single node or multi-node cluster) and how to install Spark on an existing YARN (Hadoop) cluster.

I have also explored the components included with Spark, many of which you will have used by the end of this book.

You're now up and running with Spark. You can use your Spark installation for most of the exercises throughout this book.

Q&A

Q. What are the factors involved in selecting a specific deployment mode for Spark?

A. The choice of deployment mode for Spark is primarily dependent upon the environment you are running in and the availability of external scheduling frameworks such as YARN or Mesos. For instance, if you are using Spark with Hadoop and you have an existing YARN infrastructure, Spark on YARN is a logical deployment choice. However, if you are running Spark independent of Hadoop (for instance sourcing data from S3 or a local filesystem), Spark Standalone may be a better deployment method.

Q. What is the difference between the `yarn-client` and the `yarn-cluster` options of the `--master` argument using `spark-submit`?

A. Both the `yarn-client` and `yarn-cluster` options execute the program in the Hadoop cluster using YARN as the scheduler; however, the `yarn-client` option uses the client host as the driver for the program and is designed for testing as well as interactive shell usage.

Workshop

The workshop contains quiz questions and exercises to help you solidify your understanding of the material covered. Try to answer all questions before looking at the "Answers" section that follows.

Quiz

1. **True or false:** A Spark Standalone cluster consists of a single node.

2. Which component is not a prerequisite for installing Spark?

    A. Scala

    B. Python

    C. Java

3. Which of the following subdirectories contained in the Spark installation contains scripts to start and stop master and slave node Spark services?

    A. `bin`

    B. `sbin`

    C. `lib`

4. Which of the following environment variables are required to run Spark on Hadoop/YARN?

    A. `HADOOP_CONF_DIR`

    B. `YARN_CONF_DIR`

    C. Either `HADOOP_CONF_DIR` or `YARN_CONF_DIR` will work.

Answers

1. **False.** Standalone refers to the independent process scheduler for Spark, which could be deployed on a cluster of one-to-many nodes.

2. **A.** The Scala assembly is included with Spark; however, Java and Python must exist on the system prior to installation.

3. **B.** `sbin` contains administrative scripts to start and stop Spark services.

4. **C.** Either the `HADOOP_CONF_DIR` or `YARN_CONF_DIR` environment variable must be set for Spark to use YARN.

Exercises

1. Using your Spark Standalone installation, execute `pyspark` to open a PySpark interactive shell.

2. Open a browser and navigate to the SparkUI at **http://localhost:4040**.

3. Click the Environment top menu link or navigate to Environment page directly using the url: **http://localhost:4040/environment/**.

4. Note some of the various environment settings and configuration parameters set. I will explain many of these in greater detail throughout the book.

HOUR 4

Understanding the Spark Application Architecture

What You'll Learn in This Hour:

▶ The components of a Spark application
▶ How the different Spark application components work together
▶ How Spark applications run on YARN

In this hour, I will dive into the details of Spark's application architecture, describing each application component, its function, and its relationship to other Spark application components.

By the end of this hour, you should be familiar with the Spark application and cluster architecture and understand how programs are executed in Spark. These are fundamental concepts you will see in action throughout this book.

Anatomy of a Spark Application

A Spark application contains several components, all of which exist whether you are running Spark on a single machine or across a cluster of hundreds or thousands of nodes.

Each component has a specific role in executing a Spark program. Some of these roles are passive during execution such as the client components, and other roles are active in the execution of the program, including components executing computation functions.

The components of a Spark application are the *driver*, the *master*, the *cluster manager*, and the *executor(s)*, which run on *worker nodes* or *workers*. Figure 4.1 shows all of the Spark components in the context of a Spark Standalone application. I will describe each component and its function in more detail later in the hour.

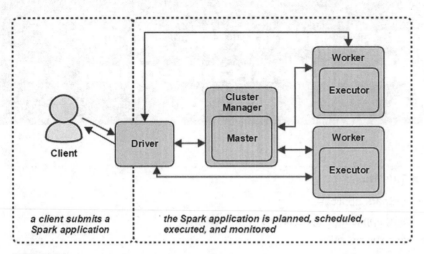

FIGURE 4.1
Spark Standalone runtime application components.

All of the Spark components, including the driver, master, and executor processes, run in *Java virtual machines (JVMs)*. A JVM is a cross-platform runtime engine that can execute instructions compiled into Java *bytecode*. Scala, which Spark is written in, compiles into bytecode and runs on JVMs.

It is important to distinguish between Spark's runtime application components and the locations and node types on which they run. These components run in different places using different deployment modes, so don't think of these components in physical node or instance terms. For instance, when you are running Spark on YARN, there would be several variations of Figure 4.1. However, all the components pictured are still involved in the application and have the same roles. I will discuss this in detail in the section "**Spark Applications Running on YARN.**"

Spark Driver

The life of Spark application starts (and finishes) with the Spark driver. The Spark driver is the process clients use to submit applications in Spark. The driver is also responsible for planning and coordinating the execution of the Spark program and returning status and/or results (data) to the client.

The Spark Context

The Spark driver is responsible for creating the *SparkContext*. The Spark Context, which is referred to as `sc` in all of our Spark examples, is the application instance representing the connection to the Spark master (and Spark workers). The Spark Context is instantiated at the beginning of a Spark application (including the interactive shells) and is used for the entirety of the program.

NOTE

The object name for the SparkContext instance is arbitrary. I have used the convention `sc` in this book—this is the default instantiation in the Spark interactive shells. In texts or examples elsewhere, you may see this referred to as `spark` or `spark_context`. It is up to the developer's discretion.

Application Planning

One of the main functions of the driver is to plan the application. The driver takes the application processing input and plans the execution of the program. The driver takes all of the requested *transformations* (data manipulation operations) and *actions* (requests for output or a prompt to execute the program) and creates a *directed acyclic graph (DAG)*.

NOTE

A DAG is a mathematical construct that is commonly used in computer science to represent dataflows and their dependencies. DAGs contain *vertices* or *nodes* and *edges*. Vertices or nodes, in a dataflow context, are steps in the process flow. Edges in a DAG connect vertices to one another in a directed orientation in such a way that it is impossible to have circular references.

The DAG consists of *tasks* and *stages*. Tasks are the smallest unit of schedulable work in a Spark program. Stages are sets of tasks that can be run together. Stages are dependent upon one another.

DAGs, in a process scheduling sense, are not unique to Spark. For instance, they are used in other big data ecosystem projects such as Tez, Drill, and Presto for scheduling. DAGs are fundamental to Spark, so it is worth being familiar with the concept.

Application Scheduling

The driver also coordinates the running of stages and tasks defined in the DAG. Key driver activities involved in the scheduling and running of tasks include the following:

▶ Keeping track of available resources to execute tasks

▶ Scheduling tasks to run "close" to the data where possible (the data locality concept is discussed in **Hour 2, "Understanding Hadoop"**)

▶ Coordinating the location and movement of data in between processing stages

Other Driver Functions

In addition to planning and orchestrating the execution of a Spark program, the driver also is responsible for returning the results from an application. These could be return codes or data in the case of an action that requests data to be returned to the client (for example, an interactive query).

The driver also serves the *Application UI* on port 4040, as shown in Figure 4.2. This UI is created automatically, independent of the code submitted or how it was submitted (that is, interactive versus `spark-submit`).

FIGURE 4.2
The Spark Application UI.

If subsequent applications are launched on the same host, successive ports are used for the Application UI (for example, 4041, 4042, and so on).

Spark Executors and Workers

Spark executors are the host processes on which tasks from a Spark DAG are run. Executors reserve CPU and memory resources on slave nodes or workers in a Spark cluster. Executors are dedicated to a specific Spark application and terminated when the application completes. A Spark executor can run hundreds or thousands of tasks within a Spark program.

Typically a worker node—which hosts the executor process—has a finite or fixed amount of executors that can be allocated at any point in time, therefore a cluster—being a known number of nodes—has a finite amount of executors that can be allocated to run Spark tasks.

As I mentioned, Spark executors are hosted in JVMs. The JVMs for executors are allocated a *heap*, which is a dedicated memory space in which to store and manage objects. The amount of memory committed to the JVM Heap for an executor is set by the property `spark.executor.memory` or as a command line argument `--executor-memory` to `pyspark`, `spark-shell`, or `spark-submit`.

Executors store output data from tasks on memory or disk, I will detail this in **Hour 6, "Learning the Basics of Spark Programming with RDDs."** It's important to note that workers and executors are only aware of the tasks allocated to them, whereas the driver is responsible for understanding the complete set of tasks and their respective dependencies that comprise an application.

Worker nodes expose a user interface on port 8081, as shown in Figure 4.3.

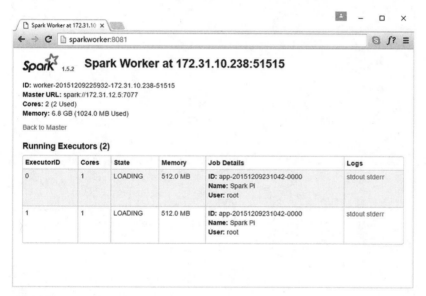

FIGURE 4.3
The Spark worker UI.

Spark Master and Cluster Manager

The Spark driver plans and coordinates the set of tasks required to run a Spark application. The tasks themselves run in executors, which are hosted on Worker nodes.

The master and the cluster manager are the central processes that monitor, reserve, and allocate the distributed cluster resources (containers in the case of YARN) on which the executors run. The master and the cluster manager can be separate processes or they can be combined into one process, as is the case when running Spark in Standalone mode.

Spark Master

The Spark master is the process that requests resources in the cluster and makes these available to the Spark driver. In either deployment mode, the master negotiates resources or containers with worker nodes or slave nodes and tracks their status and monitors their progress.

The Spark master process serves a web user interface on port 8080 on the master host, as shown in Figure 4.4.

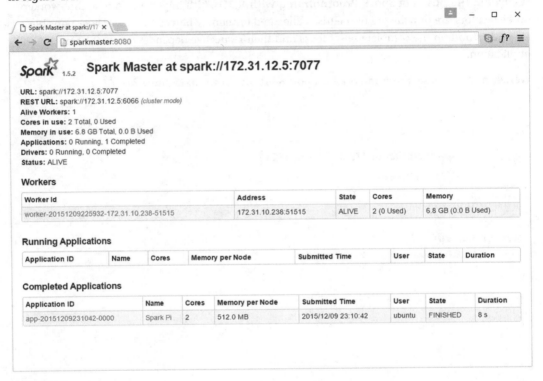

FIGURE 4.4
The Spark master UI.

NOTE

It's important to distinguish the runtime functions of the driver and the master. The name "master" can be inferred to mean that this process is governing the execution of the application. This is not the case.

The master simply requests resources and makes these resources available to the driver for the lifetime of the application. Although the master monitors the status and health of these resources, it is not involved in the execution of the application and the coordination of its tasks and stages. That is the job of the driver.

Cluster Manager

The cluster manager is the process responsible for monitoring the worker nodes and reserving resources on these nodes upon request by the master. The master then in turn makes these cluster resources available to the driver in the form of executors.

As discussed, the cluster manager can be separate from the master process. This is the case when running Spark on Mesos or YARN, which I discuss further in the next section, "**Spark Applications Running on YARN.**"

In the case of Spark running in Standalone mode, the master process also performs the functions of the cluster manager. Effectively, it acts as its own cluster manager.

Spark Applications Running on YARN

Hadoop is a very popular and common deployment platform for Spark. Some industry pundits see Spark as soon to supplant MapReduce as the primary processing platform for applications in Hadoop. With YARN being the resource scheduling backbone of Hadoop, it's important to understand how Spark applications run on YARN, and thus how they run on Hadoop.

ResourceManager as the Cluster Manager

You will recall that the cluster manager in a distributed Spark application is the process that governs, monitors, and reserves resources in the form of containers on cluster worker (or slave) nodes. These containers are reserved upon request by the Spark master. The cluster manager in the case of Spark on YARN is the YARN ResourceManager.

In **Hour 2, "Understanding Hadoop,"** you learned that the ResourceManager allocates an ApplicationsMaster when an application is submitted to YARN. The ApplicationsMaster determines container requirements for the application and negotiates these resources with the ResourceManager.

A Spark Driver running in YARN mode submits an application to the ResourceManager, and then the ResourceManager designates an ApplicationsMaster for the Spark application.

An example of a Spark application managed by YARN shown in the ResourceManager UI, typically available at **http://<resource_manager>:8088**, is shown in Figure 4.5.

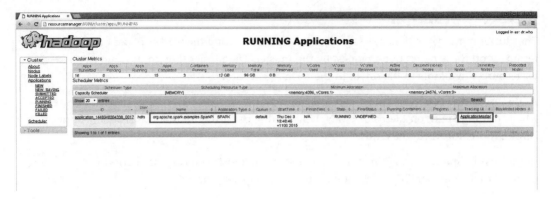

FIGURE 4.5
The Spark application shown in the YARN Resource Manager UI.

The ResourceManager continually monitors container allocation and node resources across the cluster. When new containers become available as they are released by other applications, these containers can be allocated to new or queued applications according to a scheduler policy. Common scheduler policies include the *CapacityScheduler* and *FairScheduler*. These policies determine application, queue, or user access to cluster resources and ensure that long and short running jobs can coexist.

ApplicationsMaster as the Spark Master

The ApplicationsMaster process that is instantiated by the ResourceManager upon Spark application submission acts as the Spark master. The driver informs the ApplicationsMaster of its executor requirements for the application. The ApplicationsMaster, in turn, requests containers (which are hosted on NodeManagers) from the ResourceManager to host these executors.

The ApplicationsMaster is responsible for managing these containers (executors) for the lifetime of the application. As discussed, however, the driver coordinates the application's state and processing stage transitions.

The ApplicationsMaster itself is hosted in a JVM on a slave or worker node in the cluster and is actually the first resource allocated to any application running on YARN.

The ApplicationsMaster UI for a Spark application is the Spark Master UI. This is available as a link from the ResourceManager UI. An example is shown in Figure 4.6.

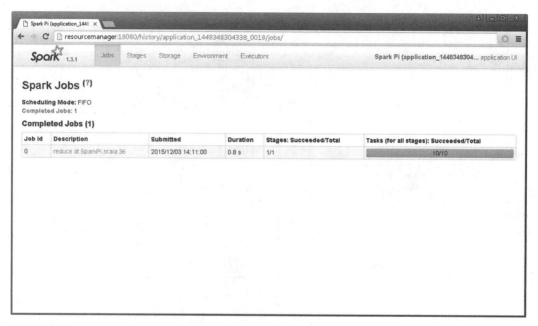

FIGURE 4.6
The ApplicationsMaster UI for a Spark application running on YARN.

Spark applications running on YARN can use two different submission modes: `yarn-client` and `yarn-cluster`. I will discuss both in more detail now.

yarn-cluster Mode

In `yarn-cluster` mode, the driver runs in the cluster; more specifically, the driver runs inside the ApplicationsMaster. This mode is best suited for production applications. The Spark interactive shells are not available using the `yarn-cluster` mode.

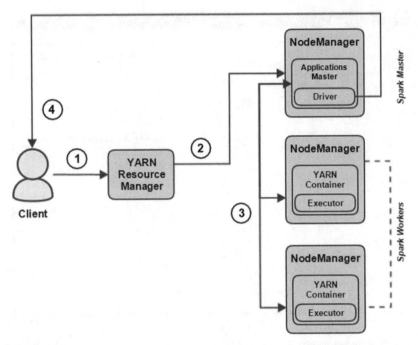

FIGURE 4.7
Spark on YARN in yarn-cluster mode.

Figure 4.7 describes a Spark application running on YARN in `yarn-cluster` mode. The steps involved at a high level are the following:

1. The client (a user process invoking `spark-submit`) submits a Spark application to the cluster manager (the YARN ResourceManager).

2. The ResourceManager assigns an ApplicationsMaster (the Spark master) for the application. The driver process is created on the same node.

3. The ApplicationsMaster requests containers for executors from the ResourceManager. The containers are assigned and the executors are spawned. The driver then communicates with the executors to marshal processing of tasks and stages of the Spark program.

4. The driver returns progress, results, and status to the client.

yarn-client Mode

In `yarn-client` mode, the driver runs on the client, which is *normally* not a node in the cluster. Because the driver is running on a client as opposed to a server process, it is not managed by YARN. The client-based driver process still communicates with the ApplicationsMaster to request executor resources. However, as opposed to `yarn-cluster` mode, in `yarn-client` mode, the client running the driver is required to be available for the entirety of the program because the driver is marshaling all of the tasks and stages in the application.

This mode is better suited to interactive applications because this is the only YARN mode that enables running the interactive Spark shell programs.

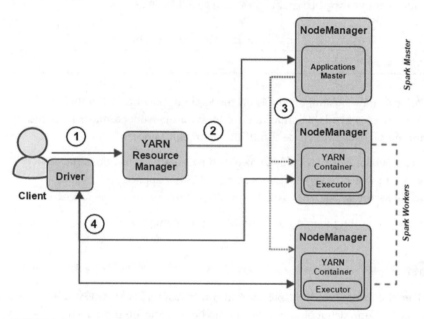

FIGURE 4.8
Spark on YARN in yarn-client mode.

Figure 4.8 describes a Spark application running on YARN in `yarn-client` mode. At a high level, the steps involved are the following:

1. The client submits a Spark application to the cluster manager (the YARN ResourceManager). The driver process is created and runs on the client.

2. The ResourceManager assigns an ApplicationsMaster (the Spark master) for the application.

3. The ApplicationsMaster requests containers for executors from the ResourceManager. The containers are assigned and the executors are spawned.

4. The driver (located on the client) then communicates with the executors to marshal processing of tasks and stages of the Spark program. The driver returns progress, results, and status to the client.

Log File Management with Spark on YARN

YARN has an important feature called *log aggregation* that collects application logs from completed applications and stores them in HDFS. These logs are then made available through a UI called the *YARN Timeline Server*. If log-aggregation is enabled, you can view a completed application through the command shown in Listing 4.1, where `<app ID>` is obtained from the ResourceManager UI: for example, `application_1448348304338_0019`.

LISTING 4.1 Obtaining Application Logs from the Command Line

```
yarn logs -applicationId <app ID>
```

During execution, Spark executor logs are available on the Spark application UI in the executors tab. These logs are also available on local directories on the NodeManager hosts that the executor(s) are running on. However, these can be more difficult to access.

The YARN Timeline Server (which was previously known as the Generic Applications History Server) is an easy interface in which to view logs for completed YARN applications including Spark. The YARN Timeline Server is typically available at `http://<resource_manager>:8188`.

We will discuss much more regarding logging in **Hour 22, "Monitoring Spark."**

Local Mode

In local mode, the driver, the master, and the executor all run in a single JVM. This is useful for development, unit testing, and debugging, but has limited use for running production applications because it is not distributed and does not scale. Furthermore, failed tasks are not re-executed by default. You can override this behavior, however. Local mode is enabled when the `--master local` parameter is supplied when submitting a program, as shown in Listing 4.2.

LISTING 4.2 Spark Pi Estimator in Local Mode

```
spark-submit --class org.apache.spark.examples.SparkPi \
--master local \
$SPARK_HOME/lib/spark-examples*.jar 10
```

Local mode can be used with interactive Spark shells as well. Listing 4.3 shows an example of launching the `PySpark` shell in local mode.

LISTING 4.3 PySpark Interactive Shell in Local Mode

```
pyspark --master local
```

There are several configuration options when launching a Spark program in local mode, all of which are available with both interactive and non-interactive Spark applications. These options can be specified from the command line as a parameter to the `--master` argument when launching an application or a shell. Table 4.1 explains these options.

TABLE 4.1   Local Mode Options

Option	Description
Local	Runs the application in local mode using *one* core.
local[n]	Runs the application in local mode using *n* cores. An asterisk (*) can be used as *n* to enable *all cores* on the system to be used.
local[n,m]	Runs the application in local mode using *n* cores, retrying failed tasks *m* times. An asterisk can be used as *n* to enable *all cores* on the system to be used.

Local mode options can also be specified within your Spark code. An example of programmatically specifying local mode for a non-interactive PySpark application is shown in Listing 4.4. The same can be achieved similarly in Scala as well.

LISTING 4.4   Specifying Local Mode in Your Code

```
from pyspark import SparkContext
sc = SparkContext("local[*]")
# your application code...
```

In local mode, the application UI is available at **http://localhost:4040**. Note that the Master and Worker UIs are not available when running in local mode.

▼ TRY IT YOURSELF

Running a Spark Program in Local Mode

Try running the following steps on a machine with Spark installed as we had set up in **Hour 3, "Installing Spark."**

1. Launch a `PySpark` shell using local mode using the following command:

```
pyspark --master local
```

2. Input the following code into the interactive shell:

```
from random import random
def sample(p):
    x, y = random(), random()
    return 1 if x*x + y*y < 1 else 0
count = sc.parallelize(xrange(0, 1000000)).map(sample) \
  .reduce(lambda a, b: a + b)
print "The result of Pi in %s mode is roughly %f" \
  % (sc.master, (4.0 * count / 1000000))
```

3. Note that the `sc.master` returns the master used by the application, in this case, `local`.

4. Explore the application UI at http://localhost:4040 and note the values in the Spark Properties section of the Environment tab.

Summary

In this hour, I have described Sparks runtime application architecture, its components, and their respective functions.

You learned that the driver is the process that the client interacts with when launching a Spark application, either through one of the interactive shells or through the spark-submit script. The driver is responsible for creating the Spark Context and planning an application by creating a DAG consisting of tasks and stages.

The driver communicates with a cluster manager to allocate application runtime resources (containers) on which executors will run. Executors are specific to a given application and remain active until the completion of the application, successful or otherwise. Executors can run many tasks within an application (hundreds or thousands in some cases).

I explained that when running Spark on YARN, a popular deployment platform for Spark, the cluster manager is the YARN ResourceManager that allocates an ApplicationsMaster to host the Spark master process. In the case of Spark Standalone, the Spark master and the cluster manager are one in the same.

I also discussed running with the --master local option, in which the Driver, Master and Executor run in a single JVM. This can be helpful for debugging Spark programs.

Q&A

Q. Why are tasks grouped into stages in a Spark DAG?

A. Stages enable sets of tasks to be parallelized where ever possible. Spark's intelligent DAG scheduling attempts to make the most efficient use of the resources available to it.

Q. What is the distinction between a worker and an executor?

A. An executor is used to run one to many Spark tasks in an application. Workers refer to the nodes on which executors run in a distributed environment.

Q. Under what circumstances would you typically use the `--master local` argument with `spark-submit`?

A. Using local mode, all Spark processes—the driver, the master, and the executor—run in a single JVM. This is useful for development and testing. However, it's not typically suited for running production applications because it doesn't scale and has limited resiliency.

Workshop

The workshop contains quiz questions and exercises to help you solidify your understanding of the material covered. Try to answer all questions before looking at the "Answers" section that follow.

Quiz

1. **True or false:** The Spark Driver serves the application UI.

2. Which is not a function of the Spark driver?

    A. Allocating resources on the cluster

    B. Initializing the SparkContext

    C. Planning the execution of a Spark program

3. What is the Spark master process called when running Spark on YARN?

4. How many JVMs are spawned in local mode?

Answers

1. **True.**

2. **A.** The Spark driver uses resources on the cluster (executors) negotiated and allocated by a cluster manager or master.

3. The ApplicationsMaster.

4. **One.** The driver, master, and executors run in a single JVM.

HOUR 5
Deploying Spark in the Cloud

What You'll Learn in This Hour:

▶ The basics of Amazon Web Services

▶ How to deploy Spark on AWS EC2 and EMR

▶ How to deploy hosted Spark with Databricks

The rise and proliferation of public and private cloud technology, Software-as-a-Service (SaaS), Infrastructure-as-a-Service (IaaS), and Platform-as-a-Service (PaaS) have truly been game-changers in the way organizations think of technology.

Deploying Spark in the cloud can provide a fast, scalable, and elastic processing environment. In this hour, I look at several methods of deploying Spark platforms, applications, and workloads in the cloud.

Amazon Web Services Primer

If you are already familiar with Amazon Web Services (AWS) and you have an account set up already, feel free to skip this section.

Amazon is one of the world's first and largest online retailers since the early 90s. Amazon has spent years designing and building scalable infrastructure, platforms, services, and application programming interfaces (APIs) to manage their vast business requirements.

In 2003, the vision for Amazon's new technology strategy to build standardized, automated infrastructure leveraging web services and virtualization was unveiled. Subsequently, Amazon realized that this model could not only fulfill the requirements of Amazon's own website but could also be sold to the public as a new, accretive business opportunity. This business ultimately became AWS.

The AWS portfolio contains dozens of different services, from IaaS products such as *Elastic Compute Cloud (EC2)*, storage services such as *Simple Storage Service (S3)*, and PaaS products such as *Elastic MapReduce (EMR)*.

In this book, I will introduce the main technologies that relate to deployment options for Spark. However, many other AWS products are available, so I encourage you to explore AWS further beyond the scope of this book.

Elastic Compute Cloud (EC2)

EC2 is Amazon's web service-enabled virtual computing platform. EC2 enables users to create virtual servers and networks in the cloud. The virtual servers are called *instances*. EC2 instances can be created with a variety of different instance permutations. The *Instance Type* property determines the number of virtual CPUs and the amount of memory and storage an EC2 instance has available to it. An example instance type is m4.large. A complete list of the different EC2 instance types available can be found at **https://aws.amazon.com/ec2/instance-types/**

EC2 instances can be optimized for compute, memory, storage and mixed purposes, and can even include GPUs (graphics processing units), a popular option for machine learning and deep analytics.

There are numerous options for operating systems with EC2 instances. All of the popular Linux distributions are supported (including Red Hat, Ubuntu, and SLES) as well various Microsoft Windows options.

EC2 instances are created in security groups. *Security groups* govern network permissions and access control lists (ACLs). Instances can also be created in a *Virtual Private Cloud (VPC)*. A VPC is a private network, not exposed directly to the Internet. This is a popular option for organizations looking to minimize exposure of EC2 instances to the public internet.

EC2 instances can be provisioned with various storage options, including *instance storage* or *ephemeral storage* (volatile storage that is lost when an instance is stopped) and *Elastic Block Store (EBS)* (persistent, fault tolerant storage). There are different options with each, such as SSD (solid state) for instance storage or provisioned IOPS with EBS.

Additionally, AWS offers *Spot instances,* which allow you to bid on spare Amazon EC2 computing capacity, often available at a discount compared to normal on-demand EC2 instance pricing.

EC2, as well as all other AWS services, is located in an AWS *region*. There are currently nine regions, which include the following:

- ▶ US East (N. Virginia)
- ▶ US West (Oregon)
- ▶ US West (N. California)
- ▶ EU (Ireland)
- ▶ EU (Frankfurt)

▶ Asia Pacific (Singapore)

▶ Asia Pacific (Sydney)

▶ Asia Pacific (Tokyo)

▶ South America (Sao Paulo)

Simple Storage Service (S3)

The AWS Simple Storage Service is storage in Amazon's cloud-based *object store*. An object store manages data (such as files) as objects. These objects exist in *buckets*. Buckets are logical, user-created containers with properties and permissions. S3 provides APIs for users to create and manage buckets as well as to create, read, and delete objects from buckets.

The S3 bucket namespace is global, meaning that any buckets created must have a globally unique name. The AWS console or APIs will let you know if you are trying to create a bucket with a name that already exists.

S3 objects, like files in HDFS, are immutable, meaning they are write once, read many. When an S3 object is created and uploaded, an *ETag* is created, which is effectively a signature for the object. This can be used to ensure integrity when the object is accessed (downloaded) in the future.

There are also public buckets in S3 containing *public data sets*. These are datasets provided for informational/educational purposes, but can be used for data operations such as processing with Hadoop or Spark. Datasets range from historical weather data to census data to astronomical data to genetic data, many of which are in the tens or hundreds of terabytes.

S3 objects can be seamlessly accessed using Spark, as I'll discuss later. More information about S3 is available at **https://aws.amazon.com/s3/**

Elastic MapReduce (EMR)

Elastic MapReduce or EMR is Amazon's Hadoop-as-a-Service platform. EMR clusters can be provisioned using the AWS Management Console or via the AWS APIs. Options for creating EMR clusters include number of nodes, node instance types, Hadoop distribution, and additional applications to install (which include Spark).

EMR clusters can read data and output results directly to and from S3. They are intended to be provisioned on demand run a discrete work flow, a job flow, and terminate. They do have local storage, but as they are not intended to run in perpetuity. You should only use this local storage for transient data.

EMR is a quick and scalable deployment method for Spark. More information about EMR can be found at **https://aws.amazon.com/elasticmapreduce/**

AWS Pricing and Getting Started

EC2 and EMR are charged based upon usage. Each instance type within each region has an instance/hour cost associated with it. The usage costs per hour are usually relatively low and the medium- to long-term costs are quite reasonable, but the more resources you use for longer, the more you are charged.

If you have not already signed up with AWS, you're in luck! AWS has a free tier available for new accounts that enables you to use certain instance types and services for free for the first year. You can find out more at **https://aws.amazon.com/free/**

This page walks you through setting up an account with no ongoing obligations.

Spark on EC2

The Spark installation includes a set of scripts and libraries to deploy Spark on EC2. The Spark EC2 deployment scripts deploy a fully functional Spark cluster with a user-defined number of instances in Standalone mode using AWS EC2 instances. In addition, the Spark EC2 deployment scripts also install and configure

- ▶ An HDFS cluster co-located with the Spark slave nodes
- ▶ An *Alluxio* (formerly called *Tachyon*) cluster co-located with the Spark slave nodes (as in-memory distributed file system)
- ▶ Scala
- ▶ R with an instance of R-Studio server
- ▶ Ganglia (optionally installed for monitoring)

To set up Spark on EC2, you will need the following:

- ▶ An AWS Account
- ▶ An AWS User with an `AWS_ACCESS_KEY_ID` and `AWS_SECRET_ACCESS_KEY`
- ▶ A host with a Spark installation

After you are signed up with AWS and signed in for the first time, you will typically be using your *root* account. Best practice is to create one or more additional *Identity and Access Management (IAM)* user accounts. These user accounts can be be delegated granular permissions in AWS such as the permission to create and terminate instances.

After you create an account, you can use the IAM console to create AWS access keys and AWS secret keys. These are API keys that you can use to create and manage AWS products without using the AWS Management Console. There are SDKs available for AWS in a number of languages such as Python, Ruby, Java, and more that can be used to deploy any product in the AWS portfolio.

Before you get started, you can get more info relating to the Spark on EC2 at
http://spark.apache.org/docs/latest/ec2-scripts.html

In your Spark installation in $SPARK_HOME/ec2, you will find the spark-ec2 shell script. This is a wrapper script for a Python program in the same directory. This program is self-contained and will download all of its dependencies at runtime. The syntax for the spark-ec2 script is shown in Listing 5.1.

LISTING 5.1   spark-ec2 Syntax

```
spark-ec2 [options] <action> <cluster_name>
```

The *cluster_name* is a user-defined name for the cluster. This name will be used to manage and terminate the cluster after creation. The *actions* available for the spark-ec2 program are listed in Table 5.1.

TABLE 5.1   spark-ec2 Actions

Action	Description
launch	Creates a Spark EC2 cluster
start	Starts a Spark EC2 cluster
login	Login to a Spark EC2 cluster
Stop	Stops a Spark EC2 cluster
destroy	Deletes a Spark EC2 cluster
get-master	Get the master hostname for a Spark EC2 cluster
reboot-slaves	Reboot slave nodes in a Spark EC2 cluster

The launch option will create a Spark cluster with the options specified and will also create the security groups *<cluster_name>_*master and *<cluster_name>_*slaves, which will contain all of the inbound and outbound network rules to allow the cluster to function (for example, which incoming and outgoing IP addresses and ports are allowed). You can also specify to launch a Spark cluster in a VPC to provide further isolation from the public Internet.

More than 30 different options are available for the `spark-ec2` script. To keep things simple, I have listed the most commonly used options in Table 5.2.

TABLE 5.2   spark-ec2 Options

Option	Description
`-s,--slaves`	Number of slaves to launch (default: 1)
`-k,--key-pair`	Key pair to use on instances
`-i,--identity-file`	SSH private key file to use for logging into instances
`-t,--instance-type`	Type of instance to launch: must be 64-bit and small instances are not supported (default: `m1.large`)
`-r, --region`	EC2 region used to use (default: `us-east-1`)
`--ebs-vol-num`	Number of EBS volumes to attach to each node for additional storage (up to eight volumes are supported)
`--ebs-vol-size`	Size (in GB) of each EBS volume
`--copy-aws-credentials`	Add AWS credentials to Hadoop configuration to allow Spark to access S3

By default, the instances are launched using an *Amazon Machine Image (AMI),* which consists of Amazon Linux (Amazon's distribution of Linux based on Centos).

Deploying Spark on EC2

In this exercise, you will set up a Spark cluster in Standalone mode with one master and three slave nodes using `m1.large` instances:

1. Create a *keypair* that will be used to authenticate and manage EC2 instances. From the AWS Management Console home, select the EC2 option, as shown in Figure 5.1.

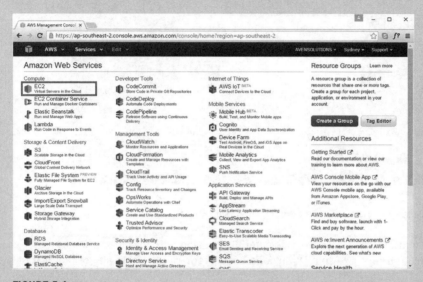

FIGURE 5.1
The AWS Management Console, EC2 management.

2. From the EC2 Management Console, select Key Pairs from the Network & Security section on the menu on the left. Then select Create Key Pair. Name the keypair `spark-cluster` and select Create, as shown in Figure 5.2.

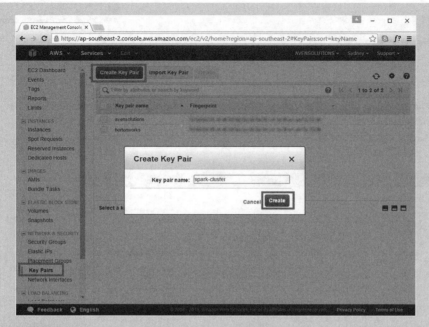

FIGURE 5.2
The EC2 Management Console—Key Pair creation dialog box.

This will create the keypair in your selected EC2 region and download a file called `spark-cluster.pem` to your Downloads folder. You will need this file for the next step.

3. Copy the `spark-cluster.pem` file to the `$SPARK_HOME/ec2` directory of a host (any host) with Spark installed.

4. Set permissions on the file `spark-cluster.pem`, which allows read-only for the owner only using the following command:

```
sudo chmod 400 $SPARK_HOME/ec2/spark-cluster.pem
```

5. Obtain your access key and secret key by selecting Identity & Access Management from the AWS Management Console, as shown in Figure 5.3.

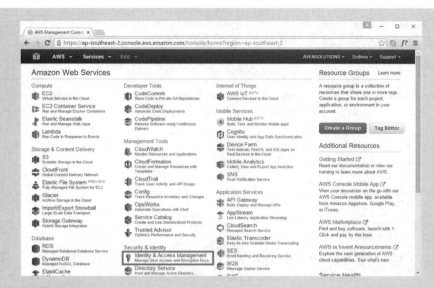

FIGURE 5.3
The AWS Management Console—Identity & Access Management.

6. In the IAM Console, select Users from the left menu, highlight your desired user, and go to the Security Credentials tab. Click Create Access Key, and then select Download Credentials, as shown in Figure 5.4. This downloads a comma-separated value (.CSV) file containing the access key and secret key you will use in subsequent steps.

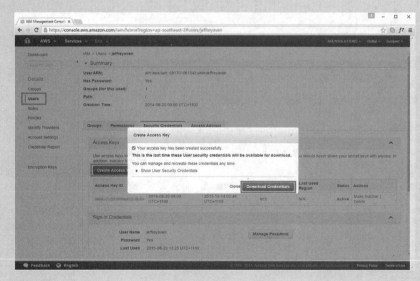

FIGURE 5.4
The IAM Console: Create and download API keys.

7. From the Spark host where you will be running the launch scripts, set the `AWS_ACCESS_KEY_ID` and `AWS_SECRET_ACCESS_KEY` environment variables as shown:

```
export AWS_ACCESS_KEY_ID=YOURACCESSKEY
export AWS_SECRET_ACCESS_KEY=YOURSECRETKEY
```

8. From the `$SPARK_HOME/ec2` directory, execute the following command (substitute the value for `--region` with the AWS region you will be using):

```
./spark-ec2 --key-pair=spark-cluster \
--identity-file=spark-cluster.pem \
--region=your-region \
--slaves=3 \
--instance-type=m1.large \
--copy-aws-credentials \
--no-ganglia \
launch my-spark-cluster
```

9. View the EC2 instances created in the AWS Management Console, as shown in Figure 5.5.

FIGURE 5.5
Spark cluster instances in AWS Management Console.

10. Run the following command to return the master instance public DNS name:

```
./spark-ec2 --region=your-region \
get-master my-spark-cluster
```

This command should return something like this:

```
Searching for existing cluster my-spark-cluster in region ap-southeast-2...
Found 1 master, 3 slaves.
ec2-52-62-56-83.ap-southeast-2.compute.amazonaws.com
```

11. Use the public DNS name returned by the command run in Step 8 to open the Spark Master UI for the EC2 cluster. The Spark Master UI can be found at port 8080 of the master node instance, as shown in Figure 5.6.

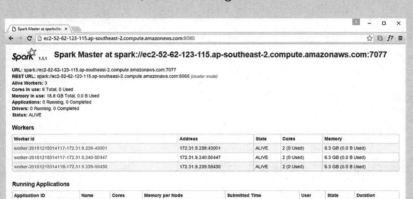

FIGURE 5.6
The Spark Master UI.

12. Click one of the worker nodes listed in the Workers section of the Spark master UI to view a worker UI (located on port 8081 of a cluster slave node), as shown in Figure 5.7.

FIGURE 5.7
The Spark Worker UI.

▼

13. View the HDFS NameNode UI for the HDFS cluster deployed with Spark, which is located on port 50070 of the Master node (which you obtained the hostname for in Step 8). The NameNode UI is shown in Figure 5.8.

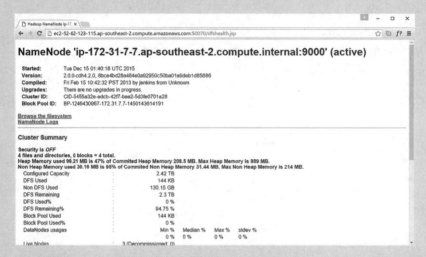

FIGURE 5.8
The HDFS NameNode UI.

14. As discussed, an Alluxio (Tachyon) distributed in memory filesystem cluster is also installed by default by the `spark-ec2` scripts. You can view the Alluxio (Tachyon) Master UI on port 19999 of the Spark master instance, as shown in Figure 5.9.

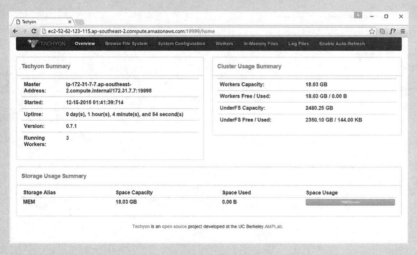

FIGURE 5.9
The Alluxio (Tachyon) Master UI.

15. SparkR and R-Studio are also installed by default. I discuss Spark and R more in **Hour 15, "Getting Started with Spark and R,"** but you can view the R-Studio UI on port 8787 of the Spark master instance, as shown in Figure 5.10.

FIGURE 5.10
The R Studio UI.

16. Now stop your Spark EC2 cluster by executing the following command:

```
./spark-ec2 --region=your-region \
stop my-spark-cluster
```

17. You can restart your cluster at any time by executing the following command:

```
./spark-ec2 --key-pair=spark-cluster \
--identity-file=spark-cluster.pem \
--region=your-region \
start my-spark-cluster
```

18. You can also login to run commands, such `spark-submit`, `spark-shell`, and `pyspark`, by using the `login` action, as shown here:

```
./spark-ec2 --key-pair=spark-cluster \
--identity-file=spark-cluster.pem \
--region=your-region \
login my-spark-cluster
```

Congratulations! You have just set up a fully functional three-node Spark cluster on AWS EC2!

Spark on EMR

Spark can also be deployed on AWS using the AWS Elastic MapReduce (EMR) Hadoop PaaS offering. EMR provides a wizard-driven console interface and numerous APIs to provision a Hadoop cluster complete with HDFS, YARN, and Spark, as well as other ecosystem projects such as Hive, Pig, HUE, Presto, and Zepplin.

To deploy Spark on EMR, you will need the following:

▶ An AWS account

▶ An AWS user with an `AWS_ACCESS_KEY_ID` and `AWS_SECRET_ACCESS_KEY`. These are required if you intend to use the APIs to deploy Spark on EMR, such as the AWS CLI (command line interface) or an AWS SDK (software development kit)

▶ A key pair created. You can use the key pair created in the previous section's Try It Yourself exercise (`spark-cluster`)

EMR allows you to deploy either Amazon's distribution of Hadoop or the MapR distribution of Hadoop. Clusters can be launched in *cluster mode*, which creates a cluster that remains active until you terminate it, or in *step execution mode,* when the cluster will launch run one or more processes (steps), including Spark applications, typically using data from S3, and then terminate automatically.

EMR clusters can include any number of nodes; however, there is usually a default limit of 20 nodes. You can apply to AWS to remove this limit. Node instances can run most of the available instance types (including memory optimized, compute optimized, or dense storage instance types). EMR has three node types available, as shown in Table 5.3.

TABLE 5.3 **EMR Node Types**

Node Type	Description
Master node	Hadoop combined master node, including YARN ResourceManager and HDFS NameNode. Only one master mode is allowed in an EMR cluster.
Core node	Hadoop slave node running NodeManager and DataNode functions, capable of processing and storing data.
Task node	Hadoop slave node running NodeManager function only, capable of processing but not storing data. Useful if your inputs and outputs consist only of S3 objects.

Task nodes, core nodes, and master nodes can also run different instance types.

Access to your EMR cluster can be obtained via SSH into the Master node or via one of the web UIs associated with one or more of the installed applications such as HUE (Hadoop User Environment). These web UIs are not directly accessible via the public network. To access these, you must use an SSH tunnel created through the master node.

Your AWS API keys are automatically added to the Hadoop config files to allow you seamlessly read and write to and from S3 buckets that you have permissions to access. S3 is the intended primary storage medium for EMR because this will persist independent of the EMR cluster.

Deploying Spark on AWS EMR

In this exercise, you will create an EMR cluster consisting of one master and two core nodes including Spark and Zeppelin. *Apache Zeppelin* is a web-based, multi-language, interactive notebook application with native Spark integration. Zeppelin provides a query environment for Spark as well as providing data visualization capabilities.

For this exercise, you will need the key pair created in the previous exercise, **"Deploying Spark on EC2."**

NOTE
_____

If you use the AWS APIs (such as the AWS CLI) to deploy the EMR cluster, you will need the access key and secret keys created in the previous exercise as well.
_____

1. From the AWS Management Console, select the EMR option, as shown in Figure 5.11.

FIGURE 5.11
The AWS Management Console: EMR option.

2. From the EMR home page, click Create Cluster, as shown in Figure 5.12.

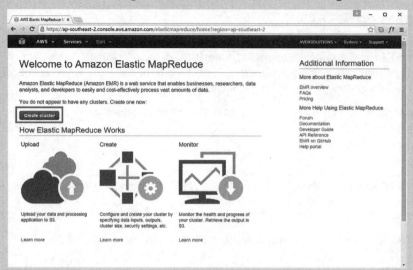

FIGURE 5.12
Click Create Cluster.

3. From the Create Cluster home page, select Go to Advanced Options.

4. From the Advanced Options Step 1: Software and Steps dialog box, select the Zeppelin and Spark options under Software Configuration, as shown in Figure 5.13. Then click Next.

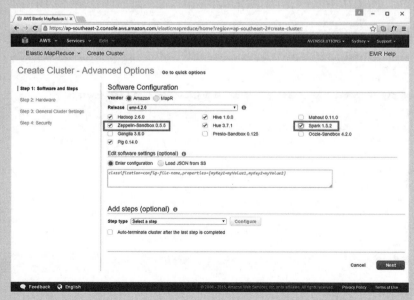

FIGURE 5.13
Select the Zeppelin and Spark software options in EMR.

5. On the Step 2: Hardware dialog box, accept the default options on one master and two core nodes and click Next, as shown in Figure 5.14.

FIGURE 5.14
The EMR hardware dialog box.

6. From the Step 3: General Cluster Settings dialog box in the General Options section, change the Cluster name to *My Spark EMR Cluster,* as shown in Figure 5.15. Then click Next.

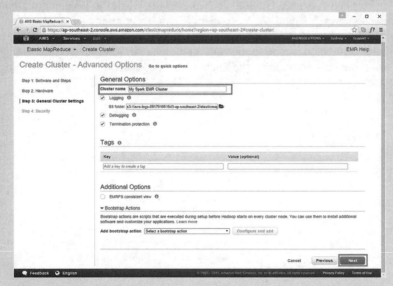

FIGURE 5.15
The cluster name setting.

7. On the Step 4: Security dialog box in the Security Options section, select `spark-cluster` from the EC2 key pair drop-down list, as shown in Figure 5.16. Then click Create Cluster.

FIGURE 5.16
The key pair setting.

8. After your EMR cluster has been provisioned, you will see the cluster in a waiting state in the EMR console, as shown in Figure 5.17. Connect to the Master node via SSH using the Master public DNS hostname and your `spark-cluster.pem` file. Instructions can be found by clicking the SSH link provided in the AWS EMR console. After an SSH session is established, follow the instructions using the Enable Web Connection link to create an SSH tunnel for web access.

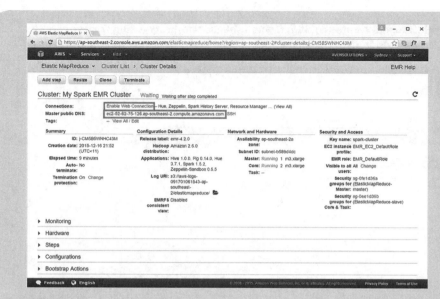

FIGURE 5.17
Connecting to your EMR cluster.

9. Your SSH session created in Step 8 should look like Figure 5.18.

FIGURE 5.18
The EMR terminal prompt.

From the terminal prompt, type `pyspark`. You will see that a PySpark session has been instantiated using YARN as the scheduler.

10. Using the SSH tunnel created in Step 8 and configuring a proxy (using FoxyProxy for
example) as detailed in the Enable Web Connection link, open a browser session using
`<master_public_dns>:8890`. This will display the Zeppelin home page, as shown
in Figure 5.19.

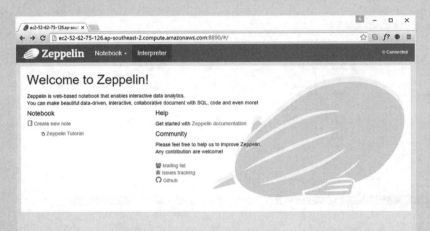

FIGURE 5.19
The Zeppelin home page.

11. From the top line menu of the Zeppelin home page, select Notebook, Create New Note.
Accept the default note name. Click the Notebook link again and then select the notebook
you just created. (It will be something like NOTE *XXXXXXXXX*.) Enter the code shown below
and click Shift+Enter.

```
val textFile = sc.textFile("s3://sty-spark/shakespeare.txt")
textFile.count()
```

This is the works of Shakespeare stored in a text file in a publicly available S3 bucket
named `sty-spark`. You are simply counting the lines of text in the file using the `count()`
action.

12. You should see a result of `Long = 129107`.

Congratulations. You have just set up an EMR cluster complete with Spark and Zeppelin!

To terminate your cluster, select Terminate in the EMR home page with your EMR cluster selected.
You will need to follow the prompts to disable termination protection, which protects you from
inadvertent termination of the cluster.

Hosted Spark with Databricks

Databricks is an integrated cloud-based Spark workspace that allows users to launch managed Spark clusters and ingest and interact with data from S3 or other relational database or flat file data sources, either in the cloud or from your environment.

The Databricks platform uses your AWS credentials to create its required infrastructure components, so you effectively have ownership of these assets in your AWS account. Databricks provides the deployment, management, and user/application interface framework for a cloud-based Spark platform in AWS.

Databricks has several pricing plans available with different features including different support levels, security and access control options, GitHub integration, and more. Pricing is subscription based with a flat monthly fee plus nominal utilization charges (charged per hour per node). Databricks offers a 14-day free trial period to get started. You will also be responsible for the instance costs incurred in AWS for Spark clusters deployed using the Databricks platform; however, Databricks allows you to use discounted spot instances to minimize AWS costs. For the latest pricing and subscription information, go to **https://databricks.com/product/pricing**

Databricks provides a simple deployment and user interface abstracting the underlying infrastructure and security complexities involved with setting up a secure Spark environment in AWS. Moreover, the Databricks management console allows you to create notebooks (similar to the Zeppelin notebook deployed with AWS EMR in the previous section). These notebooks are automatically associated with your Spark cluster and allow you seamless programmatic access to Spark functions using Python, Scala, SQL, or R.

Databricks also deploys its own distributed file system called the Databricks File System (DBFS). DBFS allows you to mount existing S3 buckets and make these seamlessly available in your Spark workspace. You can also cache data on the solid-state disks (SSDs) of your worker nodes to speed up access. The `dbutils` library included in your Spark workspace allows you configure and interact with the DBFS.

The Databricks platform and management console allows you to create data objects as *tables* (conceptually similar to tables in a relational database) from a variety of sources including AWS S3 buckets, JDBC data sources, the Databricks File Systems (DBFS), or by uploading your own files using the drag-and-drop functionality.

You can also create *jobs* using the Databricks console, which can be run noninteractively on a user-defined schedule.

▼ TRY IT YOURSELF

Deploying Spark Using Databricks

You need to register with Databricks to get started. During the registration process, you will select a username and password that will be used to access the Databricks console and any Spark clusters and notebooks you create. You will also need to supply your billing information because this is a subscription-based service.

You can register using the Sign Up link at https://databricks.com/

After you are registered with Databricks and have selected a plan (in this case, I'm using the starter plan), you can create a Spark cluster and notebook workspace using the following steps:

1. Supply your AWS account information and access credentials to Databricks. This can be done in one of two ways:

   a. By using a cross-account role in AWS, which will delegate the required privileges to create the Spark environment; or

   b. By using your AWS account, your access key ID, and your secret access key

Because you've already created an AWS IAM account and downloaded the credentials in the Spark on EC2 Try It Yourself exercise, go ahead and reuse these, as shown in Figure 5.20.

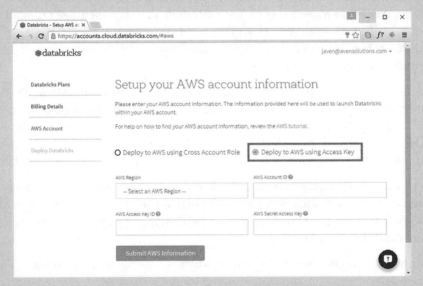

FIGURE 5.20
Supplying your AWS account information to Databricks.

Note that you will also need to provide your AWS Account ID. This can be obtained from the AWS Management Console by selecting My Account from the drop-down list as shown in Figure 5.21, and then copying the 12-digit Account ID from the dialog box shown in Figure 5.22.

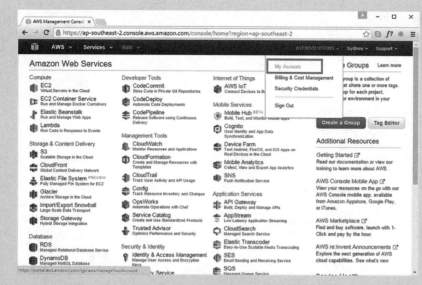

FIGURE 5.21
The AWS Management Console—My Account option.

FIGURE 5.22
The AWS Account ID.

2. After you have entered all of the required information, select Submit AWS Information. If all of your information is correct, you should see a dialog box similar to Figure 5.23.

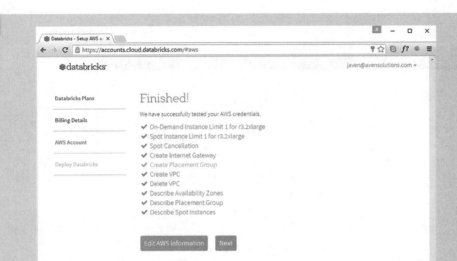

FIGURE 5.23
Databricks AWS account verification.

If you don't see any errors, click **Next**. If there are errors you should get a message indicating what the errors are and how to resolve them.

3. Launch the Databricks environment in AWS by clicking the Deploy button on the Deploy Databricks dialog box, as shown in Figure 5.24.

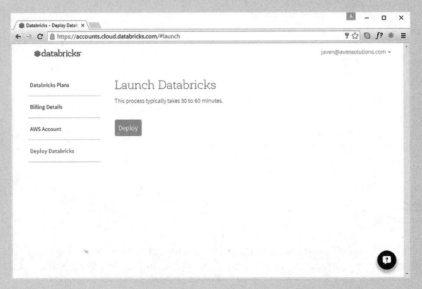

FIGURE 5.24
Deploy Databricks.

This operation creates the necessary supporting AWS infrastructure components required to create one or more Spark clusters. These components include

- A VPC with associated network ACLs

- VPC security groups to be associated with Spark nodes

- Associated VPC subnets and route tables

- Keypairs to allow instance-level access

After the supporting components have been deployed, you will receive an email with a link to access your environment. Note: At this stage, no instances are created.

4. After you have received your deployment confirmation, click the link supplied in the email. This will take you to your Databricks console. Click the **Cluster** link to create a new Spark cluster, as shown in Figure 5.25.

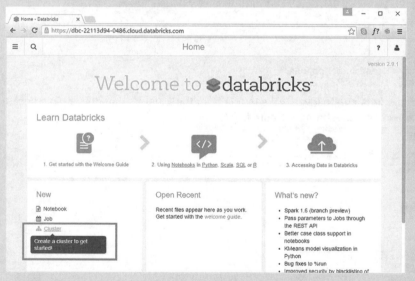

FIGURE 5.25
Create a Databricks Spark cluster.

5. From the ensuing Create Cluster dialog box (as shown in Figure 5.26), enter a name for your cluster, select the Spark Version required (this example uses Spark 1.5.2, but you can select earlier versions or the latest development releases), and select the number of workers desired. If you wish to use Spot instances to save AWS EC2 instance costs, select the Use Spot Instances option. Then click Confirm.

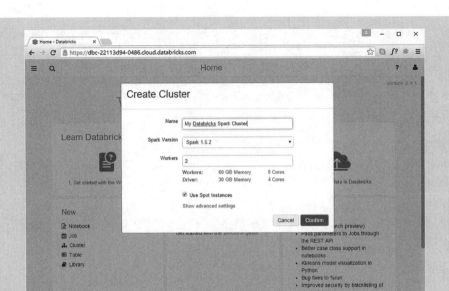

FIGURE 5.26
The Databricks Spark cluster options.

6. After your cluster is created, you will see this from the Clusters link of your Databricks console home page, as shown in Figure 5.27.

FIGURE 5.27
The Databricks Clusters list.

7. Create a notebook associated with your cluster by selecting New Notebook from your Databricks console home page. You should see a dialog box similar to Figure 5.28. Give your notebook a Name, select Python as the Language, and ensure that the cluster you just created is selected in the Cluster drop-down list. Click Create.

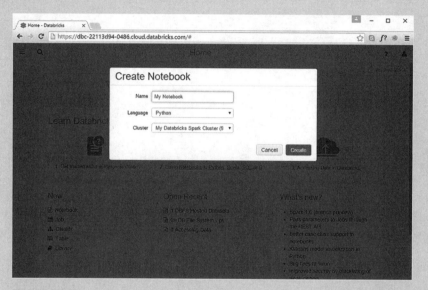

FIGURE 5.28
Create a new notebook.

8. Open your new notebook and use your Spark cluster to count the number of lines in the `shakespeare.txt` file in the `sty-spark` S3 bucket as you did in the Try It Yourself exercise in the previous section, "Spark on EMR." Do this using the Databricks File System (DBFS) and the `dbutils.fs.mount` command. Copy and paste the following Python code into your notebook, supplying your AWS credentials. Press Shift+Enter to execute the script. You should see the result as shown in Figure 5.29.

```
dbutils.fs.mount("s3n://%s:%s@%s" % ("YOURACCESSKEY" \
, "YOURSECRETKEY" \
, "sty-spark"), "/mnt/%s" % "sty-spark")
textFile = sc.textFile("/mnt/sty-spark/shakespeare.txt")
count = textFile.count()
dbutils.fs.unmount("/mnt/%s" % "sty-spark")
print "There are %s lines in the shakespeare file" % count
```

FIGURE 5.29
Testing the Databricks cluster and notebook.

You will need to escape any forward slashes in your AWS secret key by replacing these with %2F.

9. You can terminate your cluster by selecting the Terminate option, as shown in Figure 5.27. Note that this will terminate the associated EC2 instances. Any data stored locally on these instances will be lost. All other Databricks infrastructure components will remain (VPC, security groups, and so on) and will be used for any future Spark clusters.

You are now up and running with Databricks, using Spark in the cloud!

Summary

In this hour, you have learned several methods to deploy Spark in the cloud, including Amazon Web Services Elastic Compute Cloud (EC2) and Elastic MapReduce (EMR), and hosted Spark using Databricks' subscription-based offering.

The capability to deploy Spark on AWS EC2 is built in to the Spark install using the spark-ec2 script. The spark-ec2 script lets you start up, run applications, manage, and terminate Spark clusters of various sizes, using various instance types, in EC2. Storage options available to you using Spark on EC2 include HDFS (ephemeral and persistent) and Amazon S3.

Spark can be easily deployed as a processing engine to accompany Amazon Elastic MapReduce (EMR), Amazon's Hadoop-as-a-Service offering. Spark can be used in EMR job flows to process data local to the EMR cluster in HDFS or data in S3. EMR give you access to a massively scalable Hadoop platform, enabling Spark as well as additional processing engines such as Presto and others.

Databricks provides a hosted subscription-based solution for running Spark. The Databricks solution not only provides the Spark Core platform as a managed service, but also provides integrated access to visualization and exploration tools as well as the ability to create workflows and production data processing pipelines.

Q&A

Q. What is the primary difference between instance storage and EBS in AWS?

A. Instance storage is terminated when its associated EC2 instance is terminated, whereas an EBS volume is persistent independent of the instance and can be reattached to another instance.

Q. What is the difference between a task node and a core node in AWS Elastic MapReduce?

A. A task node can only process data, whereas a core node can process and store data. You would typically use task nodes in favor of core nodes if you were writing to and from S3 exclusively.

Q. What is `dbutils.fs` used for with Databricks?

A. `dbutils.fs` is a utility module that allows you to programatically interact with the Databricks File System (DBFS) including mounting and unmounting S3 buckets and caching files.

Workshop

The workshop contains quiz questions and exercises to help you solidify your understanding of the material covered. Try to answer all questions before looking at the "Answers" section that follows.

Quiz

1. Which `spark-ec2` action is used to get the hostname of the master instance for a Spark EC2 cluster?

2. Which of the the following applications can be deployed using AWS Elastic MapReduce?

    A. Spark

    B. Zeppelin

    C. HUE

    D. All of the above

3. What is the name of the integrated programming and visualization tool associated with a Databricks Spark cluster?

4. **True or false:** Deploying a Spark cluster using Databricks does not require an AWS account.

Answers

1. The `get-master` action returns the hostname for the Spark Master EC2 instance.

2. **D.** All three can be deployed using AWS Elastic MapReduce.

3. A notebook.

4. **False.** Databricks is deployed on AWS and requires an AWS account and user credentials to create a Spark cluster.

HOUR 6
Learning the Basics of Spark Programming with RDDs

What You'll Learn in This Hour:

▶ What Resilient Distributed Datasets (RDDs) are
▶ Types of RDDs
▶ How to load data into an RDD
▶ How RDDs are evaluated and processed
▶ How fault tolerance is achieved with RDDs

I've covered Spark's runtime architecture and how to deploy Spark not only locally on multiple different platforms, but also different methods of deploying Spark in the cloud. I've also discussed the basics of Hadoop as a platform that often accompanies Spark. Now I will show you how to program in Spark, starting with the basics.

In this hour, I will introduce the Resilient Distributed Dataset (RDD), the most fundamental concept in Spark programming and execution.

Introduction to RDDs

The Resilient Distributed Dataset (RDD) is the most fundamental data object used in Spark programming. RDDs are datasets within a Spark application, including the initial dataset(s) loaded, any intermediate dataset(s), and the final resultant dataset(s). Most Spark programming consists of creating new RDDs by performing operations on existing RDDs.

RDDs use various types of elements, from primitive data types such as integers, floating point numbers, and strings, to complex types such as lists or hashes, including nested objects, as well as serialized Scala and Java objects.

Although there are options for persisting RDDs to disk, RDDs are predominantly stored in memory (or intended to be stored in memory at least). As one of the initial intended uses for Spark was to support machine learning, Spark's RDDs provided a restricted form of shared memory that could make efficient reuse of data for successive/iterative operations.

Moreover, one of the main downsides of Hadoop's implementation of MapReduce was its persistence of intermediate data to disk and the copying of this data between nodes at runtime. This distributed processing method of sharing data did provide resiliency and fault tolerance; however, it was at the cost of latency. As data volumes increased along with the necessity for real-time data processing and insights, Spark's (mainly) in-memory processing framework based on the RDD grew in popularity.

The term *Resilient Distributed Dataset* is an accurate and succinct descriptor for the concept. Here's how it breaks down:

- ▶ **Resilient:** RDDs are *resilient,* meaning that if a node performing an operation in Spark is lost, the dataset can be reconstructed. This is because Spark knows the *lineage* of each RDD, which is the sequence of steps to create the RDD.

- ▶ **Distributed:** RDDs are *distributed,* meaning the data in RDDs is divided into one or many *partitions* and distributed as in-memory collections of objects across worker nodes in the cluster. As mentioned, RDDs provide an effective form of shared memory to exchange data between processes (executors) on different nodes (workers).

- ▶ **Dataset:** RDDs are *datasets* that consist of *records.* Records are uniquely identifiable data collections within a dataset. Records could be a collection of fields similar to a row in a table in a relational database, a line of text in a file, or multiple other formats. I cover records in greater detail in **Hour 7, "Understanding MapReduce Concepts."** RDDs are partitioned such that each partition contains a unique set of records and can be operated on independently: It's known as the *shared nothing* approach.

Another key property of RDDs is their immutability, which means that after they are instantiated and populated with data, they cannot be updated. Instead, new RDDs are created by performing *transformations* such as map or filter functions on existing RDDs.

Actions are the other operations that can be performed on RDDs. Actions produce output that can be in the form of data from an RDD returned to a driver program or saving the content of an RDD to a filesystem (local, HDFS, S3, or other). There are many other actions as well, including returning a count of the number of records in a RDD. I will cover transformations and actions in much greater detail later in this book. Listing 6.1 shows a sample Spark program loading data into an RDD, creating a new RDD using a filter transformation, and then using an action to save the resultant RDD to disk.

LISTING 6.1 PySpark Program to Search for Errors in Log Files

```
# load log files from local filesystem
logfilesrdd = sc.textFile("file:///var/log/hadoop/hdfs/hadoop-hdfs-*")
# filter log records for errors only
onlyerrorsrdd = logfilesrdd.filter(lambda line: "ERROR" in line)
# save onlyerrorsrdd as a file
onlyerrorsrdd.saveAsTextFile("file:///tmp/onlyerrorsrdd")
```

NOTE

The `saveAsTextFile()` action actually creates a directory containing multiple text files. This is because the RDD is partitioned and processed in parallel. In the preceding example, each individual text file in the output directory is the filtered result from a particular partition of the data loaded in the initial RDD.

More detail about RDD concepts can be found in the University of California, Berkeley paper, "Resilient Distributed Datasets: A Fault-Tolerant Abstraction for In-Memory Cluster Computing," which can be obtained at following location:
http://www.cs.berkeley.edu/~matei/papers/2012/nsdi_spark.pdf

Loading Data into RDDs

RDDs are effectively created after they are populated with data. This can be the result of transformations on an existing RDD being written into a new RDD as part of a Spark program. However, to start any Spark routine, you need to initialize at least one RDD with data from an external source. This can be done in several ways, including

▶ Loading data from a file or files

▶ Loading data from a datasource (such as a SQL or NoSQL datastore)

▶ Loading data programatically

▶ Loading data from a stream

Loading data from a stream is covered in detail in **Hour 14, "Stream Processing with Spark."** In the meantime, I will cover the other methods now.

Creating an RDD from a File or Files

Spark provides API methods to create RDDs from a file, files, or the contents of a directory. Files can be of various formats, from unstructured text files, to semi-structured files such as JSON files, to structured data sources such as .CSV files. Spark also provides support for several common serialized binary encoded formats such as `SequenceFiles` and Protocol Buffers (`protobufs`).

Spark and File Compression

Spark includes native support for several lossless compression formats. Spark can seamlessly read from common compressed file formats including GZip and Zip (or any other compressed archives created using the DEFLATE compression method), as well as BZip2 compressed archives.

Spark also provides native *codecs* (libraries for compression and decompressing data) that enable both reading and writing of compressed files. Built-in codecs include LZ4 and LZF (LZ77-based lossless compression formats) and *Snappy*.

Snappy is a fast, splittable, low CPU data compression and decompression library written by Google that is commonly used within the Hadoop core and ecosystem projects. Snappy is used by default for compressing data internal to Spark, such as the data in RDD partitions exchanged across the network between workers.

CAUTION

Splittable versus Non-splittable Compression Formats

It's important to distinguish between *splittable* and *non-splittable* compression formats when using distributed processing platforms such as Spark or Hadoop.

Splittable compression formats are indexed so that they can be split—typically on block boundaries—without compromising the integrity of the archive. Non-splittable formats, on the other hand, are not indexed and cannot be split. This means that a non-splittable archive must be read in its entirety by one system because it cannot be distributed.

Common desktop compression formats such as Zip and GZip, although they can achieve high rates of compression, are not splittable. This may be okay for small files containing lookup data, but for larger datasets, splittable compression formats such as Snappy or LZO are preferred. In some cases, you are better off decompressing the files altogether before ingesting into a distributed file system such as HDFS.

Data Locality with RDDs

By default, Spark tries to read data into an RDD from the nodes that are close to it. Because Spark usually accesses distributed partitioned data (such as data from HDFS or S3), to optimize transformation operations, it creates partitions to hold the underlying blocks from the distributed file system. Figure 6.1 depicts how blocks from a file in a distributed file system (like HDFS) are used to create RDD partitions on workers, which are co-located with the data.

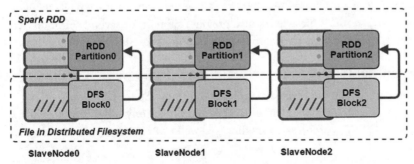

FIGURE 6.1
Loading an RDD from a text file in a distributed file system.

NOTE

If you are not using a distributed filesystem (for instance, if you are creating an RDD from a file on your local filesystem), you need to ensure that the file you are loading is available in the same relative path on all worker nodes in the cluster; otherwise, you will get the following error:

```
java.io.FileNotFoundException: File does not exist
```

For this reason, it's preferable to use a distributed filesystem such as HDFS or S3 as a file-based source for Spark RDDs, uploading the file from your local filesystem to the distributed system first, and then creating the RDD from the distributed object if possible. Another alternative approach to a local filesystem would be to use a shared network filesystem instead.

Methods for Creating RDDs from a Text File or Files

The Spark methods for creating an RDD from a file or files support several different file systems. These are specified by the *scheme* in the URI. The scheme in a URI is the prefix followed by a colon `://`. You see this all the time with Internet resources referred to by the scheme `http://` or `https://`. Schemes and URI structures for common filesystems supported by Spark are summarized in Table 6.1.

TABLE 6.1 Filesystem Schemes and URI Structures

Filesystem	URI Structure
Local Filesystem	file:///path
HDFS[*]	hdfs://*hdfs_path*
Amazon S3[*]	s3://*bucket/path* (also used are s3a and s3n)
OpenStack Swift[*]	swift://*container.PROVIDER/path*

[*] *Requires filesystem configuration parameters to be set*

Text files can be used to create RDDs using the following methods:

textFile()

Syntax:

```
sc.textFile(name, minPartitions=None, use_unicode=True)
```

The `textFile()` method is used to create RDDs from files (compressed or uncompressed), directories, or *glob* patterns (file patterns with wildcards).

The `name` argument specifies the path or glob to be referenced, including the filesystem scheme, as shown in Table 6.1.

The `minPartitions` argument determines the number of partitions to create. By default, if you are using HDFS, each block of the file (typically 64MB or 128MB) creates a single partition, as demonstrated in Figure 6.1. You can request more partitions than there are blocks; however, any number or partitions specified that is less than the number of blocks will revert to the default behavior of one block to one partition.

The use_unicode argument specifies whether to use Unicode or UTF-8 as the character encoding scheme.

The minPartitions and use_unicode arguments are optional as they have default values configured. In most cases, it's not necessary to supply these parameters explicitly unless you need to override the defaults.

Consider the Hadoop filesystem directory shown in Figure 6.2.

```
[root@sandbox ~]# hadoop fs -ls /demo/data/website/website-Logs
Found 2 items
-rwxrwxrwx   1 hdfs hdfs        355 2015-08-19 13:00 /demo/data/we
bsite/Website-Logs/IB_WebsiteLog_1000.txt
-rwxrwxrwx   1 hdfs hdfs        373 2015-08-19 13:00 /demo/data/we
bsite/Website-Logs/IB_WebsiteLog_1001.txt
```

FIGURE 6.2
An HDFS directory listing.

To read files in HDFS, the HADOOP_CONF_DIR environment variable must be set on all worker nodes of the cluster. The Hadoop config directory contains all of the information used by Spark to connect to the appropriate HDFS cluster. This can set automatically using the spark-env.sh script. The command used to set this variable on Linux systems is as follows:

```
export HADOOP_CONF_DIR=/etc/hadoop/conf
```

Examples of the textFile() method loading the data from the HDFS directory pictured in Figure 6.2 are provided in Listing 6.2.

LISTING 6.2   Creating RDDs Using the textFile() Method

```
# load the contents of the entire directory
logs = sc.textFile("hdfs:///demo/data/Website/Website-Logs/")
# load an individual file
logs = sc.textFile("hdfs:///demo/data/Website/Website-Logs/IB_WebsiteLog_1001.txt")
# load a file or files using a glob pattern
logs = sc.textFile("hdfs:///demo/data/Website/Website-Logs/*_1001.txt")
```

In each of the examples given in Listing 6.2, an RDD is created with each line of the file representing a record.

wholeTextFiles()

Syntax:

```
sc.wholeTextFiles(path, minPartitions=None, use_unicode=True)
```

The wholeTextFiles() method lets you read a directory containing multiple files. Each file will be represented as a record containing a key containing the filename and a value containing the contents of the file. In contrast, when reading all files in a directory with the textFile() method, each line of each file represents a separate record with no context as to which file the line originated from. Typically, with event processing, the originating filename is not required because the record contains a timestamp field.

As with the wholeTextFiles() method each record contains the contents of entire file, this method is intended to be used with small files. The minPartitions and use_unicode arguments behave similarly to the textFile() method.

Using the HDFS directory shown in Figure 6.3, an example of the method is shown in Listing 6.3.

LISTING 6.3   Creating RDDs Using the wholeTextFiles() Method

```
logs = sc.wholeTextFiles("hdfs:///demo/data/Website/Website-Logs/")
```

We will contrast the textFile() and wholeTextFiles() methods in the next Try-It-Yourself exercise.

TRY IT YOURSELF

Creating an RDD from TextFiles in a Local Directory

In this exercise, we will examine the behavior of the textFile() and wholeTextFiles() methods using local text files included with the Spark installation.

1. Launch a pyspark shell in local mode using the following command:

   ```
   $SPARK_HOME/bin/pyspark --master local
   ```

   Recall from **Hour 3** that SPARK_HOME was set to our Spark installation directory (/opt/spark).

2. The Spark installation includes a directory named licenses that contains license files for all of the open source projects used within the Spark project (Scala, and so on). Use this as a source of text files to load different RDDs. Enter the following code in the pyspark shell:

   ```
   licensefiles = sc.textFile("file:///opt/spark/licenses/")
   ```

You could also execute the following code using file globs; in this case, the two statements are equivalent because the directory only contains `.txt` files:

```
licensefiles = sc.textFile("file:///opt/spark/licenses/*.txt")
```

3. Execute the following command to describe the RDD created:

```
licensefiles
# you should see a return value like this:
# MapPartitionsRDD[1] at textFile at NativeMethodAccessorImpl.java:-2
```

4. Execute the `getNumPartitions()` method to return the number of partitions contained in the `licensefiles` RDD:

```
licensefiles.getNumPartitions()
# you should see a return value like this:
# 35
```

Each individual file is allocated a partition. Because the licenses directory contained 35 files, our `licensefiles` RDD contains 35 partitions.

5. Count the total number of lines in all of the files combined using the following command:

```
licensefiles.count()
# you should see a return value like this:
# 1061
```

6. Now use the `wholeTextFiles()` method to load the same files into an RDD called `licensefile_pairs` using the following command:

```
licensefile_pairs = sc.wholeTextFiles("file:///opt/spark/licenses/")
```

7. Execute the following command to describe the RDD created:

```
licensefile_pairs
# you should see a return value like this:
# org.apache.spark.api.java.JavaPairRDD@4f3d0c68
```

Note that this is a different object type to the one that was returned in Step 3 as a result of the `textFile()` method.

8. Examine the partitioning behavior of `wholeTextFiles()` by running the following command:

```
licensefile_pairs.getNumPartitions()
# you should see the following output:
# 1
```

Note the key difference between the two approaches. In Step 4, 35 partitions were created using the `textFile()` method to load the same data as there were 35 different files. The `wholeTextFiles()` method combines all of the files (which are quite small in this case) into a single partition.

9. Count the number of records in the RDD using the following command:

```
licensefile_pairs.count()
# should return 35
```

Recall from Step 5 that the same data loaded using `textFile()` returned a count of 1061, each line of each file representing a single record. In the case of `wholeTextFiles()`, each file is a single record.

10. Use the `keys()` method to create a new RDD named `filenames` containing only a list of the keys from the `licensefile_pairs` RDD.

```
filenames = licensefile_pairs.keys()
filenames.collect()
# the last command will return an array of filenames like..
#[u'file:/opt/spark/licenses/LICENSE-scala.txt', ...]
```

11. Use the `values()` method to create a new RDD named filedata containing an array of records containing the entire contents of each text file, and then return one record using the following commands:

```
filedata = licensefile_pairs.values()
filedata.take(1)
# should return the contents of one of the license files, eg
# [u'Copyright (c) 2002-2013 EPFL\nCopyright (c) 2011-2013 Typesafe, Inc...
```

You've now created an RDD using both the `textFile()` and `wholeTextFiles()` methods and observed the differences between each approach. We will use the `textFile()` method extensively throughout the rest of this book.

Creating an RDD from an Object File

Spark supports several common object file implementations. *Object files* refer to serialized data structures, not normally human readable, designed to provide structure and context to data, making access to the data more efficient for the requesting platform.

Sequence files are encoded, serialized files commonly used in Hadoop. Sequence files can be used to create RDDs using the `sequenceFile()` method. There is also a similar method called `hadoopFile()`. For brevity, I won't cover sequence files in detail in this book because it would require more knowledge about serialization in Hadoop, which is beyond the scope of this book.

Additionally, there is support for reading and writing *Pickle files*, a special serialization format for Python that will be covered in **Hour 9, "Functional Programming with Python."** Similar functionality is available for serialized Java objects using the `objectFile()` method.

I will cover examples using JSON files later in this section.

Creating an RDD from a Datasource

It is commonly required to load data from a database into an RDD in a Spark program as a source of historical data, master data, or reference/lookup data. This data could be coming from a variety of host systems and database platforms including Oracle, MySQL, Postgres, SQL Server, and others. I will focus on conventional relational database systems for now because we will cover NoSQL integration with Spark in **Hour 19, "Using Spark with NoSQL Systems."**

Similar to the creation of RDDs using external files, RDDs created using data from an external database (like a MySQL database for example) will attempt to partition the data into multiple partitions across multiple workers. This maximizes parallelism during processing, especially during the initial stages. Additionally, by dividing the table (typically by key space) into different partitions, these partitions can be loaded in parallel as well, with each partition responsible for fetching a unique set of rows. This concept is depicted in Figure 6.3.

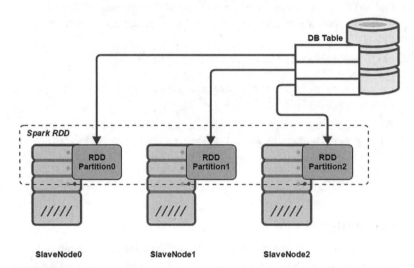

FIGURE 6.3
Loading an RDD from a table in a relational database.

The preferred methods of creating an RDD from a relational database table or query use functions from a special SparkContext called the SQLContext. The SQLContext is Spark's entry point for working with tabular data. The SQLContext allows the creation of DataFrames (formerly known as SchemaRDDs) as well as the execution of SQL queries. I will discuss this in much more detail in **Hour 13, "Using SQL with Spark."**

Creating an RDD from a JDBC Datasource

Java Database Connectivity (JDBC) is a popular Java API for accessing different (mainly relational) database management systems (DBMS), managing functions such as connecting and disconnecting from the DBMS and running queries. Database vendors typically provide drivers or connectors to provide access to their database platforms via JDBC. As Spark processes run in Java Virtual Machines (JVMs), JDBC is natively available to Spark.

Consider a MySQL Server called `mysqlserver` with a database named `employees` with a table called `employees`. The employees table has a primary key named `emp_no` that is a logical candidate to use to divide the key space from the table into multiple partitions. To access the MySQL database via JDBC, you need to launch `pyspark`, providing the `mysql-connector.jar`. An example of this is shown in Listing 6.4.

LISTING 6.4   Launching pyspark Supplying JDBC MySQL Connector JAR File

```
$SPARK_HOME/bin/pyspark \
--driver-class-path /usr/share/java/mysql-connector-java-5.x-bin.jar \
--master local
```

To create a `SQLContext`, use the code snippet provided in Listing 6.5.

LISTING 6.5   Initializing a SQLContext

```
from pyspark.sql import SQLContext
sqlctx = SQLContext(sc)
```

From within the `pyspark` shell, the following methods can be used to load the data from the employees table into an RDD named `employeesdf`.

load()
Syntax:

> `sqlContext.load(path=None, source=None, schema=None, **options)`

The `load()` function can be used for various different input types, including a relational database source. In the case of a JDBC source, the options represent a Python *dictionary* (a set of name value pairs representing the various configuration options). An example of the `load` function used to load the `employees` table is shown in Listing 6.6.

LISTING 6.6   Creating an RDD from a JDBC Datasource Using the load() Function

```
employeesdf = sqlctx.load(source="jdbc",
  url="jdbc:mysql://localhost:3306/employees?user=<user>&password=<pwd>",
  dbtable="employees",
  partitionColumn="emp_no",
  numPartitions="2" ,
  lowerBound="10001",
  upperBound="499999"
  )
employeesdf.rdd.getNumPartitions()
# should return 2 the following as we specified numPartitions=2
```

The partitionColumn argument helps Spark choose the appropriate column (preferably a long or int datatype) to create the number of partitions specified by numPartitions. The upperBound and lowerBound arguments are used to assist Spark in creating the partitions. These represent the minimum and maximum values for the partitionColumn in the source table. If any one of these arguments is supplied with the load() function, all must be supplied.

Check the API documentation for the version of Spark you are using, in more recent releases you are encouraged to use the load method from the DataFrameReader object instead of the SQLContext (I will discuss this further when we discuss DataFrames in **Hour 13, "Using SQL with Spark"**).

CAUTION

Creating too Many Partitions Using the load() or jdbc() Functions

Be careful not to specify too many partitions when loading a DataFrame from a relational data source. Each partition running on each individual worker node will connect to the DBMS independently and query its designated portion of the dataset. If you have hundreds or thousands of partitions, this could be misconstrued as a distributed denial-of-service (DDoS) attack on the host database system.

The load() function returns the special object called a DataFrame. I will discuss DataFrames in much greater detail in **Hour 13, "Using SQL with Spark."** SQL queries can be executed against DataFrames as shown in Listing 6.7.

LISTING 6.7   Running SQL Queries Against Spark DataFrames

```
sqlctx.registerDataFrameAsTable(employeesdf, "employees")
df2 = sqlctx.sql("SELECT emp_no, first_name, last_name FROM employees LIMIT 2")
df2.show()
# will return a 'pretty printed' result set similar to:
#+------+----------+---------+
#|emp_no|first_name|last_name|
#+------+----------+---------+
#| 10001|    Georgi|  Facello|
#| 10002|   Bezalel|   Simmel|
#+------+----------+---------+
```

A similar method for creating an RDD (DataFrame) from a JDBC datasource is the read.jdbc() method. This method is supported in Spark 1.4 and higher.

`read.jdbc()`

Syntax:

```
sqlContext.read.jdbc(url, table, column=None,
                     lowerBound=None,
                     upperBound=None,
                     numPartitions=None,
                     predicates=None,
                     properties=None)
```

The arguments to the `read.jdbc()` function are synonymous to the `load()` method with the additional optional argument `predicates`, which allow for including WHERE conditions to filter unneeded records while loading partitions. The `properties` argument can be used to pass parameters to the JDBC API.

Listing 6.8 shows the creation of an RDD using the `read.jdbc()` method.

LISTING 6.8 Creating an RDD from a JDBC Datasource Using the read.jdbc() Function

```
employeesdf = sqlctx.read.jdbc(
  url="jdbc:mysql://localhost:3306/employees",
  table="employees",
  column="emp_no",
  numPartitions="2" ,
  lowerBound="10001",
  upperBound="499999",
  properties={"user":"<user>", "password":"<pwd>"}
  )
employeesdf.rdd.getNumPartitions()
# should return the following as we specified numPartitions=2
```

The resultant DataFrame created by the `read.jdbc()` function can be queried similarly using SQL, as shown in Listing 6.7.

Creating RDDs from JSON files

JSON (JavaScript Object Notation) is a popular data-interchange format. JSON is a "self-describing" format, which is human-readable and commonly used to return responses from web services and RESTful APIs. JSON objects are treated as datasources and accessed using the SQLContext.

The following methods are used to create `DataFrame` RDDs from JSON files:

jsonFile()

syntax:

```
sqlContext.jsonFile(path, schema=None)
```

Or the new synonymous method supported in Spark 1.4 and higher:

read.json()

Syntax:

```
sqlContext.read.json(path, schema=None)
```

Consider a JSON file named `people.json` containing the names and optionally the ages of people. This file is included in the examples directory of the Spark install as shown in Figure 6.4.

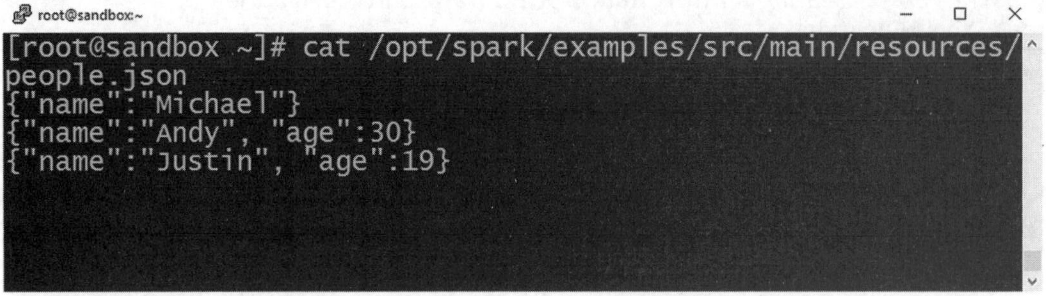

FIGURE 6.4
JSON file.

Listing 6.9 demonstrates the creation of an RDD named `people` using the people.json file.

LISTING 6.9 Creating and Working with an RDD Created from a JSON File

```
from pyspark.sql import SQLContext
sqlctx = SQLContext(sc)
people = sqlctx.jsonFile("/opt/spark/examples/src/main/resources/people.json")
people
# notice that the RDD created is a DataFrame which includes a schema
# DataFrame[age: bigint, name: string]
people.dtypes
# the dtypes method returns the column names and datatypes
#[('age', 'bigint'), ('name', 'string')]
```

```
people.show()
# you should see the following output
#+----+-------+
#| age|   name|
#+----+-------+
#|null|Michael|
#|  30|   Andy|
#|  19| Justin|
#+----+-------+
# as with all DataFrames you can create use them to run SQL queries
sqlctx.registerDataFrameAsTable(people, "people")
df2 = sqlctx.sql("SELECT name, age FROM people WHERE age > 20")
df2.show()
# you should see the resultant output below
#+----+---+
#|name|age|
#+----+---+
#|Andy| 30|
#+----+---+
```

I will also cover another special columnar file format called *Parquet* in detail in **Hour 13**, **"Using SQL with Spark."** This is another file type available for reading and writing using the SQLContext which is commonly used to store relational, structured data.

Creating an RDD Programatically

It's also possible to create an RDD in process from data in your program (lists, arrays, or collections). The data from your collection is partitioned and distributed in much the same way as the previous methods discussed. However, creating RDDs this way can be limiting because it requires all of the dataset to exist or be created in memory on one system.

The following methods allow you to create RDDs from lists in your program:

parallelize()

Syntax:

```
sc.parallelize(c, numSlices=None)
```

The parallelize() method assumes that you have a list created already and you supply this as the c (for collection) argument. The numSlices argument specifies the desired number of partitions to create. An example of the parallelize() method is shown in Listing 6.10.

LISTING 6.10   Creating an RDD Using the parallelize() Method

```
parallelrdd = sc.parallelize([0, 1, 2, 3, 4, 5, 6, 7, 8])
parallelrdd
# notice the type of RDD created
# ParallelCollectionRDD[0] at parallelize at PythonRDD.scala:423
parallelrdd.min()
# will return 0 as this was the min value in our list
parallelrdd.max()
# will return 8 as this was the max value in our list
parallelrdd.collect()
# will return the parallel collection as a list
# [0, 1, 2, 3, 4, 5, 6, 7, 8]
```

range()

Syntax:

```
sc.range(start, end=None, step=1, numSlices=None)
```

The range() method will generate a list for you and create and distribute the RDD. The start, end, and step arguments define the sequence of values and the numSlices specifies the desired number of partitions. An example of the range() method is shown in Listing 6.11.

LISTING 6.11   Creating an RDD Using the range() Method

```
# create an RDD using the range() function
# with 1000 integers starting at 0 in increments of 1
# across 2 partitions
rangerdd = sc.range(0, 1000, 1, 2)
rangerdd
# note the PythonRDD type, as range is a native Python function
# PythonRDD[1] at RDD at PythonRDD.scala:43
rangerdd.getNumPartitions()
# should return 2 as we requested numSlices=2
rangerdd.min()
# should return 0 as this was out start argument
rangerdd.max()
# should return 999 as this is 1000 increments of 1 starting from 0
rangerdd.take(5)
# should return [0, 1, 2, 3, 4]
```

Operations on RDDs

You've learned how to create RDDs from files in various file systems, from relational data sources and programatically. I've introduced the operations that can be performed on

RDDs: transformations and actions. I will discuss these in much further detail in **Hour 10,** **"Working with the Spark API (Transformations and Actions)."** However, you need to understand some further concepts relating to RDDs first.

Coarse-Grained versus Fine-Grained Transformations

Operations performed against RDDs are considered to be *coarse-grained* as they apply a transformation (typically either a map or filter function) against every element in the dataset. Coarse-grained is in contrast to "fine grained" transformations that can manipulate a single record or data cell, such as single row updates in a relational database, or put operations in a NoSQL database. Coarse-grained transformations are a concept I will revisit in **Hour 7,** **"Understanding MapReduce Concepts,"** as the coarse-grained transformations implemented with RDDs in Spark are conceptually similar to Hadoop's implementation of the MapReduce programming model.

Transformations, Actions, and Lazy Evaluation

Transformations are operations performed against RDDs that result in the creation of new RDDs. Common transformations include map and filter functions. The following example shows a new RDD being created from a transformation of an existing RDD:

```
originalrdd = sc.parallelize([0, 1, 2, 3, 4, 5, 6, 7, 8])
newrdd = originalrdd.filter(lambda x: x % 2)
```

The originalrdd was created from a parallelized collection of numbers. The filter() transformation was then applied to each element in the originalrdd to bypass even numbers in the collection. The results of this transformation are created in the new RDD called newrdd.

In contrast to transformations, which return new RDD objects, Actions return values or data to the Driver program. Common Actions include reduce(), collect(), count() and saveAsTextFile(). The following example uses the collect() action to display the contents of the newrdd:

```
newrdd.collect()
# will return [1, 3, 5, 7]
```

Spark uses lazy evaluation (also called lazy execution) in processing Spark programs. *Lazy evaluation* defers processing until an action is called (therefore when output is required). This is easily demonstrated using one of the interactive shells, where you can enter one or transformation methods to RDDs one after the other without any processing starting. Instead, each statement is parsed for syntax and object references only. After an action such as count() or saveAsTextFile() is requested, a DAG is created along with logical and physical execution plans. These are then orchestrated and managed across executors by the driver.

This lazy evaluation allows Spark to combine operations where possible, thereby reducing processing stages and minimizing the amount of data transferred between Spark executors, a process called the *shuffle*.

RDD Persistence and Re-use

RDDs are created and exist (predominantly) in memory on executors. By default, RDDs are transient objects that exist only while they are required. Once they are transformed into new RDDs and no longer needed for any other operations, they are removed permanently. This may be problematic if an RDD is required for more than one action because it must be reevaluated in its entirety each time. An option to address this is to cache or persist the RDD using the persist() method. Listings 6.12 and 6.13 demonstrate the effects of persisting an RDD.

LISTING 6.12   Using a RDD for Multiple Actions Without Persistence

```
originalrdd = sc.parallelize([0, 1, 2, 3, 4, 5, 6, 7, 8])
newrdd = originalrdd.filter(lambda x: x % 2)
noelements = newrdd.count()
# processes newrdd
listofelements = newrdd.collect()
# reprocesses newrdd
print "There are %s elements in the collection %s" % (noelements, listofelements)
# returns:
# There are 4 elements in the collection [1, 3, 5, 7]
```

LISTING 6.13   Using a RDD for Multiple Actions with Persistence

```
originalrdd = sc.parallelize([0, 1, 2, 3, 4, 5, 6, 7, 8])
newrdd = originalrdd.filter(lambda x: x % 2)
newrdd.persist()
noelements = newrdd.count()
# processes and persists newrdd in memory
listofelements = newrdd.collect()
# does not have to recompute newrdd
print "There are %s elements in the collection %s" % (noelements, listofelements)
# returns:
# There are 4 elements in the collection [1, 3, 5, 7]
```

After a request is made to persist the RDD using the persist() method (there is also a similar cache() method as well), the RDD will be kept in memory on all of the nodes in the cluster where it is computed after the first action called on it. You can see the persisted RDD in your Spark application (driver) UI in the Storage tab, as shown in Figure 6.5.

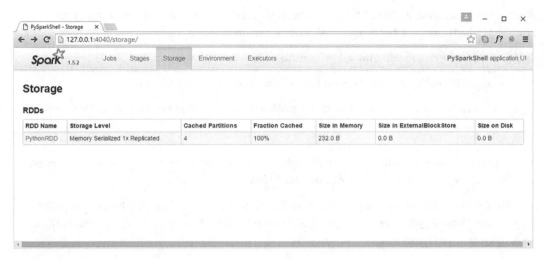

FIGURE 6.5
Persisted RDD in the Spark application UI.

I will discuss details about caching and persistence in much more detail in **Hour 11, "Using RDDs: Caching, Persistence, and Output."**

RDD Lineage

Spark keeps track of each RDD's *lineage*: that is, the sequence of transformations that resulted in the RDD. As I've discussed previously, every RDD operation recomputes the entire lineage by default unless RDD persistence is requested.

In an RDD's lineage, each RDD will have a *parent* RDD and/or a *child* RDD. Spark creates a DAG (directed acyclic graph) consisting of dependencies between RDDs. RDDs are processed in stages, which are sets of transformations. RDDs and stages have dependencies that can be narrow or wide.

Narrow dependencies or narrow operations are categorized by the following traits:

> ▶ Operations can be collapsed into a single stage; for instance, a map() and filter() operation against elements in the same dataset can be processed in a single pass of each element in the dataset.

> ▶ Only one child RDD depends on the parent RDD; for instance, an RDD is created from a text file (the parent RDD), with one child RDD to perform the set of transformations in one stage.

> ▶ No shuffling of data between nodes is required.

Narrow operations are preferred because they maximize parallel execution and minimize shuffling, which can be a bottleneck and is quite expensive.

Wide dependencies of wide operations, in contrast, have the following traits:

▶ Operations define a new stage and often require a shuffle operation.

▶ RDDs have multiple dependencies; for instance, `join()` requires an RDD to be dependent upon two or more parent RDDs.

Wide operations are unavoidable when grouping, reducing, or joining datasets, but you should be aware of the impacts and overheads involved with these operations.

Lineage can be visualized using the DAG Visualization option link from the Jobs or Stage detail page in the Spark Application UI. Figure 6.6 shows a DAG with multiple stages as the result of a wide operation (`reduceByKey()`, in this case).

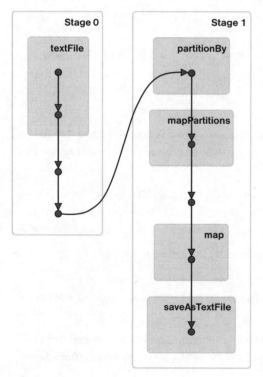

FIGURE 6.6
DAG Visualization through the Spark UI.

Fault Tolerance with RDDs

As Spark records the lineage of each RDD, including the lineage of all parent RDDs (and parent's parents and so on). Any RDD with all of its partitions can be reconstructed to the state it was at the time of the failure (which could have resulted from a node failure, for example). Because RDDs are distributed, they can tolerate and recover from the failure of any single node.

CAUTION

Non-deterministic Functions and Fault Tolerance

The use of non-deterministic functions in your Spark program—that is, functions that can produce different output given the same inputs (for example, `random()`)—will affect the ability to recreate RDDs to a consistent, repeatable state. This is further complicated if the non-deterministic function is used as a condition which affects the logic or flow of the program. Use caution when implementing non-deterministic functions.

You can avert long recovery periods for complex processing operations by *checkpointing*, or saving the data to a persistent file-based object. I will discuss checkpointing in more detail in **Hour 11, "Using RDDs: Caching, Persistence, and Output."**

Types of RDDs

Aside from the base RDD class that contains *members* (properties or attributes and functions) common to all RDDs, there are some specific RDD implementations that enable additional operators and functions. These additional RDD types include

- ▶ **PairRDD:** RDD of key value pairs (I will discuss key value pairs in more detail in **Hour 7, "Understanding MapReduce Concepts"**). You've already used this type of RDD because it's created automatically by using the `wholeTextFiles()` method.

- ▶ **DoubleRDD:** RDD consisting of a collection of double values only. Because the values are of the same numeric type, several additional statistical functions are available, including `mean()`, `sum()`, `stdev`, `variance`, and `histogram`, among others.

- ▶ **DataFrame (formerly known as SchemaRDD):** A distributed collection of data organized into named columns. A `DataFrame` is equivalent to a relational table in Spark SQL. We have created a `DataFrame` using the `load()` and `read.jdbc()` functions from the `SQLContext` in the **"Loading Data into RDDs"** section of this hour.

- ▶ **SequenceFileRDD:** An RDD created from a `SequenceFile` (compressed or uncompressed).

- ▶ **HadoopRDD:** An RDD that provides core functionality for reading data stored in HDFS using the v1 MapReduce API.

▶ **CoGroupedRDD:** A RDD that cogroups its parents. For each key in parent RDDs, the resulting RDD contains a tuple with the list of values for that key. I will discuss cogrouping in more detail in **Hour 10, "Working with the Spark API (Transformations and Actions)."**

▶ **JdbcRDD:** An RDD that executes an SQL query on a JDBC connection and reads results. Available in Scala only.

▶ **NewHadoopRDD:** An RDD that provides core functionality for reading data stored in Hadoop (for example, files in HDFS, sources in HBase, or S3), using the new MapReduce API (`org.apache.hadoop.mapreduce`).

▶ **PartitionPruningRDD:** A RDD used to prune RDD partitions/partitions to avoid launching tasks on all partitions. An example use case: If you know the RDD is partitioned by range, and the execution DAG has a filter on the key, you can avoid launching tasks on partitions that don't have the range covering the key.

▶ **ShuffledRDD:** The resulting RDD from a shuffle (for example, repartitioning of data).

▶ **UnionRDD:** An RDD resulting from a `union` operation against two or more RDDs.

There are other variants, including the ParallelCollectionRDD and the PythonRDD created from functions used to create RDDs in the previous section, **"Loading Data into RDDs."** Many of these are simple abstractions of the base RDD class.

Throughout this book, in additions to the base RDD class, we will mainly use the PairRDD, DoubleRDD, and DataFrame RDD classes, but it's worthwhile to be familiar with all of the various other RDD types. Documentation and more information about the various types of RDDs can be found in the Spark Scala API documentation at **https://spark.apache.org/docs/latest/api/scala/index.html**

Summary

In this hour, we have explored the Resilient Distributed Dataset (the RDD): the most fundamental, atomic data object in the Spark programming model. You have learned that RDDs are distributed across workers in the cluster into partitions. These partitions can then be processed in parallel. You have also learned that RDDs are fault tolerant or resilient to node failure because Spark keeps track of the lineage used to create each partition of an RDD. That means that, at any stage of the process, upon failure, any given partition can be recreated by sequentially re-executing the functions that originally created it.

You learned the various ways to initially load data into an RDD, including the common pattern of loading data from a distributed file system such as HDFS or S3, as well as loading data from a relational datasource (RDBMS), loading data programatically, and loading data from a stream.

You also learned about how Spark uses lazy evaluation to process RDDs and the key differences between coarse-grained transformations implemented in Spark and fine-grained transformations used in other in memory distributed data stores.

I have also covered the various types of RDDs that extend the base RDD construct and offer extended functionality through additional members, such as statistical functions available on numeric or DoubleRDDs.

Now that you understand the fundamental concept of the RDD, you can progressively build upon this.

Q&A

Q. Explain how RDDs are *resilient*.

A. Spark keeps track of the lineage of each RDD, that is, the steps and data operations in sequence that were used to create the RDD. An RDD can be reconstructed at any stage of the process using any other executors on any other worker node of the cluster, thereby being resilient to failure.

Q. How does Spark optimize the loading of data from a distributed file system such as HDFS?

A. Spark attempts to achieve data locality by loading data into partitions from nodes which are colocated with the blocks to be processed, minimizing the transfer of data across the network at run time.

Q. Explain the difference between *splittable* and *non-splittable* compression formats.

A. Splittable compression formats are indexed and typically compressed on block or record boundaries, meaning that parts of the compressed archive can be distributed and decompressed by different processes in a distributed computing environment. Non-splittable formats, on the other hand, can only be extracted by a single system, making them less suited for clustered computing systems such as Spark or Hadoop.

Workshop

The workshop contains quiz questions and exercises to help you solidify your understanding of the material covered. Try to answer all questions before looking at the "Answers" section that follows.

Quiz

1. **True or false:** RDDs are updateable after they're initialized.

2. Which function is used to create an RDD programatically from a collection or list of values?

   A. `textFile()`

   B. `parallelize()`

   C. `sequenceFile()`

3. What URI scheme is used to reference files stored in Amazon S3?

4. **True or false:** JSON files are accessed to create RDDs using the `SQLContext` in Spark.

Answers

1. **False.** RDDs are immutable objects. New RDDs can be created as a result of "coarse-grained" operations on existing RDDs, but RDDs do not support updates.

2. **B.** `parallelize` is used to distribute a local collection or list of values to form an RDD.

3. `s3://` (also `s3A.//` or `s3n://`)

4. **True.** The `jsonFile()` method from the `SQLContext` class is used to create RDDs from JSON files. JSON is considered to be a datasource including a schema and data. The SQLContext enables SQL query access to JSON data loaded into RDDs.

Understanding MapReduce Concepts

MapReduce is a platform- and language-independent programming model at the heart of most big data and NoSQL platforms. Although many abstractions of MapReduce, such as Spark SQL and Hive, allow us to process data without explicitly implementing map or reduce functions, understanding the concepts behind MapReduce is fundamental to truly understanding distributed programming and data processing in Spark.

MapReduce History and Background

Following Google's release of the "The Google File System" whitepaper in 2003 (which influenced the Hadoop Distributed File System), Google released another whitepaper called "MapReduce: Simplified Data Processing on Large Clusters" in December 2004.

The MapReduce whitepaper gave a high-level description of Google's approach to processing (indexing and ranking) large volumes of text data for search-engine processing. This whitepaper had a major influence on the Nutch project, which was underway at the time at Yahoo!. The creators of the Nutch project, including Doug Cutting, incorporated the principles outlined in the Google MapReduce and Google FileSystem papers into the project now known as Hadoop.

The Motivation for MapReduce

When the original scale-up approach to increasing processing capacity started to reach its limits, a new paradigm emerged: *distributed systems*. Distributed programming frameworks have existed for decades before the Google MapReduce paper was released in 2004, including Message Passing Interface (MPI), Parallel Virtual Machine (PVM), HTCondor, and others.

The early distributed computing and grid computing frameworks had several limitations, including:

▶ Complexity in programming: Developers would often need to concern themselves with state and synchronization between distributed processes, including temporal dependencies.

▶ Partial failures, which are difficult to recover from: Synchronization and data exchange between processes in a distributed system made dealing with partial failures much more challenging.

▶ Bottlenecks in getting data to the processor: Many distributed systems sourced data from shared or remote storage. Movement of this data along with the data exchanged between remote processes would ultimately result in a processing bottleneck.

▶ Limited scalability: Finite bandwidth between processes would ultimately limit the extent at which early distributed systems could scale.

As the synchronization and data movement overheads increased with every node added, at a certain point, adding additional nodes resulted in diminishing performance returns. This concept is pictured in Figure 7.1.

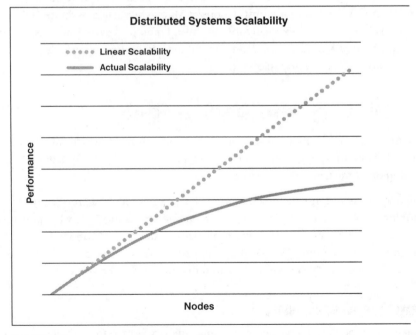

FIGURE 7.1
Diminishing returns with early distributed systems.

The Design Goals for MapReduce

Existing distributed systems before the seminal Google whitepapers were adequate to handle the scale of data at that time. At that stage, the Internet was in its formative years (or not in existence at all) and data volumes were modest. This was all about to change.

The search engine providers, including Google and Yahoo!, had a requirement to collect, store, and index an exponentially expanding number of unstructured text documents. This was the beginning of the "data deluge." The expansion of mobile data networks and social media would further exacerbate the issues.

Google set out to address the scalability limitations and develop a storage and processing platform that could scale linearly to hundreds of thousands of nodes running on commodity hardware and leverage thousands of CPUs, running thousands of concurrent tasks. The design goals outlined in the 2004 Google MapReduce white paper included

- ▶ Automatic parallelization and distribution: The programming model should make it easy to parallelize and distribute computations.

- ▶ Fault tolerance: The system must be able to handle partial failure. If a node or process fails, its workload should be assumed by other functioning components in the system.

- ▶ Input/output (I/O) scheduling: Task scheduling and allocation aims to limit the amount of network bandwidth used. Tasks are dynamically scheduled on available workers so that faster workers process more tasks.

- ▶ Status and monitoring: Status (including progress and counters) of each component and its running tasks are reported to a master process. This makes it easy to diagnose issues, optimize jobs, or perform system capacity planning.

In the subsequent sections, I will describe the MapReduce programming model in detail, but the Google whitepaper established some key distributed processing framework concepts that are still present in Hadoop and Spark today. The Google MapReduce whitepaper is available at http://research.google.com/archive/mapreduce.html

Records and Key Value Pairs

Before diving into MapReduce the model, you will first need to understand some basic data elements that I will frequently refer to. These elements include *datasets*, *records*, and *key-value pairs*.

A *dataset*, for the purposes of describing MapReduce, refers to a collection of *records*. This collection is often parallelized and distributed, as is the case with Spark RDDs or blocks in HDFS.

NOTE

There is a Dataset API that is available in Spark SQL (currently Java and Scala only). Datasets as a concept as discussed in this hour and this book in general should not be confused with this specific API construct in Spark.

Key Value Pairs and Records

Input, output, and intermediate records in MapReduce are represented in the form of *key value pairs (KV or KVP),* also known as *name value pairs* or *attribute value pairs.* Key value pairs are commonly used in programming to define a unit of data. The *key* is an identifier, for instance, the name of the attribute. In some systems, the key needs to be unique with respect to other keys in the same system—such is the case with most distributed NoSQL key value stores. However, in the case of Hadoop and Spark, the key is not required to be unique, as you will see later in the hour. The *value* is the data itself corresponding to the key. This value can be a simple, scalar value such as an integer, or a complex object such as a list of other objects. Some example key value pairs are shown in Table 7.1.

TABLE 7.1 Example Key Value Pairs

Key	Value
City	Chicago
Temperatures	[35,38,27,16]

Key value pairs are implemented in many programming languages and often used to express configuration parameters and metadata. In Python, dictionaries or dicts are sets of key value pairs. Similarly, Ruby hashes are collections of key value pairs.

Often, the implementation of key value pairs is abstracted from the programmer; however, in low-level programming in Hadoop (MapReduce implemented in Java, for example), key value pairs are the atomic data unit against which all processing is done. Key value pairs are also integral to PairRDDs in Spark.

You will need to be comfortable with key value pairs because this concept is central MapReduce and frequently referred to in schema-on-read platforms including Hadoop and Spark. You will often decompose complex problems in Spark into a series of operations against key value pairs.

MapReduce Explained

There is some ambiguity between MapReduce the programming model and MapReduce the processing framework in Hadoop. Unfortunately, the two concepts are unavoidably conflated. I will mainly discuss MapReduce in the context of a programming model while making reference to how it's implemented as framework in Hadoop.

MapReduce, the programming model (or programming abstraction), was inspired by the map and reduce primitives in Lisp and other functional programming languages.

NOTE

Lisp is a programming language that was originally specified in 1958. The name is believed to be an abbreviation for *list processor*. Lisp was created by John McCarthy, an artificial intelligence (AI) researcher at the Massachusetts Institute of Technology (MIT). Lisp was inspired by *lambda calculus* to represent a practical mathematical notation for computer programs. In previous chapters I have shown examples of the lambda notation in Python's implementation of functional programming used to express function abstraction and variable binding.

MapReduce includes two developer implemented processing phases, the *Map phase* and the *Reduce phase*, along with a *Shuffle phase*, which is implemented by the framework (in Hadoop this is implemented by the MapReduce processing framework in a phase called the *Shuffle and Sort phase*). Figure 7.2 describes the overall MapReduce process. This is an adaptation of the diagram provided in the original Google MapReduce whitepaper.

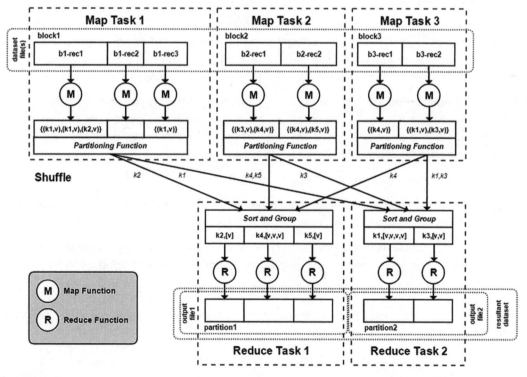

FIGURE 7.2
A MapReduce overview.

Map Phase

The Map phase is the initial phase of processing in which you'll use an input dataset as a datasource for processing. The Map phase uses *input format* and *record reader* functions in its specific implementation to derive records in the form of key value pairs for the input data.

The Map phase then applies a function or functions to each key value pair over a *portion* of the dataset. In the case of a dataset hosted in files in HDFS or S3, this portion would be a block in the filesystem. If there were *n* blocks of data in the input dataset, there would be *n* Map tasks (also referred to as *Mappers*). In reality, there may be be more Map task *attempts* as a task may fail due to node failure. Another way of looking at this is that the input data dictates the number of Map tasks implemented, whereas the number of Reduce tasks in the Reduce phase, as I will explain later, is explicitly specified by the developer.

The Map phase is purposely designed not to share state between processes; in other words, it is a true shared nothing processing stage. Each Map task iterates through its portion of the dataset in parallel to the other Map tasks in such a way that every record (key value pair) is processed once and only once (with exceptions only for task failure or speculative execution, which I will discuss later).

In the diagram in Figure 7.2, there are three Map tasks operating against three filesystem blocks (`block1`, `block2`, and `block3`). Each Map task will call its `map()` function, represented by *M* in the diagram—once for each record (key value pair), for example, `b1-rec1`, `b1-rec2`, and so on.

Each `map()` function call accepts one key value pair and emits (or outputs) zero of more key value pairs. The key value pairs emitted from the Map phase are considered to be *intermediate data* because there may be subsequent processing or mutation of the data in the Reduce phase. The `map()` function is described in pseudo-code as follows:

map (in_key, in_value) → *list (intermediate_key, intermediate_value)*

The *list* refers to the output from a `map()` function producing a list of outputs, with a list length of *n* output key value pairs (where *n* could be zero).

Common `map()` functions include filtering of specific keys, such as filtering log messages if you only wanted to count or analyze ERROR log messages. Here's a psuedo-coded example:

let map (k, v) = if (ERROR in v) then emit (k, v)

Another example of a `map()` function would be to manipulate values, such as a `map()` function that converts a text value to lowercase:

let map (k, v) = emit (k, v. toLower ( ))

There are many other examples of `map()` functions, which can be chained into a pipeline or sequence of individual functions, including conditional logic. Any `map()` function is valid as long as the function can be executed against a record contained in a portion of the dataset in isolation of other Map tasks in the application processing other portions of the dataset.

The Map task then collects all of the individual lists of intermediate data key value pairs emitted from each map function (or each input record of the Map task's unique portion of the input dataset) into a single list grouped by the intermediate key. The combined list of intermediate values grouped by their intermediate keys is then passed to a partitioning function.

Partitioning Function

The role of the *partitioning function* (or *partitioner*) is to ensure each key and its list of values is passed to one and only one *Reduce task* or *Reducer*. The most common implementation is a *hash partitioner*, which creates a hash (or unique signature) for the key and then arbitrarily divides the hashed key space into *n* number of partitions. The number of partitions is directly related to the number of Reducers specified by the developer.

A developer could implement a custom Partitioner for various reasons. For example, if you were processing a years' worth of data and you wanted each month to be processed by its own Reducer, you would implement a Partitioner to partition by the month.

The partitioning function is called for each key with an output representing the target Reducer for the key (typically, a number between 0 and $n - 1$, where n is the number of Reducers requested by the developer).

Shuffle

So far, all of the processing you've done has been fully parallelized and individual nodes or processes did not need to communicate or exchange data or state with one another. Now you need to know how to combine intermediate keys and their associated intermediate values from multiple Map tasks (in many cases running on different nodes of the cluster) in order to perform further processing in the Reduce phase.

During the Shuffle phase, the output from each separate Map task is sent to a target Reduce task as specified by the applications partitioning function. This is typically the most expensive phase of the overall MapReduce process because it requires data to be physically transferred between nodes, requiring network I/O and consuming bandwidth, which is finite at best and scarce at worst.

Reduce Phase

After all of the Map tasks have completed and the Shuffle phase has transferred all of the intermediate keys and their lists of intermediate values to their target Reducer (or Reduce task), the Reduce phase can begin.

Each Reduce task (or Reducer) executes a `reduce()` function for each intermediate key and its list of associated intermediate values. The output from each `reduce()` function is zero or more key value pairs considered to be part of the final output. In reality, this output may be the input to another Map phase in a complex multistage computational workflow, but in the context of the individual MapReduce application, the output from the Reduce task is final. Here is a pseudo-code representation of the `reduce()` function:

$$reduce \ (key, \ list \ (intermediate\_value)) \ \rightarrow \ key, \ out\_value$$

`reduce()` functions are often aggregate functions such as sums, counts, and averages. The most simplest and common `reduce()` function is the Sum Reducer, which simply sums a list of values for each key. Here's a pseudo-coded `sum reduce` function:

$$let \ reduce \ (k, \ list \ \langle v \rangle) = sum = 0 \quad for \ int \ i \ in \ list \ \langle v \rangle : \ sum \ += i \ emit \ (k, \ sum)$$

A count operation is as simple as summing a set of ones representing instances of the values you which to count. I will present examples of this in the next section on word count.

NOTE

All Map tasks and the Shuffle phase must complete before the first `reduce()` function of any Reducer can be executed. This is because any portion (block) of the input data could contain keys and values that could affect the final output from the application. For instance, if our Reduce phase is implementing an aggregate function such as an `average()` or `sum()` of values by key, the output of this function would be erroneous if intermediate values from unfinished Map tasks are not included.

Fault Tolerance

The MapReduce model allows for fault tolerance. In fact, it was purposely designed with the expectation of node failure because it was originally intended to run at scale on commodity (or even cheap, unreliable) hardware.

In Hadoop, for instance, if a Map task fails, it will automatically be rescheduled by the master process on another node (preferably a node that has a copy of the same block(s) maintaining data locality). By default, a task can fail and be rescheduled four times before the job is deemed to have failed. Similarly, because intermediate data is retained for the life of the job, if a reduce task fails, it also can be rescheduled and its input data resupplied.

Combiner Functions

In the case of commutative and associative reduce operations such as sums or counts, these operations can often be performed after the Map task is complete on the node executing the Map task; that is, before the Shuffle phase. This is done by the use of a *Combiner function* or *Combiner*.

Because the Map phase is naturally more distributed, using a Combiner where possible can be advantageous. It will reduce the amount of data transferred in the Shuffle phase and reduce the computational load in the Reduce phase. The Combiner function is the same function as the `reduce()` function; it's simply executed on the Map task node against the output from the Map task.

A Combiner function can be implemented as long as running the function on the Mapper as well as running the function more than once have no effect on the final result. For example, a sum function could be implemented in a Combiner because summing a list of sums would still provide the same result. However, an average function could not be used as a combiner function because averaging a list of averages would give an erroneous result.

Figure 7.3 depicts a Combiner function.

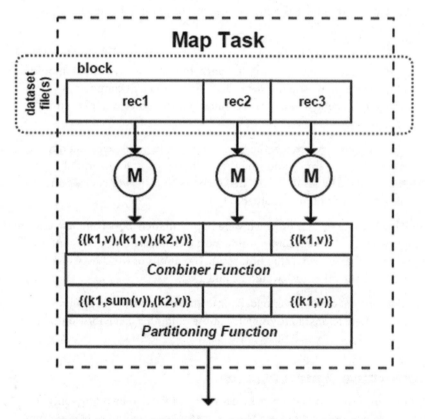

Pre-aggregated, Partitioned Data Sent to a Reducer

FIGURE 7.3
The Combiner function.

Asymmetry and Speculative Execution

The Map and Reduce phases are respectively asymmetrical in nature. For instance, one instance of a Map task may do more processing than other Map tasks mapping over the same dataset. This may be a result of more relevant keys existing in one portion or block of the input dataset.

An example would be MapReduce application looking at weblogs and filtering for a particular IP address and then doing some subsequent processing. Records with the desired IP address may be clustered in multiple contiguous records in one of the blocks in the dataset and not present in others. Therefore, one of the Map tasks would naturally have more processing to do than the others. Similarly, a Reducer may work harder than others because there are more keys (and therefore more values) in its partition.

This asymmetry can lead to some Map and/or Reduce tasks running much slower than others. Because completion of the entire Map phase is a prerequisite for beginning the Reduce phase, this asymmetry could be a bottleneck.

MapReduce implementations in Hadoop and Spark have a governing process. In Hadoop, this is the `ResourceManager` and `ApplicationsMaster`. In Spark, this is the driver, which monitors the status and progress of a collection of Map and/or Reduce Tasks. You can configure a behavior called *speculative execution,* which looks for a configurable tolerated difference in progress between tasks.

If a task falls outside of the configured tolerance, the governing process would create a duplicate task to run simultaneously against the same data (the same block, that is) to the initial (comparatively) slow-running task. The results of the first task to complete will be used and the other task would be killed and its output discarded.

For instance, if you had five Map tasks, four of which were approximately 80% complete and the fifth task was 20% complete, speculative execution would start a duplicate task to the fifth task (looking at the same portion of the dataset as the fifth task). The results of whichever task finished first would be used and the other task would be killed.

This behavior is designed to prevent a slow, overloaded, or unstable node from becoming a bottleneck. If the issue was solely related to asymmetry in the data, this behavior would have little or no effect.

Map-only MapReduce Applications

A MapReduce application can have zero Reduce tasks: This is considered to be a Map-only MapReduce application. Common applications for Map-only MapReduce jobs are ETL routines where the data is not intended to be summarized, aggregated, or reduced; file format conversion jobs; image processing jobs, and more. With Map-only applications, there is no partitioning function and the output from the Map Task in this case is considered to be the final output. Map-only jobs have the advantage of massive parallelization and avoiding the expensive shuffle operation. Figure 7.4 depicts a Map-only MapReduce application.

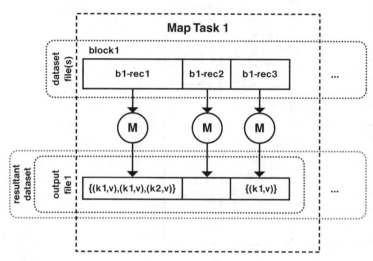

FIGURE 7.4
A Map-only application.

An Election Analogy for MapReduce

Think about the analogy of an election and a simulation of manually tallying votes to incorporate all of the MapReduce concepts together. In an election, there are multiple polling booths located in different areas that produce completed ballot papers containing votes for candidates (the input data to our analogy). Each polling booth will have a teller, who groups and tallies the votes generated in their polling booth, including the filtering out of incomplete ballot papers (the Map and Combiner functions in our analogy). The votes grouped and counted for each candidate at each booth are then sent to a counting station for a particular candidate or candidates (the partitioning function and Shuffle phase). Vote counters from the central counting station now collect all of the votes for their particular candidate or candidates from all of the polling booths and tally these up (the Reduce phase in our analogy). The respective candidates' tallies can then be easily compared against one another to determine the winner of the election. This example is shown in Figure 7.5.

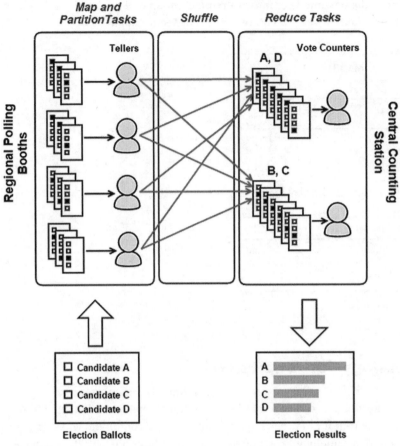

FIGURE 7.5
A MapReduce election analogy.

Word Count: The "Hello, World" of MapReduce

Word Count is a simple algorithm that is often used to represent and demonstrate the MapReduce programming model. In this section, I will break it down and then look at its implementation in both Spark and Hadoop.

Why Count Words?

If you have previously read any Hadoop training material or tutorials, you are probably sick and tired of seeing word count examples, or you may be scratching your head trying to work out what the fixation with counting words is (a seemingly uninteresting task). Word count is the most prevalent example used when describing the MapReduce programming model because it is easy to understand and demonstrates all of the components of the MapReduce model.

Having said that, many real-life problems solved with MapReduce are simply derivations of word count: for instance, counting occurrences of events in a large corpus of log files, or text mining functions such as TF-IDF (Term Frequency-Inverse Document Frequency). After you understand word count, you understand MapReduce too, and the problem-solving possibilities are endless.

How It Works

Counting words requires us to read a text file and count occurrences of each word and then rank these counts to determine the most frequently occurring words in the body of text being analyzed. Consider a text document containing the works of Shakespeare.

> O Romeo , Romeo ! wherefore art thou Romeo ?
>
> Deny thy father, and refuse thy name
>
> William Shakespeare

The first question you need to answer is how to derive a key and value from this unstructured collection of text to form an input record. Fortunately, both Hadoop and Spark have a mechanism for this; it's called the *text input format*. The text input format considers each newline terminated line of text to be a record. Each record (line) is assigned an arbitrary key (usually a byte offset representing the start of the line) and the value is the complete line of text. So in the Shakespeare excerpt from Romeo and Juliet, the input records would be as shown in Listing 7.1.

LISTING 7.1   Input to the Map Task

```
(0, 'O Romeo , Romeo ! wherefore art thou Romeo ?')
(45, 'Deny thy father, and refuse thy name')
```

You will soon see that the input key is not used in further processing; therefore, anything could have been used. Now you have your input records, which will be processed in the Map phase. Recalling that this is a distributed phase, each Mapper will have a unique set of lines of text, represented as records. Each Mapper or Map task running on a worker or slave node calls a map() function for each record in their set of records (which is called an *input split*). For each record, you split the line of text into a collection of words based upon whitespace or punctuation, a process known as *tokenization*. You then output each individual word or token as the intermediate key and the number 1 as the value. The resulting output of the map() functions for each record in the input split from Listing 7.1 would be as shown in Listing 7.2.

NOTE

You can access the Text Input Format key (the byte offset) when programming low-level Java MapReduce in Hadoop, although this is rarely required. In Spark, using the `textFile()` method, this key is normally abstracted from the user who just deals with a line of text, as you will see in the Try It Yourself exercise. You can see this key using the `newAPIHadoopFile()` method, however. I will show an example of this using Scala in **Hour 8, "Getting Started with Scala."**

LISTING 7.2   Output from the Map Task

```
('O', 1)
('Romeo', 1)
('Romeo', 1)
('wherefore', 1)
('art', 1)
('thou', 1)
('Romeo', 1)
('Deny', 1)
('thy', 1)
('father', 1)
('and', 1)
('refuse', 1)
('thy', 1)
('name', 1)
```

As an aside, if you were doing this seriously, you would filter out *stopwords* (such as "and," "a," "the," and so on) in the Map phase, you would generally also normalize the case—either all uppercase or all lowercase—and perform a process called *stemming*, which removes pluralization and possession to make related terms uniform.

You will note that the output from our `map()` functions has changed the keyspace from the arbitrary byte offset to the individual word. This demonstrates that they key can change during phases of the application. The output from each Map Task is then grouped and sorted into a key (word) and list of values (1's). The resultant output—which is the input to the Reduce task—is shown in Listing 7.3.

LISTING 7.3   Intermediate Sent to the Reducer

```
('and', [1])
('art', [1])
('Deny', [1])
('father', [1])
('name', [1])
('O', [1])
```

```
('refuse', [1])
('Romeo', [1,1,1])
('thou', [1])
('thy', [1,1])
('wherefore', [1])
```

The output from a Map task, along with similar output from every other Map task running in parallel, is the intermediate data for the job. If you have more than one Reducer specified by the developer, this is the stage when you would apply the partitioning function. For simplicity, assume there is a single Reduce task in this example, so all intermediate keys and their values go to this one Reducer. Now the intermediate data output from the Map tasks gets sent to the Reducer and merged into one set of keys and their associated list of values. The Reducer runs its reduce() function for each intermediate record and simply sums the list of ones for each key and outputs a key (word) and the sum of the 1's for that word (the count). Our final output from the Reduce task, which is the final output for the job, is shown in Listing 7.4.

LISTING 7.4   **Final Output**

```
('and', 1)
('art', 1)
('Deny', 1)
('father', 1)
('name', 1)
('O', 1)
('refuse', 1)
('Romeo', 3)
('thou', 1)
('thy', 2)
('wherefore', 1)
```

And that's Word Count! Now get ready to take a look at the specific API methods in Spark that will be used for the map() and reduce() functions.

Map and Reduce Functions in Spark

The map() and reduce() functions in Spark operate as transformations against an RDD. These can be combined or pipelined into a single statement using functional programming (which I will detail in the coming hours on Scala and Python). Consider the first five lines of the works of Shakespeare text file as shown in Listing 7.5, and then the code used to load this data into an RDD in Spark in Listing 7.6.

LISTING 7.5   First Five Lines of the Shakespeare File

```
A MIDSUMMER-NIGHT'S DREAM
Now, fair Hippolyta, our nuptial hour
Draws on apace: four happy days bring in
Another moon; but O! methinks how slow
```

LISTING 7.6   Shakespeare RDD

```
sc.textFile("hdfs:///user/training/shakespeare.txt").take(5)
# Result:
# [u"A MIDSUMMER-NIGHT'S DREAM",
#  u'',
#  u'Now, fair Hippolyta, our nuptial hour',
#  u'Draws on apace: four happy days bring in',
#  u'Another moon; but O ! methinks how slow']
```

Notice that loading the file into an RDD creates a list or array of elements, each element representing a line of text in the original file. Refer to Listing 7.6 for examples of commonly used map and reduce transformations used in Spark described in Table 7.2. The Python regular expression (regex) module re module is used in these examples to split the line of text based upon a regex.

TABLE 7.2   Map and Reduce Transformations in Spark

Transformation	Description and Example
map()	Returns a new RDD with the results of a function applied to each element in the originating RDD. Example:

```
import re
sc.textFile("hdfs:///user/training/shakespeare.txt") \
  .map(lambda line: re.split('\W+', line)) \
  .take(5)
# Result:
# [[u'A', u'MIDSUMMER', u'NIGHT', u'S', u'DREAM'],
#  [u''],
#  [u'Now', u'fair', u'Hippolyta', u'our',
#     u'nuptial', u'hour', u''],
#  [u'Draws', u'on', u'apace', u'four',
#     u'happy', u'days', u'bring', u'in', u''],
#  [u'Another', u'moon', u'but', u'O',
#     u'methinks', u'how', u'slow', u'']]
```

Transformation	Description and Example

flatMap()	Runs a function against each element in the RDD, returning a new RDD that is a single collection of elements. Whereas map() returns a list of lists when we use the split function, flatMap() returns one "flattened" list. Example:
	
	``python
	import re
	sc.textFile("hdfs:///user/training/shakespeare.txt") \
	  .flatMap(lambda line: re.split('\W+', line)) \
	  .take(30)
	# Result:
	# [u'A', u'MIDSUMMER', u'NIGHT', u'S', u'DREAM',
	# u'', u'Now', u'fair', u'Hippolyta', u'our',
	# u'nuptial', u'hour', u'', u'Draws', u'on',
	# u'apace', u'four', u'happy', u'days', u'bring',
	# u'in', u'', u'Another', u'moon', u'but', u'O',
	# u'methinks', u'how', u'slow', u'']
	``

reduceByKey()	Runs against a dataset of key value pairs (K, V). Performs a summary function for each value associated with a key. For example:
	
	``python
	# First we need to create the KV input for the reducer
	import re
	kvrdd = sc.textFile("hdfs:///user/training/shakespeare.txt") \
	    .flatMap(lambda line: re.split('\W+', line)) \
	    .map(lambda word: (word, 1))
	kvrdd.take(5)
	# Result:
	#[(u'A', 1),
	# (u'MIDSUMMER', 1),
	# (u'NIGHT', 1),
	# (u'S', 1),
	# (u'DREAM', 1)]
	# Now we can run our reduce function against kvrdd
	kvrdd.reduceByKey(lambda v1, v2: v1 + v2) \
	  .take(5)
	# Result:
	# [(u'', 130028),
	``

(Continued)

TABLE 7.2   *Continued*

Transformation	Description and Example
	`#  (u'fawn', 13),`
	`#  (u'mustachio', 2),`
	`#  (u'Debts', 1),`
	`#  (u'Florentius', 1)]`

`reduceByKey()` also takes an optional `numTasks` parameter that is the number of Reduce Tasks requested, this parameter will default to the configured default parallelism level if it is not explicitly specified.

NOTE

You would have observed the notation used in the results provided in the examples. Lists or arrays are represented by square brackets (`[ ]`) as is common in many programming languages. In the previous `reduceByKey()` example, the key value pair outputs are represented as *tuples*—an ordered set of values—using parentheses `()`. Tuples used to represent key value pairs are in the form of `(k,v)`. Tuples and lists are represented differently using Scala, but the construct is the same.

▼ TRY IT YOURSELF

Word Count in Spark

In this exercise, you will run the Word Count example using PySpark. In this case, you will run some additional transformations to clean up and sort the output by word. I will discuss these additional functions in **Hour 10, "Working with Spark API (Transformations and Actions)."**

1. Using your single node Spark installation, download the `shakespeare.txt file` using the link:
   https://s3.amazonaws.com/sty-spark/shakespeare/shakespeare.txt

   Place the file in the `/opt/spark/data` directory.

   If you have HDFS available to you (for example, using AWS EMR, Databricks, or a Hadoop distribution that includes Spark), you can upload the file to HDFS and use this as an alternative.

2. Open a `PySpark` shell in local mode:

   `pyspark --master local`

   As with Step 1, if you have a Hadoop cluster or distributed Spark standalone cluster accessible, you are free to use these instead.

3. Import the Python `re` (Regular Expression) module:

   `import re`

4. Load the file:

```
doc = sc.textFile("file:///opt/spark/data/shakespeare.txt")
```

5. Inspect the RDD created:

```
doc
# Result
MapPartitionsRDD[1] at textFile ...
```

6. Filter empty lines from the RDD, split lines by whitespace, and flatten the lists of words into one list:

```
# use the filter function to remove lines with no text
flattened = doc.filter(lambda line: len(line) > 0) \
.flatMap(lambda line: re.split('\W+', line))
```

7. Inspect the RDD:

```
flattened.take(6)
# Results (first six words):
# [u'A', u'MIDSUMMER', u'NIGHT', u'S', u'DREAM', u'Now']
```

8. Map text to lowercase, remove empty strings, and then convert to key value pairs in the form of (word, 1):

```
kvpairs = flattened.filter(lambda word: len(word) > 0) \
.map(lambda word:(word.lower(),1))
```

9. Inspect the RDD. Notice the RDD created is a PairRDD representing a collection of key value pairs:

```
kvpairs.take(5)
# Results
[(u'a', 1),
 (u'midsummer', 1),
 (u'night', 1),
 (u's', 1),
 (u'dream', 1)]
```

10. Count each word and sort results in reverse alphabetic order:

```
countsbyword = kvpairs.reduceByKey(lambda v1, v2: v1 + v2) \
.sortByKey(ascending=False)
```

11. Inspect the RDD:

```
countsbyword.take(5)
# Results
[(u'zwaggered', 1),
 (u'zur', 2),
 (u'zounds', 19),
 (u'zone', 1),
 (u'zodiacs', 1)]
```

12. Display the top five most-used words:

```
# invert the kv pair to make the count the key and sort
topwords = countsbyword.map(lambda (w, c): (c, w)) \
 .sortByKey(ascending=False)
topwords.take(5)
# Results (top 5 most used words):
[(26856, u'the'),
 (24116, u'and'),
 (22412, u'i'),
 (19225, u'to'),
 (16018, u'of')]
```

Note how you can use the `map()` function to invert the key and value. This is a common approach to performing an operations known as a secondary sort, a means to sort values that are not sorted by default.

13. Run the entire following script. Notice that it explicitly specifies the `numTasks` option to the `reduceByKey()` transformation and saves the results to a directory:

```
import re

doc = sc.textFile("file:///opt/spark/data/shakespeare.txt")

flattened = doc.filter(lambda line: len(line) > 0) \
.flatMap(lambda line: re.split('\W+', line))

kvpairs = flattened.filter(lambda word: len(word) > 0) \
 .map(lambda word:(word.lower(),1))

# repartition into 5 partitions
countsbyword = kvpairs.reduceByKey(lambda v1, v2: v1 + v2, \
numPartitions=5)

topwords = countsbyword.map(lambda (w, c): (c, w)) \
.sortByKey(ascending=False)

topwords.saveAsTextFile("file:///opt/spark/data/wordcounts")
```

Browse the `wordcounts` directory. Note that the number of output files created is directly related to the `numTasks` specified.

You have now run a complete, end-to-end Word Count example in Spark using `flatMap()`, `map()`, `filter()`, `reduceByKey()`, and `sortByKey()` functions.

Summary

In this hour, I have covered MapReduce, a fundamental programming model and framework at the heart of most big data processing systems including Hadoop and Spark. The MapReduce model is a programming abstraction that maximizes parallelization and takes full advantage of distributed data and data locality during execution.

You learned about how MapReduce uses key value pairs to represent input, intermediate, and output data, and how the different phases of processing (the Map and Reduce phases) interact with one another. I discussed the expensive (but often unavoidable) aspects of the Shuffle phase. I also discussed speculative execution and how fault tolerance is implemented in MapReduce. I used the Word Count example to demonstrate the MapReduce model and show examples of the map(), flatMap(), and reduceByKey() functions in Spark.

A solid understanding of MapReduce and the concepts behind MapReduce allows you to solve complex, nonrelational problems in schema-on-read environments not possible using other conventional approaches. It will also make you a much more efficient Spark programmer and a better cluster citizen!

Q&A

Q. Why is the Shuffle phase considered to be the most expensive operation in a distrusted MapReduce application?

A. The Shuffle phase physically moves data between multiple Map task nodes and one or more Reduce task nodes. This data movement has a high network I/O overhead as well as impacting network bandwidth. The Map and Reduce phases, on the other hand, both perform operations on local data, either in memory or on local disk, making these operations less expensive by comparison.

Q. What purpose does speculative execution serve?

A. Speculative execution "speculates" about the cause of a Map or Reduce task node running comparatively slowly in contrast to other Map or Reduce task nodes running tasks for the same application. It assumes that these nodes are running slower due to being overloaded or underresourced and dispatches the same task(s) on different nodes to prevent these slow nodes from becoming a bottleneck in the overall process.

Q. Consider an RDD (named rdd) containing lines of text. What is the difference between rdd.map(lambda x: x.split(' ')) and the rdd.flatMap(lambda x: x.split(' '))?

A. map takes a each line of input text as input and produces a list of words for each line as output, whereas flatMap takes the same input and produces one single list of words from all lines of text as output.

Workshop

The workshop contains quiz questions and exercises to help you solidify your understanding of the material covered. Try to answer all questions before looking at the "Answers" section that follows.

Quiz

1. **True or false:** A Partitioner ensures each key will be passed to one and only one Reducer.

2. `reduceByKey()` is used to

    A. Group values with the same key

    B. Combine values with the same key

    C. Apply a function to each value having the same key

3. What is the input to a `reduce()` function in generalized form?

4. **True or false:** A Combiner function implements a different function than a Reducer in the same application.

Answers

1. **True.**

2. **B.**

3. The `reduce()` function of a Reduce task takes a key and a list of values as input.

4. **False.** If a Combiner is implemented, it will run the same function as the Reducer, but this function will be run on the node executing the Map task.

HOUR 8
Getting Started with Scala

What You'll Learn in This Hour:

▶ The history and background of Scala
▶ Scala programming basics
▶ Object-oriented programming with Scala
▶ Functional programming with Scala
▶ Programming Spark using Scala

Scala is a popular multi-paradigm programming language incorporating both object-oriented programming and functional programming in one succinct, type-safe language. Spark itself is written in Scala, and Scala is a first-class programming language for writing Spark applications. Although for most of this book you will use Python in the examples and exercises, it is definitely worthwhile to get comfortable with Scala or at least to have a basic understanding of Scala. This hour gives you a great start!

Scala History and Background

The name Scala is a blend of the words *scalable* and *language*, which aptly states the key intention of Scala. Scala was created to meet the scalability, extensibility, and portability requirements of both today's and tomorrow's applications.

Scala Beginnings

Scala's beginnings can be traced many years from when it was first publicly released in 2004. During the mid-90s, German computer scientist Martin Odersky worked on several projects to add the functional programming paradigm and constructs to the object-oriented Java platform. Early projects created by Odersky included *Pizza* (https://en.wikipedia.org/wiki/Pizza_(programming_language). Odersky's work led to *Generic Java (GJ)* and to the new `javac` compiler.

In 1999, Odersky joined École Polytechnique Fédérale de Lausanne (EPFL)—English translation: Swiss Federal Institute of Technology—in Lausanne, Switzerland as a professor and continued his work with Java, compilers, and functional programming. His advancements in this area led to the Funnel project, a functional programming platform influenced by Join Calculus. Funnel complied to bytecode that could run on the Java Runtime Environment (JRE) and had a design goal of minimalism.

In 2001, the design of the ultimate successor to Funnel began; the project was named Scala (a portmanteau of *scalable* and *language*). Scala took many of the ideas from Funnel but opted for succinctness and interoperability instead of minimalism. A summary of Scala's design goals include

▶ Unification of functional and object-oriented programming paradigms: Scala is a pure object-oriented language, in which every value is an object, and which provides built-in support for functional programming constructs, treating every function as a value and supporting anonymous (unnamed) functions and nested functions.

▶ Interoperability: Scala programs compile to Java bytecode to run in the Java Virtual Machine (JVM), as well as compiling to .NET object code and run on the Common Language Runtime (CLR). Scala programs can also seamlessly import and instantiate Java classes.

▶ Type safety: Scala provides strong static typing, supporting only valid, well-defined operations on objects and providing safety and performance.

▶ Succinctness: Scala features a concise, lightweight syntax, providing excellent readability and programming agility.

▶ Pattern matching: Scala has built-in general pattern-matching capabilities, allowing it to match on any type of data; this is particularly useful in functional programming.

In 2011, Odersky founded Typesafe, Inc., a company to support and promote Scala. Scala remains one of the fastest growing and most popular programming languages today and is at the core of significant open source projects such as Apache Kafka and, of course, Apache Spark.

Scala Basics

Before you develop Spark applications in Scala, you will first need to understand some of the basics of Scala programming, including how to compile and run Scala programs, as well as some of the basic programming constructs in Scala.

Scala's Compile Time and Run Time Architecture

As previously mentioned, Scala programs compile to Java bytecode. After it's compiled, the Java bytecode runs in a Java Virtual Machine (JVM)—a virtual machine that abstracts the operating system and hardware from the application—which is what enables Java (and Scala) to be portable across different platforms (such as, for instance, Windows or Linux). The JVM has an instruction set and uses memory allocated to it to execute programs.

Standalone installations of Scala include a compiler application called *scalac*. Alternatively, *sbt* (or the *Simple Build Tool for Scala and Java*) can be used to compile, test, and package Scala (and Java) applications. Sbt is a full-featured build tool similar to other popular Java build tools, including Maven and Ant.

Figure 8.1 depicts the process of compiling a Scala or Java program into bytecode and running this in a JVM on various underlying systems.

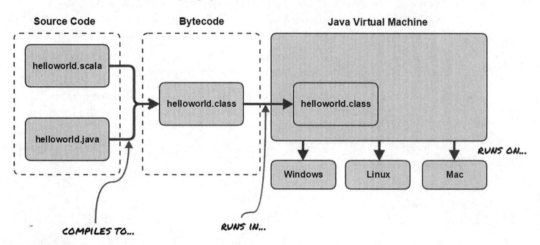

FIGURE 8.1
Compiling and running a Java or Scala program.

Compiling and Packaging Scala Programs

Your Spark installation includes a Scala runtime; however, it does not include a Scala compiler. To be able to compile Scala programs that you can use `spark-submit` or `scala` to run, you will need to install a compiler. To accomplish this, you must install a separate standalone installation of Scala.

1. Download the Scala release for your target platform (Scala 2.10 is recommended for Spark 1.6), this can be obtained from: www.scala-lang.org/download/

A Java Runtime (JRE) version 1.6 or above is a prerequisite for installing Scala. Because you will be installing on one of the systems on which you have already installed Spark, this requirement is satisfied already.

2. Install Scala using one of the following methods:

   ▶ Linux: Unpack the binaries from the downloaded tgz archive from Step 1, move these into the `/usr/lib` directory, and add the Scala bin directory to the system `$PATH`. An example is provided below (change the Scala version to match the version you have downloaded):

   ```
   tar xvf scala-2.10.6.tgz
   sudo mv scala-2.10.6 /usr/lib
   sudo ln -s /usr/lib/scala-2.10.6 /usr/lib/scala
   export PATH=$PATH:/usr/lib/scala/bin
   ```

   You can also download Debian- and Centos-based packages (deb and rpm respectively) from www.scala-lang.org/files/archive/ and use the package manager for your target platform (`apt-get`, `yum`, `zypper`, and so on) to install Scala.

   ▶ Windows: Simply install using the downloaded Scala MSI. One of the install dialogs will prompt you to add the Scala bin directory to the system `%PATH%`.

   ▶ Mac: You can use the method of unpacking the binaries, placing them into the `/usr/lib` directory, and updating the system path described for the Linux installation, or, alternatively, you can use Homebrew, as follows:

   ```
   brew update
   brew install scala
   ```

3. Test the Scala installation:

   ```
   $ scala -version
   Scala code runner version 2.10.6 -- Copyright 2002-2011, LAMP/EPFL
   ```

4. Create a simple "Hello, World" Scala program by using a text editor, creating a file called `helloworld.scala`, and saving the file with the contents below:

   ```
   object HelloWorld {
     def main(args: Array[String]) {
     println("Hello World!")
     }
   }
   ```

5. Compile the program:

   ```
   $ scalac helloworld.scala
   ```

   This creates two additional files in the current directory, `HelloWorld.class` and `HelloWorld$.class`. These files contain the program bytecode.

6. Test the program:

```
$ scala HelloWorld
Hello World!
```

7. Disassemble both class files using `javap` (Java Class File Disassembler); this program is included with the Java JDK release you installed as a precursor to installing Spark.

```
$ javap HelloWorld.class
Compiled from "helloworld.scala"
public final class HelloWorld {
  public static final void main(java.lang.String[]);
}
$ javap HelloWorld$.class
Compiled from "helloworld.scala"
public final class HelloWorld$ implements scala.ScalaObject {
  public static final HelloWorld$ MODULE$;
  public static {};
  public void main(java.lang.String[]);
}
```

More detailed information is available using the `-c` and `-v` options for the `javap` command.

8. Package the application using the `jar` command included with the Java JDK; use the `e` option to specify the main entry point for the program:

```
$ jar cvfe helloworld.jar HelloWorld *.class
added manifest
adding: HelloWorld.class(in = 637) (out= 532)(deflated 16%)
adding: HelloWorld$.class(in = 605) (out= 389)(deflated 35%)
```

9. Run the packaged program using `spark-submit`:

```
$ spark-submit --master local helloworld.jar
Hello World!
```

You could perform analogous operations using `sbt` or other Java/Scala build tools and IDEs. If you intend on building production Spark applications in Scala, you should familiarize yourself with these tools as well. More information about `sbt` is available at http://www.scala-sbt.org/.

Variables and Primitives in Scala

Scala is a true object-oriented programming language (OOP) in the sense that every value is an object. As such, there are *no primitives in Scala;* all data types are objects, meaning that all data types have defined properties and callable methods. Table 8.1 summarizes the built-in value classes akin to primitive types in Java.

TABLE 8.1   Scala Value Classes

Scala Value	Description	Java Equivalent
Byte	8-bit signed integer	byte
Short	16-bit signed integer	short
Int	32-bit signed integer	int
Long	64-bit signed integer	long
Char	16-bit single Unicode character	char
String	Array of characters	String
Float	32-bit single-precision float	float
Double	64-bit double-precision float	double
Boolean	True or false	boolean
Unit	Disregarded return value	void

TIP

Capitalization Conventions

By general convention, the first letter of a class name is capitalized, whereas identifiers for object instantiations of the class are typically lowercase. Member names are typically lowercase or mixed case for compound names, but the first letter is usually lowercase, such as, for example, toString(). This is consistent across all object-oriented programming languages, most notably Java and Scala. For example, note that in Table 8.1 String is capitalized in the Java Equivalent column; this is because String is an object (not a primitive type) in Java representing a sequenced list of characters.

Value classes in Scala are subclasses of the AnyVal class, which itself is a subclass of the root Any class. Subclasses inherit members (methods or properties) from their parent classes. Figure 8.2 shows the class hierarchy for the Scala value classes.

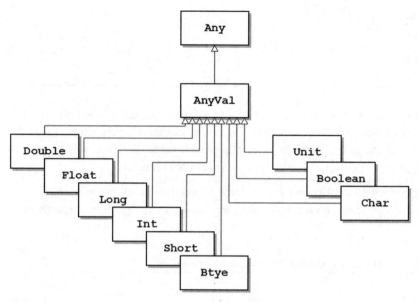

FIGURE 8.2
Scala class hierarchy for value classes.

Every object in Scala can be compared using the equality and inequality operators == and !=
respectively. The code in Listing 8.1 demonstrates methods called on an integer object.

LISTING 8.1   Int Methods

```
scala> 46
res0: Int = 46

scala> 46.toString()
res1: String = 46

scala> 46 == 47
res2: Boolean = false

scala> 46 != 47
res3: Boolean = true

scala> 46.abs
res4: Int = 46

scala> 46.toString
res5: String = 46
```

```
scala> 46.toHexString
res6: String = 2e
```

```
scala> 46.isValidInt
res7: Boolean = true
```

Note that 46 in Listing 8.1 is an object not a primitive and, as such, has all the methods available for an object instantiation of the Int class. Moreover, Listing 8.1 demonstrates how Scala uses local type inference: in this example, the value associated to the object was inferred to be of the Int class. Type inference tends to make source code more succinct.

Variables in Scala are classified as either *mutable* (capable of being updated) or *immutable* (incapable of being updated). These are declared using the var and val operators respectively, as shown in Listing 8.2.

LISTING 8.2   Mutable and Immutable Variables in Scala

```
scala> var mutablevar = 21
mutablevar: Int = 21
```

```
scala> mutablevar = mutablevar + 1
mutablevar: Int = 22
```

```
scala> val immutablevar = 21
immutablevar: Int = 21
```

```
scala> immutablevar = immutablevar + 1
:21: error: reassignment to val
```

```
scala> val immutablevar2 = immutablevar + 1
immutablevar2: Int = 22
```

As you can see from Listing 8.2, you will get an error when you try to reassign a new value to an immutable variable declared using the val operator; however, you can create a new immutable variable from an operation on an existing immutable variable as demonstrated.

It is worth noting that val creates an immutable reference, but the object it references may be mutable (capable of being updated).

Data Structures in Scala

Scala supports several common data structures referred to as *collections*. Collections can be thought of as containers for objects—typically containing data. Some collection types can be mutable or immutable as can the items stored inside a collection, in some cases. Collections supported in Scala include lists, sets, tuples, and maps.

Lists

Lists in Scala are sequenced, linear sets of items. Lists contain an arbitrary number of (zero or more) elements. List elements can be the same type, as shown in Listing 8.3.

LISTING 8.3   Lists in Scala

```
scala> val listofints = List(1, 2, 3)
listofints: List[Int] = List(1, 2, 3)
```

Scala lists can also contain elements of mixed types, as shown in Listing 8.4.

LISTING 8.4   Lists with Mixed Types

```
scala> val listofanys = List("Jeff", "Aven", 46)
listofanys: List[Any] = List(Jeff, Aven, 46)
```

Lists in Scala are *linked lists*. Linked lists are data structures in which each element is an object containing its own data and a reference to the next element or node in the list. The final element contains a reference to an empty node (represented by null or Nil). Scala lists can be used in functional programming and can be dynamically declared element by element; an example of this is shown in Listing 8.5.

LISTING 8.5   Declaring Lists and Using Functions

```
scala> val listofints = 1 :: 2 :: 3 :: Nil
listofints: List[Int] = List(1, 2, 3)

scala> listofints.filter(_ > 1)
res0: List[Int] = List(2, 3)
```

Listing 8.6 demonstrates how elements within a list can be accessed.

LISTING 8.6   Accessing Elements in a List

```
scala> listofints(0)
res2: Int = 1
```

Scala lists are immutable, meaning that after you create a list, you cannot make any changes to it. You can, however, create new lists by appending or prepending to existing list objects using the :: and ::: operators, as demonstrated in Listing 8.7.

LISTING 8.7   Appending and Prepending to Lists

```scala
scala> var listofints = 1 :: 2 :: 3 :: Nil
listofints: List[Int] = List(1, 2, 3)

scala> val listofints2 = listofints ::: 4 :: Nil
listofints2: List[Int] = List(1, 2, 3, 4)

scala> val listofints3 = 0 :: listofints2
listofints3: List[Int] = List(0, 1, 2, 3, 4)

scala> val listofints4 = listofints3 ::: 5 :: Nil
listofints4: List[Int] = List(0, 1, 2, 3, 4, 5)
```

Sets

Sets in Scala contain a set of unique elements. In contrast to lists, sets are unordered and cannot contain duplicates. Because sets are unordered, you cannot access their elements by position as you can with lists. Sets can be instantiated as shown in Listing 8.8.

LISTING 8.8   Sets in Scala

```scala
scala> val setofints1 = Set(1,2,3,4)
setofints: scala.collection.immutable.Set[Int] = Set(1, 2, 3, 4)

scala> val setofints2 = Set(4,5,6,7)
setofints: scala.collection.immutable.Set[Int] = Set(1, 2, 3, 4)

scala> val setofints3 = Set(1,2,3,4,4)
setofints: scala.collection.immutable.Set[Int] = Set(1, 2, 3, 4)
```

Sets in Scala are analogous to mathematical sets because they are based upon this concept.

> A set is a well defined collection of distinct objects.
> Wikipedia

Sets provide methods for min, max, count, find, and filter, as well as set operations such as diff, intersect, and union. Some examples of Set operations are shown in Listing 8.9.

LISTING 8.9   Example Set Operations

```scala
scala> setofints1.min
res0: Int = 1

scala> setofints1.max
res1: Int = 4
```

```
scala> setofints1.intersect(setofints2)
res2: scala.collection.immutable.Set[Int] = Set(4)

scala>  setofints1.union(setofints2)
res3: scala.collection.immutable.Set[Int] = Set(5, 1, 6, 2, 7, 3, 4)

scala> setofints1.diff(setofints2)
res4: scala.collection.immutable.Set[Int] = Set(1, 2, 3)
```

Sets are immutable but can be mutable specifying the `scala.collection.mutable.Set` class explicitly, as demonstrated in Listing 8.10.

LISTING 8.10 Mutable Sets

```
scala> var mutableset = scala.collection.mutable.Set(1,2,3,4)
mutableset: scala.collection.mutable.Set[Int] = Set(2, 1, 4, 3)

scala> mutableset += 5
res0: scala.collection.mutable.Set[Int] = Set(2, 1, 4, 3, 5)
```

Tuples

Tuples are ordered sets of values; you can think of tuples like records in a table in a relational database, where each element or value can be referenced by position. The position of the value in the tuple has some relevance, unlike the position of an element in a list. Tuples can contain objects with a mixture of data types. Also like lists, tuples are immutable data structures.

Tuples in Scala are inferred by an unqualified set of parenthesis—" ( ) ". Listing 8.11 shows some examples of instantiating tuples in Scala.

LISTING 8.11 Tuples in Scala

```
scala> val a_tuple = ("Jeff", "Aven", 46)
a_tuple: (java.lang.String, java.lang.String, Int) = (Jeff,Aven,46)

scala> val another_tuple = new Tuple3("Jeff", "Aven", 46)
another_tuple: (java.lang.String, java.lang.String, Int) = (Jeff,Aven,46)
```

Note in the last example that I used the class name `Tuple3`; if the tuple contained four elements, I would use the class name `Tuple4`, and so on.

After you have created a tuple, you can access any of the fields positionally by using `_<field_no>`; unlike lists or arrays, which are zero-based (meaning 0, 1, 2), element position in a tuple is one-based (meaning 1, 2, 3). You can also declare field names and access elements by name; examples of both access methods are shown in Listing 8.12.

LISTING 8.12   Accessing and Using Tuples

```
scala> println(a_tuple._1)
Jeff

scala> val(fname, lname, age) = a_tuple
fname: java.lang.String = Jeff
lname: java.lang.String = Aven
age: Int = 46

scala> fname
res1: java.lang.String = Jeff
```

Tuples can be embedded in other types; for instance, it is sometimes useful to have a list of tuples or an array of tuples.

Maps

Maps are collections of key value pairs, similar to dicts in Python or Hashes in Ruby. Keys in a map are unique, and any value can be retrieved based upon a key. Values in a map do not have to be unique, however. Maps have methods to return a collection containing keys or values. Listing 8.13 shows an example of creating a map and using the keys and values methods.

LISTING 8.13   Maps in Scala

```
scala> val a_map = Map("fname" -> "Jeff","lname" -> "Aven","age" -> 46)
a_map: scala.collection.immutable.Map[java.lang.String,Any] =
Map(fname -> Jeff, lname -> Aven, age -> 46)

scala> a_map.keys
res0: Iterable[java.lang.String] = Set(fname, lname, age)

scala> a_map.values
res1: Iterable[Any] = MapLike(Jeff, Aven, 46)
```

Maps are immutable by default but can mutable using the scala.collection.mutable.Map class. Mutable maps can then be appended to or updated, as shown in Listing 8.14:

LISTING 8.14   Mutable Maps

```
scala> var mutablemap = scala.collection.mutable.Map(
       "fname" -> "Jeff", "lname" -> "Aven", "age" -> 46)
mutablemap: scala.collection.mutable.Map[java.lang.String,Any] =
Map(fname -> Jeff, age -> 46, lname -> Aven)
```

```
scala> mutablemap.keys
res0: Iterable[java.lang.String] = Set(fname, age, lname)

scala> mutablemap += ("city" -> "Melbourne")
res1: mutablemap.type = Map(city -> Melbourne, fname -> Jeff, age -> 46, lname ->
Aven)

scala> mutablemap.keys.foreach(x => println(x))
city
fname
age
lname
```

NOTE

Take note of the capitalization as mentioned before; `Map`, the class, is different from `map`, the method.

Control Structures in Scala

Scala contains the conventional procedural control structures you are used to using in most programming languages; the difference is that Scala provides functional programming extensions to these structures. Take a look at some commonly used control structures in Scala.

If Expressions

Scala includes a succinct `if` construct, including an inline `if` expression, as well as support for `elseif` and `else` conditions. The `if` expression evaluates a Boolean expression and performs an operation or operations if the expression evaluates to true. Some examples of `if` expressions are shown in Listing 8.15.

LISTING 8.15   If Expressions in Scala

```
scala> val name = "Jeff"
name: java.lang.String = Jeff

scala> if (name == "Jeff")
            {
              println("Hello " + name + "!")
            }
Hello Jeff!

scala> if (name == "Jeff"){ println("Hi " + name + "!") }
Hi Jeff!
```

```
scala> if (name == "John"){
          println("Hello " + name + "!")
          } else {
          println("Hello Someone Else!")
          }
Hello Someone Else!

scala> if (name == "Juan") {
          println("Hola Juan!")
          } else if (name == "Jeff"){
          println("Hello Jeff!")
          } else {
          println("Hello Someone Else!")
          }
Hello Jeff!
```

For Loops

A `for` loop in Scala is a simple control structure that allows you to iterate through items or elements in a collection or a range while performing operations on each element. A `for` loop can be implemented in several different ways; some examples are shown in Listing 8.16.

LISTING 8.16   For Loops in Scala

```
scala> var listofstrings = "Scala" :: "is" :: "fun" :: Nil
listofstrings: List[java.lang.String] = List(Scala, is, fun)

scala> for(value : String <- listofstrings) {
          println(value);
          }
Scala
is
fun

scala> for(value <- listofstrings){println(value);}
Scala
is
fun
```

In Scala, filters can be applied to `for` loops so that they operate only on certain elements in a collection; an example of using a filter with a `for` loop is shown in Listing 8.17.

LISTING 8.17 For Loops with Filters

```
scala> for(value : String <- listofstrings if value.startsWith("S")) {
            println(value);
        }
Scala
```

It is possible to break out of a `for` loop based upon a specified condition by using the `break` control abstraction available in Scala 2.8 and higher, prior to which you would need to use a less elegant approach involving `try`, `catch`, and `throw`. An example of the `break` control abstraction is shown in Listing 8.18.

LISTING 8.18 For Loop Break

```
scala> import scala.util.control.Breaks._
import scala.util.control.Breaks._

scala> breakable {for (i <- 0 to 10) {
            println(i)
            if (i >= 5) break
        }}
0
1
2
3
4
5
```

The `yield` operator can be used to implement a *"for comprehension"* construct, providing a powerful way of iterating over collections. An example of this is shown in Listing 8.19.

LISTING 8.19 Yield Operator

```
scala> var lengthof3 = for{value <- listofstrings
                            if value.length == 3
                        }yield value
lengthof3: List[java.lang.String] = List(fun)

scala> lengthof3.foreach(x => println(x))
fun
```

Do While and While Loops

In Scala, `while` loops can be implemented using the `do while` and `while` statements. Both statements operate similarly except that `while` checks a condition at the top of a loop and do while checks a condition at the bottom of a loop. The simplest demonstration of the contrasting behaviors is shown in Listing 8.20.

LISTING 8.20   While and Do While Loops in Scala

```
scala> while(a_number <= 5){
            println(a_number);
            a_number += 1;
        }
0
1
2
3
4
5

scala> do{
            println(a_number);
            a_number += 1;
        }while(a_number <= 5)

6
```

Pattern Matching using case

Pattern matching involves evaluating a set of options in a match block, each beginning with the keyword case. Each option includes a pattern and an statement or statements to be invoked if the pattern matches. An example of match case is shown in Listing 8.21.

LISTING 8.21   Pattern Matching in Scala Using Case

```
scala> val monthno = 9
monthno: Int = 9

scala> val monthname = monthno match {
            case 8 => "August"
            case 9 => "September"
            case _ => "Another Month"
        }
monthname: java.lang.String = September

scala> println("the month is " + monthname)
the month is September
```

The match case construct can also implement *destructuring binds* (sometimes called *tuple extraction*) so they are more than just a simple switch statement.

Named Functions

Named functions in Scala are declared using the def keyword. By default, parameters to Scala named functions are passed "by-value" (meaning the arguments—which could be themselves functions or variables—are evaluated prior to being passed to the function). The return type is specified in the function signature. A return value can either be explicitly specified using the return keyword or inferred using the last expression in the body of the function. Some named function examples are shown in Listing 8.22.

LISTING 8.22   Named Functions in Scala

```
scala> def milestofeet(miles: Int): Int = {
           val feet = miles * 5280
           return feet
       }
milestofeet: (miles: Int)Int

scala> milestofeet(3)
res1: Int = 15840

scala> def milestofeet(miles: Int): Int = {
           val feet = miles * 5280
           feet
       }
milestofeet: (miles: Int)Int

scala> milestofeet(3)
res2: Int = 15840
```

You will learn more about anonymous (or unnamed) functions when you look at functional programming in Scala later in this hour.

Object-Oriented Programming in Scala

The core principles and ideals of object-oriented programming including classes, objects, polymorphism, and inheritance, are all core to Scala. I will cover these further in this section with some examples.

Classes and Inheritance

Classes are the most fundamental concept in object-oriented programming. Classes in Scala behave much the same as their Java counterparts. Classes are templates that are used to define properties and behaviors (methods) of an entity; these templates are then used to instantiate objects in your Scala program.

Scala classes can be extended, inheriting members from a *superclass*—a class from which another class is derived in part or in whole. Consider the example shown in Figure 8.3.

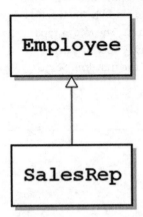

FIGURE 8.3
Employee and SalesRep classes.

A `SalesRep` is an an extension of an `Employee` sharing some common attributes but also having some unique attributes and behaviors. A simple class implementation demonstrating inheritance is provided in Listing 8.23.

LISTING 8.23   Class and Inheritance Example in Scala

```
scala> class Employee(val fname: String,
     val lname: String,
     val daily_rate: Float) {
     def calculate_wage(days_worked: Int): Float =
     days_worked.toFloat * daily_rate
     }
defined class Employee

scala> class SalesRep(fname: String,
     lname: String,
     daily_rate: Float,
     val comm_pct: Float) extends Employee(fname, lname, daily_rate){
     def calculate_comm(sales: Float): Float =
     sales * comm_pct
     }
defined class SalesRep

scala> val office_manager = new Employee("John", "Williamson", 250.0F)
office_manager: Employee = Employee@163f3c30
```

```
scala> val sales_rep = new SalesRep("Ricky", "Roma", 250.0F, 0.03F)
sales_rep: SalesRep = SalesRep@3ebfe943

scala> println("Office Manager, " +
    office_manager.fname + " " +
    office_manager.lname +
    " earns $" +
    office_manager.calculate_wage(200) +
    " per year")
Office Manager, John Williamson earns $50000.0 per year

scala> println("Sales Rep, " +
    sales_rep.fname + " " +
    sales_rep.lname +
    " earns $" +
    (sales_rep.calculate_wage(200) +
    sales_rep.calculate_comm(1000000.0F)) +
    " per year")
Sales Rep, Ricky Roma earns $80000.0 per year
```

Mixin Composition

Multiple inheritance—that is, one subclass inheriting from multiple superclasses—is achieved in Scala using mixin composition (or mixin class composition). *Mixins* are a programming concept enabling you to add methods or variables to a class without creating a strict single parent to child class relationship.

Scala uses Traits to implement mixin composition. Traits are similar to Interfaces in Java, with the key difference that traits can have values as well as methods. Listing 8.24 shows an example definition and use of Traits.

LISTING 8.24   Mixin Composition Using Traits

```
scala> trait SparkBook {
        def type_desc {println("This is a book about Spark")}
        }
defined trait SparkBook

scala> class Book (
        val name: String,
        val pages: Int
    ) {
        def book_desc {println(name + " has " + pages.toString +
" pages")}
        }
defined class Book
```

```
scala> val styspark = new Book("STY Spark", 500) with SparkBook
styspark: Book with SparkBook = $anon$1@31f57f58

scala> styspark.book_desc
STY Spark has 500 pages

scala> styspark.type_desc
This is a book about Spark
```

Singleton Objects

A *singleton object* represents a class that is instantiated to one object only. A singleton object is effectively a single-use object, as opposed to a generalized class, which can be used many times as a template to create multiple object instantiations. Singleton objects are declared using the object keyword.

A simple use for singleton objects is the main entry object and its main method used to run a Scala program. Similar to the main entry point method in Java, which accepts an array of String arguments and returns void, the main method in Scala accepts a String array and returns the Scala equivalent, Unit (note the capitalization and recall that everything is an object in Scala).

Listing 8.25 shows some examples of singleton objects, including a singleton object used to run a Scala program.

LISTING 8.25   Singleton Objects in Scala

```
scala> object SparkBook {
        val book_msg = "This is a book about Spark"
      }
defined module SparkBook

scala> object Main {
        def main(args: Array[String]): Unit = {
          println(SparkBook.book_msg)
        }
      }
defined module Main

scala> Main.main(Array())
This is a book about Spark

scala> SparkBook.book_msg
res0: java.lang.String = This is a book about Spark
```

Singleton objects cannot be created with parameters and cannot be instantiated using the `new` keyword used to instantiate normal classes. As demonstrated by the last statement in Listing 8.25, methods can be invoked directly on singleton objects by using the syntax `ObjectName.method`. Singleton objects would be used in Scala as opposed to static methods in Java.

Polymorphism

Another defining characteristic of object-oriented programming is polymorphism. *Polymorphism* is the ability to redefine objects or methods under different circumstances. Parametric polymorphism is the simplest example of this concept in Scala. Listing 8.26 demonstrates parametric polymorphism.

LISTING 8.26   Parametric Polymorphism in Scala

```scala
scala> class MultiType[T](val value: T) {
         def add_one(intvalue: Int): Int = {intvalue + 1}
         def concat_one(strvalue: String): String = {strvalue + "1"}
       }
defined class MultiType

scala> val a_string = new MultiType("String")
a_string: MultiType[java.lang.String] = MultiType@26d5e01d

scala> println(a_string.concat_one(a_string.value))
String1

scala> val an_int = new MultiType(1)
an_int: MultiType[Int] = MultiType@3d762a6

scala> println(an_int.add_one(an_int.value).toString)
2
```

Functional Programming in Scala

Scala's functional programming support incorporated into a pure object-oriented language is what clearly sets it apart from many other languages. Take a look at some of the key functional programming properties of Scala.

First-class Functions

Scala functions are first-class functions, meaning that functions can be passed as arguments to other functions and can be returned as values from other functions. Functions in Scala are "first-class citizens," in that they are treated the same as any other variable or object in a Scala application. This is a core tenet of any true functional programming language.

Anonymous Functions

Anonymous functions (or *unnamed functions*) are an integral construct in functional programming. Scala provides several methods to define and use anonymous functions. Anonymous functions are referred to as function literals at compile time; at runtime, these functions are objects referred to as *function values*. Some examples of anonymous functions in Scala are shown in Listing 8.27.

LISTING 8.27   Anonymous Functions in Scala

```
scala> val feet: Int => Int = _ * 5280
feet: Int => Int = <function1>

scala> feet(3)
res27: Int = 15840
```

As you can see, this is the same function you had declared previously as a named function, instead using the notation x => func(x). The underscore "_" is shorthand for the anonymous function input. As you will see in Spark applications written in Scala, anonymous functions are often used in transformations such as map, filter, and reduce.

Higher-order Functions

Functions that take one or more functions as input arguments or functions that return a function as a result are considered to be *higher-order functions*. Examples of higher-order functions in Spark programming can be found in most common transformations. Consider the function shown in Listing 8.28. This is an obvious example of a function, map, which takes another function as its input. Each element in the RDD is passed through the function by the map transformation.

LISTING 8.28   Higher-order Functions in Scala

```
scala> val listofints = List(3,-11,8,-12,4)
listofints: List[Int] = List(3, -11, 8, -12, 4)

scala> val absvalues = listofints.map(i => i.abs)
absvalues: List[Int] = List(3, 11, 8, 12, 4)
```

Closures

A *closure* is a function that uses one or more variables declared outside of the function. Variables defined inside of a function are referred to as *bound variables*, whereas variables used in a function but declared outside of the function are called *free variables*. Closures are functions that use both bound and free variables; the function is essentially enclosed with the variables from its enclosing lexical scope.

Listing 8.29 shows an example of a closure using the `absvalues` List created in the previous listing, the variable `one` is a free variable, and the variable `i` used in the anonymous function is a bound variable.

LISTING 8.29   Closures in Scala

```
scala> var one = 1
one: Int = 1

scala> val add_one = absvalues.map(i => i + one)
add_one: List[Int] = List(4, 12, 9, 13, 5)

scala> add_one
List[Int] = List(4, 12, 9, 13, 5)

scala> var one = 2
one: Int = 2

scala> add_one
List[Int] = List(4, 12, 9, 13, 5)
```

As you can see from Listing 8.29 although the value for the variable `one` was changed, the `add_one` function which was enclosed with the original value has not changed.

Currying

Currying allows you to take a function with multiple parameters and represent it as a function accepting a single parameter. Currying and curried functions were named after Haskell Curry, the creator of the Haskell programming language (a pure functional programming language). Curried functions return a function that can be in turn called with a single argument, as shown in Listing 8.30.

LISTING 8.30   Currying in Scala

```
scala> def add_n_to_each(listofints: List[Int])(n: Int) = {
         listofints.map(i => i + n)
      }
add_n_to_each: (listofints: List[Int])(n: Int)List[Int]

scala> val add_to_list = add_n_to_each(absvalues)_
add_to_list: Int => List[Int] = <function1>

scala> add_to_list(1)
res0: List[Int] = List(4, 12, 9, 13, 5)
```

Lazy Evaluation

Lazy evaluation, which I discussed in **Hour 6, "Learning the Basics of Spark Programming with the RDDs,"** in the context of RDD processing, is another key feature used in functional programming. Lazy evaluation allows a program to compute or evaluate an expression only when a result is required, meaning that if a value is never required, the function or expression is never evaluated. In contrast to lazy evaluation, many non-functional languages use *strict evaluation,* whereby all expressions are evaluated upon declaration. Listing 8.31 demonstrates the use of lazy evaluation using the keyword `lazy`.

LISTING 8.31   Lazy Evaluation in Scala

```
scala> lazy val lazyval = 1 + 2
lazyval: Int = <lazy>

scala> lazyval
res0: Int = 3
```

Immutable Data Structures

Immutable data structures, such as Lists in Scala, are integral to functional programming. Immutable data structures allow data to be shared between functions as well as between other data structures ensuring an object won't be modified during evaluation.

Spark Programming in Scala

To demonstrate Spark programming in Scala, let's implement the Word Count application you had developed in **Hour 7, "Understanding MapReduce Concepts,"** (previously written in PySpark) using Scala.

▼ TRY IT YOURSELF

Spark Word Count in Scala

In this exercise, you will rewrite the Word Count example (counting unique words from the works of Shakespeare) from **Hour 7** using Scala. I will walk you through and discuss each Spark transformation using Scala individually, then put it all together in one script at the end.

1. Use your existing single node Spark installation with the `shakespeare.txt` file downloaded to the `/opt/spark/data` directory in the **Hour 7** exercise. If you need to download the file again, you can use the link: https://s3.amazonaws.com/sty-spark/shakespeare/shakespeare.txt

As with the exercise in the previous hour, if you have HDFS available to you (as when using AWS EMR, Databricks, or a Hadoop distribution that includes Spark) you are free to upload the file to HDFS and use this as an alternative.

2. Open a Scala spark shell in local mode:

```
spark-shell --master local
```

As with Step 1, if you have a Hadoop cluster or distributed Spark standalone cluster accessible, you are free to use these instead.

3. Load the file:

```
val doc = sc.textFile("file:///opt/spark/data/shakespeare.txt")
```

4. Inspect the RDD created:

```
doc
res0: org.apache.spark.rdd.RDD[String] = MapPartitionsRDD[1] at textFile at
<console>:21
```

5. Filter empty lines:

```
val noempties = doc.filter(line => line.length > 0)
```

6. Split by whitespace and flatten into one list:

```
val flattened = noempties.flatMap(line => line.split("\\W+"))
```

7. Inspect the RDD:

```
flattened.take(5)
res2: Array[String] = Array(A, MIDSUMMER, NIGHT, S, DREAM)
```

8. Filter zero-length words:

```
val noemptystr = flattened.filter(word => word.length > 0)
```

9. Map text to lowercase and convert to key value pairs in the form of (word, 1):

```
val kvpairs = noemptystr.map(word => (word.toLowerCase,1))
```

10. Inspect the RDD:

```
kvpairs.take(5)
res4: Array[(String, Int)] = Array((a,1), (midsummer,1), (night,1), (s,1),
(dream,1))
```

11. Count each word and sort results in reverse alphabetic order:

```
val byworddsc = kvpairs.reduceByKey(_ + _).sortByKey(false)
```

12. Inspect the RDD:

```
byworddsc.take(5)
res6: Array[(String, Int)] = Array((zwaggered,1), (zur,2), (zounds,19),
(zone,1), (zodiacs,1))
```

13. Display the top five most used words:

```
// invert the kv pair to make the count the key and sort
val topwords = byworddsc.map(kv => kv.swap).sortByKey(false)
topwords.take(5)
res7: Array[(Int, String)] = Array((26856,the), (24116,and), (22412,i),
(19225,to), (16018,of))
```

14. Combine the code into one succinct command with a sequence of functions; note that to do this in the interactive shell you will need to use the `:paste` command first, copy and paste the entire code block, and then use Ctrl+D to exit paste mode. This allows you to enter a multi-line command in the Scala shell without each line being interpreted as an individual statement. This program saves the entire results to a directory called `/opt/spark/data/scalawc`:

```
val topwords = sc.textFile("file:///opt/spark/data/shakespeare.txt")
  .filter(line => line.length > 0)
  .flatMap(line => line.split("\\W+"))
  .filter(word => word.length > 0)
  .map(word => (word.toLowerCase,1))
  .reduceByKey(_ + _)
  .map(kv => kv.swap)
  .sortByKey(false)
  .saveAsTextFile("file:///opt/spark/data/scalawc")
```

Browse the `part-00000` file created in the `scalawc` directory. You should see the following output:

```
(26856,the)
(24116,and)
(22412,i)
(19225,to)
(16018,of)
(14097,you)
(13986,a)
(12283,my)
(11171,that)
(10640,in)
...
```

You have now written and tested a Spark application written in Scala. It is interesting to compare and contrast the Scala version with the functionally equivalent PySpark version from Hour 7.

Summary

Scala is a rich, extensible, and eloquent programming language. Scala is a dual-paradigm language, being both a true object-oriented language as well as a rich, functional programming language.

In this hour, I have covered some basic Scala concepts and programming constructs as well as complex types (Collections) including lists, sets, tuples, and maps. I have covered functional programming, first-class functions, and anonymous functions in Scala. You also learned about the runtime architecture of Scala, how to compile Scala programs, and how to use Scala in Spark applications.

By no means have I exhaustively covered Scala; there are entire books written on this topic alone. For the remainder of this book, I will use Python for my examples and exercises where possible because it is generally a more well known and commonly used language; however, there are many advantages to using Scala for Spark programming. For example, many new features in Spark are released in the Scala API first (and, in some cases, are only exposed using the Scala API). If you wish to use Scala beyond this book, many resources are available to you.

Q&A

Q. What are the key differences between lists and sets in Scala?

A. Lists are ordered, can contain duplicates, and their elements can be accessed positionally. Sets, on the other hand, are unordered, unique collections of objects that do not support positional access. Sets in Scala are analogous to the properties of mathematical sets.

Q. Why are functions considered "first-class citizens" in Scala?

A. Functions in Scala are objects or function values. These functions can be passed as arguments to other functions or returned as values from other functions. In other words, functions are treated as "first-class citizens" or no differently than any other variable or object in a Scala program.

Q. What is the difference between a *function literal* and a *function value* in Scala?

A. Anonymous functions are referred to as function literals at compile time; at runtime, these functions are objects referred to as function values.

Workshop

The workshop contains quiz questions and exercises to help you solidify your understanding of the material covered. Try to answer all questions before looking at the "Answers" section that follows.

Quiz

1. **True or false:** Scala Sets can be mutable or immutable and can contain duplicates.

2. Which primitive types are *not* supported in Scala?

    A. `int`

    B. `long`

    C. `char`

    D. All of the above

3. Mixin class composition is expressed in Scala using which keyword?

    A. `Class`

    B. `Trait`

    C. `Interface`

4. A curried function in Scala takes _____ argument and returns _____.

Answers

1. **False.** Sets can be declared as mutable or immutable; however, Sets cannot contain duplicate values.

2. **D.** Trick question! Scala does not support primitives; all of the base value types are objects inheriting members from their respective classes. For example, `Int` is a class for objects containing integer values.

3. **B.**

4. A curried function in Scala takes **one** argument list and returns **a function**.

HOUR 9
Functional Programming with Python

What You'll Learn in This Hour:

▶ Python runtime architecture
▶ Complex data structures in Python
▶ Object serialization in Python
▶ Anonymous and higher-order functions in Python
▶ `map`, `reduce`, and `filter` Python functions
▶ Closures, currying, and partial functions in Python
▶ Interactive Python programming with IPython and Jupyter
▶ Functional programming with PySpark

Python is an amazingly useful language. Its uses range from automation to web services to machine learning and everything in between. Python has risen to be one of the most widely used languages available today.

Functional Python extends this utility. In this hour, you will examine the functional programming elements included in Python, including anonymous functions, common higher-order functions, and immutable and iterable data structures. You will explore the Python runtime, learn about object serialization in Python using pickling, and further explore Spark programming in Python using PySpark. You will also get introduced to IPython as an interactive Python environment.

Python Overview

Python is a multi-paradigm programming language combining the imperative and procedural programming paradigms with full support for the object-oriented and functional paradigms. Python is a very readable language, which makes it easy to learn, adopt, and extend.

Python Background

Python was created by Guido van Rossum at Centrum Wiskunde & Informatica (CWI), the National Research Institute for Mathematics and Computer Science in the Netherlands.

Python was based upon a predecessor language called ABC, a language developed earlier at CWI that was designed to address the productivity issues with C. Python was released in 1991 as a further attempt to increase programmer productivity.

Python has always had a strong open source and community ethos. The Python Software Foundation (PSF) was created to promote, protect, and advance the Python programming language and to support the global community of Python programmers. The PSF considers recommendations through the Python Enhancement Proposals (PEPs). There are numerous conferences, user groups, wikis, and more dedicated to Python and its extensions.

Python is an incredibly rich language that is both succinct and intuitive, yet equally powerful and adaptable. Python's runtime supports both interactive and script-processing modes. Python is extensible, shipping with hundreds of library modules for tasks that in other languages often require loading external libraries. For this reason, Python is referred to as the "batteries included" language.

The next section gives you a look at the Python runtime architecture before you explore functional programming in Python.

Python Runtime Architecture

Python is an interpreted language, meaning that the Python interpreter—a program itself—reads your Python program, and executes the instructions contained in it. This is as opposed to a compiled language, which is explicitly compiled with an external compiler before it can be run.

In actuality, the Python interpreter does actually compile your Python program's source code into Python byte code, which is cross-platform machine code that is executed in the Python Virtual Machine (PVM), Python's runtime engine. The PVM is actually a function of the interpreter.

You can see the bytecode file that is generated, because it appears in your script directory as `<script_name>.pyc` when you first execute your Python program. Figure 9.1 illustrates the Python runtime, including Python bytecode, the Python interpreter, and the Python Virtual Machine.

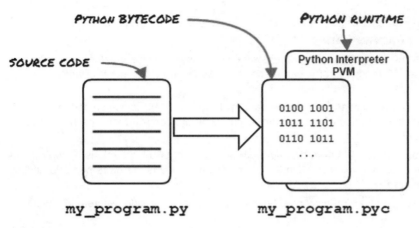

FIGURE 9.1
Python runtime.

NOTE

Python source code files are named with a .py extension by convention. Although this naming convention is not necessary for programs that you directly execute using the Python interpreter, it is highly recommended because it is required for Python modules you wish to import into your program.

The .pyc bytecode file created by the Python interpreter can be reused to bypass the compilation step for subsequent executions if there have been no source code modifications (based upon timestamp comparisons). In cases where the .pyc file cannot be written to the script directory, the bytecode will be generated in memory and discarded when the program exits.

There are several implementations of the Python runtime, the primary implementations being CPython and Jython, with other implementations such as IronPython and Python.NET. The next few sections look at some of the major implementations.

CPython

CPython is the standard and most common implementation of Python. CPython is the reference implementation of Python, which is built upon the portable ANSI C language, making it the most performant of all of the Python variants. CPython is the implementation that is usually provided by default with most common Linux distributions. The CPython runtime executes Python bytecode instructions on the Python Virtual Machine, which is written in C.

NOTE

Bytecode versus Machine Code

I have mentioned bytecode quite a bit in this book, whether it was that Scala programs compile to Java bytecode or that CPython programs can be compiled as Python bytecode. It is worth distinguishing bytecode from machine code.

Machine code is a set of instructions to be carried out by the system CPU; machine code is therefore directly reliant on the underlying hardware. C programs are compiled into machine code using the `make` program.

Bytecode, on the hand, is abstracted from the hardware and specific CPU instructions by the runtime (either the JVM, in the case of Java, or PVM, in the case of Python) and is therefore portable and, in many cases, cross-platform.

Machine code is generally faster than bytecode; however, bytecode is portable, whereas machine code is not.

Consider the code in Listing 9.1 saved as a file named `convert_temps.py`. Listing 9.2 demonstrates disassembly of the Python program into a human readable representation of the Python bytecode using the Python `dis` module.

LISTING 9.1 Sample Python Program

```
tempc = [38.4, 19.2, 12.8, 9.6]
tempf = map(lambda x: (float(9)/5)*x + 32, tempc)
for temp in tempf:
    print("%.2f" % temp)
```

LISTING 9.2 Human Readable Representation of Python Bytecode

```
$ python -m dis convert_temps.py
  1           0 LOAD_CONST              0 (38.4)
              3 LOAD_CONST              1 (19.2)
              6 LOAD_CONST              2 (12.8)
              9 LOAD_CONST              3 (9.6)
             12 BUILD_LIST              4
             15 STORE_NAME              0 (tempc)

  2          18 LOAD_NAME               1 (map)
             21 LOAD_CONST              4 (<code object <lambda> at...>)
             24 MAKE_FUNCTION           0
             27 LOAD_NAME               0 (tempc)
             30 CALL_FUNCTION           2
             33 STORE_NAME              2 (tempf)

  3          36 SETUP_LOOP             23 (to 62)
             39 LOAD_NAME               2 (tempf)
```

```
              42 GET_ITER
       >>     43 FOR_ITER              15 (to 61)
              46 STORE_NAME             3 (temp)

 4            49 LOAD_CONST             5 ('%.2f')
              52 LOAD_NAME              3 (temp)
              55 BINARY_MODULO
              56 PRINT_ITEM
              57 PRINT_NEWLINE
              58 JUMP_ABSOLUTE         43
       >>     61 POP_BLOCK
       >>     62 LOAD_CONST             6 (None)
              65 RETURN_VALUE
```

The CPython PVM performs all memory management functions—including managing virtual memory—and manages the *garbage collection* process, which is the process that detects memory no longer in use and frees this memory to be used again. Garbage collection in CPython is accomplished using an algorithm called *reference counting,* which tracks references to an object and frees memory when an object has no references.

Don't confuse CPython with Cython; this is a completely different project, which provides C extensions for Python.

Jython

Jython, which was originally called JPython, converts Python source code to Java bytecode to run on the Java Virtual Machine (JVM). As Jython compiles to Java bytecode, Jython can import and use native Java classes (in much the same way Scala does). Jython manages memory, heap management, and garbage collection through the JVM runtime. Jython may be a suitable option if interoperability with Java is desired.

Python.NET and IronPython

Python.NET and *IronPython* are developed on Microsoft's .NET platform and run in Microsoft's Common Language Runtime (CLR). IronPython and Python.NET are written entirely in C# and are supported by Microsoft's development tools such as Visual Studio. IronPython and Python.NET are suited for developers who need integration with Windows or who develop exclusively in .NET.

Psyco and PyPy

PyPy and its predecessor project, *Psyco,* were projects based upon a Just-in-Time (JIT) compiler for Python, essentially compiling some or all of your Python program directly into machine code, making it much faster and possibly using less memory that the bytecode equivalent. PyPy is designed to be code compatible with CPython and supports many popular Python external libraries.

PySpark (Python for Spark)

PySpark uses the standard CPython implementation; therefore, CPython or simply Python must be available on all systems where Spark is to be installed. Fortunately, Python is included by default on most commercial distributions of Linux and is readily available for other platforms. PySpark uses *Py4J*, which enables Python programs using a standard CPython interpreter to access Java objects in a JVM. Py4J also enables Java applications to call back Python objects. The Py4J libraries are included with the Spark installation.

Data Structures and Serialization in Python

Python RDDs in Spark are simply distributed collections of Python objects, so it is important to understand the various data structures available in Python. I will cover the main data structures and serialization in Python here.

Lists

Lists in Python are (zero-based) indexed sequences of mutable values with the first value numbered zero. You can remove or replace elements in a list as well as append elements to the end of a list.

Lists support the three primary functional programming constructs, `map()`, `reduce()`, and `filter()`. The usage differs slightly between pure Python and PySpark, as shown in Listing 9.3.

LISTING 9.3   map(), reduce(), and filter() in Python and PySpark

```
# pure python
tempc = [38.4, 19.2, 12.8, 9.6]
tempf = map(lambda x: (float(9)/5)*x + 32, tempc)

# pyspark
tempc = sc.parallelize([38.4, 19.2, 12.8, 9.6])
tempf = tempc.map(lambda x: (float(9)/5)*x + 32)
```

Lists support several other built in methods including `count()`, `sort()`, `reverse()`, `append()`, `extend()`, `insert()`, `remove()`, and more. Individual list elements can be accessed using the index number in square brackets, such as, for example, `firstelem = tempc[0]`. Although Python lists are mutable by default, list objects contained within Python RDDs in Spark are immutable—as is the case with any objects created within Spark RDDs.

Sets

Sets in Python are analogous to Set objects in Scala, which are based upon the set mathematical abstraction. Sets are unordered collections of unique values. By default, sets in Python are mutable collections, elements can be added to or removed from sets.

Sets can be created as immutable objects, as is the case with Python RDDs using set objects. In native Python, immutable sets are created as *frozensets,* which are like sets except that they cannot be updated.

Set objects support mathematical set operations such as union, intersection, difference, and others. Listing 9.4 demonstrates instantiation of a frozenset in Python and in PySpark and various common set operations.

LISTING 9.4 Immutable Sets in Python and PySpark

```
# python
tempc0 = frozenset([38.4, 19.2])
tempc1 = frozenset([12.8, 9.6])
tempc2 = frozenset([23.7, 9.6])

tempc1.intersection(tempc2)
frozenset([9.6])

tempc1.difference(tempc2)
frozenset([12.8])

tempc0.union(tempc1)
frozenset([9.6, 38.4, 19.2, 12.8])

# pyspark
tempc = sc.parallelize(set([38.4, 19.2, 12.8, 9.6]))
tempc
ParallelCollectionRDD[0] at parallelize at PythonRDD.scala:423
```

Tuples

Tuples are an immutable sequence objects (the objects contained in a tuple can themselves be immutable or mutable). Tuples can contain different underlying object types, such as a mixture of `string`, `int`, and `float` objects, or other sequence types, such as sets and other tuples. For simplicity, tuples can be thought of as similar to immutable lists. However, they are different constructs and have very different purposes.

Tuples are similar to records in a relational database table, where each record has a structure and each field defined with an ordinal position in the structure has a meaning. List objects simply have an order, and because they are mutable by default, this order is not directly related to the structure.

Tuples consist of one or more values separated by commas enclosed in parentheses. Elements are accessed from Python tuples similarly to the way they are accessed from lists—using square brackets with a zero-based index referencing the specific element.

Tuple objects have methods for comparing tuples with other tuples, as well as returning the length of a tuple (the number of elements in the tuple) as well as other methods. You can also convert a list in Python to a tuple using the `tuple(list)` function. Listing 9.5 shows the creation and usage of tuples in native Python.

LISTING 9.5 Tuples in Python

```
rec0 = "Jeff", "Aven", 46
rec1 = "Barack", "Obama", 54
rec2 = "John F", "Kennedy", 46
rec3 = "Jeff", "Aven", 46

rec0
('Jeff', 'Aven', 46)
len(rec0)
3
print("first name: " + rec0[0])
first name: Jeff

# compare tuples
cmp(rec0, rec1)
1 ## no fields match

cmp(rec0, rec2)
-1 ## some fields match

cmp(rec0, rec3)
0 ## all fields match

# create tuple of tuples
all_recs = rec0,rec1,rec2,rec3
all_recs
(('Jeff', 'Aven', 46), ('Barack', 'Obama', 54),
('John F', 'Kennedy', 46), ('Jeff', 'Aven', 46))

# create list of tuples
list_of_recs = [rec0,rec1,rec2,rec3]
list_of_recs
[('Jeff', 'Aven', 46), ('Barack', 'Obama', 54),
('John F', 'Kennedy', 46), ('Jeff', 'Aven', 46)]
```

As you can see from Listing 9.5, it is very important to distinguish your square brackets from your parentheses because these have very different structural meanings.

Tuples in PySpark are often (but not always) created as resultant output data structures from a `map()` function. Listing 9.6 demonstrates this; I will create a list of tuples using a map function containing a temperature in Celsius as the first element and the corresponding Fahrenheit temperature as the second element.

LISTING 9.6   Tuples in PySpark

```
tempc = sc.parallelize([38.4, 19.2, 12.8, 9.6])
temp_tups = tempc.map(lambda x: (x,(float(9)/5)*x + 32))
temp_tups
PythonRDD[1] at RDD at PythonRDD.scala:43
temp_tups.take(4)
# RDD containing a list of Tuples
[(9.6, 49.28), (19.2, 66.56), (38.4, 101.12), (12.8, 55.04)]
```

Tuples are an integral object type in functional programming. After you get comfortable with tuples, you will find many uses for them in data manipulation and analysis in Spark.

Dictionaries

Dictionaries or *dicts* in Python are unordered mutable sets of key value pairs. Dict objects are denoted by curly braces ({ }), which can be created as empty dictionaries by simply executing a command like `my_empty_dict = {}`. Unlike lists and tuples, where an element is accessed by its ordinal position in the sequence—by its index, that is—an element in a dict is accessed by its key. Keys are separated from their values with a colon (:), whereas key value pairs in a dict are separated by commas.

Dicts are useful because their elements are self-describing rather than relying on a predefined schema or ordinality. Dict elements are accessed by key, as shown in Listing 9.7. This listing also shows how to add or remove elements from a dict and some useful dict methods including `keys()`, `values()`, `cmp()`, and `len()`.

LISTING 9.7   Dictionaries in Python

```
dict0 = {'fname':'Jeff', 'lname':'Aven', 'pos':'author'}
dict1 = {'fname':'Barack', 'lname':'Obama', 'pos':'president'}
dict2 = {'fname':'Ronald', 'lname':'Reagan', 'pos':'president'}
dict3 = {'fname':'John', 'mi':'F', 'lname':'Kennedy', 'pos':'president'}
dict4 = {'fname':'Jeff', 'lname':'Aven', 'pos':'author'}

len(dict0)
3

dict0['fname']
'Jeff'

dict0.keys()
['lname', 'pos', 'fname']

dict0.values()
['Aven', 'author', 'Jeff']
```

```
# compare dictionaries
cmp(dict0, dict1)
1 ## keys match but values dont

cmp(dict0, dict4)
0 ## all key value pairs match

cmp(dict1, dict2)
-1 ## some key value pairs match
```

Dicts can be used as immutable objects within a PythonRDD. Consider the dictionary objects created in Listing 9.7. We can create the same objects in PySpark and then embed them into a Spark RDD. Listing 9.8 shows an example that creates an RDD as a list of dicts and then performs `filter()` and `map()` operations to return a list of presidents.

LISTING 9.8   Using Dictionary Objects in PySpark

```
people = sc.parallelize([dict0, dict1, dict2, dict3])
people
ParallelCollectionRDD[0] at parallelize at PythonRDD.scala:423
presidents = people.filter(lambda x: x['pos'] == 'president') \
                .map(lambda x: x['fname'] + " " + x['lname'])
presidents.take(3)
['Barack Obama', 'Ronald Reagan', 'John Kennedy']
```

Python Object Serialization

To recap, serialization is the process of converting an object into a structure that can be unpacked (or deserialized) at a later point in time on the same system or on a different system. Serialization (or the ability to serialize and deserialize data) is a necessary characteristic of any distributed processing system and features heavily throughout the Hadoop and Spark projects.

JSON

Object serialization can be achieved in several ways using Python. The first is a serialization format we see the most often, *JSON* or *(Java Script Object Notation)*. JSON has extended well beyond JavaScript and is used in a multitude of different platforms with support in nearly every programming language as well as being a common response structure returned from web services.

JSON is supported natively in Python using the `json` object, a built-in module used to encode and decode JSON. JSON objects consist of key value pairs (dictionaries) and/or arrays (lists), which can be nested within each other. The Python JSON object includes methods for searching, adding and deleting keys, updating values, and printing objects. Listing 9.9 demonstrates creating a JSON object in Python and performing various actions.

LISTING 9.9 Using JSON Objects in Python

```
import json
from pprint import pprint

json_str = '''{
  "people" : [
    {"fname": "Jeff",
     "lname": "Aven",
     "tags": ["big data","hadoop"]},
    {"fname": "Doug",
     "lname": "Cutting",
     "tags": ["hadoop","avro","apache","java"]},
    {"fname": "Martin",
     "lname": "Odersky",
     "tags": ["scala","typesafe","java"]},
    {"fname": "John",
     "lname": "Doe",
     "tags": []}
    ]}'''

people = json.loads(json_str)
len(people["people"])
4

people["people"][0]["fname"]
u'Jeff'

# add tag item to the first person
people["people"][0]["tags"].append(u'spark')

# delete the fourth person
del people["people"][3]

# pretty print json object
pprint(people)
{u'people': [{u'fname': u'Jeff',
u'lname': u'Aven',
u'tags': [u'big data', u'hadoop', u'spark']},
{u'fname': u'Doug',
u'lname': u'Cutting',
u'tags': [u'hadoop', u'avro', u'apache', u'java']},
{u'fname': u'Martin',
u'lname': u'Odersky',
u'tags': [u'scala', u'typesafe', u'java']}]}
```

JSON objects can be used within RDDs in PySpark similar to the way I had demonstrated using dict objects. Listing 9.10 demonstrates using JSON objects in PySpark.

LISTING 9.10 Using JSON Objects with PySpark

```
import json
json_str = json_str from listing 9.10
people_obj = json.loads(json_str)
people = sc.parallelize(people_obj["people"])
ParallelCollectionRDD[0] at parallelize at PythonRDD.scala:423
hadoop_tags = people.filter(lambda x: "hadoop" in x['tags']) \
              .map(lambda x: x['fname'] + " " + x['lname'])
hadoop_tags.take(2)
[u'Jeff Aven', u'Doug Cutting']
```

I will also discuss JSON as a serialization format for Spark SQL dataframes in **Hour 13, "Using SQL with Spark."**

Pickle

Pickle is an alternative serialization method that is proprietary to Python. Pickle is faster that JSON. However, it lacks the portability of JSON, which is a universally interchangeable serialization format.

The Python `pickle` module converts a Python object or objects into a byte stream that can be transmitted, stored, and reconstructed into its original state.

cPickle, as the name suggests, is implemented in C instead of Python and is thus much faster than the Python implementation. There are some limitations, however. The `cpickle` module does not support subclassing, which is possible using the `pickle` module.

Pickling and unpickling an object in Python is a straightforward process, as shown in Listing 9.11. Note that I will attempt to use cPickle if this is available. Also notice that the load and dump idioms are analogous to the way you serialize and deserialize objects using JSON. The `pickle.dump` approach saves the pickled object to a file, whereas `pickle.dumps` returns the pickled representation of the object as a string that may look strange (although it is not designed to be human readable).

LISTING 9.11 Object Serialization Using Pickle in Python

```
try:
    import cPickle as pickle
except:
    import pickle
```

```
obj = { "fname": "Jeff", \
        "lname": "Aven", \
        "tags": ["big data","hadoop"]}
str_obj = pickle.dumps(obj)
pickled_obj = pickle.loads(str_obj)
pickled_obj["fname"]
'Jeff'
pickled_obj["tags"].append('spark')
str(pickled_obj["tags"])
"['big data', 'hadoop', 'spark']"
pickled_obj_str = pickle.dumps(pickled_obj)
"(dp1\nS'lname'\np2\nS'Aven'\np3\nsS'fname'\np4\nS'Jeff'
\np5\nsS'tags'\np6\n(lp7\nS'big data'\np8\naS'hadoop'\np
9\naS'spark'\np10\nas."
pickle.dump(pickled_obj, open('object.pkl', 'wb'))
```

PySpark uses PickleSerializer by default to serialize objects using cpickle. Other serializers, such as the MarshalSerializer, are available, but these may be more limited in their functionality. The PickleSerializer is used in PySpark to load objects into a pickled format and to unpickle objects; this includes reading preserialized objects from other systems (such as SequenceFiles in Hadoop) and converting them into a format usable by Python.

The PySpark Spark context includes two methods for handling pickled input and output files, pickleFile and saveAsPickleFile. This is an efficient format to store and transfer files between PySpark processes. The next sections give you a look at the syntax and usage of each PySpark method.

saveAsPickleFile()

Syntax:

```
RDD.saveAsPickleFile(path, batchSize=10)
```

The saveAsPickleFile method is used to save the contents of an RDD to a directory containing data files serialized with Pickle, which are then readable by other PySpark processes. The file is actually saved as a SequenceFile (a Java serialization format discussed briefly in **Hour 6, "Learning the Basics of Spark Programming with RDDs,"**) that encapsulates serialized Python objects.

The path argument refers to the fully output directory path, which cannot exist at runtime (recall that we assume our filesystem is immutable and directories and files cannot be overwritten). The batchSize argument is the batch size used by the BatchedSerializer to call the PickleSerializer. Changes to this option may have an impact on performance—it is an optional argument as it defaults to 10.

Listing 9.12 shows the usage of the `saveAsPickleFile` method.

LISTING 9.12   Using the saveAsPickleFile() Method in PySpark

```
file = sc.textFile("file:///opt/spark/data/shakespeare.txt")
pklfile = shakespeare.saveAsPickleFile("file:///opt/spark/data/pickled")
```

pickleFile()

Syntax:

```
sc.pickleFile(name, minPartitions=None)
```

The `pickleFile` method is used to load a Spark RDD from a previously saved Pickle file. Note that the `pickleFile` method only works with Pickle files created and saved with the `saveAsPickleFile` PySpark method previously discussed. The `minPartitions` argument is an optional directive to Spark to create a specified number of partitions, used to optimize parallelism.

Listing 9.13 demonstrates creating an RDD from a previously generated directory containing Pickle file(s) (created in Listing 9.12).

LISTING 9.13   Using the pickleFile() Method in PySpark

```
pklfile = sc.pickleFile("file:///opt/spark/data/pickled")
pklfile.count()
129107
```

Python Functional Programming Basics

Python's functional support embodies all of the functional programming paradigm characteristics that you would expect, including:

▶ Functions are the fundamental unit of programming

▶ Functions have input and output only, statements (which could result in side effects) are not allowed

▶ First-class and higher-order functions

▶ Support for anonymous functions

The next few sections look at some of the functional programming concepts and their implementation in Python using PySpark.

Anonymous Functions and lambda

You have already seen several examples of anonymous functions in Python and PySpark in this book, so this concept should be familiar by now. Anonymous functions, or unnamed functions, are a consistent feature of functional programming languages such as Lisp, Scala, JavaScript, Erlang, Clojure, Go, and many more.

Anonymous functions in Python are implemented using the `lambda` construct rather than using the `def` keyword for named functions in Python. Anonymous functions accept any number of input arguments but return just one value (which could be another function, a scalar value, or a data structure such as a list). Listing 9.14 shows two similar functions; one is a named function and another an anonymous function.

LISTING 9.14   Named Functions and Anonymous Functions in Python

```
# named function
def plusone(x): return x+1
plusone(1)
2
type(plusone)
<type 'function'>

# anonymous function
plusonefn = lambda x: x+1
plusonefn(1)
2
type(plusonefn)
<type 'function'>
```

Both methods for creating a function shown in the previous listing are similar and in this case functionally equivalent.

LISTING 9.15   Named Versus lambda Functions in Python

```
plusone.func_name
'plusone'

plusonefn.func_name
'<lambda>'
```

As you can see in Listing 9.15, the named function `plusone` keeps a reference to the function name whereas the anonymous function `plusonefn` keeps a `<lambda>` name reference.

Named functions can contain statements such as `print`, anonymous functions can only contain a single or compound expression (which could be a call to another named function which is in scope). Named functions can also use the return statement, which is not supported with anonymous functions.

The true power of anonymous functions is evident when you look at higher-order functions such as map, reduce, and filter, and start chaining single-use functions together in a processing pipeline, as you will do in Spark.

Higher-order Functions

Higher-order functions accept functions as arguments and are able to return a function as their result. map, reduce, and filter are examples of higher-order functions. These functions accept a function as an argument.

The flatMap, filter, map, and reduceByKey functions in Listing 9.16 are all examples of higher-order functions because they accept (expect) an anonymous function as input.

LISTING 9.16   Higher-order Functions

```
lines = sc.textFile("file:///opt/spark/data/shakespeare.txt")
counts = lines.flatMap(lambda x: x.split(' ')) \
    .filter(lambda x: len(x) > 0) \
    .map(lambda x: (x, 1)) \
    .reduceByKey(lambda x, y: x + y) \
    .collect()
for (word, count) in counts:
    print("%s: %i" % (word, count))
```

Functions that return functions as a return value are also considered higher-order functions. *Callback* functions are defined by this characteristic.

Tail Calls

Tail calls are functions which call themselves. *Tail call recursion* involves functions which recursively call themselves under certain conditions. In Listing 9.17, I create a named function gcd to return the greatest common denominator between two integer values. The function is called recursively until the modulo (remainder) is equal to zero, the point at which we have found the greatest common denominator between the two numbers. Note that we have done this in PySpark, generating a list of random pairs (a list of tuples), which we then map over, producing a list of tuples containing the first number (*x*), the second number (*y*) and the greatest common denominator between the two.

LISTING 9.17   Tail Call Recursion

```
def gcd(x, y):
    if x < y: return gcd(y, x)
    r = x%y
```

```
        if r == 0: return y
        else: return gcd(y, r)

import random
low = 1
high = 100
numpairs = sc.parallelize([[(random.randint(low, high), \
        random.randint(low, high)) for k in range(10)])
numpairs_gcd = numpairs.map(lambda x: (x[0], x[1], gcd(x[0], x[1])))
numpairs_gcd.take(5)
[(81, 3, 3), (91, 100, 1), (99, 18, 9), (28, 34, 2), (90, 99, 9)]
```

Short-circuiting

Another Python feature that is useful in functional programming is *short-circuiting*, which avoids unnecessary computation or evaluation within functions. The and/or Boolean operators serve as short-circuit operators. Consider Listing 9.18. We have modified the `filter` function from Listing 9.16 to include a Boolean short-circuit operator.

LISTING 9.18 Short-circuit Operators in Python

```
...
.filter(lambda x: (len(x) > 0) and (len(x) < 3)) \
...
```

The and operator only evaluates the second function if the first function evaluates to True. If an or operator was used, the second function would not be evaluated if the first function evaluated to True.

Parallelization

Pure functional programming discourages, and in some cases disallows, functions that produce "side effects." Side effects refer to any action that is outside of the function's scope, such as printing, writing to an external file or database, or maintaining state.

If a function produces no side effects and there is no dependency between two functions (for example, if one function does not use another function as an argument), then the two functions can be run in parallel. The in-built parallelization capabilities in functional Python are well suited to distributed processing platforms such as Spark.

Closures in Python

Closures in Python are conceptually identical to their Scala equivalents, as discussed in the last hour. Closures are function objects that *enclose* the scope at the time they were instantiated.

This can include any external variables or functions that were used when the function was created. Closures "remember" the values by enclosing the scope. Listing 9.19 is a simple example of closures in Python.

LISTING 9.19   Closures in Python

```
def generate_message(concept):
    def ret_message():
            return 'This is an example of ' + concept
        return ret_message

# create closure
call_func = generate_message('closures in Python')

call_func
<function ret_message at 0x7f2a52b72d70>
call_func()
'This is an example of closures in Python'

# inspect closure
call_func.__closure__
(<cell at 0x7f2a557dbde0: str object at 0x7f2a557dbea0>,)
type(call_func.__closure__[0])
<type 'cell'>
call_func.__closure__[0].cell_contents
'closures in Python'

# delete function
del generate_message

# call closure again
call_func()
'This is an example of closures in Python'
# the closure still works!
```

In Listing 9.19, the function ret_message() is the closure, and the value for concept is enclosed in the function scope. You can use the __closure__ function member to see information about the closure. The references enclosed in the function are stored in a tuple of cells. You can access the cell contents using the cell_contents function as shown.

To prove the concept of closures, you can delete the outer function, generate_message, and you'll find the referencing function, call_func, still works.

Interactive Programming Using IPython

IPython, which is the shortened name for Interactive Python, provides an enhanced interactive development environment for Python. IPython and its derivative projects provide an additional set of tools, interfaces, and capabilities that are of particular use to data analysts, data scientists, and Spark enthusiasts!

IPython History and Background

IPython was created in 2001 by Fernando Pérez, a graduate student in physics at the University of Colorado Boulder. IPython was inspired by Mathematica, a symbolic mathematical computation program used in the scientific, engineering, and mathematical fields. Mathematica enabled users to embed code alongside familiar word-processing elements to create "computational documents," referred to as Notebooks.

IPython incorporated support for notebooks as well as some other key enhancements to the standard Python interpreter and REPL shell, including:

▶ Integrated system shell access

▶ TAB completion

▶ Numbered input/output prompts with command history and search capability

▶ Lightweight persistence framework enabling you to save Python variables and use them in new sessions

▶ Integrated filesystem navigation

▶ Extensible *magic* commands, special built-in commands ranging from plotting a graph using program data to timing and profiling operations

▶ Dynamic object introspection using easy shortcut commands

▶ Capability to assign custom aliases to program elements

▶ Session logging and restoring

▶ GUI integration

▶ Enhanced debugging and profiling capabilities

▶ and more . . .

Figure 9.2 shows an example IPython session, including an example of object introspection using the ? directive.

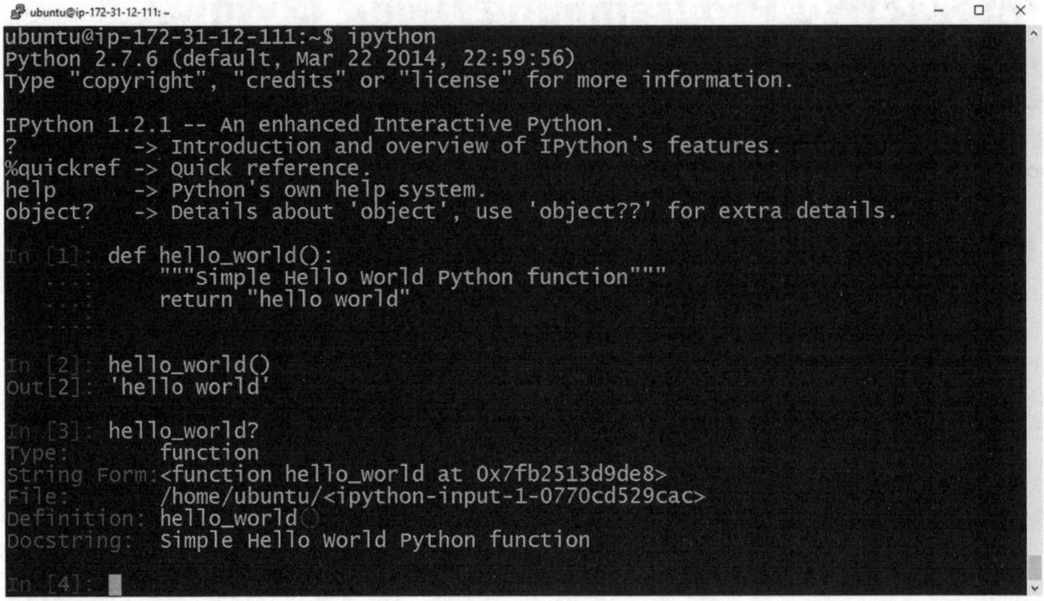

```
ubuntu@ip-172-31-12-111: ~                                          –  □  ×
ubuntu@ip-172-31-12-111:~$ ipython
Python 2.7.6 (default, Mar 22 2014, 22:59:56)
Type "copyright", "credits" or "license" for more information.

IPython 1.2.1 -- An enhanced Interactive Python.
?         -> Introduction and overview of IPython's features.
%quickref -> Quick reference.
help      -> Python's own help system.
object?   -> Details about 'object', use 'object??' for extra details.

In [1]: def hello_world():
   ...:     """Simple Hello world Python function"""
   ...:     return "hello world"
   ...:

In [2]: hello_world()
Out[2]: 'hello world'

In [3]: hello_world?
Type:       function
String Form:<function hello_world at 0x7fb2513d9de8>
File:       /home/ubuntu/<ipython-input-1-0770cd529cac>
Definition: hello_world()
Docstring:  Simple Hello World Python function

In [4]:
```

FIGURE 9.2
IPython session.

IPython is an open source project released under the BSD licensing scheme. Its features make it a powerful development and exploration environment.

Using IPython with Spark

IPython can easily be configured as the default PySpark interactive shell environment, providing all of the benefits or IPython to your Spark programming environment. You can try it out here.

▼ TRY IT YOURSELF

Using IPython with Spark

In this exercise, you install IPython and configure an IPython profile to use for a PySpark development environment. You follow this by running an example PySpark program in IPython.

1. Install IPython on your system. This can be done on any system with Python installed using `pip` (Python's package management system). Simply run the following:

   ```
   pip install ipython
   ```

   You may need to run this command with elevated privileges on Linux systems.

2. Test the IPython installation:

   a. Execute `ipython` from the terminal or command prompt.

   b. You should have an IPython shell. Test the shell by typing the simple `print "hello world"` command at the prompt.

   c. Press Ctrl+D followed by `y` to exit the IPython shell

3. Create a new profile in IPython for PySpark, by running the following:

```
ipython profile create pyspark
```

This creates a default config file in your local user directory.

4. Set environment variables for `SPARK_HOME` (may be set already) and `PYSPARK_SUBMIT_ARGS`:

```
export SPARK_HOME=/opt/spark
export PYSPARK_SUBMIT_ARGS="--master local pyspark-shell"
```

5. Create an environment startup configuration file for the IPython PySpark profile (I will use `vi` for this example, but you could use analagous text editors on other platforms):

```
vi ~/.ipython/profile_pyspark/startup/00-pyspark-setup.py
```

Add the following code to the `00-pyspark-setup.py` file:

```
import os, sys, glob

print 'configuring IPython PySpark environment..'

# get environment vars and update path
SPARK_HOME = os.environ.get('SPARK_HOME', None)
sys.path.insert(0, SPARK_HOME + "/python")

# Get Py4J version and add to the system path
libpath = os.path.join(SPARK_HOME,'python/lib/py4j*src.zip')
py4js = glob.glob(libpath)
if len(py4js) > 0:
    py4j = py4js[0]
    sys.path.insert(0, py4j)

# Initialize PySpark
execfile(os.path.join(SPARK_HOME,'python/pyspark/shell.py'))
```

Save the script and exit the text editor.

6. Open IPython using the PySpark profile:

```
ipython --profile=pyspark
```

You should see the familiar PySpark initialization messages in the IPython shell, as shown in Figure 9.3.

FIGURE 9.3
PySpark using the IPython interpreter.

7. Try some of the magic commands below. The `%profile` command displays the current profile used with IPython (in this case, the pyspark profile). The `%quickref` command displays a "Quick Reference Card" showing shortcuts, magic commands, and general help for getting started with IPython.

```
In [1]: %profile
pyspark
In [2]: %quickref
IPython - enhanced Interactive Python - Quick Reference Card
=============================================================
...
```

8. Execute our PySpark word count program from **Hour 7, "Understanding MapReduce Concepts,"** in the IPython interpreter by entering the following commands one by one in the IPython shell:

```
In [3]: import re
In [4]: doc = sc.textFile("file:///opt/spark/data/shakespeare.txt")
In [5]: flattened = doc.filter(lambda line: len(line) > 0) \
         .flatMap(lambda line: re.split('\W+', line))
In [6]: kvpairs = flattened.filter(lambda w: len(w) > 0) \
         .map(lambda w:(w.lower(),1))
In [7]: countsbyword = kvpairs.reduceByKey(lambda v1, v2: v1 + v2)
In [8]: topwords = countsbyword.map(lambda (w, c): (c, w)) \
         .sortByKey(ascending=False)
In [9]: topwords.take(5)
```

You should see the output shown in Figure 9.4.

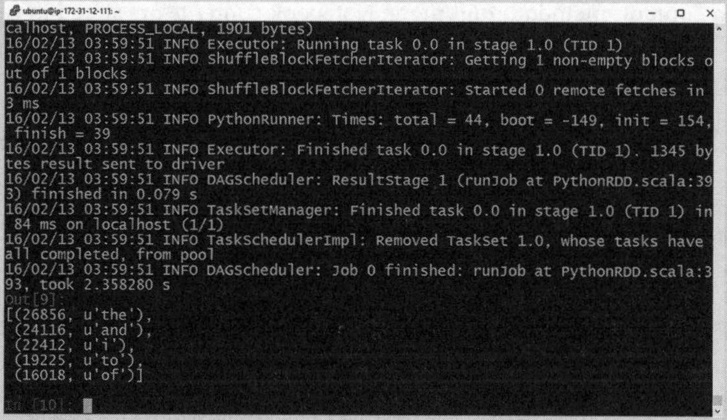

FIGURE 9.4
Word count results in IPython.

Now that I have introduced you to IPython, I encourage you to explore the IPython enhanced shell further and experience some of the many features available. When you are familiar with IPython, you may choose to use this as your default shell environment for PySpark!

TIP

IPython Profile Startup Files

The `00-pyspark-setup.py` file you created in Step 5 from the preceding Try it Yourself exercise is an example of a IPython profile startup file. This script will be run automatically at the beginning of every IPython session for the relevant profile. This script can be used to initialize any other session or environment variables or perform and set up operations prior to executing any other IPython commands or running any other scripts. The directory can contain multiple scripts that will be executed in lexicographical order, which is why I prefixed the script with `00-`.

Jupyter, the IPython Notebook

Notebooks have become a popular tool, widely in use today in the Spark development community. The capability to combine different languages along with markup facilities makes it easy to explore and visualize data in an interactive environment. Jupyter, formally known as the IPython notebook, provides a web-based notebook experience that includes extensions for Ruby, R, and other languages.

Notebook Documents

Jupyter notebook files are an open document format using JSON. Notebook files contain source code, text, markup, media content, metadata and more. Notebook contents are stored in cells in the document. Figure 9.5 and Listing 9.20 show an example Jupyter notebook and an excerpt from the associated JSON document.

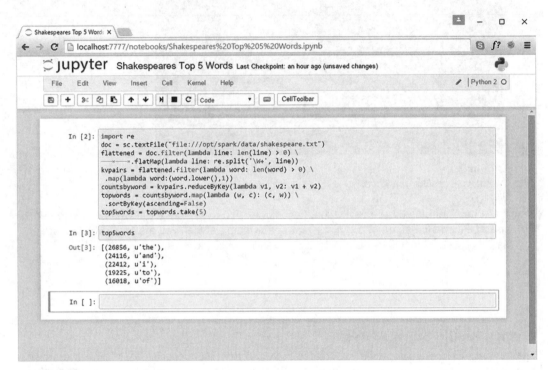

FIGURE 9.5
Jupyter notebook.

LISTING 9.20   Jupyter Notebook JSON Document

```
{
 "cells": [
 {
   "cell_type": "code",
   "execution_count": 2,
   "metadata": {
   "collapsed": true
 },
 "outputs": [],
 "source": [
  "import re\n",
  "doc = sc.textFile(\"file:///opt/spark/data/shakespeare.txt\")\n",
```

```
"flattened = doc.filter(lambda line: len(line) > 0) \\\n",
"\t\t.flatMap(lambda line: re.split('\\W+', line))\n",
"kvpairs = flattened.filter(lambda word: len(word) > 0) \\\n",
" .map(lambda word:(word.lower(),1))\n",
"countsbyword = kvpairs.reduceByKey(lambda v1, v2: v1 + v2)\n",
"topwords = countsbyword.map(lambda (w, c): (c, w)) \\\n",
" .sortByKey(ascending=False)\n",
"top5words = topwords.take(5) "
]
},...]}
```

Jupyter/IPython Kernels

Jupyter/IPython notebooks communicate with back-end systems using kernels. *Kernels* are processes that run interactive code in a particular programming language and return output to the user. Kernels also respond to tab completion and introspection requests. Kernels communicate with notebooks using the *Interactive Computing Protocol,* which is an open network protocol based on JSON data over ZMQ and WebSockets.

Kernels are currently available for Scala, Ruby, Javascript, Erlang, Bash, Perl, PHP, PowerShell, Clojure, Go, Spark, and many more. Of course there is a kernel used to communicate with IPython (because this was the basis of the Jupyter project). The IPython kernel is referred to as Kernel Zero and is the reference implementation for all other kernels.

Next, try out Jupyter with PySpark.

TRY IT YOURSELF ▼

Spark Notebooks with Jupyter

You will install Jupyter alongside your IPython installation from the previous exercise and create and execute a notebook to be used with Spark.

1. Install prerequisites for Jupyter (commands shown for Debian based Linux systems; however, the same packages are available for other distributions and platforms as well):

   ```
   sudo apt-get update
   sudo apt-get install python-dev build-essential
   ```

2. Install Jupyter using Python `pip`:

   ```
   sudo pip install jupyter
   ```

3. Configure Jupyter to listen on all IP addresses (required if you are not using your localhost):

```
jupyter notebook --generate-config
```

This creates a file called: `~/.jupyter/jupyter_notebook_config.py`.

Use a text editor such as `vi` to add the following line to the beginning of this file:

```
c.NotebookApp.ip = '*'
```

This file can be used to set many other configurations options for Jupyter such as the port Jupyter listens on, security options, and more.

4. Install matplotlib, a Python 2D plotting library that produces publication quality visualizations:

```
sudo apt-get build-dep python-matplotlib
sudo pip install matplotlib
```

You will use matplotlib to demonstrate magic commands and rendering visualizations in Jupyter notebooks.

5. Start PySpark environment in Jupyter:

```
PYSPARK_DRIVER_PYTHON=ipython \
PYSPARK_DRIVER_PYTHON_OPTS="notebook --no-browser \
--port=7777" pyspark --master local
```

You should see the output shown in Figure 9.6 in the console:

```
ubuntu@ip-172-31-39-62:~                                          -  □  ×
ubuntu@ip-172-31-39-62:~$ PYSPARK_DRIVER_PYTHON=ipython PYSPARK_DRIVER_PYTHON_OP
TS="notebook --no-browser --port=7777" pyspark --master local
[TerminalIPythonApp] WARNING | Subcommand `ipython notebook` is deprecated and w
ill be removed in future versions.
[TerminalIPythonApp] WARNING | You likely want to use `jupyter notebook`... cont
inue in 5 sec. Press Ctrl-C to quit now.
[I 06:26:43.741 NotebookApp] Writing notebook server cookie secret to /run/user/
1000/jupyter/notebook_cookie_secret
[W 06:26:43.763 NotebookApp] WARNING: The notebook server is listening on all IP
 addresses and not using encryption. This is not recommended.
[W 06:26:43.763 NotebookApp] WARNING: The notebook server is listening on all IP
 addresses and not using authentication. This is highly insecure and not recomme
nded.
[I 06:26:43.766 NotebookApp] Serving notebooks from local directory: /home/ubunt
u
[I 06:26:43.766 NotebookApp] 0 active kernels
[I 06:26:43.766 NotebookApp] The Jupyter Notebook is running at: http://[all ip
addresses on your system]:7777/
[I 06:26:43.766 NotebookApp] Use Control-C to stop this server and shut down all
 kernels (twice to skip confirmation).
```

FIGURE 9.6
Jupyter terminal output.

6. Open a browser to `http://<jupyter_host>:7777`, you should be directed to the Jupyter home page.

7. Create a new notebook by using the top right menu options:

New -> Notebooks -> Python 2

8. Rename the notebook using the following top menu options:

File -> Rename

Rename the notebook "Shakespeares Top 5 Words"

9. Enter the following code in the first input prompt area (as shown in Figure 9.7):

```python
import re
doc = sc.textFile("file:///opt/spark/data/shakespeare.txt")
flattened = doc.filter(lambda line: len(line) > 0) \
   .flatMap(lambda line: re.split('\W+', line))
kvpairs = flattened.filter(lambda word: len(word) > 0) \
   .map(lambda word:(word.lower(),1))
countsbyword = kvpairs.reduceByKey(lambda v1, v2: v1 + v2)
topwords = countsbyword.map(lambda (w, c): (c, w)) \
   .sortByKey(ascending=False)
top5words = topwords.take(5)
```

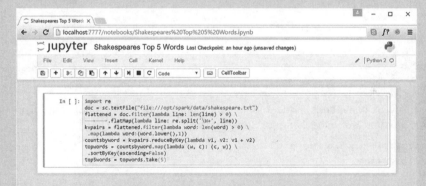

FIGURE 9.7
Jupyter notebook input.

10. Press the Ctrl+Enter shortcut to execute the cell (you can also press the play button on the top menu), the commands will be executed in the background.

11. Enter the following command in the next input cell to display the top5words list:

```
top5words
```

You should see the output shown in Figure 9.8.

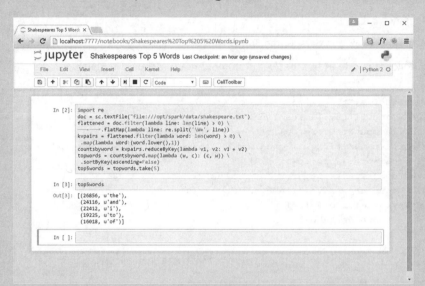

FIGURE 9.8
Jupyter notebook output.

12. Enter the following commands in the subsequent input cell to render a bar chart displaying the top five words used in the works of Shakespeare:

```python
import matplotlib.pyplot as plt
%matplotlib inline
xValue = []
yValue = []
for tup in top5words:
    xValue.append(tup[1])
    yValue.append(int(tup[0]))
# Plot the data
topN = list(range(1,6))
plt.xlabel('Word')
plt.ylabel('Count')
plt.title('Top 5 Used Words')
plt.bar(topN,yValue)
plt.xticks()
plt.xticks(topN, xValue)
plt.show()
```

13. Press Ctrl+Enter to execute the cell; you should see output similar to Figure 9.9.

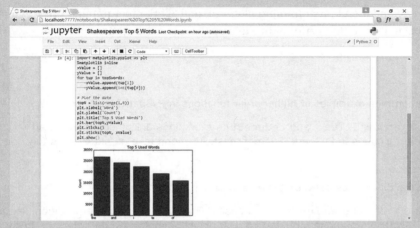

FIGURE 9.9
Visualizations with matplotlib.

14. From the terminal where you started Jupyter, press Ctrl+C to exit.

15. Navigate to your home directory and inspect the `Shakespeares Top 5 Words.ipynb` file; this is the JSON document representing the notebook you just created.

Congratulations, you are now up and running with Jupyter. If you are running Jupyter in a production environment, there would be additional tasks required to secure Jupyter such as configuring authentication and SSL.

Summary

To understand PySpark, you need to fully understand Python and, in particular, functional programming in Python. In this hour, you learned about the CPython interpreter and the CPython runtime architecture, which is the reference implementation of Python and the implementation used in PySpark.

You looked at the various sequence types and data structures available natively in Python, including lists, sets, tuples, and dicts. You also learned about object serialization in Python using JSON and Pickle, showing examples in both Python and PySpark.

You have learned about the foundational functional programming concepts implemented by Python including anonymous lambda functions, examples of higher-order functions, and closures.

Finally, you looked at data analysis in Spark using IPython as an extended interactive Python shell and Jupyter as a notebook computational environment.

Python is a diverse and useful programming platform, and Spark programming using Python provides a functionally rich and performant rapid application development platform.

Q&A

Q. What are common examples of higher-order functions in PySpark?

A. The `map`, `flatMap`, `filter`, and `reduceByKey` functions are all commonly used higher-order functions in PySpark. Each of these functions take an anonymous function as input.

Q. What are the differences between tuples and lists in Python?

A. Tuples have a structure with each ordinal position having a specific interpretation, like a field in a relational database table record. List objects simply have an order, and because they are mutable by default, this order is not directly related to the structure.

Q. What are some of the advantages of using the IPython interpreter and/or Jupyter Notebooks?

A. IPython provides an enhanced interactive shell environment for Python and PySpark programming, including shell access, TAB completion, command history and search capability, extensible magic commands, debugging and profiling capabilities, and more. Jupyter provides a web-based interactive Python and PySpark programming environment with the capability to create reusable notebooks, containing commands, markup, visualizations, and more.

Workshop

The workshop contains quiz questions and exercises to help you solidify your understanding of the material covered. Try to answer all questions before looking at the "Answers" section that follows.

Quiz

1. **True or false:** Tuples are an immutable sequence of objects (which themselves can be mutable or immutable).

2. The `pickleFile` method is used for what purpose in PySpark?

   A. To create a Spark RDD from a previously saved Pickle file.

   B. To save a Spark RDD to a Pickle file.

3. A function which recursively calls itself while a condition is met is called what?

4. **True or false:** Closures maintain references to the enclosed function scope in a list with each reference contained in a list element.

Answers

1. **True.**

2. **A.** The `saveAsPickleFile` method is used to save a Spark RDD as a Pickle file.

3. Tail call recursion.

4. **False.** References are maintained in a tuple, with each reference referred to as a cell.

HOUR 10
Working with the Spark API (Transformations and Actions)

What You'll Learn in This Hour:

▶ Data sampling with Spark
▶ Additional Spark transformations and their usage
▶ Additional Spark actions and their usage
▶ Numerical RDD functions

You have seen and used the most common transformations already, including map, flatMap, filter, and reduceByKey, as well as the common actions take and saveAsTextFile. You are now going to explore the many other transformations and actions provided by the Spark API, including usage examples. You will look at sampling techniques in Spark that are useful for processing large data sets as well as specific statistical functions available for numeric RDDs. By the end of this hour, you will have the complete toolbox of basic Spark functions to build virtually any application.

RDDs and Data Sampling

We first introduced Resilient Distributed Datasets (RDDs) in **Hour 6, "Learning the Basics of Spark Programming with RDDs,"** as the basic data abstraction in Spark. Lets quickly recap some of the basic RDD concepts.

RDD Refresher

RDDs are distributed collections of immutable objects that can be operated on in parallel. RDDs are divided into one or more partitions, which are usually located on different nodes.

There are two types of operations that can be performed on RDDs: transformations, which perform functions (map, filter, and so on) against each element in an RDD and result in a new RDD being created; and actions, which return a value to the Spark driver. RDD transformation operations are lazily evaluated, meaning they are only evaluated when an action is requested to return a result.

Also recall that Spark plans, tracks, and manages the lineage of each RDD—that is, it plans, tracks, and manages the sequence of transformations that resulted in the RDD. This sequence is used to recover from process failure (such as, for example, a worker node or executor failure).

There are virtually no restrictions on the types of objects or data that can be used to create RDDs. Because Spark is a schema-on-read system, the structure and interpretation of the data are defined when the data is accessed.

Data Sampling with Spark

During development and discovery, you may need to sample data in RDDs before running a process across the entirety of an input data set or sets. The Spark API includes several functions to sample RDDs and produce new RDDs from the sampled data. These sample functions include transformations that return new RDDs and actions that return data to the Spark driver program. Let's look at some of the sampling transformations and actions provided by Spark.

sample()

syntax:

```
RDD.sample(withReplacement, fraction, seed=None)
```

The sample transformation is used to create a sampled subset RDD from an original RDD based upon a percentage of the overall dataset.

The withReplacement argument is a Boolean value specifying whether elements in an RDD can be sampled multiple times.

The fraction argument is a double value between 0 and 1 that represents the probability that an element will be chosen. Effectively, this represents the approximate percentage of the dataset you wish to be returned to the resultant sampled RDD. Note that if you specify a value larger than 1 for this argument it will default back to 1.

The optional seed argument is an integer representing a seed for the random number generator that is used to determine whether to include an element in the return RDD.

Listing 10.1 shows an example of the sample transformation used to create an approximate 10 percent subset of web log events from a corpus of web logs.

LISTING 10.1   Using sample()

```
logs = sc.textFile('file:///opt/spark/data/weblogs')
logs.count()
# returns 1,051,105
sampled_logs = logs.sample(False, 0.1, seed=None)
sampled_logs.count()
# returns 106,020 (10.09% of the orginal RDD)
```

There is also a similar `sampleByKey` function that operates on a key value pair RDD. I will discuss key value pair RDDs in more detail later in this hour.

takeSample()

Syntax:

```
RDD.takeSample(withReplacement, num, seed=None)
```

The `takeSample` action is used to return a random list of values (elements or records) from the RDD being sampled.

The `num` argument is the number of randomly selected records to be returned.

The `withReplacement` and `seed` arguments behave similarly to the aforementioned `sample` function.

Listing 10.2 shows an example of the `takeSample` action.

LISTING 10.2   Using takeSample()

```
dataset = sc.parallelize([1,2,3,4,5,6,7,8,9,10])
dataset.takeSample(False, 3)
# returned [6, 10, 2]
```

Spark Transformations

You have seen several examples of `map`, `flatMap`, `filter`, and `reduceByKey` in this book thus far. You will use these again in combination with many of the other transformations available in the Spark RDD API. Spark is a fast-moving project that continually adds new functionality, so by no means is this an exhaustive list of transformations. However, here I will attempt to cover some of the most common and useful Spark transformations with some practical examples.

Functional Transformations

Functional transformations include the mapping and filtering functions, which should already look familiar to you. These are the most commonly used Spark functions. They operate against an RDD and evaluate each record using a function to either manipulate data or exclude data from the resultant RDD.

map()

Syntax:

```
RDD.map(<function>, preservesPartitioning=False)
```

The map transformation is the most basic of all transformations. It evaluates a named or anonymous function for each element within a partition of a dataset. One or many map functions can run asynchronously because they shouldn't produce any side effects, maintain state, or attempt to communicate or synchronize with other map operations.

The preservesPartitioning argument is an optional Boolean argument intended for use with RDDs with a Partitioner defined, typically a key value pair RDD (which I will discuss later in this hour) in which a key is defined and grouped by a key hash or key range. If this parameter is set to True, the partitions are kept intact. This parameter can be used by the Spark scheduler to optimize subsequent operations (such as joins based upon the partitioned key).

Consider Figure 10.1. The map transformation evaluates a function for each input record and emits a transformed output record. In this case, the split function takes a string and produces a list, and each string element in the input data is mapped to a list element in the output. The result, in this case, is a list of lists.

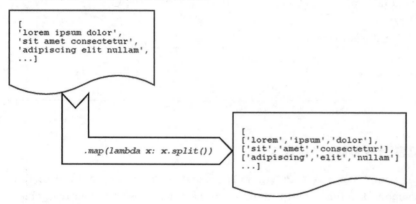

FIGURE 10.1
The map transformation.

flatMap()

Syntax:

```
RDD.flatMap(<function>, preservesPartitioning=False)
```

The flatMap transformation is similar to the map transformation in that it runs a function against each record in the input dataset. However, flatMap "flattens" the output, meaning it removes a level of nesting (for example given a list containing lists of strings, flattening would result in a single list of strings—"flattening" all of the nested lists). Figure 10.2 shows the effect of a flatMap transformation using the same lambda function as the map operation shown in Figure 10.1. Notice that instead of each string producing a respective list object, all elements are flattened into one list. In other words, flatMap, in this case, produces one combined list as output (in contrast to the list of lists in the map example).

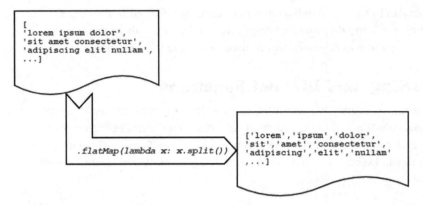

FIGURE 10.2
The flatMap transformation.

The `preservesPartitioning` argument works the same as it does in the `map` function.

filter()

Syntax:

> `RDD.filter(<function>)`

The `filter` transformation evaluates a Boolean expression against each element (record) in the dataset. The Boolean value returned determines whether or not the record is included in the resultant output RDD. This is another common transformation used to remove records from an RDD that are not required for intermediate processing and are not included in the final output.

Listing 10.3 shows an example of the `map`, `flatMap`, and `filter` transformations used together to convert input text to uppercase using `map`, to split the text into a combined list of words using `flatMap`, and then to filter the list to return only words that are greater than four characters long using `filter`.

LISTING 10.3   The map, flatMap, and filter Transformations in Spark

```
lorem = sc.textFile('file:///opt/spark/data/lorem.txt')
lorem.map(lambda x: x.upper()) \
    .flatMap(lambda x: x.split()) \
    .filter(lambda x: len(x) > 4) \
    .collect()
# Returns:
# ['LOREM', 'IPSUM', 'DOLOR', 'CONSECTETUR', 'ADIPISCING', 'NULLAM']
```

There is a standard axiom in the world of big data programming, *"filter early, filter often,"* because there is no value in carrying records or fields through a process where they are not needed. Both the `filter` and `map` functions can be used to achieve this objective.

Grouping, Sorting, and Distinct Functions

Grouping data is a normal precursor to performing aggregation or summary functions (such as, for instance, summing, counting, and so on). Sorting data is another useful operation for preparing output or for looking at the top or bottom records in a dataset. Some of these functions should look familiar to you because you have used them in a previous Word Count example.

groupBy()

Syntax:

```
RDD.groupBy(<function>, numPartitions=None)
```

The `groupBy` transformation returns an RDD of items grouped by a specified function. The function can simply nominate a key by which to group all elements or to specify an expression to be evaluated against elements to determine a group (such as when grouping elements by odd or even numbers of a numeric field in the data).

The `numPartitions` argument can be used to create a specified number of partitions created automatically by computing hashes from the output of the grouping function. For instance, if you wanted to group an RDD by the days in a week and process each day separately, you would specify `numPartitions=7`. You will see `numPartitions` specified in numerous Spark transformations, where its behavior is exactly the same.

CAUTION

Consider Other Functions If You Are Grouping to Aggregate

If your ultimate intention in using `groupBy` is to aggregate values (such as when performing a sum or count) there are more efficient operators for this purpose in Spark, including `aggregateByKey` and `reduceByKey` (which I will discuss in the section on **Key Value Pair Transformations**).

The `groupBy` transformation does not perform any aggregation prior to shuffling data, resulting in more data being shuffled. Furthermore, `groupBy` requires that all the values for a given key fit into memory. The `groupBy` transformation is useful in some cases, but you should consider these factors before deciding to use this function.

sortBy()

Syntax:

```
RDD.sortBy(<keyfunc>, ascending=True, numPartitions=None)
```

The `sortBy` transformation sorts an RDD by the function that nominates the key for a given dataset. It sorts according to the sort order of the key object type (such as, for instance, int values would be sorted numerically, whereas string values would be sorted in lexicographical order).

The `ascending` argument is a Boolean argument defaulting to True that specifies the sort order to be used. A descending sort order is specified by setting `ascending=False`.

distinct()

Syntax:

```
RDD.distinct(numPartitions=None)
```

The `distinct` transformation returns a new RDD containing distinct elements from the input RDD. It is used to remove duplicates where duplicates are defined as *all* elements or fields within a record that are the same as another record in the dataset.

Take a look at an example of `groupBy`, `sortBy`, and `distinct`.

Consider a directory containing web logs delimited by white space with fields as described in Listing 10.4. Listing 10.5 demonstrates the use of the `groupBy`, `sortBy`, and `distinct` transformations to return tuples containing unique response codes (such as 200, 500, and so on) and a list of tuples containing the response code and the unique ports (such as 80, 443) for each response code.

LISTING 10.4   Sample Web Log Schema

```
# field 0  : date
# field 1  : time
# field 2  : ip
# field 3  : username
# field 4  : sitename
# field 5  : computername
# field 6  : ip
# field 7  : port
# field 8  : method
# field 9  : uri-stem
# field 10 : uri-query
# field 11 : status
# field 12 : time-taken
# field 13 : version
# field 14 : host
# field 15 : user-agent
# field 16 : referer
```

LISTING 10.5   The distinct, sortBy, and groupBy Transformations

```
logs = sc.textFile('file:///opt/spark/data/weblogs')
logrecs = logs.map(lambda x: x.split(' '))
reqfieldsonly = logrecs.map(lambda x: (x[7], x[11]))
# [(u'80', u'200'), (u'80', u'200'), (u'80', u'200'), ...]
distinctrecs = reqfieldsonly.distinct()
# [(u'80', u'200'), (u'443', u'200'), (u'443', u'500'), ...]
sorted = distinctrecs.sortBy(lambda x: x[1]) \
         .map(lambda x: (x[1], x[0]))
# [(u'200', u'443'), (u'200', u'80'), (u'206', u'80'), ...]
grouped = sorted.groupBy(lambda x: x[0]) \
         .map(lambda x: (x[0], list(x[1])))
# [(u'200', [(u'200', u'443'), (u'200', u'80')]), ...]
```

Set Operations

Set operations are conceptually similar to mathematical set operations. Set functions operate against two RDDs and result in one RDD. Consider the Venn diagram in Figure 10.3 showing a set of odd integers and a subset of Fibonacci numbers. I will use these two sets to demonstrate the various set transformations available in the Spark API.

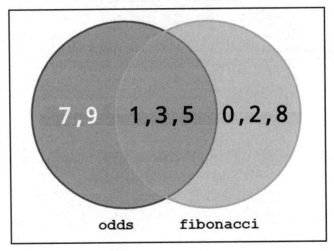

FIGURE 10.3
Set Venn diagram.

union()

Syntax:

```
RDD.union(<otherRDD>)
```

The union transformation takes one RDD and appends another RDD to it resulting in a combined output RDD. The RDDs are not required to have the same schema or structure. (For instance, the first RDD can have five fields whereas the second can have more or less than five fields.)

The union transformation does not filter duplicates from the output RDD, in the case that two unioned RDDs have records that are identical to one another. To filter duplicates, you could follow the union transformation with the distinct function discussed previously.

The resultant RDD from a union operation is not sorted either, but this could be accomplished by following union with a sortBy function.

Listing 10.6 shows an example using union.

LISTING 10.6   The union Transformation

```
odds = sc.parallelize([1,3,5,7,9])
fibonacci = sc.parallelize([0,1,2,3,5,8])
odds.union(fibonacci).collect()
# [1, 3, 5, 7, 9, 0, 1, 2, 3, 5, 8]
```

intersection()

Syntax:

```
RDD.intersection(<otherRDD>)
```

The intersection transformation returns elements that are present in both RDDs. In other words, it returns the overlap between two sets. The elements or records must be identical in both sets, with each respective record's data structure and all of its fields being identical in both RDDs.

Listing 10.7 demonstrates the intersection transformation.

LISTING 10.7   The intersection Transformation

```
odds = sc.parallelize([1,3,5,7,9])
fibonacci = sc.parallelize([0,1,2,3,5,8])
odds.intersection(fibonacci).collect()
# [1, 3, 5]
```

subtract()

Syntax:

```
RDD.subtract(<otherRDD>, numPartitions=None)
```

The `subtract` transformation (see Listing 10.8) returns all elements from the first RDD that are not present in the second RDD. This is an implementation of a mathematical set subtraction.

LISTING 10.8   The subtract Transformation

```
odds = sc.parallelize([1,3,5,7,9])
fibonacci = sc.parallelize([0,1,2,3,5,8])
odds.subtract(fibonacci).collect()
# [7, 9]
```

Spark Actions

Actions in Spark return values to the Spark driver program. They are typically the final step in a Spark program. Recall that with lazy evaluation, the complete set of Spark transformations in a program are only processed when an action is requested. In the next hour, I will be discussing Spark actions used to output data to files, such as `saveAsTextFile`, but right now let's look at some of the other common Spark actions.

The count Action

The `count` action returns the number of elements or records in an RDD. It can be called at any time against any Spark RDD, causing the RDD and all of the RDDs in its lineage to be evaluated. For this reason, `count` is often a convenient way to force evaluation of an RDD.

count()
Syntax:

> `RDD.count()`

The `count` action takes no arguments, Listing 10.9 shows a simple `count` example. Note that with actions that take no arguments, you will need to include empty parentheses, " ( ) ", after the action name.

LISTING 10.9   The count Action

```
lorem = sc.textFile('file:///opt/spark/data/lorem.txt')
words = lorem.flatMap(lambda x: x.split())
words.count()
# 9
```

The collect, take, top, and first Actions

Whereas the `count` action returns a count of data elements in the RDD, the `collect`, `take`, `top`, and `first` actions return data from the RDD. Let's look at these actions with some simple examples.

collect()

Syntax:

> `RDD.collect()`

The `collect` action returns a list that contains all of the elements in an RDD to the Spark driver. Because `collect` does not restrict the output, which can be quite large and can potentially cause out-of-memory errors on the driver, it is typically useful only for small RDDs or development. Listing 10.10 demonstrates the `collect` action.

LISTING 10.10   The collect Action

```
lorem = sc.textFile('file:///opt/spark/data/lorem.txt')
words = lorem.flatMap(lambda x: x.split())
words.collect()
# [u'lorem', u'ipsum', u'dolor', u'sit', u'amet', u'consectetur',
# u'adipiscing', u'elit', u'nullam']
```

take()

Syntax:

> `RDD.take(n)`

The `take` action returns the first *n* elements of an RDD. The elements taken are not in any particular order; in fact, the elements returned from a `take` action are non-deterministic, meaning they can differ if the same action is run again (particularly in a fully distributed environment). There is a similar Spark function, `takeOrdered`, which takes the first *n* elements ordered based upon a key supplied by a key function.

For RDDs that span more than one partition, `take` scans one partition and uses the results from that partition to estimate the number of additional partitions needed to satisfy the number requested.

Listing 10.11 shows an example of the `take` action.

LISTING 10.11   The take Action

```
lorem = sc.textFile('file:///opt/spark/data/lorem.txt')
words = lorem.flatMap(lambda x: x.split())
words.take(3)
# [u'lorem', u'ipsum', u'dolor']
```

top()

Syntax:

> *RDD*.top(n, key=None)

The top action returns the top *n* elements from an RDD, but unlike take, the elements are ordered and returned in descending order. Order is determined by the object type, such as, for example, numerical order for integers or dictionary order for strings.

The key argument specifies the key by which to order the results to return the top *n* elements.

Listing 10.12 shows the top three words sorted in descending lexicographical order.

LISTING 10.12   The top Action

```
lorem = sc.textFile('file:///opt/spark/data/lorem.txt')
words = lorem.flatMap(lambda x: x.split())
words.top(3)
# [u'sit', u'nullam', u'lorem']
```

first()

Syntax:

> *RDD*.first()

The first action returns the first element in this RDD. Similar to take and collect and unlike top, first does not consider the order of elements and is a non-deterministic operation (in fully distributed environments specifically).

As you can see from Listing 10.13, the primary difference between first and take(1) is that first returns an atomic data element, take (even if *n*=1) returns a *list* of data elements. The first action is useful for inspecting the output of an RDD as part of development or data exploration.

LISTING 10.13   The first Action

```
lorem = sc.textFile('file:///opt/spark/data/lorem.txt')
words = lorem.flatMap(lambda x: x.split())
words.first()
# u'lorem'
```

The reduce and fold Actions

The reduce and fold actions are aggregate actions, each of which executes a commutative and associative operation (such as summing a list of values, for example) against an RDD. *Commutative* and *associative* are the operative terms here. This makes the operations independent of the order in which they run, and this is integral to distributed processing because the order cannot be guaranteed. The commutative and associative characteristics are summarized here in general form:

$$commutative \Rightarrow x + y \ = \ y + x \ associative \ \Rightarrow (x + y) + z \ = \ x + (y + z)$$

Take a look at the main Spark actions that perform aggregations.

reduce()
Syntax:

```
RDD.reduce(<function>)
```

The reduce action reduces the elements of an RDD using a specified commutative and associative operator. The function supplied specifies two inputs (lambda x, y: ...) that represent values in a sequence from the specified RDD. Listing 10.14 shows an example of a sum reduce operation against a list of numbers.

LISTING 10.14   The reduce Action

```
numbers = sc.parallelize([1,2,3,4,5,6,7,8,9])
numbers.reduce(lambda x, y: x + y)
# 45
```

As you may recall, we previously looked at another aggregate operation, reduceByKey, which appears to behave similarly. There are some significant differences, however.

First, reduceByKey is a transformation that returns an RDD, whereas reduce is an action that returns a value.

Second, reduce aggregates partitions locally, whereas reduceByKey can force a *shuffle* or a potential repartitioning, because data with the same key will need to be reduced by the same node.

fold()

Syntax:

```
RDD.fold(zeroValue, <function>)
```

The `fold` action aggregates the elements of each partition of an RDD, and then performs the aggregate operation against the results for all using a given associative and commutative function and a `zeroValue`. A simple example is a `fold` action with `zeroValue=0`, as shown in Listing 10.15.

LISTING 10.15   The fold Action

```
numbers = sc.parallelize([1,2,3,4,5,6,7,8,9])
numbers.fold(0, lambda x, y: x + y)
# 45
```

The `fold` action in Listing 10.15 looks exactly the same as the `reduce` action in Listing 10.14. However, Listing 10.16 demonstrates a clear functional difference in the two actions. The `fold` action provides a `zeroValue` that will be added to the beginning and the end of the commutative and associative function supplied as input to the `fold` action. This allows `fold` to operate on an empty RDD, whereas `reduce` will produce an exception with an empty RDD.

$$result = zeroValue + (1+2)+3.. + zeroValue$$

LISTING 10.16   The fold Action Compared with reduce

```
empty = sc.parallelize([])

empty.reduce(lambda x, y: x + y)
# ValueError: Can not reduce() empty RDD

empty.fold(0, lambda x, y: x + y)
# 0
```

There is also a similar `aggregate` action in the RDD API.

The foreach Action

Unlike the previous actions, which either return a count, an aggregation of the data, or part or all of the data in an RDD, `foreach` is an action which performs a function on each element of an RDD. Let's examine `foreach`.

foreach()

Syntax:

```
RDD.foreach(<function>)
```

The `foreach` action applies a function (anonymous or named) to all elements of an RDD. Because `foreach` is an action rather than a transformation, you can perform functions otherwise not possible (or intended) in transformations, such as a `print` function. Although Python `lambda` functions will not allow you to execute a `print` statement directly, you can use a named function that executes a `print` instead. An example of this is given in Listing 10.17.

LISTING 10.17   The foreach Action

```
def printfunc(x): print(x)
lorem = sc.textFile('file:///opt/spark/data/lorem.txt')
words = lorem.flatMap(lambda x: x.split())
words.foreach(lambda x: printfunc(x))
# lorem
# ipsum
# dolor
# sit
# amet
# consectetur
# adipiscing
# elit
# nullam
```

Keep in mind that `foreach` is an action, as such it will trigger evaluation of the RDDs entire lineage. If this is not what you intend then `map` may be a better option.

Key Value Pair Operations

Key value pair RDDs, or simply *pair RDDs,* contain records consisting of (surprise) keys and values. The keys can be simple objects such as integer or string objects or complex objects such as tuples. The values can range from scalar values to data structures such as lists, tuples, dictionaries, or sets. This is a common data representation in multi-structured data analysis on schema-on-read and NoSQL systems, as I had discussed in **Hour 7, "Understanding MapReduce Concepts,"** when I introduced you to the Map Reduce programming approach.

Pair RDDs are very useful in functional Spark programming. Let's look at some of the available transformations and actions used with RDDs consisting of key value pairs, many of which are simple adaptions of the transformations and actions I have already discussed.

Key Value Pair RDD Dictionary Functions

Dictionary functions return a set of keys or values from a key value pair RDD. Let's look at these functions.

keys()

Syntax:

```
RDD.keys()
```

The keys transformation returns an RDD with the keys from a key value pair RDD, or the first element from each tuple in a key value pair RDD. Listing 10.18 demonstrates using the keys function.

LISTING 10.18   The keys Transformation

```
kvpairs = sc.parallelize([('city','Hayward')
                         ,('state','CA')
                         ,('zip',94541)
                         ,('country','USA')])
kvpairs.keys().collect()
# ['city', 'state', 'zip', 'country']
```

values()

Syntax:

```
RDD.values()
```

The values transformation returns an RDD with values from a key value pair RDD or the second element from each tuple in a key value pair RDD. Listing 10.19 demonstrates using the values function.

LISTING 10.19   The values Transformation

```
kvpairs = sc.parallelize([('city','Hayward')
                         ,('state','CA')
                         ,('zip',94541)
                         ,('country','USA')])
kvpairs.values().collect()
# ['Hayward', 'CA', 94541, 'USA']
```

Functional Key Value Pair RDD Transformations

Functional transformations available for key value pair RDDs work similarly to the more general functional transformations you learned about earlier in this hour. The difference is that these functions operate specifically on either the key or value element within a tuple (the key value pair, in this case).

keyBy()

Syntax:

```
RDD.keyBy(<funtion>)
```

The `keyBy` transformation creates tuples (consisting of a key and a value) from the elements in the RDD by applying a function. The value is the complete tuple from which the key was derived.

Consider a list of locations as tuples with a schema of *city, country, location_no*. We want the *location_no* to be our key. The example in Listing 10.20 demonstrates the use of the `keyBy` function to create new tuples in whicih the first element is the key and the second element, the value, is a tuple containing all fields from the original tuple.

LISTING 10.20 The keyBy Transformation

```
locations = sc.parallelize([['Hayward', 'USA', 1)
                            ,('Baumholder','Germany', 2)
                            ,('Alexandria','USA', 3)
                            ,('Melbourne','Australia', 4)])
bylocno = locations.keyBy(lambda x: x[2])
bylocno.collect()
# [(1, ('Hayward', 'USA', 1)),
#  (2, ('Baumholder', 'Germany', 2)),
#  (3, ('Alexandria', 'USA', 3)),
#  (4, ('Melbourne', 'Australia', 4))]
```

mapValues()

Syntax:

```
RDD.mapValues(<function>)
```

The `mapValues` transformation passes each value in a key value pair RDD through a function without changing the keys. Like its generalized equivalent, `map`, `mapValues` outputs one element for each input element.

The original RDD's partitioning is not affected.

flatMapValues()

Syntax:

```
RDD.flatMapValues(<function>)
```

The `flatMapValues` transformation passes each value in a key value pair RDD through a function without changing the keys and produces a flattened list. It works exactly like `flatMap`, which I have discussed in the previous section, returning zero to many output elements per input element.

Similar to `mapValues`, the original RDD's partitioning is retained.

The easiest way to contrast `mapValues` and `flatMapValues` is with a practical example. Consider a text file containing a city and a pipe delimited list of temperatures as shown here:

```
Hayward,71|69|71|71|72
Baumholder,46|42|40|37|39
Alexandria,50|48|51|53|44
Melbourne,88|101|85|77|74
```

Listing 10.21 simulates the loading of this data into an RDD and then uses `mapValues` to create a list of key value pair tuples containing the city and a list of temperatures for the city. It shows the use of `flatMapValues` with the same function against the same RDD to create tuples containing the city and a temperature for each temperature recorded for the city.

A simple way to describe this is that `mapValues` creates *one* element per city containing the city name and a list of five temperatures for the city, whereas `flatMapValues` flattens the lists to create *five* elements per city with the city name and a temperature value.

LISTING 10.21   The mapValues and flatMapValues Transformations

```
locwtemps = sc.parallelize(['Hayward,71|69|71|71|72',
                            'Baumholder,46|42|40|37|39',
                            'Alexandria,50|48|51|53|44',
                            'Melbourne,88|101|85|77|74'])
kvpairs = locwtemps.map(lambda x: x.split(','))
# [[u'Hayward', u'71|69|71|71|72'],[u'Baumholder', u'46|42|40|37|39'],
# [u'Alexandria', u'50|48|51|53|44'],[u'Melbourne', u'88|101|85|77|74']]
locwtemplist = kvpairs.mapValues(lambda x: x.split('|')) \
                    .mapValues(lambda x: [int(s) for s in x])
# [(u'Hayward', [71, 69, 71, 71, 72]),
#  (u'Baumholder', [46, 42, 40, 37, 39]),
#  (u'Alexandria', [50, 48, 51, 53, 44]),
#  (u'Melbourne', [88, 101, 85, 77, 74])]
locwtemps = kvpairs.flatMapValues(lambda x: x.split('|')) \
                   .map(lambda x: (x[0], int(x[1])))
# [(u'Hayward', 71),
#  (u'Hayward', 69),
#  (u'Hayward', 71),
#  (u'Hayward', 71),
#  (u'Hayward', 72)]
```

Grouping, Aggregation, Sorting, and Set Operations

These operations are functionally analogous to their more generalized forms discussed earlier in this hour, again with the difference that these functions operate specifically on RDDs comprised of key value pairs.

groupByKey()

Syntax:

```
RDD.groupByKey(numPartitions=None, partitionFunc=<hash_fn>)
```

The groupByKey transformation groups the values for each key in a key value pair RDD into a single sequence.

The numPartitions argument specifies how many partitions—how many *groups*, that is—to create. The partitions are created using the partitionFunc argument, which defaults to Spark's built-in hash partitioner. If numPartitions is None, as it defaults to, then the configured system default number of partitions is used (spark.default.parallelism).

Consider the output from Listing 10.21. If you wanted to calculate the average temperature by city, you would first need to group all of the values together by their city, then compute the averages. Listing 10.22 shows how you can use groupBy to accomplish this

LISTING 10.22   The groupBy Transformation

```
# locwtemps = [('Hayward', 71), ('Hayward', 69), ('Hayward', 71),...]
grouped = locwtemps.groupByKey()
# [('Melbourne', <pyspark.resultiterable.ResultIterable object...>),...]
avgtemps = grouped.mapValues(lambda x: sum(x)/len(x))
# [('Melbourne',85),('Baumholder',40),('Alexandria',49),('Hayward',70)]
```

Notice that groupBy returns a ResultIterable object for the grouped values. An Iterable object, in Python, is a sequence object that can be looped over. Many functions in Python accept iterables as input, such as the sum and len functions used in the previous example.

TIP

Consider Using reduceByKey or foldByKey Instead of groupByKey

If you are grouping values for the purposes of aggregation (such as a sum or count for each key) then using `reduceByKey` or `foldByKey` will provide much better performance in many cases. This is because the results of the aggregation function will be combined before the shuffle, resulting in a reduced amount of data shuffled.

reduceByKey()

Syntax:

```
RDD.reduceByKey(<function>, numPartitions=None,
                partitionFunc=<hash_fn>)
```

The `reduceByKey` transformation merges the values for each key using an associative function. The `reduceByKey` method is called on a dataset of key value pairs and returns a dataset of key value pairs, aggregating values for each key. The reduce function is expressed as: $v_n, v_{n+1} => v_{result}$.

The `numPartitions` and `partitionFunc` arguments behave exactly the same as in the `groupByKey` function. The `numPartitions` value is effectively the number of reduce tasks to execute, and this can be increased to obtain a higher degree of parallelism. The `numPartitions` value also affects the number of files produced with the `saveAsTextFile` or other file-producing Spark actions. For instance, `numPartitions=2` produces two output files when the RDD is saved to disk.

Listing 10.23 takes the same input key value pairs and produces the same results (average temperatures per city) as our previous `groupByKey` example by using the `reduceByKey` function instead. This method is preferred for reasons I will discuss shortly.

LISTING 10.23   The reduceByKey Transformation to Average Values by Key

```
# locwtemps = [('Hayward', 71), ('Hayward', 69), ('Hayward', 71),...]
temptups = locwtemps.mapValues(lambda x: (x, 1))
# [('Hayward', (71, 1)), ('Hayward', (69, 1)), ('Hayward', (71, 1)),..]
inputstoavg = temptups.reduceByKey(lambda x, y: (x[0]+y[0], x[1]+y[1]))
# [('Melbourne', (425, 5)), ('Baumholder', (204, 5)),...]
averages = inputstoavg.map(lambda x: (x[0], x[1][0]/x[1][1]))
# [('Melbourne',85),('Baumholder',40),('Alexandria',49),('Hayward',70)]
```

Averaging is not an associative operation, so I got around this in Listing 10.23 by creating tuples containing the sum total of values for each key and the count for each key (operations that are associative and commutative) and then computing the average as a final step.

If you recall the MapReduce hour earlier in this book (**Hour 7, "Understanding MapReduce Concepts,"**), the `reduceByKey` transformation is analogous to the `reduce` method (used with a combiner) from our MapReduce examples. Recall that the combiner combines values locally (on each worker node) before each of the combined lists are sent to a remote worker or workers running the final reduce stage (a shuffle operation).

Because the combiner and reducer are using the same associative and commutative function, in the previous case a sum function, you can think of this as summing a list of sums as opposed to summing a bigger list of individual values. Because there is less data sent in the shuffle phase, reduceByKey with a sum function generally performs better than a groupByKey followed by a sum function.

foldByKey()

Syntax:

```
RDD.foldByKey(zeroValue, <function>, numPartitions=None,
              partitionFunc=<hash_fn>)
```

The foldByKey transformation is functionally similar to the fold action discussed in the previous section. However, foldByKey is a transformation that works with predefined key value pair elements. Both foldByKey and fold provide a zeroValue argument of the same type to be used should the RDD be empty.

The function supplied is in the generalized aggregate function form $v_n, v_{n+1} => v_{result}$, which you also use for the reduceByKey transformation.

The numPartitions and the partitionFunc arguments have the same effect as they do with the groupByKey and reduceByKey transformations.

LISTING 10.24 The foldByKey Example to Find Maximum Value by Key

```
# locwtemps = [('Hayward', 71), ('Hayward', 69), ('Hayward', 71), ...]
maxbycity = locwtemps.foldByKey(0, lambda x, y: x if x > y else y)
maxbycity.collect()
# [('Melbourne',101), ('Baumholder',46), ('Alexandria',53), ('Hayward',72)]
```

There is also a similar method called aggregateByKey in the RDD API.

sortByKey()

Syntax:

```
RDD.sortByKey(ascending=True, numPartitions=None,
              keyfunc=<function>)
```

The sortByKey transformation sorts a key value pair RDD by the predefined key. The sort order is dependent upon the underlying key object type (numeric types are sorted numerically, and so on). The difference between sort, which you looked at earlier, and sortByKey is that sort requires you to identify the key by which to sort, whereas sortByKey is aware of the key already.

Keys are sorted in the order provided by the `ascending` argument, defaulting to True. The `numPartitions` argument specifies how many resultant partitions to output using a range partitioning function. The `keyfunc` argument is an optional parameter used if you wanted to derive a key from passing the predefined key through another function, as, for example, `keyfunc=lambda k: k.lower()`.

Listing 10.25 shows the use of the `sortByKey` transformation. In the first example, I do a simple sort based upon the key, a string representing the city name, sorted alphabetically. In the second example, I have inverted the keys and the values to make the temperature the key and then use `sortByKey` to list the temperatures in descending numerical order (the highest temperatures first).

LISTING 10.25   **The sortByKey Transformation**

```
# locwtemps = [('Hayward', 71), ('Hayward', 69), ('Hayward', 71), ...]
sortedbykey = locwtemps.sortByKey()
# [('Alexandria', 50), ('Alexandria', 48), ('Alexandria', 51), ..]
sortedbyval = locwtemps.map(lambda x: (x[1],x[0])) \
                        .sortByKey(ascending=False)
# [(101, 'Melbourne'), (88, 'Melbourne'), (85, 'Melbourne'), ...]
```

subtractByKey()

Syntax:

> `RDD.subtractByKey(<otherRDD>, numPartitions=None)`

The `subtractByKey` transformation is a set operation similar to the `subtract` transformation I discussed earlier in this hour. The `subtractByKey` transformation returns key value pair elements from an RDD with keys that are not present in key value pair elements from the `otherRDD`.

The `numPartitions` argument specifies how many output partitions to be created in the resultant RDD, defaulting to the configured `spark.default.parallelism` value.

Listing 10.26 demonstrates `subtractByKey` by using two RDDs containing city names as the key and a tuple containing location data for the city.

LISTING 10.26   **The subtractByKey Transformation**

```
cities1 = sc.parallelize([('Hayward',(37.668819,-122.080795)),
                          ('Baumholder',(49.6489,7.3975)),
                          ('Alexandria',(38.820450,-77.050552)),
                          ('Melbourne', (37.663712,144.844788))])
cities2 = sc.parallelize([('Boulder Creek',(64.0708333,-148.2236111)),
                          ('Hayward',(37.668819,-122.080795)),
                          ('Alexandria',(38.820450,-77.050552)),
                          ('Arlington', (38.878337,-77.100703))])
```

```
cities1.subtractByKey(cities2).collect()
# [('Melbourne',(37.663712,144.844788)),('Baumholder',(49.6489,7.3975))]
cities2.subtractByKey(cities1).collect()
# [('Boulder Creek',(64.0708333,-148.2236111)),('Arlington',(38.878337, -77.100703))]
```

Join Functions

Join operations are analogous to the join operations we routinely see is SQL programming. Join functions combine records from two RDDs based on a common field, a key. Because join functions in Spark require a key to be defined, they operate on key value pair RDDs (discussed in the previous section). Here I will describe the various join functions available in Spark with examples of each.

Join Types

A quick refresher on joins—you can skip this if you have a relational database background. Joins operate on two different datasets where one field in each dataset is nominated as a key (or a join key). The datasets are referred to in the order they are specified in. For instance, the first dataset specified is considered as the *left* entity or dataset, the second dataset specified is considered as the *right* entity or dataset.

An *inner join*, often simply called a *join* (where the "inner" is inferred), returns all elements or records from both datasets where the nominated key is present in both datasets.

An *outer join* does not require keys to match in both datasets. Outer joins are implemented as either a left outer join, right outer join, or a full outer join.

A *left outer join* returns all records from the *left* (or first) dataset along with matched records only (by the specified key) from the *right* (or second) dataset.

A *right outer join* returns all records from the *right* (or second) dataset along with matched records only (by the specified key) from the *left* (or first) dataset.

A *full outer join* returns all records from both datasets whether there is a key match or not.

Join Transformations

After map, joins are some of the most commonly required transformations in the Spark API, so it is imperative that you understand these functions and become comfortable in using them. Let's look at the available join transformations in Spark, their usage, and some examples.

join()
Syntax:

```
RDD.join(<otherRDD>, numPartitions=None)
```

The `join` transformation is an implementation of an inner join, matching two key value pair RDDs by their key.

The optional `numPartitions` argument determines how many partitions to create in the resultant dataset. If this is not specified, the default value for the `spark.default.parallelism` configuration parameter is used. The `numPartitions` argument has the same behavior for the other types of join operations in the Spark API as well.

The RDD returned is a structure containing the matched key and a value that is a tuple containing the entire matched records from both RDDs as a list object.

This is where it may sound a bit foreign to you if you are used to performing join operations in SQL—which returns a flattened list of columns from both entities. Let's work through an example.

For the examples in this section, I will use a fictitious retailer with a list of stores and a list of salespeople with the stores they are assigned to. Figure 10.4 is a logical depiction of how a join operation works in Spark.

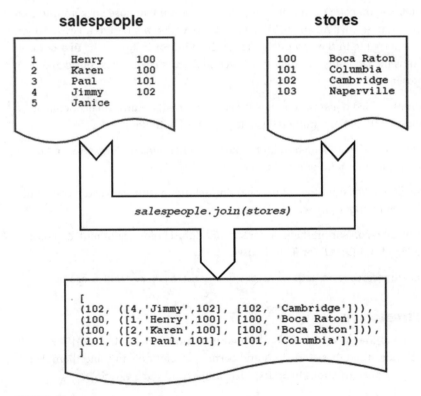

FIGURE 10.4
(Inner) join in Spark.

Take a look at the code behind this example in Listing 10.27.

LISTING 10.27 The join Transformation

```
stores = sc.parallelize(['100\tBoca Raton', '101\tColumbia',
                         '102\tCambridge', '103\tNaperville']) \
                  .map(lambda x: x.split('\t')) \
                  .keyBy(lambda x: x[0])
salespeople = sc.parallelize(['1\tHenry\t100', '2\tKaren\t100',
                              '3\tPaul\t101', '4\tJimmy\t102',
                              '5\tJanice\t']) \
                  .map(lambda x: x.split('\t')) \
                  .keyBy(lambda x: x[2])
salespeople.join(stores).collect()
#[('102', (['4', 'Jimmy', '102'], ['102', 'Cambridge'])),
# ('100', (['1', 'Henry', '100'], ['100', 'Boca Raton'])),
# ('100', (['2', 'Karen', '100'], ['100', 'Boca Raton'])),
# ('101', (['3', 'Paul', '101'], ['101', 'Columbia']))]
```

Our join operation returned all salespeople who were assigned to stores keyed by the store ID (the join key) along with the entire store record and salesperson record. Notice that the resultant RDD contains duplicate data. You could (and should in many cases) follow the join with a map transformation to prune fields or project only the fields required for further processing.

TIP

Optimizing Joins in Spark

Joins involving RDDs that span more than one partition (of which many will) will require a shuffle. Spark will generally plan and implement this activity to achieve the most optimal performance possible; however, a simple axiom to remember is *"join large by small."* This means reference the large RDD (the one with the most elements if this is known) first followed by the smaller of the two RDDs.

This will seem strange for users coming from relational database programming backgrounds but unlike relational database systems, joins are relatively inefficient in Spark. Unlike most databases, there are no indexes or statistics to optimize the join so the optimizations you can provide are essential to maximizing performance.

leftOuterJoin()

Syntax:

> RDD.leftOuterJoin(<otherRDD>, numPartitions=None)

The leftOuterJoin transformation returns all elements or records from the first RDD referenced. If keys from the first (or left) RDD are present in the right RDD then the right RDD record is returned along with the left RDD record. Otherwise, the right RDD record is None (or empty).

Look at a logical diagram in Figure 10.5.

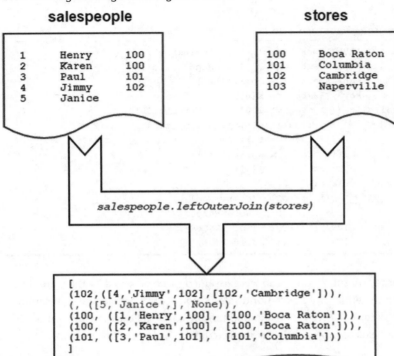

FIGURE 10.5
Using leftOuterJoin in Spark.

In the example in Figure 10.5 and the associated code in Listing 10.28, you can use
leftOuterJoin to identify salespeople with no stores.

LISTING 10.28   The leftOuterJoin Transformation

```
salespeople.leftOuterJoin(stores) \
        .filter(lambda x: x[1][1] is None) \
        .map(lambda x: "salesperson " + x[1][0][1] + " has no store") \
        .collect()
# ['salesperson Janice has no store']
```

rightOuterJoin()

Syntax:

> RDD.rightOuterJoin(<otherRDD>, numPartitions=None)

The rightOuterJoin transformation returns all elements or records from the second RDD
referenced. If keys from the second (or right) RDD are present in the left RDD, then the left

RDD record is returned along with the right RDD record. Otherwise the left RDD record is None (or empty).

Figure 10.6 shows a logical diagram describing the rightOuterJoin followed by the associated code in Listing 10.29.

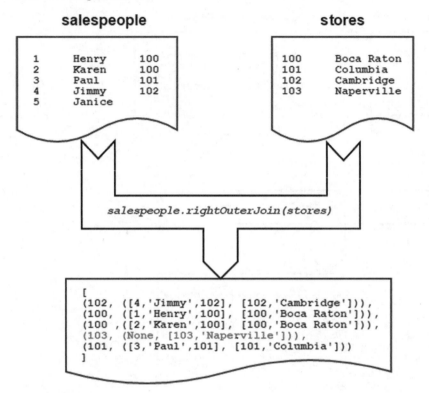

FIGURE 10.6
Using rightOuterJoin in Spark.

LISTING 10.29   The rightOuterJoin Transformation

```
salespeople.rightOuterJoin(stores) \
        .filter(lambda x: x[1][0] is None) \
        .map(lambda x: x[1][1][1] + " store has no salespeople") \
        .collect()
# ['Naperville store has no salespeople']
```

fullOuterJoin()
Syntax:

```
RDD.fullOuterJoin(<otherRDD>, numPartitions=None)
```

The `fullOuterJoin` transforms all elements from both RDDs whether there is a key matched or not. Keys not matched from either the left or right dataset are represented as None or empty.

Figure 10.7 depicts the result of a `fullOuterJoin` with our example datasets, followed by the associated code in Listing 10.30.

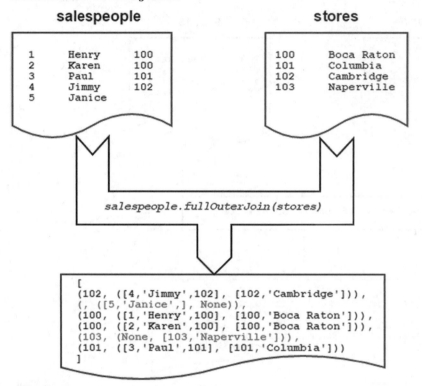

salespeople

```
1    Henry    100
2    Karen    100
3    Paul     101
4    Jimmy    102
5    Janice
```

stores

```
100    Boca Raton
101    Columbia
102    Cambridge
103    Naperville
```

salespeople.fullOuterJoin(stores)

```
[
(102, ([4,'Jimmy',102], [102,'Cambridge'])),
(, ([5,'Janice',], None)),
(100, ([1,'Henry',100], [100,'Boca Raton'])),
(100, ([2,'Karen',100], [100,'Boca Raton'])),
(103, (None, [103,'Naperville'])),
(101, ([3,'Paul',101], [101,'Columbia']))
]
```

FIGURE 10.7
Using fullOuterJoin in Spark.

LISTING 10.30   The fullOuterJoin Transformation

```
salespeople.fullOuterJoin(stores) \
        .filter(lambda x: x[1][0] is None or x[1][1] is None) \
        .collect()
# [(, ([5,'Janice',], None)),(103,(None,[103,'Naperville']))]
```

`cogroup()`

Syntax:

```
RDD.cogroup(<otherRDD>, numPartitions=None)
```

The cogroup transformation groups multiple key value pair datasets by a key. It is somewhat similar conceptually to a fullOuterJoin, but there are a few key differences in its implementation:

▶ The cogroup transformation returns an *Iterable* object, similar to the object returned from the groupByKey function you saw earlier.

▶ The cogroup transformation groups multiple elements from both RDDs into Iterable objects, whereas fullOuterJoin created separate output elements for the same key.

▶ The cogroup transformation can group three or more RDDs (using the Scala API or the groupWith function alias).

The resultant RDD output from a cogroup operation of two RDDs *(A, B)* with a key *K* could be summarized as:

$$[K, \textit{Iterable}(K, V_{A}, ...), \textit{Iterable}(K, V_{B}, ...)]$$

If an RDD does not have elements for a given key that is present in the other RDD, the corresponding Iterable is empty. Listing 10.31 shows a cogroup transformation using our example salespeople and stores RDDs.

LISTING 10.31   The cogroup Transformation

```
salespeople.cogroup(stores).collect()
# [(102, (<pyspark.resultiterable.ResultIterable object...>,
#          <pyspark.resultiterable.ResultIterable object...>)),
#  (, (<pyspark.resultiterable.ResultIterable object...>,
#      <pyspark.resultiterable.ResultIterable object...>)),
# ...]
salespeople.cogroup(stores) \
  .mapValues(lambda x: [item for sublist in x for item in sublist]) \
  .collect()
# [(102, [[4,'Jimmy',102], [102,'Cambridge']]),
#  (, [[5,'Janice',]]), ...]
```

cartesian()

Syntax:

> RDD.cartesian(<otherRDD>)

The cartesian transformation (sometimes referred to by its colloquial name, *cross join*) generates every possible combination of records from both RDDs. The number of records produced by this transformation is equal to the number of records in the first RDD multiplied by the number of records in the second RDD.

Listing 10.32 demonstrates the use of the `cartesian` transformation.

LISTING 10.32   The cartesian Transformation

```
salespeople.cartesian(stores).collect()
# returns 5 x 4 = 20 records
# [((100, [1,'Henry',100]), (100, [100,'Boca Raton']))),...]
```

CAUTION

The cartesian Transformation Can Create Large Amounts of Data

Cartesian or cross-product operations can yield excessively large amounts of data. Although this is a useful function for testing multiple combinations of items for machine learning, there is a likelihood that you could create a big data problem where one otherwise did not exist!

▼ TRY IT YOURSELF

Join Functions in Spark

For this example we will be using data from the Bay Area Bike Share Data Challenge. The Bay Area Bike Share program enables members to pick up bikes from designated stations, which they can then drop off at the same or a different station. Bay Area Bike Share has made their trip data available for public use through their Open Data program. More information can be found at:

http://www.bayareabikeshare.com/open-data

The data for this exercise has also been made available in our AWS S3 bucket:

s3://sty-spark/bike-share

Data from the Bay Area Bike Share program is in comma delimited text files. We have summarized the files we will use in this exercise in Tables 10.1 and 10.2.

TABLE 10.1   Fields in status.csv

Field Name	Description
station_id	station ID number
bikes_available	number of available bikes
docks_available	number of available docks
time	date and time, PST

TABLE 10.2   Fields in stations.csv

Field Name	Description
station_id	station ID number
name	name of station
lat	latitude
long	longitude
dockcount	number of docks at station
landmark	city
installation	original date that station was installed

In this exercise, I will use Spark to return the average number of bikes available by the hour for one week (February 22 to February 28), for stations located in the San Jose area only.

1. Download the data. This can be done in several different ways:

   ▶ Download the data from the **s3://sty-spark** bucket listed above, and store this on your local Spark installation.

   ▶ Use the Databricks or AWS EMR platforms covered in **Hour 5, "Deploying Spark in the Cloud,"** which have direct access to the S3 bucket.

   ▶ From a Spark instance on Hadoop and access the files directly from the S3 buckets.

2. Open a `pyspark` shell.

3. Load the data into RDDs.

```
stations = sc.textFile('/bike-share/stations')
status = sc.textFile('/bike-share/status')
```

   or, if you are using one of the direct S3 methods above:

```
stations = sc.textFile('s3a://sty-spark/bike-share/stations')
status = sc.textFile('s3a://sty-spark/bike-share/status')
```

4. Split the status data into discrete fields projecting only the fields necessary. Also, decompose the date string so that you can filter records by date more easily in the next step:

```
status2 = status.map(lambda x: x.split(',')) \
.map(lambda x: (x[0], x[1], x[2], x[3].replace('"',''))) \
.map(lambda x: (x[0], x[1], x[2], x[3].split(' '))) \
.map(lambda x: (x[0], x[1], x[2], x[3][0].split('-'), x[3][1].split(':'))) \
.map(lambda x: (int(x[0]), int(x[1]), int(x[3][0]), int(x[3][1]), int(x[3][2]),
  int(x[4][0])))
# [(10, 7, 2014, 12, 30, 15),...]
# [(station_id,bikes_available,year,month,day,hour),...]
# tuple:(x[0],x[1],x[2],x[3],x[4],x[5])
```

5. Because `status.csv` is the biggest of your datasets (over 36M records), restrict the dataset to only the dates required, and then drop the date fields because they are no longer necessary:

```
status3 = status2.filter(lambda x: x[2]==2015 and \
                                   x[3]==2 and \
                                   x[4]>=22) \
             .map(lambda x: (x[0], x[1], x[5]))
# [(10, 9, 23),...]
# [(station_id,bikes_available,hour),...]
# tuple:(x[0],x[1],x[2])
```

6. Filter the stations dataset to only include stations where the `landmark='San Jose'`:

```
stations2 = stations.map(lambda x: x.split(',')) \
                .filter(lambda x: x[5] == 'San Jose') \
              .map(lambda x: (int(x[0]), x[1]))
# [(2, u'San Jose Diridon Station'),...]
# tuple:(x[0],x[1])
```

7. Convert both RDDs to key value pair RDDs to prepare for a join operation:

```
status_kv = status3.keyBy(lambda x: x[0])
# [(10, (10, 9, 23)),...]
# tuple:(k,(v[0],v[1],v[2]))

stations_kv = stations2.keyBy(lambda x: x[0])
# [(2, (2, u'San Jose Diridon Station')),...]
# tuple:(k,(v[0],v[1]))
```

8. Join the filtered status key value pair RDD to the filtered stations key value pair RDD by their keys (`station_id`):

```
joined = status_kv.join(stations_kv)
# [(2,((2,20,0),(2,u'San Jose Diridon Station'))),...]
# tuple:(k,((v[0][0],v[0][1],v[0][2]),(v[1][0],v[1][1])))
```

9. Clean the joined RDD:

```
cleaned = joined.map(lambda x: (x[0], x[1][0][1], x[1][0][2], x[1][1][1]))
# [(2, 20, 0, u'San Jose Diridon Caltrain Station'),...]
# [(station_id,bikes_available,hour,name),...]
# tuple:(x[0],x[1],x[2],x[3])
```

10. Create a key value pair with the key being a tuple consisting of the station name and the hour, and then compute the averages by each hour for each station:

```
avgbyhour = cleaned.keyBy(lambda x: (x[3],x[2])) \
    .mapValues(lambda x: (x[1], 1)) \
    .reduceByKey(lambda x, y: (x[0] + y[0], x[1] + y[1])) \
    .mapValues(lambda x: (x[0]/x[1]))
# [((u'SJSU 4th at San Carlos', 2), 11)]
# [((name,hour),bikes_available),...]
# tuple:((k[0],k[1]),v[0])
```

11. Find the top 10 averages by station and hour using the sortBy function:

```
topavail = avgbyhour.keyBy(lambda x: x[1]) \
        .sortByKey(ascending=False) \
        .map(lambda x: (x[1][0][0], x[1][0][1], x[0]))
topavail.take(5)
# [(u'San Jose Diridon Caltrain Station', 18, 16),
# (u'San Jose Diridon Caltrain Station', 6, 16),
# (u'San Jose Diridon Caltrain Station', 7, 16),
# (u'San Jose Diridon Caltrain Station', 17, 16),
# (u'San Jose Diridon Caltrain Station', 4, 15)]
# [(name,hour,bikes_available),...]
# tuple:(x[0],x[1],x[2])
```

You can also try combining all of this code into a single Python script and use spark-submit to execute it as a batch.

You could take this much further of course, including using Jupyter notebooks, which I introduced you to in the previous hour, to plot graphs based upon transformations and aggregations in Spark.

Numerical RDD Operations

Numerical RDDs consist only of numerical values. These are commonly used for statistical analysis, so you will see many of the functions available to numeric RDDs are your common statistical functions. Let's look at these functions with some simple examples.

min()

Syntax:

```
RDD.min(key=None)
```

The min function is an action that returns the minimum value for a numerical RDD.
The key argument is a function used to generate a key for comparing. Listing 10.33 shows the use of the min function.

LISTING 10.33   The min Function

```
numbers = sc.parallelize([0,1,1,2,3,5,8,13,21,34])
numbers.min()
# 0
```

max()
Syntax:

> *RDD*.max(key=None)

The max function is an action that returns the maximum value for a numerical RDD. The key argument is a function used to generate a key for comparing. Listing 10.34 shows the use of the max function.

LISTING 10.34   The max Function

```
numbers = sc.parallelize([0,1,1,2,3,5,8,13,21,34])
numbers.max()
# 34
```

mean()
Syntax:

> *RDD*.mean()

The mean function computes the arithmetic mean from a numeric RDD. Listing 10.35 demonstrates the use of the mean function.

LISTING 10.35   The mean Function

```
numbers = sc.parallelize([0,1,1,2,3,5,8,13,21,34])
numbers.mean()
# 8.8
```

sum()
Syntax:

> *RDD*.sum()

The sum function returns the sum of a list of numbers from a numeric RDD. Listing 10.36 shows the use of the sum function.

LISTING 10.36   The sum Function

```
numbers = sc.parallelize([0,1,1,2,3,5,8,13,21,34])
numbers.sum()
# 88
```

stdev()

Syntax:

> RDD.stdev()

The stdev function is an action that computes the standard deviation for a series of numbers from a numeric RDD. An example of stdev is given in Listing 10.37.

LISTING 10.37   The stdev Function

```
numbers = sc.parallelize([0,1,1,2,3,5,8,13,21,34])
numbers.stdev()
# 10.467091286503619
```

variance()

Syntax:

> RDD.variance()

The variance function computes the variance in a series of numbers in a numeric RDD. *Variance* is a measure of how far a set of numbers are spread out. An example of variance is provided in Listing 10.38.

LISTING 10.38   The variance Function

```
numbers = sc.parallelize([0,1,1,2,3,5,8,13,21,34])
numbers.variance()
# 109.55999999999999
```

stats()

Syntax:

> RDD.stats()

The stats function returns a *StatCounter* object, which is a structure containing the count, mean, standard deviation, max, and min in one operation. Listing 10.39 demonstrates the stats function.

LISTING 10.39   The stats Function

```
numbers = sc.parallelize([0,1,1,2,3,5,8,13,21,34])
numbers.stats()
# (count: 10, mean: 8.8, stdev: 10.4670912865, max: 34.0, min: 0.0)
```

Summary

The set of transformations and actions exposed through the Spark functional programming API is the foundation of all of the capabilities available using Spark. Virtually all of the extensions and abstractions I will discuss as you progress through this book (such as Spark SQL for instance) will be built upon this basic set of transformations and actions.

You looked at the various sampling transformations and actions available in the Spark API—including sample, sampleByKey, and takeSample—which can be used to randomly select elements from an RDD; this is useful for development and for creating test sets of data for modelling.

In this hour, I further detailed basic transformations such as map, flatMap, and filter, and introduced set operations including union, intersection, and subtract. You learned more about key value pair RDDs and their available functions and compared the behavior of some of the shuffle operations such as groupByKey and reduceByKey. I have covered the basic Spark actions such as count, collect, take, top, and first as well.

Additionally, I have detailed the full set of join transformations available when working with key value pair RDDs—join, leftOuterJoin, rightOuterJoin, and fullOuterJoin.

I have also covered the statistical functions available when working with numeric RDDs such as min, max, stdev, variance and stats.

You now have the foundational set of Spark programming tools with which you can implement most data processing patterns or build nearly any Spark application.

Q&A

Q. What is the difference between the map and flatMap transformations?

A. The map transformation produces an output element for each input element, whereas flatMap produces zero or more output elements for each input element and can be used to flatten (or remove a level of nesting) from the output. An example of the last point is the str.split() function. When used with map, the output is a list of lists. When the same function is used with flatMap, the result is a single flattened list.

Q. The `foreach` and `map` operations operate on each element of an RDD. What are the differences between these two operations?

A. The `map` operation is a transformation, meaning it operates on an RDD and returns an RDD. The `foreach` operation is an action meaning it operates on an RDD and returns data to the Driver.

Q. What considerations do you need to be aware of when using `groupByKey` or `reduceByKey`?

A. In a fully distributed processing environment, `groupByKey` and `reduceByKey` may require a shuffle to occur to transfer all data with the same key to the same worker node. If you are grouping records specifically to aggregate values, then `reduceByKey` is favored over `groupByKey` because it will reduce the amount of data shuffled over the network by combining values for each key locally before the shuffle.

Workshop

The workshop contains quiz questions and exercises to help you solidify your understanding of the material covered. Try to answer all questions before looking at the "Answers" section that follows.

Quiz

1. **True or false:** A full outer join returns all records from two datasets whether there is a key match or not.

2. Which numerical RDD function returns the min, max, count, mean, and standard deviation for all values in the RDD?

    A. `min`

    B. `variance`

    C. `stats`

    D. `stdev`

3. What is the difference between the `take(1)` and `first()` actions?

4. **True or false:** The `keys` transformation returns an RDD with ordered keys from a key value pair RDD.

Answers

1. **True.**

2. **C.**

3. The `take(1)` action returns a list with one element from an RDD, whereas `first()` returns one element (not in a list).

4. **False.** The `keys` transformation returns an RDD with the keys from a key value pair RDD, but the keys are not ordered.

What You'll

▶ RDD stor

▶ Caching

▶ Checkpoi

▶ Saving RD

▶ Introductio

This hour is focused upon RDD storage. You will learn about the various storage functions available to you as a Spark programmer that can be used for program optimization, durability or process restart/recovery. You will also further explore the available Spark actions that save RDDs to persistent storage such as HDFS, S3, local storage, or Alluxio—a memory-centric storage system. These tools build upon the Spark API transformations you have learned about in the previous hour and gives you the additional tools required to build efficient end-to-end Spark processing pipelines.

RDD Storage Levels

Thus far, I have discussed RDDs as distributed immutable collections of objects that reside in memory on cluster worker nodes. There are, however, other storage options for RDDs that are beneficial for a number of reasons. Before I discuss the various RDD storage levels that lead into caching and persistence, let's review the concept of RDD lineage.

RDD Lineage Revisited

Recall from **Hour 6, "Learning the Basics of Spark Programming with RDDs,"** that Spark plans the execution of a program as a DAG (directed acyclic graph), which is a set of operations separated into stages with stage dependencies. Some operations, such as map operations, can be completely parallelized, and some operations, such as reduceByKey, require a shuffle. This naturally introduces a stage dependency.

The Spark driver keeps track of every RDD's lineage, that is, the series of transformations performed to yield an RDD (or a partition thereof). This enables every RDD at every stage to be reevaluated in the event of a failure (this provides the *resiliency* in Resilient Distributed Datasets).

Consider a simple example involving only one stage, as represented in Figure 11.1.

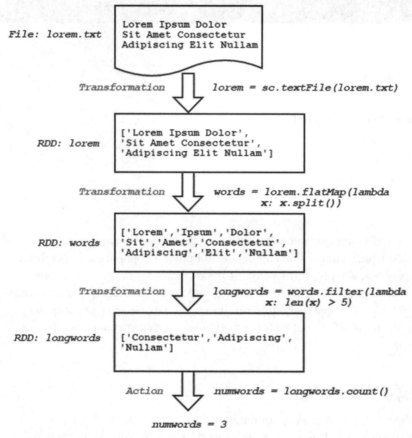

FIGURE 11.1
RDD lineage.

A summary of a physical execution plan created by Spark using the `toDebugString()` function is shown in Listing 11.1.

LISTING 11.1 The toDebugString() Function

```
>>> print(longwords.toDebugString())
(1) PythonRDD[6] at collect at <stdin>:1 []
 |  MapPartitionsRDD[1] at textFile at ..[]
 |  file://lorem.txt HadoopRDD[0] at textFile at ..[]
```

The action `longwords.count()` forces evaluation of each of the parent RDDs to longwords. If this (or any other action, such as `longwords.take(1)` or `longwords.collect()`) is called a subsequent time, the entire lineage is reevaluated. In simple cases, with small amounts of data with one or two stages, these reevaluations are not an issue, but in many circumstances they can be inefficient and can impact recovery times in the event of a failure.

RDD Storage Levels

RDDs are stored in their partitions on various worker nodes in the Spark (YARN or Mesos) cluster. RDDs have six basic storage levels available, which are summarized in Table 11.1.

TABLE 11.1   RDD Storage Levels

Storage Level	Description
MEMORY_ONLY	(Default) RDD partitions are stored in memory only.
MEMORY_AND_DISK	RDD partitions that do not fit in memory are stored on disk.
MEMORY_ONLY_SER	RDD partitions are stored as serialized objects in memory. This option can be used to save memory (as serialized objects may consume less space than their deserialized equivalent).
MEMORY_AND_DISK_SER	RDD partitions are stored as serialized objects in memory. Objects that do not fit into memory are spilled to disk.
DISK_ONLY	RDD partitions are stored on disk only.

There is also an OFF_HEAP storage level , which I will discuss in the **Introduction to Alluxio (Tachyon)** section later in this hour.

Additionally, there are replicated storage options available with each of the basic storage levels listed in Table 11.1. These replicate each partition to more than one cluster node. Replication of RDDs consumes more space across the cluster but enables tasks to continue to run in the event of a failure without having to wait for lost partitions to be reprocessed. Although fault tolerance is provided for all Spark RDDs regardless of their storage level, replicated storage levels provide much faster fault recovery.

Storage Level Flags

Storage levels are implemented as a set of flags that control the RDD storage. There are flags that determine whether to use memory, whether to spill data to disk if it does not fit in memory, whether to store objects in serialized format, and whether to replicate the RDD partitions to multiple nodes. Flags are implemented in the StorageClass constructor, as shown in Listing 11.2.

LISTING 11.2   StorageClass Constructor

```
StorageLevel(useDisk,
             useMemory,
             useOffHeap,
             deserialized,
             replication=1)
```

The useDisk, useMemory, useOffHeap, and deserialized arguments are Boolean values, whereas replication is an integer value defaulting to 1. The RDD storage levels listed in Table 11.1 are actually static constants that can be used for common storage levels. Table 11.2 shows these static constants with their respective flags.

TABLE 11.2   StorageLevel Constants and Flags

Constant	useDisk	useMemory	useOffHeap	deserialized	replication
MEMORY_ONLY	False	True	False	True	1
MEMORY_AND_DISK	True	True	False	True	1
MEMORY_ONLY_SER	False	True	False	False	1
MEMORY_AND_DISK_SER	True	True	False	False	1
DISK_ONLY	True	False	False	False	1
MEMORY_ONLY_2	False	True	False	True	2
MEMORY_AND_DISK_2	True	True	False	True	2
MEMORY_ONLY_SER_2	False	True	False	False	2
MEMORY_AND_DISK_SER_2	True	True	False	False	2
DISK_ONLY_2	True	False	False	False	2
OFF_HEAP	False	False	True	False	1

The Spark API includes a function called getStorageLevel that can be used to inspect the storage level for an RDD.

getStorageLevel()

Syntax:

```
RDD.getStorageLevel()
```

The getStorageLevel function returns the different storage option flags set for an RDD. The return value, in the case of PySpark, is an instance of the class pyspark.storagelevel. StorageLevel. Listing 11.3 shows how to use the getStorageLevel function.

LISTING 11.3   The getStorageLevel() Function

```
>>> lorem = sc.textFile('file://lorem.txt')
>>> lorem.getStorageLevel()
StorageLevel(False, False, False, False, 1)
# get individual flags
>>> lorem_sl = lorem.getStorageLevel()
>>> lorem_sl.useDisk
False
>>> lorem_sl.useMemory
False
>>> lorem_sl.useOffHeap
False
>>> lorem_sl.deserialized
False
>>> lorem_sl.replication
1
```

Choosing a Storage Level

RDD storage levels enable you to tune Spark jobs and to accommodate large scale operations that would otherwise not fit into the aggregate memory available across the cluster. Additionally, replication options for the available storage levels can reduce recovery times in the event of a task or node failure.

Generally speaking, if your RDD fits into the available memory across the cluster, then the default memory only storage level is sufficient and will provide the best performance.

Caching, Persistence, and Checkpointing

You have learned about different RDD storage options available in the previous section. In this section, you will learn how to implement different storage options to optimize Spark applications or to reduce recovery times in the event of failure.

Caching RDDs

A Spark RDD (including all of its parent RDDs) is normally recomputed for each action called in the same session or application. Caching an RDD persists the data in memory, which can then be reused multiple times in the same routine when subsequent actions are called, without requiring reevaluation.

Caching does not trigger execution or computation but is, rather, a suggestion. If there is not enough memory available to cache the RDD, it will be reevaluated for each lineage triggered by an action. Caching will never spill to disk because it only ever uses memory. The cached RDD will be persisted using the MEMORY_ONLY_SER storage level.

Under the appropriate circumstances, caching is a useful tool to increase application performance. Listing 11.4 shows an example of caching with RDDs.

LISTING 11.4 Caching RDDs

```
doc = sc.textFile("file:///opt/spark/data/shakespeare.txt")
words = doc.flatMap(lambda x: x.split()) \
           .map(lambda x: (x,1)) \
           .reduceByKey(lambda x, y: x + y)
words.cache()
words.count() # triggers computation
# 33505
words.take(3) # no computation required
# [(u'fawn', 12), (u'mustachio', 1), (u'Debts', 1)]
words.count() # no computation required
# 33505
```

Persisting RDDs

Cached partitions (partitions of an RDD where the `cache` method was run) are stored in memory on executor JVMs on Spark worker nodes. If one of the worker nodes were to fail or become unavailable, Spark would need to recreate the cached partition from its lineage.

The `persist` method offers additional storage options including MEMORY_AND_DISK, DISK_ONLY, MEMORY_ONLY_SER, MEMORY_AND_DISK_SER, as well as MEMORY_ONLY (which is the same as the `cache` method). When using persistence with one of the disk storage options, the persisted partitions are stored as local files on the worker nodes running Spark executors for the application. The persisted data on disk can be used to reconstitute partitions lost due to executor or memory failure.

Additionally, `persist` can use replication to persist the same partition on more than one node. Replication makes reevaluation less likely because more than one node would need to fail or be unavailable to trigger recomputation.

Persistence offers additional durability over caching, while still offering increased performance. It is worth reiterating, however, that Spark RDDs are fault-tolerant regardless of persistence and can always be recreated in the event of a failure. Persistence simply expedites this process.

Persistence, as is the case with caching, is a suggestion, not an imperative, and only takes place after an action is called to trigger evaluation of an RDD. If sufficient resources are not available — for instance, if there is not enough memory available — persistence will not be implemented. You can inspect the persistence state and current storage levels from any RDD at any stage using the `getStorageLevel` method discussed in the previous section.

The methods available for persisting and unpersisting RDDs are documented in the following sections.

persist()

Syntax:

```
RDD.persist(storageLevel=StorageLevel.MEMORY_ONLY_SER)
```

The persist method specifies the desired storage level and storage attributes for an RDD. The desired storage options will be implemented the first time the RDD is evaluated. If this is not possible (as when, for example, there is insufficient memory to persist the RDD in memory), then Spark will revert to its normal behavior retaining only required partitions in memory.

The storageLevel argument is expressed as either a static constant or a set of storage flags (see both methods discussed in the previous section on RDD Storage Levels). For example, to set a storage level of MEMORY_AND_DISK_SER_2, you could do either of the following:

```
myrdd.persist(StorageLevel.MEMORY_AND_DISK_SER_2) # or;
myrdd.persist(StorageLevel(True, True, False, False, 2))
```

The default storage level is MEMORY_ONLY_SER.

unpersist()

Syntax:

```
RDD.unpersist()
```

The unpersist method unpersists the RDD. This is used if you no longer need the RDD to be persisted. Also, if you want to change the storage options for a persisted RDD, you must unpersist the RDD first. If you attempt to change the storage level of a RDD marked for persistence you will get the exception "Cannot change storage level of an RDD after it was already assigned a level."

TIP

Removing an RDD from Cache

The unpersist method can also be used to remove an RDD that was cached using the cache method.

Listing 11.5 shows several examples of persistence.

LISTING 11.5 Persisting an RDD

```
doc = sc.textFile("file:///opt/spark/data/shakespeare.txt")
words = doc.flatMap(lambda x: x.split()) \
          .map(lambda x: (x,1)) \
          .reduceByKey(lambda x, y: x + y)
```

```
words.persist()
words.count()
words.take(3)
print(words.toDebugString())
(1) PythonRDD[8] at ... [Memory Serialized 1x Replicated]
 |  MapPartitionsRDD[5] at ... [Memory Serialized 1x Replicated]
 |  ShuffledRDD[4] at ... [Memory Serialized 1x Replicated]
+-(1) PairwiseRDD[3] at ... [Memory Serialized 1x Replicated]
    |  PythonRDD[2] at ...[Memory Serialized 1x Replicated]
    |  MapPartitionsRDD[1] ... [Memory Serialized 1x Replicated]
    |  HadoopRDD[0] ... [Memory Serialized 1x Replicated]
```

Persisted RDDs can also be viewed in the Spark Application UI in the Storage tab, as shown in Figures 11.2 and 11.3.

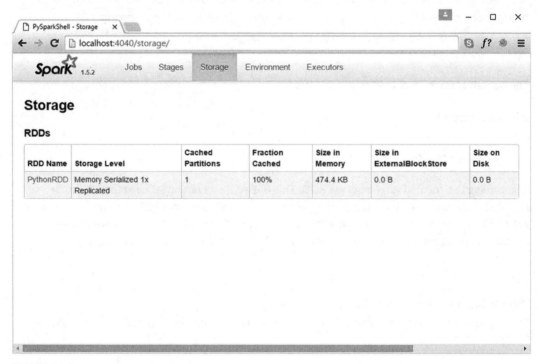

FIGURE 11.2
Viewing persisted RDDs in the Spark Application UI.

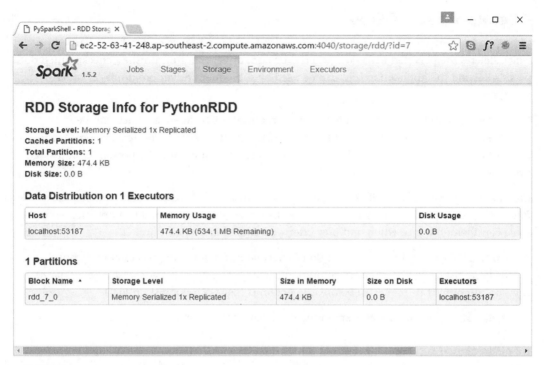

FIGURE 11.3
Viewing details of a persisted RDD in the Spark Application UI.

Choosing When to Persist or Cache RDDs

Caching can improve performance or reduce recovery times. If an RDD is likely to be reused and if sufficient memory is available on worker nodes in the cluster, it is typically beneficial to cache these RDDs. Iterative algorithms such as those used in machine learning routines are often good candidates for caching.

Caching reduces recovery times in the event of failure because RDDs only need to be recomputed starting from the cached RDDs. However, if you require a higher degree of in-process durability, consider one of the disk-based persistence options or a higher replication level—which increases the likelihood that a persisted replica of an RDD exists somewhere in the Spark cluster.

Checkpointing RDDs

Checkpointing saves data to a file. Unlike the disk-based persistence option just discussed, which deletes the persisted RDD data when the Spark driver program finishes, checkpointed data persists beyond the application and can be used by subsequent driver programs (or other programs).

Checkpointing eliminates the need for Spark to maintain RDD lineage, which can be problematic when the lineage gets quite long (such as with streaming or iterative processing applications). Long lineage typically leads to long recovery times and the possibility of a stack overflow.

Checkpointing data to a distributed filesystem (such as HDFS) provides additional storage fault tolerance as well. Checkpointing is expensive, however, so it should be implemented with some consideration as to when and how often you should checkpoint an RDD.

As with the caching and persistence options, checkpointing only happens after an action is called against an RDD to force computation (such as `count()`). If you wish to checkpoint, checkpointing must be requested before any action is requested against an RDD.

The methods associated with checkpointing are documented here:

setCheckpointDir()

Syntax:

```
SparkContext.setCheckpointDir()
```

The `setCheckpointDir` method sets the directory under which RDDs will be checkpointed. If you are running Spark on a Hadoop cluster, the directory must be a HDFS path.

checkpoint()

Syntax:

```
RDD.checkpoint()
```

The `checkpoint` method marks the RDD for checkpointing. It will be checkpointed upon the first action executed against the RDD and the files saved to the directory configured using the `setCheckpointDir` method. The `checkpoint` method must be called before any action is requested against the RDD.

After checkpointing is complete, the complete RDD lineage, including all references to the RDDs parent RDDs will be removed.

NOTE

You must specify the checkpoint directory using the `setCheckpointDir` method before attempting to checkpoint an RDD; otherwise, you will receive the following error:

```
org.apache.spark.SparkException:
Checkpoint directory has not been set in the SparkContext
```

The checkpoint directory is only valid for the current Spark Context, so you will need to execute `setCheckpointDir` for each separate Spark application. Additionally, the checkpoint directory should not be shared across multiple Spark applications.

isCheckpointed()

Syntax:

```
RDD.isCheckpointed()
```

The `isCheckpointed` function returns a Boolean response as to whether or not the RDD has been checkpointed.

getCheckpointFile()

Syntax:

```
RDD.getCheckpointFile()
```

The `getCheckpointFile` function returns the name of the file to which the RDD was checkpointed.

Listing 11.6 demonstrates the use of checkpointing.

LISTING 11.6   Checkpointing RDDs

```
sc.setCheckpointDir('file:///opt/spark/data/checkpoint')
doc = sc.textFile("file:///opt/spark/data/shakespeare.txt")
words = doc.flatMap(lambda x: x.split()) \
         .map(lambda x: (x,1)) \
         .reduceByKey(lambda x, y: x + y)
words.checkpoint()
words.count()
...
... Done checkpointing RDD to ..., new parent is RDD 8
33505
words.isCheckpointed()
True
words.getCheckpointFile()
u'file:/.../d7a8269e-cbed-422f-bf1a-87f3853bd218/rdd-6'
```

▼ TRY IT YOURSELF

Checkpointing RDDs

In this exercise, you will look at the impact checkpointing can have on an iterative routine. You can use any installation of Spark for this exercise.

1. You will be running a script in noninteractive mode and would like to suppress informational log messages. Spark uses log4j as its logging framework. To create a log4j profile to suppress noncritical messages, perform the following steps:

   a. Make a copy of the default log4j.properties template file as follows:

   ```
   cd /opt/spark/conf
   cp log4j.properties.template log4j.properties.erroronly
   ```

   b. Use a text editor (such as `vi` or `nano`) to open the newly created `log4j.properties.erroronly` file. Locate the following line:

   ```
   log4j.rootCategory=INFO, console
   ```

   c. Change the line to:

   ```
   log4j.rootCategory=ERROR, console
   ```

   and save the file.

2. Create a new PySpark script called `looping_test.py`, and copy and paste the code below into the file:

   ```python
   import sys
   from pyspark import SparkConf, SparkContext
   sc = SparkContext()
   sc.setCheckpointDir("file:///tmp/checkpointdir")
   rddofints = sc.parallelize([1,2,3,4,5,6,7,8,9,10])
   try:
       # this will create a very long lineage for rddofints
       for i in range(1000):
           rddofints = rddofints.map(lambda x: x+1)
           if i % 10 == 0:
               print("Looped " + str(i) + " times")
               #rddofints.checkpoint()
               rddofints.count()
   except Exception as e:
       print("Exception : " + str(e))
       print("RDD Debug String : ")
       print(rddofints.toDebugString())
       sys.exit()
   print("RDD Debug String : ")
   print(rddofints.toDebugString())
   ```

   Save the file locally

3. Execute the `looping_test.py` script using `spark-submit` (suppressing informational messages) as follows:

```
spark-submit \
--driver-java-options \
"-Dlog4j.configuration=log4j.properties.erroronly" \
looping_test.py
```

4. You should have seen an exception after a certain number of iterations. The exception will look something like the following:

PicklingError: Could not pickle object as excessively deep recursion required.

5. Now open the `looping_test.py` file again with a text editor and uncomment the following line:

```
#rddofints.checkpoint()
```

So the file should now read:

```
...
print("Looped " + str(i) + " times")
rddofints.checkpoint()
rddofints.count()
...
```

6. Execute the script again using the same command as in step 3.

7. You should now see that all 1,000 iterations have completed, thanks to periodically check-pointing the RDD. Furthermore, note the debug string printed after the routine:

```
(1) PythonRDD[301] at RDD at PythonRDD.scala:43 []
|  PythonRDD[298] at RDD at PythonRDD.scala:43 []
|  ReliableCheckpointRDD[300] at count at ...
```

Checkpointing, caching, and persistence are useful functions in Spark programming and can not only improve performance, but in some cases (as you have just seen) can be the difference between a program completing successfully or not.

Saving RDD Output

After you have processed a series of RDD transformations, the final step is often to save the final dataset to external storage, typically HDFS, S3, or a local filesystem. In this section, I will go through the various Spark actions to save RDDs externally.

External Storage Systems

Spark RDDs can be written back as files to most filesystems. These include local and NFS file systems; distributed file systems such as HDFS; cloud, block, or object storage systems such as S3 or Swift; and in-memory filesystems such as Alluxio/Tachyon, which I will discuss in the next section.

Distributed filesystems or block storage systems are often preferred as they naturally partition and distribute the data, enabling greater parallelism in the first (normally) "shared nothing" stage. This is why Spark is often accompanied by Hadoop.

Furthermore, Spark RDD can be written back to key value stores or NoSQL platforms such as Cassandra, HBase or Couchbase—which I discuss in more detail in **Hour 19, "Using Spark with NoSQL Systems."**

Storage Formats

Thus far you have seen how Spark RDDs can be saved to directories containing plain text files using the `saveAsTextFile` action. You also looked at saving Python serialized objects as Pickle files using the `saveAsPickleFile` action in **Hour 9, "Functional Programming with Python."** There are several other options when it comes to saving Spark RDDs as external datasets.

Before I discuss compression options, let's look again at the primary Spark action to save RDDs to text files on an external system.

saveAsTextFile()

Syntax:

```
RDD.saveAsTextFile(path, compressionCodecClass=None)
```

The `saveAsTextFile` method is the Spark action saves the RDD to a directory containing text files (with one file for each partition). The individual text file contain string representations of elements.

The `path` argument refers to a fully qualified path to the output directory, including the filesystem scheme. The `compressionCodecClass` argument specifies the codec to be used to write out the files in compressed format. The default behavior is not to compress text file output.

NOTE

The directory specified by the `path` argument to the `saveAsTextFile` must not exist when the Spark job is run. Because Spark assumes an immutable filesystem, it cannot overwrite an existing directory.

Compressed Storage Options

Spark (and Hadoop) include built-in support for compression and decompression of several compression formats. Support for compression and decompression is provided through libraries called *codecs*. Spark ships with codecs for the LZ4, LZF, and Snappy compression algorithms and formats. The LZ4, LZF, and Snappy formats were chosen as the preferred compression alternatives for Spark because they provide very fast, low CPU compression as well as because they are splittable compression formats.

Through the Hadoop compression codecs often available to Spark, programmers can also access common compression formats such as GZip and BZip.

CAUTION

Splittable versus Non-Splittable Compression Formats Revisited

In Hour 6, "Learning the Basics of Spark Programming with RDDs," I discussed splittable versus non-splittable compression formats in the context of external datasources from which to create RDDs. It is worthwhile reiterating the differences between the two formats and the performance penalties or advantages of choosing one over the other.

Splittable compression formats such as Snappy and LZO are compressed on block boundaries and include indexes so they can be processed independently (in parallel on different nodes). They also often sacrifice higher compression rates for lower CPU utilization (and thus faster throughput).

Non-splittable compression formats are more common as interchange formats (such as GZip). They typically get much better rates of compression but use much more CPU and take much longer during the compression process. The fact that they are non-splittable, however, means that they must be processed entirely on one node (because they cannot be split into blocks and processed in parallel).

As an example, if you were to create an RDD from a 30GB compressed Gzip archive on HDFS containing several text files files with an aggregate uncompressed size of 120GB, all blocks would need to be processed by a single Spark executor because blocks from the archive cannot be decompressed independently. As you can imagine, this will have a great impact on network IO and will most likely result in a stack overflow on the Spark worker processing the data.

Subject to understanding the potential performance impact at scale of using unsplittable compression types such as GZip, these formats can be useful for relatively small amounts of output data intended for end users. Listing 11.7 shows an example of using the GZip compression codec (through the Hadoop codec library) to save an RDD to compressed text files.

LISTING 11.7   Saving RDDs as Compressed Text Files Using the GZip Codec

```
doc = sc.textFile("file:///opt/spark/data/shakespeare.txt")
words = doc.flatMap(lambda x: x.split())
words.saveAsTextFile("file:///opt/spark/data/gzip",
                     "org.apache.hadoop.io.compress.GzipCodec")
# produces file: part-00000.gz
```

If the output files created are likely to be used for further processing (for instance, if they will serve as potential input for another Spark routine) then Snappy, LZ4, or LZF used with either the serialized object files or columnar storage formats I will discuss next are preferred approaches for compression.

Sequence Files

Sequence files are files containing serialized binary encoded key value pairs. Sequence files are commonly used in Hadoop MapReduce, particularly when the output of one job is the input to another job. Sequence files work seamlessly with Hadoop writable key and value types (efficient, compact, self-describing "wire transfer" formats). Sequence files are useful with Spark processing as well, for the same reasons.

As sequence files include the key and value types, if the definition of the key or value object changes, the file becomes unusable. The action used to save RDDs as sequence files is documented here:

saveAsSequenceFile()

Syntax:

```
RDD.saveAsSequenceFile(path, compressionCodecClass=None)
```

The saveAsSequenceFile method is the Spark action that saves the RDD to a directory containing Sequence Files consisting of uniform key value pairs. The keys are values implementing the org.apache.hadoop.io.Writable interface.

Pyrolite, a lightweight library enabling Java to interface with Python, is used to convert pickled Python RDD into RDD of Java objects. Keys and values of this Java RDD are converted to Writables and written out. The path and compressionCodecClass behave the same as the saveAstextFile method.

Listing 11.8 demonstrates the use of the saveAsSequenceFile method.

LISTING 11.8 Saving RDDs to Sequence Files

```
doc = sc.textFile("file:///opt/spark/data/shakespeare.txt")
words = doc.flatMap(lambda x: x.split()) \
          .keyBy(lambda x: x)
words.saveAsSequenceFile("file:///opt/spark/data/seqfiles")
```

If you intend on using sequence files in Hadoop, you should consider using the Hadoop file specific actions in Spark as these will provide you with more fine-grained control. I will discuss these actions next.

Hadoop Input and Output Formats

Hadoop input and output formats are used by Hadoop (Java) MapReduce to define how to handle files, including how to interpret records (or key value pairs) from the data in files. Common Hadoop input formats include the following:

▶ `TextInputFormat`

▶ `SequenceFileInputFormat`

▶ `KeyValueTextInputFormat`

The default input format for Hadoop is the `TextFileInputFormat`, which is used to derive key value pairs from plain text files. The key is the byte offset for the beginning of each line in the file, and the value is the line of text itself. This enables plain free text files to be used in MapReduce programs where a key is not naturally obvious.

The compression codecs discussed previously can also be used with Hadoop input and output formats. Also, Hadoop's built-in support for projects such as HBase (a distributed key value store built on HDFS) can be leveraged by Spark Hadoop file and dataset methods—I discuss this further in **Hour 19, "Using Spark with NoSQL Systems."**

The Spark actions used with Hadoop files are as follows:

saveAsHadoopFile()

Syntax:

```
RDD.saveAsHadoopFile(path,
                outputFormatClass,
                keyClass=None,
                valueClass=None,
                keyConverter=None,
                valueConverter=None,
                conf=None,
                compressionCodecClass=None)
```

The `saveAsHadoopFile` method outputs a key value pair RDD to a Hadoop file system (HDFS) using the original MapReduce API output formats.

You can distinguish the older MapReduce API from the newer API by the package names. The older or original MapReduce API names reference the *mapred* package, such as:

`org.apache.hadoop.mapred.TextOutputFormat`

The newer API uses the *mapreduce* package, for example:

`org.apache.hadoop.mapreduce.lib.output.TextOutputFormat`

The `outputFormatClass` argument specifies an `OutputFormat` Java class from the *new* MapReduce API. If you wish to use an `OutputFormat` class from the original API, you need to use the `saveAsNewAPIHadoopFile` method, which I will discuss next.

NOTE

Many Hadoop installations and distributions still maintain both the original MapReduce API and the newer API. This is not to be confused with the original and new MapReduce cluster and application resource management framework, often called MR1 and MR2/YARN respectively.

The important thing to note is that the files saved with the original API OutputFormats need to be accessed using Java applications using the original API.

The `keyClass` and `valueClass` arguments specify the Hadoop `Writable` or `WritableComparable` object classes (such as `IntWritable` or `Text`). If the key and value types are not specified, they will be inferred.

Python key and value objects in the RDD will be converted to Hadoop Java Writable types using the `org.apache.spark.api.python.JavaToWritableConverter` unless a specific converter class is specified using the `keyConverter` or `valueConverter` arguments.

The `conf` argument is applied on top of the base Hadoop conf associated with the SparkContext of the RDD to create a merged Hadoop MapReduce job configuration for saving the data. This is useful for configuration arguments associated with Hadoop OutputFormats, such as setting compression properties like specifying block, record, or file level compression.

Listing 11.9 demonstrates the use of the `saveAsHadoopFile` action to save an RDD as Snappy compressed sequence files.

LISTING 11.9 The saveAsHadoopFile Action

```
doc = sc.textFile("hdfs://localhost:8020/input/shakespeare.txt")
words = doc.flatMap(lambda x: x.split()) \
            .map(lambda x: (x,1)) \
            .reduceByKey(lambda x, y: x + y)
words.saveAsHadoopFile("hdfs://localhost:8020/output/hadoopcompseqfiles",
    outputFormatClass="org.apache.hadoop.mapred.SequenceFileOutputFormat",
    keyClass="org.apache.hadoop.io.Text",
    valueClass="org.apache.hadoop.io.IntWritable",
    keyConverter=None,
    valueConverter=None,
    conf=None,
    compressionCodecClass="org.apache.hadoop.io.compress.SnappyCodec")
```

`saveAsNewAPIHadoopFile()`

Syntax:

```
RDD.saveAsNewAPIHadoopFile(path,
                    outputFormatClass,
                    keyClass=None,
                    valueClass=None,
                    keyConverter=None,
                    valueConverter=None,
                    conf=None)
```

The `saveAsNewAPIHadoopFile` method operates exactly the same as the `saveAsHadoopFile` action, except that `saveAsNewAPIHadoopFile` uses the newer MapReduce APIs. Listing 11.10 shows the use of the `saveAsNewAPIHadoopFile` action.

Note that the `OutputFormat` class is different than the previous example using the original (old) MapReduce API. Also notice that the `compressionCodecClass` is not an argument. If you wish to use compression, this will need to be defined in the target `OutputFormat` class or Hadoop configuration or merged configuration using the `conf` argument.

LISTING 11.10   The saveAsNewAPIHadoopFile Action

```
cls = "org.apache.hadoop.mapreduce.lib.output.SequenceFileOutputFormat"
doc = sc.textFile("hdfs://localhost:8020/input/shakespeare.txt")
words = doc.flatMap(lambda x: x.split()) \
            .map(lambda x: (x,1)) \
            .reduceByKey(lambda x, y: x + y)
words.saveAsNewAPIHadoopFile("hdfs://localhost:8020/output/newAPIfiles",
    outputFormatClass=cls,
    keyClass="org.apache.hadoop.io.Text",
    valueClass="org.apache.hadoop.io.IntWritable",
    keyConverter=None,
    valueConverter=None,
    conf=None)
```

There are also related Spark methods called `saveAsHadoopDataset` and `saveAsNewAPI-HadoopDataset`. These actions are used to output RDDs to key value stores such as HBase. I will discuss these methods in **Hour 19** when I cover using Spark with NoSQL platforms.

Columnar and Other Storage Formats

There are several other storage formats available, including columnar storage formats such as Parquet and ORC, as well as JSON storage options, which I will discuss in detail in **Hour 13**, "**Using SQL with Spark.**" These can be quite useful if you are using SQL as a primary access method or using Spark in tandem with projects such as Hive, Impala, or HAWQ.

Introduction to Alluxio (Tachyon)

Alluxio is an open source, distributed, in-memory storage platform that was developed at the UC Berkeley's AMPLab, the same institution that founded the Spark and Mesos projects. In fact, many of the same individual early contributors to the Spark project were also founding contributors to the Alluxio project. Let's look at the beginnings of Alluxio and its design goals.

Alluxio Background

Alluxio—or Tachyon, as it was originally named when it was first released in 2013—was designed to address the inherent bottlenecks in analytics pipelines where data needed to be shared (for example, output from an application or data resulting from a shuffle operation).

Moreover, as you have seen in this hour, in-memory persistence or caching enables much faster access, but it is not durable. Executor or worker failure results in cache loss. Also, "on heap" memory persistence—that is, memory persisted on the executor JVM from cached RDDs—can be inefficient because data may be duplicated and because large Java heaps can result in an excessive garbage collection (GC)–Java process to reclaim memory occupied by objects no longer in use by the program.

Alluxio addresses these issues and serves as an integrated companion storage solution for Spark by enabling reliable, "memory speed" data-sharing between processes (with executors on different workers in the same cluster or even processes from different clusters).

Alluxio provides reliability through its distributed architecture and through its fault-tolerance capability to recompute data from lineage (sound familiar?).

The whitepaper "Tachyon: Memory Throughput I/O for Cluster Computing Frameworks" released by AMPLab establishes the framework for Alluxio. This is a highly recommended read if you are considering using Alluxio with Spark. You can find this whitepaper at http://www.cs.berkeley.edu/~haoyuan/papers/2013_ladis_tachyon.pdf

Alluxio Architecture

Alluxio operates as a cluster of worker nodes orchestrated by a workflow manager process running on a master node. The master node tracks lineage and data locations for data persisted in the memory-centric storage system.

Alluxio clusters can be run in one of two modes: *single master mode* or *fault-tolerant mode*.

Single master has only one master node process. This is the simplest mode in which to run Alluxio, but because the master is a single point of failure, this mode is not recommended for production or SLA bound systems. Fault-tolerant mode has two or more masters running in an active/passive configuration using a quorum of Zookeeper instances to control failover of the masters in the case of failure. Zookeeper is an Apache project used to share state across different systems. It is also used by projects such as HBase.

Alluxio uses RAM disks on the worker nodes to manage data persisted in the cluster. Figure 11.4 shows a high level architectural overview of a fault tolerant Alluxio cluster with three worker nodes.

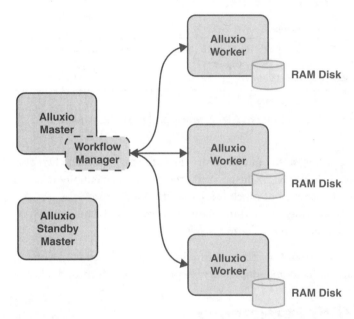

FIGURE 11.4
Alluxio cluster architecture.

Alluxio's architecture enables:

▶ Memory speed data sharing and access between nodes/processes

▶ Fault-tolerance for failed Spark executors or workers

▶ No in-memory duplication or excessive garbage collection

Alluxio as a Filesystem

Alluxio is exposed as a filesystem with the scheme *alluxio*. This allows it to be used for reads, writes, and metadata operations just as any other local or distributed filesystem. Be aware, however, that Alluxio is an immutable store, because the underlying storage systems integrated with Alluxio (such as HDFS) are immutable. So you should not try to use Alluxio as a general purpose updateable file system.

Alluxio has a file system API and shell commands to explore and interact with the filesystem. I will focus on using Alluxio with Spark specifically in this hour, but you can find more information about alternative API and shell access from the Alluxio project website (www.alluxio.org/).

Listing 11.11 demonstrates using Alluxio as a source and target filesystem for a Spark application. This particular example works with a single master mode Alluxio cluster.

LISTING 11.11   Alluxio Filesystem Access Using Spark

```
sc.hadoopConfiguration.set("fs.alluxio.impl", "alluxio.hadoop.FileSystem")
data = sc.textFile("alluxio://masternode:19998/input")
datasaveAsTextFile("alluxio://masternode:19998/output")
```

To use Alluxio in fault-tolerant mode (with multiple masters), you simply use the scheme *alluxio-ft://* in place of *alluxio://*.

Alluxio can not only be used as a persistent store but also, more importantly, as a cache layer or buffer for long-term storage such as S3, HDFS, NFS, Gluster, and others, which essentially use SSD or spinning disk and are inherently slower but much less expensive for storing large amounts of data for long periods. Alluxio—being a virtual filesystem—can also be backed by physical disk, although it is intended to be memory-centric.

Alluxio, as a reliable, persistent, and performant distributed virtual filesystem, can be used with many other projects in addition to Spark, including MapReduce, Impala, HBase, Flink, and others.

Alluxio for Off Heap RDD Persistence

Alluxio can also be used as off-heap cache or persistence for Spark RDDs. This enables multiple executors to share the same pool of memory, reducing duplication. Using Alluxio as off-heap persistence for RDDs also reduces garbage collection requirements and provides additional fault-tolerance in the case of lost or crashed Spark executors (because partitions from lost executors would not need to be reconstituted because they otherwise would be with on-heap persistence).

Listing 11.12 shows an example of using Alluxio for off-heap memory persistence with Spark.

LISTING 11.12   Alluxio as Off Heap Memory for RDD Persistence

```
sc.hadoopConfiguration.set("fs.alluxio.impl", "alluxio.hadoop.FileSystem")
data = sc.textFile("alluxio://masternode:19998/input")
data.persist(StorageLevel.OFF_HEAP)
```

Other Alluxio Features and Usages

Alluxio is a generalized system, so it offers many more benefits in addition to its seamless integration with Spark. Alluxio can be used as a distributed in-memory key value store. Alluxio also exposes an "UnderFileSystem" or "UnderStore" interface that enables storage systems such as S3, Swift, and HDFS to integrate with Alluxio. You can also configure Alluxio with tiered storage so that you can back primary storage in memory with SSD and spinning disk, keeping more frequently used data in faster storage media. These are some of the many benefits of Alluxio, but because this project is a topic on its own, I would encourage you to find more information from the Alluxio project website.

Summary

In this hour, you revisited the lifecycle of an RDD and explored how every RDD keeps track of its lineage in order to provide fault tolerance. The default behavior is for an RDD to execute its entire lineage each time it is evaluated. However, this can be affected by using the caching, persistence, and checkpointing.

I discussed caching and persistence as a method for increasing performance of RDDs, which are reused multiple times in an application, as well as being a method to reduce recovery times in the event of a failure (of an executor or a worker). You looked at all of the available storage options for persisted RDDs, including the memory and disk options and combinations thereof.

Serialization of persisted objects can provide additional read performance and can reduce the size of objects persisted in memory or on disk. Replication of persisted RDD partitions can provide additional fault tolerance and reduce recovery times.

I discussed checkpointing as a means to save data to a filesystem (HDFS or others), allowing Spark to remove the lineage from an RDD altogether. This is especially useful for periodic saving of state for iterative algorithms where elongated lineage can make recovery very expensive.

You looked further at the methods available in the Spark API to save RDD results as external file-based datasets that you will use regularly. And finally, I introduced Alluxio (formerly known as Tachyon) as a distributed in-memory store that can be used for persistence of RDDs to off heap memory or as an in-memory file system or cache layer.

Q&A

Q. What is the main benefit of replicating persisted RDD partitions to multiple nodes?

A. Replication lowers the likelihood that an RDD will need to be recomputed. Because the same RDD partition data is available on multiple nodes, node failure does not automatically require partition reevaluation, which it would require otherwise.

Q. What is the main benefit gained from checkpointing in a recursive machine learning program?

A. Checkpointing saves RDD data externally (typically to HDFS on Hadoop systems). Because the checkpointed file is considered to be a durable copy of the RDD, the RDD lineage can be removed. This is especially useful in the case of iterative algorithms that can be run hundreds of thousands of times. Periodic checkpointing can significantly reduce recovery times and avoid a potential stack overflow.

Q. What is Alluxio and what can it be used for with Spark?

A. Alluxio (formerly known as Tachyon) is a fault-tolerant distributed in-memory storage system that can be used with Spark to persist RDDs (offering more scale than conventional on heap memory persistence). Alluxio can also be used as an in memory filesystem to load external datasets into Spark RDDs or to save RDD output.

Workshop

The workshop contains quiz questions and exercises to help you solidify your understanding of the material covered. Try to answer all questions before looking at the "Answers" section that follows.

Quiz

1. True or false: Spark can save output directly to Gzip archives.

2. The `MEMORY_AND_DISK_SER` storage level specifies what storage options for an RDD?

    A. In memory (off-heap), on disk, serialized

    B. In memory, on disk, serialized

    C. In memory, on disk, serialized, and replicated

3. What do the `OFF_HEAP` storage level constant and associated `useOffHeap` storage flag refer to?

4. **True or false:** Caching can use disk if memory is not available.

Answers

1. **True.** Gzip archives can be created by the `saveAsTextFile` action by specifying `compressionCodecClass` as the Gzip codec.

2. **B.**

3. Alluxio (Tachyon).

4. **False.** Caching is memory only. Persistence can be configured to use disk, however.

HOUR 12
Advanced Spark Programming

What You'll Learn in This Hour:

▶ Shared variables in Spark—broadcast variables and accumulators
▶ Partitioning and repartitioning of Spark RDDs
▶ Processing RDD data with external programs

In this hour, I will cover the additional programming tools at your disposal with the Spark API, including broadcast variables and accumulators as shared variables across different workers. I will also dive deeper into the important topic of Spark partitioning. I will show you how to use external programs and scripts to process data in Spark RDDs in a Spark managed lineage. This hour will complete your toolbox of transformations and actions available in the core Spark API.

Broadcast Variables

Broadcast variables are read-only variables set by the Spark Driver program and are made available to the worker nodes in a Spark cluster, thereby making them available to any tasks running on executors on the workers. Broadcast variables are read-only after they are set by the driver. Broadcast variables are shared across workers using an efficient peer-to-peer sharing protocol based on BitTorrent; this enables greater scalability than simply pushing variables directly to executor processes from the Spark driver. Figure 12.1 demonstrates how broadcast variables are initialized, disseminated among workers, and accessed by nodes within tasks.

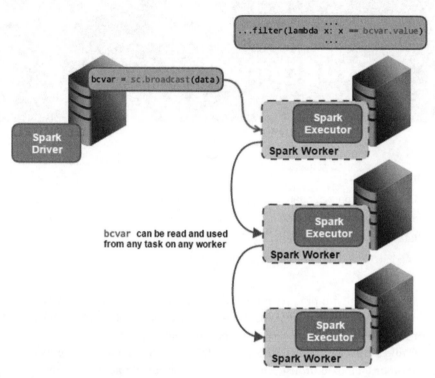

FIGURE 12.1
Spark broadcast variables.

The "Performance and Scalability of Broadcast in Spark" whitepaper that can be found at www.cs.berkeley.edu/~agearh/cs267.sp10/files/mosharaf-spark-bc-report-spring10.pdf documents the BitTorrent broadcast method as well as the other broadcast mechanisms considered for Spark, which is worth a read.

Broadcast Variable Creation and Usage

Broadcast variables are created under a SparkContext and then can be accessed as an object in the context of the Spark application. Syntax for creating and accessing broadcast variables is described here:

broadcast()

Syntax:

```
SparkContext.broadcast(value)
```

The broadcast method creates an instance of a Broadcast object within the specific SparkContext. The value is the object that is to be serialized and encapsulated in the Broadcast object; this could be any valid Python object. After they're created, these variables are available to all tasks running in the application. Listing 12.1 shows an example of the broadcast method.

LISTING 12.1 The Broadcast Method

```
>>> stations = sc.broadcast({'83':'Mezes Park', '84':'Ryland Park'})
>>> stations
<pyspark.broadcast.Broadcast object at 0x…>
```

Broadcast variables can also be created from the contents of a file (either on a local, network, or distributed filesystem). Listing 12.2 shows an example of how to do this.

LISTING 12.2 Creating a Broadcast Variable from a File

```
# stations.csv data:
# ...
# 83,Mezes Park,37.491269,-122.236234,15,Redwood City,2/20/2014
# 84,Ryland Park,37.342725,-121.895617,15,San Jose,4/9/2014
# ...
>>> stationsfile = '/opt/spark/data/stations.csv'
>>> stationsdata = dict(map(lambda x: (x[0],x[1]), \
                    map(lambda x: x.split(','), \
                    open(stationsfile))))
>>> stations = sc.broadcast(stationsdata)
>>> stations.value["83"]
'Mezes Park'
```

In Listing 12.2, you loaded a csv file (stations.csv) and created a dictionary of name value pairs consisting of the station id and the station name. You can then access this dictionary from within any map or filter RDD operations within the SparkContext.

When initialized, broadcast variable objects have the following methods that can be called within the SparkContext:

value()
Syntax:

    Broadcast.value()

You have already seen the use of the `value` function to return the value from the broadcast variable; in the example, the `value` was a dict (or map) that could access values from the map by their given key.

The `value` function can be used within a lambda function in a map or filter operation within your Spark program.

unpersist()

Syntax:

```
Broadcast.unpersist(blocking=False)
```

Similar to our use of RDD method with the same name, the Broadcast member method `unpersist` is used to remove a broadcast variable from memory on all of the workers in the cluster where it was present.

The Boolean `blocking` argument specifies whether this operation should block until the variable is unpersisted from all nodes or whether this can be an asynchronous, nonblocking operation. If you require memory released immediately, set this argument to `True`.

An example of the `unpersist` method is provided in Listing 12.3.

LISTING 12.3   The unpersist() Method

```
>>> stations = sc.broadcast({'83':'Mezes Park', '84':'Ryland Park'})
>>> stations.unpersist()
```

There are also several Spark configuration options relating to broadcast variables, which are described in Table 12.1. Typically, these can be left at their default settings, but it is useful to know about them.

TABLE 12.1   Spark Configuration Options Relating to Broadcast Variables

Configuration Option	Description
spark.broadcast.compress	Specifies whether to compress broadcast variables before transferring them to workers. Defaults to `True` (recommended).
spark.broadcast.factory	Specifies which broadcast implementation to use. Defaults to `TorrentBroadcastFactory`.
spark.broadcast.blockSize	Size of each block of the broadcast variable (used by `TorrentBroadcastFactory`). Defaults to 4MB.
spark.broadcast.port	Port for the driver's HTTP broadcast server to listen on. Defaults to random.

Advantages of Broadcast Variables

Why are broadcast variables useful or even required in some cases? As I had discussed when I covered joins, cogrouping, and other multiset operations in **Hour 10, "Working with the Spark API (Transformations and Actions),"** it is often necessary to combine two datasets together to produce a resultant dataset. This can be achieved in multiple ways.

Consider two associated datasets, *stations* (a relatively small lookup data set) and *status* (a large eventful data source). These two datasets can be joined on a natural key, *station_id*. You could...

1. Simply join the two datasets as RDDs directly in your Spark application, as shown in Listing 12.4.

LISTING 12.4 Joining Lookup Data Using an RDD join()

```
# stations.csv data:
# ...
# 10,7,8,"2014-12-30 15:37:02"
# ...
status = sc.textFile('s3://sty-spark/.../status.csv') \
            .map(lambda x: x.split(',')) \
            .keyBy(lambda x: x[0])
stations = sc.textFile('s3://sty-spark/.../stations.csv') \
            .map(lambda x: x.split(',')) \
            .keyBy(lambda x: x[0])
joined = status.join(stations) \
    .map(lambda x: (x[1][0][3],x[1][1][1],x[1][0][1],x[1][0][2])) \
    .take(3)
[("2015-01-09 17:02:02", 'Embarcadero at Sansome', '7', '8'),
 ("2014-09-01 00:00:03", 'Embarcadero at Sansome', '7', '8'),
 ("2014-09-01 00:01:02", 'Embarcadero at Sansome', '7', '8')]
```

This could (and most likely will) result in an expensive shuffle operation.

2. Better: Set a table variable in the driver for *stations;* this will then be available as a runtime variable for Spark tasks implementing map operations (eliminating the requirement for a shuffle), as shown in Listing 12.5.

LISTING 12.5 Joining Lookup Data Using a Driver Variable

```
stationsfile = 'stations.csv'
sdata = dict(map(lambda x: (x[0],x[1]), \
                 map(lambda x: x.split(','), \
                 open(stationsfile))))
status = sc.textFile('s3://sty-spark/.../status.csv') \
            .map(lambda x: x.split(',')) \
            .keyBy(lambda x: x[0])
```

```
status.map(lambda x: (x[1][3], sdata[x[0]], x[1][1], x[1][2])) \
    .take(3)
#[("2015-01-09 17:02:02", 'Embarcadero at Sansome', '7', '8'),
# ("2014-09-01 00:00:03", 'Embarcadero at Sansome', '7', '8'),
# ("2014-09-01 00:01:02", 'Embarcadero at Sansome', '7', '8')]
```

This works and is better in most cases than option 1; however, it lacks scalability. In this case, the variable is part of a closure within the function it is being referenced by. This may result in unnecessary (and less efficient) transfer and duplication of data on the worker nodes.

3. Best: Initialize a broadcast variable for the smaller *stations* table. This will use peer-to-peer replication to make the variable available to all workers, and the single copy can be used by all tasks on all executors belonging to an application running on the worker. Then use the variable in your map operations similar to option 2. An example of this is provided in Listing 12.6.

LISTING 12.6　Joining Lookup Data Using a Broadcast Variable

```
stationsfile = 'stations.csv'
sdata = dict(map(lambda x: (x[0],x[1]), \
            map(lambda x: x.split(','), \
            open(stationsfile))))
stations = sc.broadcast(sdata)
status = sc.textFile('s3://sty-spark/.../status.csv') \
            .map(lambda x: x.split(',')) \
            .keyBy(lambda x: x[0])
status.map(lambda x: (x[1][3], stations.value[x[0]], x[1][1], x[1][2])) \
    .take(3)
#[("2015-01-09 17:02:02", 'Embarcadero at Sansome', '7', '8'),
# ("2014-09-01 00:00:03", 'Embarcadero at Sansome', '7', '8'),
# ("2014-09-01 00:01:02", 'Embarcadero at Sansome', '7', '8')]
```

As you can see from the above scenario, using broadcast variables is an efficient method for sharing data at runtime between processes running on different nodes of your Spark cluster. Broadcast variables

▶ Eliminate the need for a shuffle operation.

▶ Use an efficient and scalable peer-to-peer distribution mechanism.

▶ Replicate data once per worker (as opposed to replicating once per task—there may be thousands of tasks in a Spark application).

▶ Can be reused multiple times by many tasks.

▶ Are serialized objects, so they can be read efficiently.

Accumulators

Another type of shared variables in Spark are accumulators. Unlike broadcast variables, accumulators can be updated; more specifically, they are numeric values that can be incremented. You can think of them as counters that can be used in a number of ways in Spark programming. Accumulators allow you to aggregate multiple values while your program is running.

Accumulators are set by the driver program and updated by executors running tasks within the respective Spark Context. The final value from the accumulator can then be read back by the driver, typically at the end of the program.

Accumulators are updated only once per successfully completed task in a Spark application. Worker nodes send the updates to the accumulator back to the driver, which is the only process that can read the accumulator value. Accumulators can use integer or float values. Listing 12.7 and Figure 12.2 demonstrate how accumulators are created, updated, and read.

LISTING 12.7   **Creating and Accessing Accumulators**

```
acc = sc.accumulator(0)
def addone(x):
   global acc
   acc += 1
   return x + 1
myrdd=sc.parallelize([1,2,3,4,5])
myrdd.map(lambda x: addone(x)).collect()
[2, 3, 4, 5, 6]
print("records processed: " + str(acc.value))
records processed: 5
```

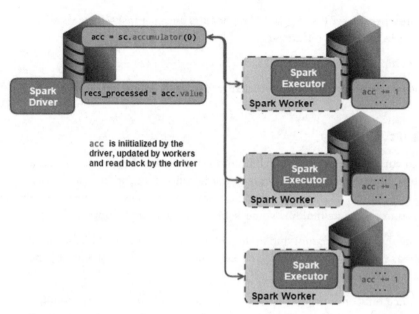

FIGURE 12.2
Accumulators.

Using Accumulators

From a programming standpoint, accumulators are very straightforward. The functions related to accumulators in Spark programming are documented here:

accumulator()

Syntax:

```
SparkContext.accumulator(value, accum_param=None)
```

The `accumulator` method creates an instance of an Accumulator object within the specific Spark Context and initializes with a given initial value specified by the `value` argument. The `accum_param` argument is used to define custom accumulators, which I will discuss shortly.

value()

Syntax:

```
Accumulator.value()
```

The `value` method retrieves the accumulator's value. This method is only usable in the driver program.

Custom Accumulators

Standard accumulators created in a Spark Context support primitive numeric data types including int and float. *Custom accumulators* can be used to perform aggregate operations on variables of types other than scalar numeric values. Custom accumulators are created using the `AccumulatorParam` helper object. The only requirement is that the operations performed are associative and commutative (meaning the order and sequence of operation is irrelevant).

A common use of custom accumulators is to accumulate vectors as either lists or dicts. Conceptually, however, the same principle applies in a non-mathematical context to non-numeric operations, as when, for instance, you create a custom accumulator to concatenate string values.

To use custom accumulators, you need to define a custom class that extends the `AccumulatorParam` class. The class needs to include two specific member functions: `addInPlace`, which is used to operate against two objects of the custom accumulators data type and to return a new value, and `zero`, which provides a "zero value" for the type, such as, for instance, an empty map for a map type .

Listing 12.8 shows an example of a custom accumulator used to sum vectors as a Python dict.

LISTING 12.8   Custom Accumulators

```
from pyspark import AccumulatorParam
class VectorAccumulatorParam(AccumulatorParam):
   def zero(self, value):
      dict1={}
      for i in range(0,len(value)):
         dict1[i]=0
      return dict1
   def addInPlace(self, val1, val2):
      for i in val1.keys():
         val1[i] += val2[i]
      return val1

rdd1=sc.parallelize([{0: 0.3, 1: 0.8, 2: 0.4}, {0: 0.2, 1: 0.4, 2: 0.2}])
vector_acc = sc.accumulator({0: 0, 1: 0, 2: 0}, VectorAccumulatorParam())

def mapping_fn(x):
   global vector_acc
   vector_acc += x
   # do some other rdd processing...

rdd1.foreach(mapping_fn)
print vector_acc.value
# {0: 0.50, 1: 1.20, 2: 0.60}
```

Uses for Accumulators

Accumulators are typically used for operational purposes, such as, for instance, counting the number of records processed or tracking the number of malformed records. They can also be used for notional counts of different types of records; an example would be a count of different response codes discovered during the mapping of log events.

In some cases, you can use accumulators for processing within an application, we will do this in our next Try-It-Yourself exercise.

CAUTION

Potential for Erroneous Results in Accumulators

If accumulators are used in transformations (for instance, when calling accumulators to perform add in place operations to calculate results inside a `map` operation), the results may be erroneous. Stage retries or speculative execution can cause accumulator values to be counted more than once, resulting in an incorrect count.

If absolute correctness is required, you should only use accumulators within actions computed by the Spark Driver, such as the `foreach` action. If you are looking only for notional or indicative counts on very large datasets, then it is OK to update accumulators in transformations. This behavior may be changed in future releases of Spark; for now, this is just a Caveat Emptor.

▼ TRY IT YOURSELF

Using Broadcast Variables and Accumulators

In this exercise, you will calculate the average word length from words in our Shakespeare text. You will remove known stop words (such as a, and, or, the, and so on) using a broadcast variable. You will then compute the averages using accumulators.

You can find the data for this exercise in the `shakespeare` and `stopwords` folders in the `s3://sty-spark` bucket.

1. Open a `pyspark` shell:

   ```
   $ pyspark
   ```

2. Import the `stop-word-list.csv` data from S3 using the https link. This is a comma-delimited list of known English stop words. You will use the built-in `urllib2` Python module to read the data, then convert the data into a Python list using the `split()` function:

   ```
   import urllib2
   stopwordsurl = "https://s3.amazonaws.com/sty-spark/stopwords/stop-word-list.csv"
   data = urllib2.urlopen(stopwordsurl).read()
   stopwordslist = data.split(",")
   ```

3. Create a broadcast variable for the `stopwordslist`:

```
stopwords = sc.broadcast(stopwordslist)
```

4. Initialize accumulators for the cumulative word count and cumulative total length of all words:

```
word_count = sc.accumulator(0)
total_len = sc.accumulator(0.0)
```

You created `total_len` as a float because you will use this as the numerator in a division operation later and you will want to keep the precision in the result.

5. Create a function to accumulate word count and the total word length:

```
def add_values(word,word_count,total_len):
    word_count += 1
    total_len += len(word)
```

6. Create an RDD by loading the text document, tokenizing and normalizing all text in the document, and filtering stop words using our `stopwords` broadcast variable:

```
words = sc.textFile('s3n://sty-spark/shakespeare/') \
    .flatMap(lambda line: line.split()) \
    .map(lambda x: x.lower()) \
    .filter(lambda x: x not in stopwords.value)
```

If you dont have AWS access, you can use the link below to download the file to your local Spark machine and reference this locally using the *file://* scheme.

https://s3.amazonaws.com/sty-spark/shakespeare/shakespeare.txt

7. Use the `foreach` action to iterate through the resultant RDD and call your accumulation function:

```
words.foreach(lambda x: add_values(x, word_count, total_len))
```

8. Calculate the average word length from your accumulator shared variables and display the final result:

```
avgwordlen = total_len.value/word_count.value
print("Total Number of Words: " + str(word_count.value))
# Total Number of Words: 966958
print("Average Word Length: " + str(avgwordlen))
# Average Word Length: 3.60872240573
```

9. Save the entire code below into a new Python script named `avgwordlen.py`:

```
from pyspark import SparkContext
sc = SparkContext()

# read stopwords list into broadcast variable
import urllib2
stopwordsurl = "https://s3.amazonaws.com/sty-spark/stopwords/stop-word-list.csv"
```

```
data = urllib2.urlopen(stopwordsurl).read()
stopwordslist = data.split(",")
stopwords = sc.broadcast(stopwordslist)

# initialize accumulators
word_count = sc.accumulator(0)
total_len = sc.accumulator(0.0)

# define function to increment word count and total length
def add_values(word,word_count,total_len):
    word_count += 1
    total_len += len(word)

# load document, tokenize text and filter stopwords
words = sc.textFile('s3n://sty-spark/shakespeare/') \
    .flatMap(lambda line: line.split()) \
    .map(lambda x: x.lower()) \
    .filter(lambda x: x not in stopwords.value)

# iterate through result set and increment accumulators
words.foreach(lambda x: add_values(x, word_count, total_len))

# calculate average word length
avgwordlen = total_len.value/word_count.value

# display result
print("Total Number of Words: " + str(word_count.value))
print("Average Word Length: " + str(avgwordlen))
```

10. Use `spark-submit` to run the average word length Spark program:

```
$ spark-submit avgwordlen.py
```

Partitioning and Repartitioning

Partitioning is integral to Spark processing in most cases. Effective partitioning can improve application performance by orders of magnitude. Conversely, inefficient partitioning can result in programs failing to complete (producing, for example, executor-out-of-memory errors for excessively large partitions).

I'll recap what we know about RDD partitions, and then I will discuss API methods that can effect partitions or access data within partitions more effectively.

Partitioning Overview

The number of partitions to create as a result of an RDD transformation is usually configurable. There are some default behaviors you should be aware of, however, which are

▶ Spark will create an RDD partition per block when using HDFS (typically the size of a block in HDFS is 128MB), as in, for instance:

```
myrdd = sc.textFile("hdfs:///dir/filescontaining10blocks")
myrdd.getNumPartitions()
10
```

▶ Shuffle operations such as the "ByKey" operations, groupByKey, reduceByKey, and other operations in which the numPartitions value is not supplied as an argument to the method will result in a number of partitions equal to the spark.default.parallelism configuration value. For example:

```
# with spark.default.parallelism=4
myrdd = sc.textFile("hdfs:///dir/filescontaining10blocks")
mynewrdd = myrdd.flatMap(lambda x: x.split()) \
    .map(lambda x:(x,1)) \
    .reduceByKey(lambda x, y: x + y)
mynewrdd.getNumPartitions()
4
```

▶ If spark.default.parallelism is not set, the number of partitions created by a transformation will be equal to the highest number of partitions defined by an upstream RDD in the current RDDs lineage. For instance:

```
# with spark.default.parallelism not set
myrdd = sc.textFile("hdfs:///dir/filescontaining10blocks")
mynewrdd = myrdd.flatMap(lambda x: x.split()) \
    .map(lambda x:(x,1)) \
    .reduceByKey(lambda x, y: x + y)
mynewrdd.getNumPartitions()
10
```

▶ The default Partitioner class used by Spark is the HashPartitioner. The HashPartitioner hashes all keys with a deterministic hashing function and then uses this key hash to create (usually approximately) equal buckets. The aim is to disperse data evenly across the specified number of partitions based on the key.

▶ Some Spark transformations, such as the filter transformation, do not allow you to change the partitioning behavior of the resultant RDD. For example, if we applied a filter function to an RDD with four partitions, this would result in a new, filtered RDD with four partitions, using the same partitioning scheme as the original RDD (that is, hash partitioned).

Although the default behavior is normally acceptable, in some circumstances it can lead to inefficiencies. I will discuss some of these circumstances and the tools Spark provides to address these potential issues.

Controlling Partitions

There are issues at both ends of the spectrum when it comes to answering the question "How many partitions should an RDD have?" Having too few, very large partitions could result in out-of-memory issues on your executors. Having too many small partitions is sub-optimal because too many tasks are spawned for trivial input sets. A mix of large and small partitions can result in speculative execution occurring needlessly (if this is enabled).

Consider the scenario in Figure 12.3.

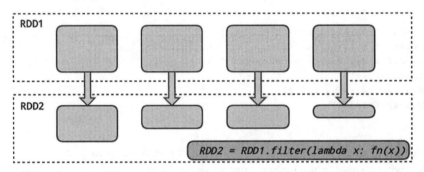

FIGURE 12.3
Skewed partitions.

The `filter` operation creates a new partition for every input partition (on a one to one basis) with only records that meet the filter condition. This can result in some partitions having significantly less data than others, which can lead to bad outcomes, such as data skewing, speculative execution, and sub-optimal performance, in subsequent stages.

In such cases, you can use one of the repartitioning methods in the Spark API; these include `partitionBy`, `coalesce`, `repartition`, and `repartitionAndSortWithinPartitions`, which I will detail shortly.

These functions take a partitioned input RDD and create a new RDD with *n* partitions; *n* could be more or less than the original number of partitions. Take the example from Figure 12.3. In Figure 12.4, I apply a `repartition` function to consolidate my four unevenly distributed partitions to two "evenly" distributed partitions (using the `HashPartitioner` by default).

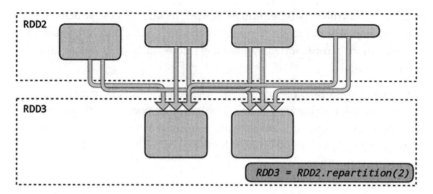

FIGURE 12.4
The repartition function.

TIP

Determining the Optimal Number of Partitions

Often, determining the optimal number of partitions involves experimenting with different values until you find the point of diminishing returns (the point at which each additional partition starts to degrade performance). As a starting point, a simple axiom is to use two times the number of cores in your cluster (that is, two times the aggregate amount of cores across all worker nodes). I will discuss this further in **Hour 24, "Improving Spark Performance."**

Repartitioning Functions

The main functions used to repartition RDDs are documented here:

partitionBy()

Syntax:

```
RDD.partitionBy(numPartitions, partitionFunc=portable_hash)
```

The partitionBy method returns a new RDD containing the same data as the input RDD, but with the number of partitions specified by the numPartitions argument, using the *portable_hash* function (HashPartitioner) by default. An example of partitionBy is shown in Listing 12.9.

LISTING 12.9 The partitionBy Function

```
kvrdd = sc.parallelize([(1,'A'),(2,'B'),(3,'C'),(4,'D')],4)
kvrdd.partitionBy(2).getNumPartitions()
2
```

The `partitionBy` function is also called by other functions, such as `sortByKey`, which calls `partitionBy` using the `rangePartitioner` instead of the `portable_hash` function. The `rangePartitioner` partitions records sorted by their key into equally sized ranges; this is an alternative to hash partitioning.

This `partitionBy` transformation is also a useful function for implementing your own custom partitioner, such as a function to bucket web logs into monthly partitions. Your custom partition function must take a key as input and must return a number between zero and the `numPartitions` specified; this return value is then used by the `partitionBy` function to direct the elements to their target partition.

repartition()
Syntax:

> `RDD.repartition(numPartitions)`

The `repartition` method returns a new RDD with the same data as the input RDD, consisting of exactly the number of partitions specified by the `numPartitions` argument. The `repartition` method may require a shuffle, and, unlike `partitionBy`, it has no option to change the partitioner (or partitioning function). The `repartition` method also allows you to create more partitions in the target RDD than existed in the input RDD. Listing 12.10 shows an example of the `repartition` function.

LISTING 12.10 The repartition Function

```
kvrdd = sc.parallelize([(1,'A'),(2,'B'),(3,'C'),(4,'D')],4)
kvrdd.repartition(2).getNumPartitions()
2
```

coalesce()
syntax:

> `RDD.coalesce(numPartitions, shuffle=False)`

The `coalesce` method returns a new RDD consisting of the number of partitions specified by the `numPartitions` argument. The `coalesce` method also allows you to control whether the repartitioning triggers a shuffle using the Boolean `shuffle` argument. The operation `coalesce(n, shuffle=True)` is functionally equivalent to to `repartition(n)`.

However, `coalesce` is an optimized implementation of `repartition`; unlike `repartition`, `coalesce` gives you more control over the shuffle behavior and, in many cases, allows you to avoid data movement. Also, unlike `repartition`, `coalesce` lets you only to *decrease* the number of target partitions from the number of partitions in your input RDD.

Listing 12.11 demonstrates the use of the `coalesce` function with the `shuffle` argument set to `False`.

LISTING 12.11   The coalesce Function

```
kvrdd = sc.parallelize([(1,'A'),(2,'B'),(3,'C'),(4,'D')],4)
kvrdd.coalesce(2, shuffle=False).getNumPartitions()
2
```

repartitionAndSortWithinPartitions()

Syntax:

```
RDD.repartitionAndSortWithinPartitions(numPartitions=None,
                partitionFunc=portable_hash,
                ascending=True,
                keyfunc=<lambda function>)
```

The `repartitionAndSortWithinPartitions` method repartitions the input RDD into the number of partitions directed by the `numPartitions` argument and is partitioned according to the function specified by the `partitionFunc` argument. Within each resulting partition, records are sorted by their keys, as defined by the `keyfunc` argument, in the sort order determined by the `ascending` argument.

The `repartitionAndSortWithinPartitions` method is commonly used to implement a *secondary sort*. The sorting capability for key value pair RDDs is normally based upon an arbitrary key hash or a range; this becomes more challenging with key value pairs with composite keys, such as, for example, $((k_1, k_2), v)$. If you wanted to sort on k_1 first and then within a partition sort the k_2 values for each k_1, this would involve a secondary sort.

Listing 12.12 demonstrates the use of the `repartitionAndSortWithinPartitions` method to perform a secondary sort on a key value pair RDD with a composite key. The first part of the key is grouped in separate partitions; I then sort the second part of the key in descending order. Note that I am using a function called `glom` to inspect partitions; I will discuss this function shortly.

LISTING 12.12   The repartitionAndSortWithinPartitions Function

```
kvrdd = sc.parallelize([((1,99),'A'),((1,101),'B'),
                        ((2,99),'C'),((2,101),'D')],2)
kvrdd.glom().collect()
[
[((1, 99), 'A'), ((1, 101), 'B')],
[((2, 99), 'C'), ((2, 101), 'D')]
]
kvrdd2 = kvrdd.repartitionAndSortWithinPartitions( \
            numPartitions=2,
            ascending=False,
            keyfunc=lambda x: x[1])
```

```
kvrdd2.glom().collect()
[
[((1, 101), 'B'), ((1, 99), 'A')],
[((2, 101), 'D'), ((2, 99), 'C')]
]
```

NOTE

Work is underway to add native secondary sort capability to RDD sorting transformations in the Spark API.

Partition-specific API Methods

Many of Spark's methods are designed to interact with partitions as atomic units; these include both actions and transformations. Some of the methods are described here:

`foreachPartition()`

syntax:

> *RDD*`.foreachPartition(func)`

The `foreachPartition` method is an action similar to `foreach`, applying a function (`func`) to each partition of an RDD. Listing 12.13 shows an example of the `foreachPartition` method.

LISTING 12.13   The foreachPartition Action

```
...
def f(x):
    for rec in x:
        print(rec)
kvrdd2.foreachPartition(f)
...
((1, 101), 'B')
((1, 99), 'A')
...
((2, 101), 'D')
((2, 99), 'C')
...
```

Keep in mind that `foreachPartition` is an action, not a transformation, and will thereby trigger evaluation of the input RDD and its entire lineage. Furthermore, the function will result in data being sent to the Driver, so be mindful of the final RDD data volumes when running this function.

glom()

Syntax:

```
RDD.glom()
```

The glom method returns an RDD created by coalescing all of the elements within each partition into a list. This is useful for inspecting RDD partitions as collated lists; you saw an example of this in Listing 12.12.

lookup()

Syntax:

```
RDD.lookup(key)
```

The lookup method returns the list of values in an RDD for the key referenced by the key argument. If used against an RDD paritioned with a known partitioner, lookup uses the partitioner to narrow its search to only the partitions where the key would be present. Listing 12.14 shows an example of the lookup method.

LISTING 12.14   The lookup Function

```
kvrdd = sc.parallelize([(1,'A'),(1,'B'),(2,'C'),(2,'D')],2)
kvrdd.lookup(1)
['A', 'B']
```

mapPartitions()

Syntax:

```
RDD.mapPartitions(func, preservesPartitioning=False)
```

The mapPartitions method returns a new RDD by applying a function (the func argument) to each partition of this RDD. Listing 12.15 demonstrates the mapPartitions method to invert the key and value within each partition.

LISTING 12.15   The mapPartitions Function

```
kvrdd = sc.parallelize([(1,'A'),(1,'B'),(2,'C'),(2,'D')],2)
def f(iterator): yield [(b, a) for (a, b) in iterator]
kvrdd.mapPartitions(f).collect()
[[('A', 1), ('B', 1)], [('C', 2), ('D', 2)]]
```

Many of Spark's other transformations use the `mapPartitions` function internally. There is also a related transformation called `mapPartitionsWithIndex`, which returns functions similarly but tracks the index of the original partition.

Processing RDDs with External Programs

Spark provides a mechanism to run functions (transformations) based upon languages other than the languages native to Spark (Scala, Python, and Java). Languages you could use include, but are by no means limited to, Ruby, Perl, or Bash. The languages do not need to be scripting languages, either; you can use Spark with C or FORTRAN, among others.

There are different reasons for wanting to do this, such as, for instance, if you want to use some existing code libraries (not in Python, Scala, or Java) in your Spark programs without having to rewrite them in a native Spark language.

Using external programs with Spark is achieved through the `pipe` function.

CAUTION
Possible Issues with External Processes in Spark

The `pipe` function should be used carefully because piped commands may fork excessive amounts of RAM. Because the forked subprocesses created by `pipe` are out of Spark's resource management scope, they may also cause performance degradation to other tasks running on worker nodes.

The `pipe` function is described here:

pipe()
Syntax:

```
RDD.pipe(command, env=None, checkCode=False)
```

The `pipe` method returns an RDD created by "piping" elements through a forked external process specified by the `command` argument. The `env` argument is a dict of environment variables that defaults to None. The `checkCode` parameter specifies whether or not to check the return value of the shell command.

The script or program you supply as the command argument needs to read from STDIN and write its output to STDOUT.

Consider the Perl script (saved as `parsefixedwidth.pl`) in Listing 12.16, which is used to parse fixed-width output data, a common file format with extracts from mainframes and legacy systems.

LISTING 12.16   Sample External Transformation Program

```perl
#!/usr/bin/env perl
my $format = 'A6 A8 A8 A20 A2 A5';
while (<>) {
  chomp;
  my( $custid, $orderid, $date,
    $city, $state, $zip) =
  unpack( $format, $_ );
  print "$custid\t$orderid\t$date\t$city\t$state\t$zip";
}
```

Listing 12.17 demonstrates the use of the `pipe` command to run the `parsefixedwidth.pl` script from Listing 12.16.

LISTING 12.17   The pipe Function

```python
sc.addFile("/home/ubuntu/parsefixedwidth.pl")
fixed_width = sc.parallelize(['384096102875222020160317Hayward               CA94541'])
piped = fixed_width.pipe("parsefixedwidth.pl")
                  .map(lambda x: x.split('\t'))
piped.collect()
[['384096', '10287522', '20160317', 'Hayward', 'CA', '94541']]
```

The `addFile` operation is required because the `parsefixedwidth.pl` Perl script will need to be distributed to all worker nodes participating in the cluster prior to running the `pipe` transformation. Note that you also need to ensure that the interpreter or host program (in this case, Perl) exists in the path of all worker nodes.

Summary

In this hour, you have wrapped up your introduction to the Spark core API. I have discussed the different shared variables available in the Spark API: broadcast variables and accumulators.

You saw that broadcast variables are useful for distributing reference information, such as lookup tables, to workers to avoid expensive "reduce side" joins. You also saw that accumulators are useful as general purpose counters in Spark applications and can also be used to optimize processing.

The following article provides further reading on broadcast variables and accumulators:

http://ampcamp.berkeley.edu/wp-content/uploads/2012/06/matei-zaharia-amp-camp-2012-advanced-spark.pdf

I went through partitioning in more detail, and discussed the methods available to repartition RDDs, including `repartition` and `coalesce`, as well as functions designed to work on partitions atomically, such as `mapPartitions`. I also discussed partitioning behavior and its influence on performance.

Finally, I finished off with the use of the `pipe` function to use external programs with Spark.

Q&A

Q. What is the main advantage of using Spark broadcast variables as opposed to simply setting variables in your driver program and referencing them in map or filter operations?

A. Broadcast variables are distributed once per worker using an efficient peer-to-peer sharing mechanism. These variables can be used by many tasks on all executors on all workers with a SparkContext. Setting variables directly in your driver program and using them within RDD functions could result in data duplication and uses a less efficient transfer mechanism.

Q. What issues can arise by having too many small partitions within an RDD?

A. Too many small partitions can result in many small tasks being scheduled by Spark; this may not be efficient because the overhead and time required to spawn the tasks may be greater than the processing work itself. You would benefit in this case with fewer, larger tasks.

Q. What issues can arise with *very* large partitions?

A. Very large partitions can lead to out-of-memory issues and executor failures. A mixture of very large and moderately sized partitions can result in *speculative execution* (if this behavior is enabled). Speculative execution occurs when some tasks are running disproportionately longer than their peer tasks, the long running tasks are then respawned on other workers consuming cluster resources and providing no net benefit.

Workshop

The workshop contains quiz questions and exercises to help you solidify your understanding of the material covered. Try to answer all questions before looking at the "Answers" section that follows.

Quiz

1. **True or false:** Accumulators are incremented and can be read from Spark workers.

2. Which command is used to remove a broadcast variable, `bcvar`, from memory?

   A. `bcvar.remove()`

   B. `bcvar.unpersist()`

   C. `bcvar = sc.broadcast(None)`

3. Which Partitioner class is used to partition keys according to the sort order for their given type?

4. **True or false:** `repartition(5)` is the same as `coalesce(5, shuffle=True)`.

Answers

1. **False.** Accumulators are incremented by worker nodes but can only be read by the Driver.

2. **B.** The `unpersist()` method is used to remove a broadcast variable from memory on all worker nodes.

3. `RangePartitioner`

4. **True.** These statements are functionally equivalent.

HOUR 13
Using SQL with Spark

What You'll Learn in This Hour:

▶ Introduction to Hive and Spark SQL
▶ Introduction to the Spark DataFrame API
▶ Using Spark with Hive
▶ Creating and accessing Spark DataFrames
▶ Using Spark SQL with external applications

SQL (Structured Query Language) is by far the most common and widely used language to define and express questions about data. The vast majority of operational data that exists today is stored in tabular format in relational database systems. Many data analysts innately decompose complex problems into a series of SQL DML (Data Manipulation Language) or SELECT statements. The founders of Spark, as a data transformation and analysis platform, recognized the benefits (and necessities) of providing a SQL interface to Spark. In this hour, I will introduce Spark SQL and the DataFrame API that have evolved to become significant components of the Spark processing framework.

Introduction to Spark SQL

Spark SQL is one of the most popular extensions to Spark. Spark SQL enables interactive queries, supporting business intelligence (BI) and visualization tools and making Spark accessible to a much wider audience of analysts. Before I deep-dive into the internals of Spark SQL, I should first cover the background and historical context behind the initiative, including the Hive project.

Background

In the summer of 2011, about two years after the inception of the Spark project, the founders of Spark at the AMPLab-UC Berkeley started a Spark extension project named Shark. Shark was designed to port the functionality of the Apache Hive project (which provided a SQL-like abstraction to Hadoop MapReduce) to use the Spark core in-memory processing engine. Shark was designed to be 100% compatible with Hive but provide performance increases in orders of magnitude (original benchmarks were on the order of 40 times speed improvement, with later benchmarks reaching as much as 100 times improvement).

Shark provided a well-known interface, SQL, to data in HDFS using Spark. Shark was the first attempt at SQL integration for Spark and was built directly on top of the Hive codebase (which I will discuss next). In 2014, the team involved with the Spark and Shark projects announced a new project, Spark SQL, which would ultimately supplant Shark as Spark's integrated solution for providing a SQL interface to Spark.

There is a separate, recent initiative, not to be confused with Spark SQL, called *Hive on Spark*. Hive on Spark is an extension of the Hive project to provide a Spark execution engine to Hive in addition to the existing execution engines, which are MapReduce and Apache Tez.

Hive Overview

The Apache Hive project started at Facebook in 2010 to provide a high level SQL-like abstraction on top of Hadoop MapReduce. Hive introduced a new language called *HiveQL* (or Hive Query Language), which implements a subset of SQL-92, an internationally agreed-upon standard specification for the SQL language, with some extensions.

The motivation for Hive was that few analysts were available with Java MapReduce programming skills, whereas most analysts were proficient in SQL. Furthermore, SQL is the common language for BI and visualization and reporting tools, which commonly use ODBC/JDBC as a standard interface.

In Hive's original implementation, HiveQL would get parsed by the Hive client and mapped to a sequence of Java MapReduce operations, which would then be submitted as jobs on the Hadoop cluster. The progress would be monitored and the results returned to the client (or written back to the desired location in HDFS). Figure 13.1 provides a high-level depiction of how Hive processes data on HDFS. I will discuss the metastore next.

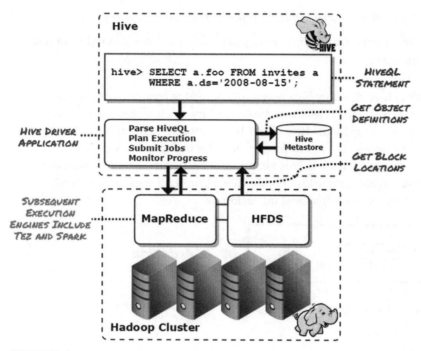

FIGURE 13.1
Hive high-level overview.

Hive Objects and the Hive Metastore

Hive implements a tabular abstraction to objects in HDFS, presenting directories and all files they contain as a table in its programming model. Just as in a conventional relational database, tables have predefined columns with designated datatypes. The data in HDFS can then be accessed via SQL Data Manipulation Language (or DML) statements just as with a normal database management system. This is where the similarity ends, however, as Hadoop is a "schema on read" platform, backed by an immutable filesystem, HDFS. The following key differences exist between Hive and a conventional database platform:

▶ UPDATE is not (really) supported

   Although UPDATE has been introduced into the HiveQL dialect, HDFS is still an immutable filesystem, so this abstraction involves applying coarse-grained transformations, whereas a true UPDATE in a RDBMS is a fine-grained operation.

▶ No transactions, no journaling, no rollbacks, no (real) transaction isolation level

▶ No declarative referential integrity (DRI), no primary keys, no foreign keys

▶ Incorrectly formatted data (for example, mistyped data or malformed records) are simply represented to the client as NULL

The mapping of tables to their directory locations in HDFS and the columns and their definitions are maintained in the Hive *metastore*. The metastore is a relational database (somewhat ironic) that is written to and read by the Hive client. The object definitions also include the input and output formats for the files represented by the table objects (for example CSVInputFormat, and so on) and *SerDes* (short for Serialization/Deserialization), which instruct Hive as to how to extract records and fields from the files. Figure 13.2 shows a high-level example of the interactions between Hive and the metastore.

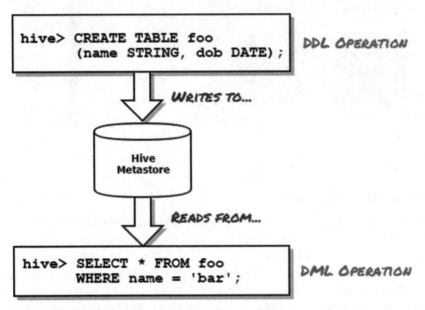

FIGURE 13.2
Hive metastore interaction.

The metastore can be an embedded Derby database (the default) or a local or remote database (such as MySQL or Postrges). In most cases, a shared database is implemented, which enables developers and analysts to share object definitions.

There is also a Hive subproject called *HCatalog*, which was an initiative to extend objects created in Hive to other projects, such as Apache Pig, with a common interface.

The Hive metastore is leveraged by Spark SQL, as I will discuss soon.

Hive CLI, HiveServer2, Beeswax, and Beeline

Hive provides a client command line interface (CLI) that accepts and parses HiveQL input commands. This is a common method for performing ad hoc queries. Figure 13.3 shows the Hive CLI.

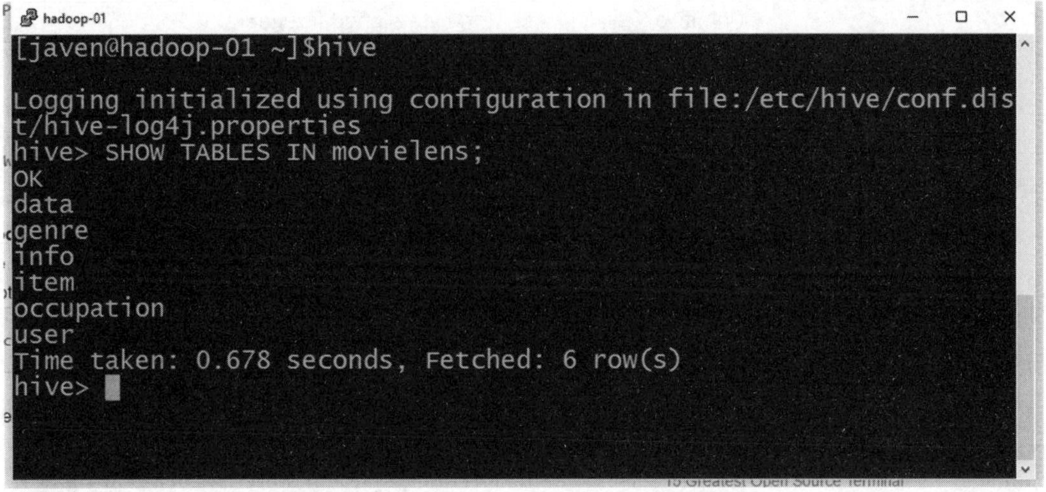

```
[javen@hadoop-01 ~]$hive

Logging initialized using configuration in file:/etc/hive/conf.dis
t/hive-log4j.properties
hive> SHOW TABLES IN movielens;
OK
data
genre
info
item
occupation
user
Time taken: 0.678 seconds, Fetched: 6 row(s)
hive>
```

FIGURE 13.3
The Hive command line interface.

The Hive CLI is used when the Hive client (or driver application) is deployed to the local machine, including the connection to the metastore. For large-scale implementations, a client/ server approach is often more appropriate because the connection details to the metastore are kept in one place (on the server) and access can be controlled to the cluster. This approach is called HiveServer2.

HiveServer2 can now act as a multi-session driver application for multiple clients. HiveServer2 provides a JDBC interface that can be used by external clients (such as visualization tools) as well as a lightweight CLI called *Beeline*. Beeline is included and can be used directly with Spark SQL.

There is also a web-based interface called *Beeswax*, which is used within the HUE (or Hadoop User Environment) project.

Hive Datatypes and Data Definition Language (DDL)

Hive supports most common primitive datatypes, similar to those found in most databases systems, as well as several complex data types. These types (which are used as the underlying types for Spark SQL) are listed in Table 13.1.

TABLE 13.1 Hive Data Types

Type	Category	Description
TINYINT	Primitive	1-btye signed integer
SMALLINT	Primitive	2-byte signed integer
INT	Primitive	4-byte signed integer
BIGINT	Primitive	8-byte signed integer
FLOAT	Primitive	4-byte single precision floating point number
DOUBLE	Primitive	8-byte double precision floating point number
BOOLEAN	Primitive	True/false value
STRING	Primitive	Character string
BINARY	Primitive	Byte array
TIMESTAMP	Primitive	Timestamp with nanosecond precision
DATE	Primitive	Year/month/day, in the form YYYYMM-DD
ARRAY	Complex	Ordered collection of fields of the same type
MAP	Complex	Unordered collection of key value pairs
STRUCT	Complex	Collection of named fields of varying types

A typical Hive DDL (Data Definition Language) statement used to create a table in Hive is shown in Listing 13.1.

LISTING 13.1 Hive CREATE TABLE Statement

```
CREATE EXTERNAL TABLE stations
(
station_id INT,
name STRING,
lat DOUBLE,
long DOUBLE,
dockcount INT,
landmark STRING,
installation STRING
)
ROW FORMAT DELIMITED
FIELDS TERMINATED BY ','
STORED AS TEXTFILE
LOCATION 'hdfs:///data/bike-share/stations';
```

CAUTION

Internal Tables versus External Tables in Hive

When you create tables in Hive, the default option is to create a Hive "internal" table. Directories for internal tables are managed by Hive, and a DROP TABLE statement for an internal table will delete the corresponding files from HDFS. It is typically recommended to use external tables by specifying the keyword EXTERNAL in the CREATE TABLE statement. This provides the schema and location for the object in HDFS, but a DROP TABLE operation does not delete the directory and files.

SQL on Hadoop

Although the Hive project was instrumental in providing the pattern of SQL-like access to unstructured data in HDFS, performance and user experience clearly fell well short of existing Relational Database Management Systems (RDBMS) and massively parallel processing (MPP) database technology performance. The batch nature of MapReduce, which was the processing engine behind Hive, was not suited to interactive queries or real-time applications.

In 2010, Google released a seminal whitepaper (yes, another one!) called "Dremel: Interactive Analysis of Web-Scale Datasets," outlining Google's approach to interactive SQL access to schema on read systems. This was a major catalyst for the "SQL on Hadoop" movement.

Pure-play Hadoop vendors including Cloudera, Hortonworks, MapR, and Pivotal all set off in different directions to develop the best mousetrap for delivering true interactive, RDBMS-like performance against data stored in HDFS. A performant, enterprise-grade SQL on Hadoop solution was seen as a key differentiator by each of the established vendors, and each made a significant investment in their chosen solution. A brief summary of the SQL on Hadoop landscape immediately after the Dremel whitepaper is provided here:

▶ Cloudera Impala: Developed by Cloudera, Impala is written in C++ and is built to short-circuit many of the operations that normally interact with blocks in HDFS. Furthermore, Impala is a memory-intensive solution performing extensive caching of metadata and block locations. Impala was designed to share the metastore with Hive and be (mostly) compatible with HiveQL, but was a completely separate project from Apache Hive.

▶ Apache Tez: As Hortonworks' preferred solution for lower-latency SQL on Hadoop operations, Tez created and implemented a smarter DAG scheduling framework to execute coarse-grained operations against data in HDFS. Tez, as an extension to the Apache Hive project, became an integrated execution engine for Hive (hot-swappable with MapReduce as an execution engine).

- ▶ Pivotal HAWQ (now Apache HAWQ): HAWQ was built by Pivotal to enable federation of queries across Greenplum (Pivotal's MPP database software solution built on top of PostgreSQL) and HDFS. HAWQ then developed into a fully fledged SQL on Hadoop solution, with a predominantly memory-centric architecture.

- ▶ Apache Drill: Adopted by MapR as their preferred approach to SQL on Hadoop, Apache Drill is an open source, low-latency query engine for Hadoop with the capability to use objects created with Hive.

Other SQL engines for Hadoop would follow later, including *Apache Presto* (Facebook's next-generation data warehousing solution) and *Apache Flink* (a generalized data processing framework with a *Table API* supporting relational-like access).

The common performance detractor addressed by all of the implementations was reducing or eliminating the need to write out intermediate data to disk, which was seen as a major shortcoming of the MapReduce architecture.

However, as the battle lines were being drawn and the Hadoop vendors were dueling each other with their respective solutions, another solution was quietly being developed that would alter the landscape of SQL on Hadoop as it was commonly understood. This solution was Shark and, ultimately, Spark SQL.

Spark SQL Architecture

Spark SQL, as a successor to the Shark project, provides a SQL (mainly HiveQL-compatible) abstraction to its RDD-based storage, scheduling, and execution model. Many of the key characteristics of the core Spark project are inherited by Spark SQL, including lazy evaluation and mid-query fault tolerance. Moreover, Spark SQL can be used in conjunction with the Spark core API within a single application.

Spark SQL includes some key extensions to the core API, however, which are designed to optimize typical relational access patterns. These include the following:

- ▶ Partial DAG execution (PDE): PDE enables DAGs to be changed (and optimized) on the fly as information is discovered about the data during processing. The DAG modifications include optimization for performing joins, handling "skew" in the data, and altering the degree of parallelism used by Spark.

- ▶ Columnar storage: Spark SQL stores objects in memory using Columnar Storage, which organizes data by columns instead of organizing data by rows. This has a significant performance impact on SQL access patterns. Figure 13.4 shows the difference between columnar and row-oriented data storage.

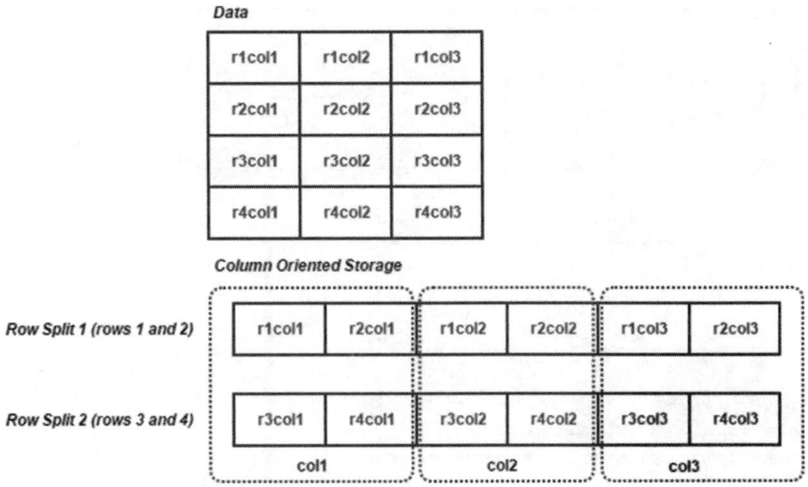

Data

r1col1	r1col2	r1col3
r2col1	r2col2	r2col3
r3col1	r3col2	r3col3
r4col1	r4col2	r4col3

Column Oriented Storage

	col1		col2		col3	
Row Split 1 (rows 1 and 2)	r1col1	r2col1	r1col2	r2col2	r1col3	r2col3
Row Split 2 (rows 3 and 4)	r3col1	r4col1	r3col2	r4col2	r3col3	r4col3

FIGURE 13.4
Column-oriented storage.

Moreover, Spark SQL includes native support for Parquet format files, which is a columnar file-based storage format optimized for relational access.

▶ Partition statistics: Spark SQL maintains statistics about data within partitions, which can be leveraged in PDE, and provides the capability to do *map pruning* (pruning or filtering partitions based upon columnar statistics) and optimize normally expensive join operations.

▶ The DataFrame API: I will discuss this in detail in the next section.

Spark SQL has been designed to be used with environments already using Hive, with a Hive metastore and Hive (or HCatalog) object definitions for data stored in HDFS, S3, or other sources. The SQL dialect supported by Spark SQL is a subset of HiveQL and supports many HiveQL built-in functions as well as supporting user-defined functions (UDFs).

Spark SQL can also be used without Hive or a Hive metastore. A high-level overview of the Spark SQL architecture along with the interfaces exposed by Spark SQL are shown in Figure 13.5.

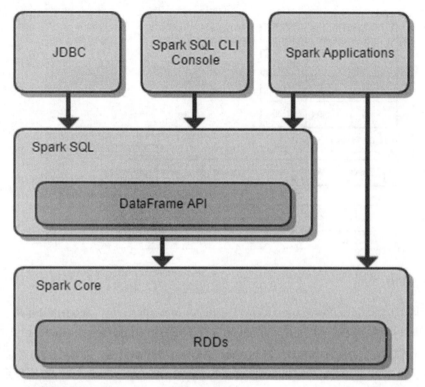

FIGURE 13.5
Spark high-level architecture.

The whitepaper titled "Spark SQL: Relational Data Processing in Spark" is recommended further reading. You can obtain this whitepaper from http://people.csail.mit.edu/matei/papers/2015/sigmod_spark_sql.pdf.

HiveContext and SQLContext

Just as the SparkContext was the main entry point for an application using the Spark Core API, the SQLContext and the HiveContext are Spark SQL's main entry points. Both the SQLContext and the HiveContext require a current instantiation of a SparkContext.

The SQLContext is the basic entry point for Spark SQL and does not require Hive to be available. Instantiation of a SQLContext is shown in Listing 13.2.

LISTING 13.2   Spark SQLContext

```
from pyspark import SparkConf, SparkContext
from pyspark.sql import SQLContext, HiveContext

sc = SparkContext()
sqlContext = SQLContext(sc)
```

The SQLContext exposes the DataFrame API (which I will discuss in the next section) and enables you to create and query table objects using SQL statements and operators.

The HiveContext is a superset of the SQLContext, enabling access to Hive, the Hive metastore, and the capability to use Hive UDFs. The HiveContext also provides a more robust SQL parser. The HiveContext does not require Hive, however. For this reason, I recommend you use the HiveContext as your Spark SQL entry point, even if you are not using Hive. An example of creating a HiveContext and performing a simple HiveQL query is shown in Listing 13.3.

LISTING 13.3   Spark HiveContext

```
from pyspark import SparkConf, SparkContext
from pyspark.sql import SQLContext, HiveContext

sc = SparkContext()
hiveContext = HiveContext(sc)
sql_cmd = """SELECT name, lat, long
FROM stations
WHERE landmark = 'San Jose'"""
sqlContext.sql(sql_cmd).show()
+--------------------+--------+-----------+
|                name|     lat|       long|
+--------------------+--------+-----------+
|    Adobe on Almaden|37.331415|  -121.8932|
|    San Pedro Square|37.336721|-121.894074|
|Paseo de San Antonio|37.333798|-121.886943|
| San Salvador at 1st|37.330165|-121.885831|
|           Japantown|37.348742|-121.894715|
|  San Jose City Hall|37.337391|-121.886995|
|         MLK Library|37.335885| -121.88566|
|       St James Park|37.339301|-121.889937|
|         Ryland Park|37.342725|-121.895617|
|                 ...|      ...|        ...|
+--------------------+--------+-----------+
```

When using the interactive REPL shells, either pyspark or spark-shell, the HiveContext is automatically instantiated as sqlContext.

Hive configuration for the HiveContext is read from the primary Hive configuration file: hive-site.xml. Most importantly, hive-site.xml includes location and connection details for the Hive metastore.

Getting Started with Spark SQL DataFrames

Spark SQL DataFrames are distributed collections of records, all with the same defined schema, conceptually analogous to a sharded table from a relational database. Spark SQL DataFrames were first introduced as SchemaRDD objects and are loosely based upon the DataFrame object constructs in R (which you will learn about in **Hour 15, "Getting Started with Spark and R"**) and Pandas (Python library for data manipulation and analysis).

DataFrames are ultimately an abstraction for Spark RDDs. However, unlike primitive RDDs, DataFrames track their schema and provide native support for many of the common SQL functions and relational operators. DataFrames, like RDDs, are evaluated as DAGs, using lazy evaluation and providing lineage and fault tolerance. Also like RDDs, DataFrames support caching and persistence using methods similar to those discussed in **Hour 11, "Using RDDs: Caching, Persistence, and Output."**

DataFrames can be created in many different ways, including creation from

- ▶ An existing RDD

- ▶ A JSON file

- ▶ A text file, Parquet file, or ORC file

- ▶ A table in Hive

- ▶ An external database

Given an existing SQLContext, take a look at some of the common methods of constructing DataFrames.

Creating a DataFrame from an Existing RDD

The main function used to create DataFrames from RDDs is the `createDataFrame` method, which is described here:

createDataFrame()
Syntax:

```
SQLContext.createDataFrame(data,
              schema=None,
              samplingRatio=None)
```

The `createDataFrame` method creates a DataFrame object from an existing RDD. The `data` argument is a reference to a named RDD object consisting of tuples or list elements. The `schema` argument refers to the schema to be projected to the DataFrame object, whereas `samplingRatio` is used to sample the data if the schema is to be inferred. I will discuss defining or inferring the schema for a DataFrame shortly. Listing 13.4 shows an example of loading a DataFrame from an existing RDD.

LISTING 13.4   Creating a DataFrame from an RDD

```
myrdd = sc.parallelize([('Jeff', 46),('Kellie', 44)])
sqlContext.createDataFrame(myrdd).collect()
[Row(_1=u'Jeff', _2=46), Row(_1=u'Kellie', _2=44)]
```

Notice that the return value from the collect action is a list of **Row** (`pyspark.sql.Row`) objects. In this case, because the schema (including the field names) was not specified, the fields are referenced by `_<fieldnumber>` where the field number starts at one.

Creating a DataFrame from a Hive Table

To load data from a Hive table into a Spark SQL DataFrame, you will need a HiveContext to be created. Recall that the HiveContext reads the Hive client configuration (`hive-site.xml`) to obtain connection details for the Hive metastore. This enables seamless access to Hive tables from a Spark application. This can be done in a couple of different ways, including the `sql` method or the `table` method. Both are described here:

sql()
Syntax:

> *HiveContext.*`sql(sqlQuery)`

The `sql` method creates a DataFrame object from a table in Hive by supplying a `sqlQuery` argument, performing a DML operation from a table in Hive. If the table is in a database other than the Hive default database, it needs to be referenced using the `<databasename>`. `<tablename>` format. The sqlQuery can be any valid HiveQL statement including `SELECT *` or a `SELECT` statement with a `WHERE` clause or `JOIN` predicate. Listing 13.5 shows an example of creating a DataFrame using a HiveQL query against a table in the Hive default database.

LISTING 13.5   sql Method for Creating a DataFrame from a Table in Hive

```
# HiveContext available as sqlContext.
sql_cmd = """SELECT name, lat, long
             FROM stations
             WHERE landmark = 'San Jose'"""
df = sqlContext.sql(sql_cmd)
df.show()
```

```
+-------------------+---------+-----------+
|               name|      lat|       long|
+-------------------+---------+-----------+
|   Adobe on Almaden|37.331415|  -121.8932|
|   San Pedro Square|37.336721|-121.894074|
|Paseo de San Antonio|37.333798|-121.886943|
| San Salvador at 1st|37.330165|-121.885831|
|           Japantown|37.348742|-121.894715|
|  San Jose City Hall|37.337391|-121.886995|
|         MLK Library|37.335885| -121.88566|
|       St James Park|37.339301|-121.889937|
|         Ryland Park|37.342725|-121.895617|
|                 ...|      ...|        ...|
+-------------------+---------+-----------+
```

table()

Syntax:

> ***HiveContext.table(tableName)***

The `table` method creates a DataFrame object from a table in Hive. Unlike the `sql` command, there is no opportunity to prune columns with a column list or filter rows with a `WHERE` clause. The entire table is loaded into the DataFrame.

LISTING 13.6   table Method for Creating a DataFrame from a Table in Hive

```
# HiveContext available as sqlContext.
df = sqlContext.table('stations')
# returns all rows and all columns from the stations table in Hive
```

There are other useful methods that can be used to interrogate the Hive system and database catalogs such as `tables` (which returns a DataFrame containing names of tables in the given database) and `tableNames` (which returns a list of names of tables in a given Hive database).

Creating a DataFrame from JSON Objects

JSON is a common, standard, human-readable serialization (or wire transfer) format that is often used in web service responses. I introduced the `jsonFile` method in **Hour 6, "Learning the Basics of Spark Programming with RDDs,"** when I discussed loading data into RDDs. Because JSON is a semi-structured source with a schema, support for JSON is included in Spark SQL. Here's a recap of the `jsonFile` method.

jsonFile()

Syntax:

```
SQLContext.jsonFile(path,
                    schema=None,
                    samplingRatio=1.0)
```

The jsonFile method creates a DataFrame object from a file containing one or more valid JSON objects. path refers to the fully qualified path to the JSON file. The schema and samplingRatio arguments behave similarly to the createDataFrame method previously discussed.

Suppose you had a file containing the following JSON data:

```
{"name":"Adobe on Almaden", "lat":37.331415, "long":-121.8932}
```

Listing 13.7 demonstrates the use of the jsonFile method to create an RDD from the JSON document.

LISTING 13.7   Creating a DataFrame from a JSON Document

```
df = sqlContext.jsonFile('file:///data/stations.json')
df.show()
+---------+----------+--------------------+
|      lat|      long|                name|
+---------+----------+--------------------+
|37.331415| -121.8932|    Adobe on Almaden|
+---------+----------+--------------------+
```

NOTE

Each line in a JSON file must be a valid JSON object. The schemas (or keys) do not need to be uniform across all JSON objects in a file. Keys that do not present in a given JSON object will be represented as NULL in the resultant DataFrame.

In addition to the jsonFile method, Spark SQL provides a method to create a DataFrame from an existing RDD consisting of a list of one or more discrete JSON objects as strings. This method is called jsonRDD and is presented here:

jsonRDD()

Syntax:

```
SQLContext.jsonRDD(rdd,
                   schema=None,
                   samplingRatio=1.0)
```

The `jsonRDD` method creates a DataFrame object from an RDD (or a parallelized collection) of JSON objects. The `rdd` argument is a reference to a named RDD containing the collection of JSON objects. The `schema` and `samplingRatio` arguments are as previously discussed.

Listing 13.8 demonstrates the use of the `jsonRDD` method.

LISTING 13.8   Creating a DataFrame from an RDD Containing JSON Objects

```
stationsrdd = sc.parallelize( \
  ['{"name":"Adobe on Almaden", "lat":37.331415, "long":-121.8932}', \
   '{"name":"Japantown", "lat":37.348742, "long":-121.894715}'])
df = sqlContext.jsonRDD(stationsrdd)
df.show()
+---------+-----------+--------------------+
|      lat|       long|                name|
+---------+-----------+--------------------+
|37.331415|  -121.8932|   Adobe on Almaden|
|37.348742|  -121.8947|           Japantown|
+---------+-----------+--------------------+
```

Creating DataFrames from Files Using the DataFrameReader

Version 1.4 of Spark introduced a new interface used to load DataFrames from external storage systems, the DataFrameReader. The DataFrameReader can be used to load from external filesystems, as well as external SQL and NoSQL data sources.

The DataFrameReader interface is accessed using `SQLContext.read()`, as I show in the examples creating DataFrames from plain text files and columnar storage files, including Parquet and ORC.

text()
Syntax:

> `SQLContext.read.text(paths)`

The `text` method of the DataFrameReader is used to load DataFrames from text files in an external filesystem (local, NFS, HDFS, S3, or others). Its behavior is similar to its RDD equivalent—`sc.textFile()`.`path` refers to a path that could be a file, directory, or file glob ("globbing" expressions are similar to regular expressions used to return a list of files satisfying the glob pattern).

Listing 13.9 demonstrates the `DataFrameReader.read.text` function.

LISTING 13.9   Creating a DataFrame from a Plain Text File or File(s)

```
# read an individual file
df = sqlContext.read.text('hdfs:///.../stations/stations.csv')
df.take(1)
[Row(value=u'9,Japantown,37.348742,-121.894715,15,San Jose,8/5/2013')]
# you can also read all files from a directory...
df = sqlContext.read.text('hdfs:///.../stations/')
```

Note that the Row object returned for each line in the text file (or files) contains one string, which is the entire line of the file.

Quick Recap of Columnar Storage and Parquet Files

You were introduced to columnar storage concepts in the previous section. These concepts extend beyond in-memory structures to persistent file formats such as Parquet and ORC (Optimized Row Columnar) files.

Apache Parquet is a popular, generalized columnar storage format that is designed to be integrated into any Hadoop ecosystem project. Parquet is a "first-class citizen" within the Spark project and is the preferred storage format for Spark SQL processing.

ORC is a successor to RCFile, which was a columnar storage format purpose-built to improve Hive read performance. If you need to share data structures with Hive and need to accommodate non-Spark access patterns (such as Tez), ORC may be an appropriate format. However, Parquet support is available through the Hive project.

parquet()

Syntax:

> *SQLContext*.read.parquet(*paths*)

The parquet method of the DataFrameReader is used to load files stored with the Parquet columnar storage format. These files will often be the output of another process (such as the output from a previous Spark process). The path argument refers to a parquet file or files or a directory containing parquet files.

The Parquet format encapsulates the schema and data in one structure, so the schema is applied and available to the resultant DataFrame.

Given an existing file in parquet format, Listing 13.10 demonstrates the use of the DataFrameReader.read.parquet method.

LISTING 13.10   **Creating a DataFrame from a Parquet File (or Files)**

```
df = sqlContext.read.parquet('hdfs:///.../stations.parquet')
df.printSchema()
root
|-- station_id: integer (nullable = true)
|-- name: string (nullable = true)
|-- lat: double (nullable = true)
|-- long: double (nullable = true)
|-- dockcount: integer (nullable = true)
|-- landmark: string (nullable = true)
|-- installation: string (nullable = true)
df.take(1)
[Row(station_id=9, name='Japantown', lat=37.348742, long=-121.894715,
 dockcount=15, landmark='San Jose', installation='8/5/2013')]
```

TIP

Parquet and Compression

By default, Spark uses the GZip codec to compress parquet files (recall the coverage of compression and decompression in **Hour 11, "Using RDDs: Caching, Persistence, and Output"**). If you require an alternative codec (for example, Snappy) to read or write compressed Parquet files, you can supply the following config:

```
sqlContext.setConf("spark.sql.parquet.compression.codec.", "snappy")
```

orc()

Syntax:

> *HiveContext.read.orc(path)*

The orc method of the DataFrameReader is used to load a DataFrame from a file or directory consisting of ORC format files. ORC is a format native to the Hive project, and support for ORC is only available from version 1.5 onward using the HiveContext. The path argument refers to a directory containing ORC files, typically associated with a table in ORC format in a Hive warehouse. Listing 13.11 shows the use of the orc method to load the ORC files associated with a Hive table stored as ORC.

LISTING 13.11   **Creating a DataFrame from Hive ORC Files**

```
# HiveContext available as sqlContext.
df = sqlContext.read.orc('hdfs:///.../stations_orc/')
df.printSchema()
root
|-- station_id: integer (nullable = true)
|-- name: string (nullable = true)
|-- lat: double (nullable = true)
```

```
|-- long: double (nullable = true)
|-- dockcount: integer (nullable = true)
|-- landmark: string (nullable = true)
|-- installation: string (nullable = true)
df.take(1)
[Row(station_id=9, name='Japantown', lat=37.348742, long=-121.894715,
 dockcount=15, landmark='San Jose', installation='8/5/2013')]
```

You can also use the DataFrameReader to load data from external datasources such as MySQL, Oracle, or others using the `SQLContext.read.jdbc` method.

Converting DataFrames to RDDs

DataFrames can be easily converted to native RDDs by using the `rdd` method, as shown in Listing 13.12. The resultant RDD will consist of `pyspark.sql.Row` objects.

LISTING 13.12 Converting a DataFrame to an RDD

```
stationsdf = sqlContext.read.parquet('hdfs:///.../stations.parquet')
stationsrdd = stationsdf.rdd
stationsrdd
MapPartitionsRDD[4] at javaToPython at ...
stationsrdd.take(1)
[Row(station_id=9, name='Japantown', lat=37.348742, long=-121.894715
 dockcount=15, landmark='San Jose', installation='8/5/2013')]
```

DataFrame Data Model

The data model for the DataFrame API is based on the Hive data model. Datatypes used with DataFrames map directly to their equivalents in Hive. This includes all of the common primitive types as well as complex, nested types such as the equivalents to lists, dictionaries, and tuples.

Primitive Types

Table 13.2 lists the primitive types encapsulated by PySpark-type objects (types derived from the base class—`pyspark.sql.types.DataType`).

TABLE 13.2 Spark SQL Primitive Types (pyspark.sql.types)

Type	Hive Equivalent	Python Equivalent
ByteType	TINYINT	int
ShortType	SMALLINT	int
IntegerType	INT	int
LongType	BIGINT	long

TABLE 13.2 *Continued*

Type	Hive Equivalent	Python Equivalent
FloatType	FLOAT	float
DoubleType	DOUBLE	float
BooleanType	BOOLEAN	bool
StringType	STRING	string
BinaryType	BINARY	bytearray
TimestampType	TIMESTAMP	datetime.datetime
DateType	DATE	datetime.date

Complex Types

Complex, nested structures are accessible in Spark SQL using native HiveQL-based operators. Table 13.3 lists the complex types in the DataFrame API with their Hive and Python equivalents.

TABLE 13.3 Spark SQL Complex Types (pyspark.sql.types)

Type	Hive Equivalent	Python Equivalent
ArrayType	ARRAY	list, tuple, or array
MapType	MAP	dict
StructType	STRUCT	list or tuple

DataFrame Schemas

The schema for a Spark SQL DataFrame can be explicitly defined or inferred. In previous examples, I didn't specify the schema, so in each case, it was inferred. Inferring the schema is the simplest method. However, it is generally better practice to define the schema in your code. I will cover examples of each method.

Inferring the Schema

Spark SQL can use *reflection* (a process of examining an object to determine its composition) to infer the schema of a DataFrame object. This can be done to interpret a schema for an RDD that has been converted to a DataFrame. In this case, the process would involve creating a Row object from each record in the RDD and assigning a datatype from each field in the RDD. The datatypes are inferred from the first record, so it's important that the first record is representative of the dataset and there are no missing values.

Listing 13.13 shows an example of schema inference for a DataFrame created from an RDD. In this example, I use the DataFrame method `printSchema` to print the schema to the console in a tree format.

LISTING 13.13   Schema Inference for a DataFrame Created from an RDD

```
rdd = sc.textFile('file://.../stations.csv') \
        .map(lambda x: x.split(',')) \
        .map(lambda x: (int(x[0]), str(x[1]),
                        float(x[2]), float(x[3]),
                        int(x[4]), str(x[5]), str(x[6])))
rdd.take(1)
[(2, 'San Jose Diridon Caltrain Station',
37.329732, -121.901782, 27, 'San Jose',
'8/6/2013')]
df = sqlContext.createDataFrame(rdd)
df.printSchema()
root
|-- _1: long (nullable = true)
|-- _2: string (nullable = true)
|-- _3: double (nullable = true)
|-- _4: double (nullable = true)
|-- _5: long (nullable = true)
|-- _6: string (nullable = true)
|-- _7: string (nullable = true)
```

Note that the fields use the `_<fieldnumber>` convention for their identifiers and have a `nullable` property value set to `True` (meaning these values do not need to be supplied). Also notice that the larger type variants are assumed. For instance, I have cast the `lat` and `long` fields to `float` in this RDD, yet the inferred schema in the resultant DataFrame uses `double` (actually, an instance of the `DoubleType`) for the same fields. Likewise, `long` was inferred from `int` values.

Schema inference is performed automatically for DataFrames created from JSON documents, as shown in Listing 13.14.

LISTING 13.14   Schema Inference for DataFrames Created from JSON

```
rdd = sc.parallelize( \
        ['{"name":"Adobe on Almaden", "lat":37.331415, "long":-121.8932}', \
         '{"name":"Japantown", "lat":37.348742, "long":-121.894715}'])
df = sqlContext.jsonRDD(rdd)
df.printSchema()
root
|-- lat: double (nullable = true)
|-- long: double (nullable = true)
|-- name: string (nullable = true)
```

The schema for a DataFrame created from a Hive table is automatically inherited from its Hive definition, as shown in Listing 13.15.

LISTING 13.15 Schema for a DataFrame Created from a Hive Table

```
# HiveContext available as sqlContext.
df = sqlContext.table("stations")
df.printSchema()
root
|-- station_id: integer (nullable = true)
|-- name: string (nullable = true)
|-- lat: double (nullable = true)
|-- long: double (nullable = true)
|-- dockcount: integer (nullable = true)
|-- landmark: string (nullable = true)
|-- installation: string (nullable = true)
```

Defining the Schema Programatically

The preferred method of defining a schema for your DataFrame objects is to explicitly supply this in your code. Creating a schema requires you to create a `StructType` object containing a collection of `StructField` objects. You then apply this schema to your DataFrame when it is created. An example of defining a schema explicitly is shown in Listing 13.16 using a previous example. Notice the difference in behavior between the inferred and defined schemas.

LISTING 13.16 Defining the Schema for a DataFrame Explicitly

```
from pyspark.sql.types import *
myschema = StructType([ \
          StructField("station_id", IntegerType(), True), \
          StructField("name", StringType(), True), \
          StructField("lat", FloatType(), True), \
          StructField("long", FloatType(), True), \
          StructField("dockcount", IntegerType(), True), \
          StructField("landmark", StringType(), True), \
          StructField("installation", StringType(), True) \
          ])
rdd = sc.textFile('file:///.../stations.csv') \
        .map(lambda x: x.split(',')) \
        .map(lambda x: (int(x[0]), str(x[1]),
                        float(x[2]), float(x[3]),
                        int(x[4]), str(x[5]), str(x[6])))
df = sqlContext.createDataFrame(rdd, myschema)
df.printSchema()
root
|-- station_id: integer (nullable = true)
|-- name: string (nullable = true)
|-- lat: float (nullable = true)
|-- long: float (nullable = true)
|-- dockcount: integer (nullable = true)
|-- landmark: string (nullable = true)
|-- installation: string (nullable = true)
```

Using Spark SQL DataFrames

The DataFrame API is currently one of the fastest-moving areas within the Spark project. New (and significant) features and functions are added with every minor release. Extensions to the Spark SQL DataFrame model, such as the Datasets API, are moving equally quickly. In fact, Spark SQL (including its core component, the DataFrame API) could nearly warrant its own book. I will cover the basics of the DataFrame API using Python in this section, enough to get you up and running with DataFrames. The rest is up to you!

DataFrame Metadata Operations

There are several metadata functions available with the DataFrame API. These are functions that return information about the data structure, not the data itself. You have already seen one of the available functions, `printSchema()`, which returns the schema defined for a `DataFrame` object in a tree format. Other metadata functions include the following:

columns

Syntax:

> `DataFrame.columns`

The `columns` method returns a list of column names for the given DataFrame. An example is provided in Listing 13.17.

LISTING 13.17 **Returning a List of Columns from a DataFrame**

```
df = sqlContext.read.parquet('hdfs:///.../stations.parquet')
df.columns
['station_id', 'name', 'lat', 'long', 'dockcount', 'landmark',
 'installation']
```

dtypes

Syntax:

> `DataFrame.dtypes`

The `dtypes` method returns a list of tuples, with each tuple consisting of the column names and the data types for a column for a given DataFrame object. This may be more useful than the `printSchema` method, which I previously discussed, because it can be accessed programatically. Listing 13.18 demonstrates the `dtypes` method.

```
df = sqlContext.read.parquet('hdfs:///.../stations.parquet')
df.dtypes
[('station_id', 'int'), ('name', 'string'), ('lat', 'double'),
 ('long', 'double'), ('dockcount', 'int'), ('landmark', 'string'),
 ('installation', 'string')]
```

Basic DataFrame Operations

Because DataFrames are a columnar abstraction of RDDs, you will see many similar functions (transformations and actions) that are direct descendants of RDD methods, with some additional relational methods like `select`, `drop`, and `where`. I will cover some of the key Spark SQL DataFrame functions now. For brevity, if the syntax and usage is analogous to functions I've already looked at in the Spark Core API, I won't describe the syntax again.

count, collect, take, foreach, and show

The `count` function is available in the DataFrame API to return the number of rows in the DataFrame. As with `count` in the RDD API, `count` is an action that will trigger evaluation of the DataFrame and its lineage.

The `collect`, `take(n)`, and `foreach` functions are all supported DataFrame methods and are functionally and syntactically analogous to the functions with the same name in the RDD API. I've already used these methods in some examples in the previous section.

Similar to the `collect` and `take` actions, you may have noticed an alternative method used in examples in the last section. `show`. `show` is an action that triggers evaluation of a DataFrame if the DataFrame does not exist in cache.

show()
Syntax:

```
DataFrame.show(n=20, truncate=True)
```

The `show` method prints the first *n* rows of a DataFrame to the console. Unlike `collect` or `take(n)`, `show` cannot be returned to a variable. It is solely intended to view the contents or a subset of the contents in the console (or notebook). The `truncate` argument specifies whether to truncate long strings and align cells to the right.

The output of the show command is "pretty printed," meaning it is formatted as a grid result set, including column headings for readability.

select, drop, filter, where, and distinct

The `select`, `drop`, `filter`, `where`, and `distinct` methods all share something in common. They can be used to either prune columns or filter rows from a `DataFrame`. In each case, the results of these operations create a new `DataFrame` object.

drop()

Syntax:

```
DataFrame.drop(col)
```

The `drop` method returns a new DataFrame with the column specified in the `col` argument removed. Listing 13.19 demonstrates the use of the `drop` method.

LISTING 13.19   Dropping Columns from a DataFrame

```
df = sqlContext.read.parquet('hdfs:///.../stations.parquet')
newdf = df.drop(df.installation)
newdf.printSchema()
root
|-- station_id: integer (nullable = true)
|-- name: string (nullable = true)
|-- lat: double (nullable = true)
|-- long: double (nullable = true)
|-- dockcount: integer (nullable = true)
|-- landmark: string (nullable = true)
```

filter()

Syntax:

```
DataFrame.filter(condition)
```

The `filter` method returns a new DataFrame containing only rows that satisfy the given *condition*. Listing 13.20 demonstrates the use of `filter`.

LISTING 13.20   Filtering Rows from a DataFrame

```
df = sqlContext.read.parquet('hdfs:///.../stations.parquet')
df.filter(df.name == 'St James Park') \
  .select(df.name,df.lat,df.long) \
  .show()
+-------------+---------+-----------+
|         name|      lat|       long|
+-------------+---------+-----------+
|St James Park|37.339301|-121.889937|
+-------------+---------+-----------+
```

`where` is an alias for `filter` and can be used interchangeably.

distinct()

Syntax:

> *DataFrame*.distinct()

The distinct method returns a new DataFrame containing the distinct rows in the input DataFrame, essentially filtering out duplicate rows. A duplicate row would be a row where all values for all columns are the same as another row in the same DataFrame. Listing 13.21 shows an example of the distinct method.

LISTING 13.21   Filtering Duplicate Rows Using distinct

```
rdd = sc.parallelize([('Jeff', 46), \
                      ('Kellie', 44), \
                      ('Jeff', 46)])
df = sqlContext.createDataFrame(rdd)
df.show()
+------+---+
|    _1| _2|
+------+---+
|  Jeff| 46|
|Kellie| 44|
|  Jeff| 46|
+------+---+
df.distinct().show()
+------+---+
|    _1| _2|
+------+---+
|Kellie| 44|
|  Jeff| 46|
+------+---+
```

drop_duplicates is a similar method that also lets you optionally consider only certain columns in the distinct operation.

select, map, and flatMap

These methods can be used to apply column-level functions to rows in Spark SQL DataFrames, as well as project-specific columns (including computed columns).

map and flatMap are available as DataFrame methods. Conceptually, they function the same as their named equivalents in the RDD API. However, dealing with DataFrames with named columns, the lambda functions are slightly different. Additionally, DataFrame map and flatMap methods operate on a DataFrame and return an RDD. Take a look at the example in Listing 13.22, which uses map to project a column from a DataFrame into a new rdd.

LISTING 13.22   map Functions with Spark SQL DataFrames

```
df = sqlContext.read.parquet('hdfs:///.../stations.parquet')
rdd = df.map(lambda r: r.name)
rdd
PythonRDD[11] at collect at<stdin>:1
rdd.take(1)
[u'San Jose Diridon Caltrain Station']
```

If you wanted the result of a mapping operation to return a new DataFrame instead of an RDD, select, which is described here, is a better option.

select()

Syntax:

>   *DataFrame.*select(*cols)

The select method returns a new DataFrame object from the list of columns specified in cols. The string * can be used to select all columns from the DataFrame with no manipulation. Listing 13.23 shows an example of the select function.

LISTING 13.23   select Method in Spark SQL

```
df = sqlContext.read.parquet('hdfs:///.../stations.parquet')
newdf = df.select((df.name).alias("Station Name"))
newdf.show(2)
+--------------------+
|        Station Name|
+--------------------+
|San Jose Diridon ...|
|San Jose Civic Ce...|
+--------------------+
only showing top 2 rows
```

As you can see from Listing 13.23, you can also apply column aliases with select using the alias operator. select is also the primary method to apply column-level functions in DataFrame transformation operations. You will see an example of this when I discuss built-in and user-defined functions shortly.

Other Useful DataFrame Operations

Some other operations in the Spark SQL DataFrame API are worth a mention. These methods include sample and sampleBy, which work similarly to their RDD equivalents, as well as the limit function, which creates a new DataFrame with a specific number of arbitrary Rows from the originating DataFrame. Both of these methods are useful for working with data at scale, limiting the working set during development.

Another useful method during development is explain. explain returns a query plan, including a logical and physical plan for evaluating the DataFrame. This can be helpful in troubleshooting or optimizing Spark SQL programs.

I won't detail these methods here, but you are encouraged to explore the documentation and experiment. *docstrings* are included with all functions in the Python Spark SQL API. These can be used to explore the syntax and usage of any function in Spark SQL (and any other functions in the Spark Python API). Python docstrings are accessible using the __doc__ method of a function with the fully qualified class path, as shown in Listing 13.24.

LISTING 13.24   Getting Help for Python API Spark SQL Functions

```
print(pyspark.sql.DataFrame.sample.__doc__)
Returns a sampled subset of this :class:'DataFrame'.
    >>> df.sample(False, 0.5, 42).count()
    2
    .. versionadded:: 1.3
```

DataFrame Built-in Functions and UDFs

There are numerous functions available in Spark SQL that are present in most other common DBMS implementations of SQL. Using the Python Spark API, these built-in functions are available through the pyspark.sql.functions module. Functions include scalar and aggregate functions and can operate on fields, columns, or rows depending upon the function. Table 13.4 shows a sampling of the functions available in the pyspark.sql.functions library.

TABLE 13.4   Some of the Built-in Functions Available in Spark SQL

Type	Sample Available Functions
String functions	startswith, substr, concat, lower, upper, regexp_extract, regexp_replace
Math functions	abs, ceil, floor, log, round, sqrt
Statistical functions	avg, max, min, mean, stddev
Date functions	date_add, datediff, from_utc_timestamp
Hashing functions	md5, sha1, sha2
Algorithmic functions	soundex, levenshtein
Windowing functions	over, rank, dense_rank, lead, lag, ntile

If you can't find a function to do what you want to do, you can create and use user-defined functions (UDFs) within Spark SQL. Column-level UDFs can be created and incorporated into your Spark program using the udf method described here.

udf()

Syntax:

```
pyspark.sql.functions.udf(func, returnType=StringType)
```

The udf method creates a column expression representing a user defined function. func is a named or anonymous function (using the lambda syntax) that operates on a column within a DataFrame Row. The returnType argument specifies the data type of the object returned from the function. This type is a member of pyspark.sql.types or a subtype of the pyspark.sql.types.DataType class.

Suppose you wanted to define functions to convert decimal latitudinal and longitudinal coordinates to their geo-positional direction with respect to the equator and the prime meridian. Listing 13.25 demonstrates creating two UDFs to take the decimal latitude and longitude coordinates and return 'N,' 'S', 'E,' or 'W' respectively.

LISTING 13.25 User-Defined Functions in Spark SQL

```
df = sqlContext.read.parquet('hdfs:///.../stations.parquet')
from pyspark.sql.functions import *
from pyspark.sql.types import *
lat2dir = udf(lambda x: 'N' if x > 0 else 'S', StringType())
lon2dir = udf(lambda x: 'E' if x > 0 else 'W', StringType())
df.select(df.lat, lat2dir(df.lat).alias('latdir'),
          df.long, lon2dir(df.lat).alias('longdir')) \
        .show()
+---------+------+-----------+-------+
|      lat|latdir|       long|longdir|
+---------+------+-----------+-------+
|37.329732|     N|-121.901782|      E|
|37.330698|     N|-121.888979|      E|
|    ...  |  ... |    ...    |  ...  |
+---------+------+-----------+-------+
```

DataFrame Set Operations

Set operations, such as join and union, are common requirements for DataFrames because they are integral operations in relational (SQL) programming.

Joining DataFrames

DataFrames support all of the types of join operations supported in the RDD API and in HiveQL, including inner joins, outer joins, and left semi joins.

join()

Syntax:

```
DataFrame.join(other, on=None, how=None)
```

The join method creates a new DataFrame from the results of a join operation against the DataFrame referenced in the other argument (the right side of the argument). The on argument specifies a column, a list of columns, or an expression to evaluate the join operation. The how argument specifies the type of join to be performed. Valid values include inner (default), outer, left_outer, right_outer, and leftsemi.

Consider a new entity from the bike-share dataset called *trips*. trips includes two fields, start_terminal and end_terminal, which correspond to station_id in the stations entity. Listing 13.26 demonstrates an inner join between these two entities using the join method.

LISTING 13.26   Joining DataFrames in Spark SQL

```
trips = sqlContext.table("trips")
stations = sqlContext.table("stations")
joined = trips.join(stations, trips.start_terminal == stations.station_id)
joined.printSchema()
root
|-- trip_id: integer (nullable = true)
|-- duration: integer (nullable = true)
|-- start_date: string (nullable = true)
|-- start_station: string (nullable = true)
|-- start_terminal: integer (nullable = true)
|-- end_date: string (nullable = true)
|-- end_station: string (nullable = true)
|-- end_terminal: integer (nullable = true)
|-- bike_num: integer (nullable = true)
|-- subscription_type: string (nullable = true)
|-- zip_code: string (nullable = true)
|-- station_id: integer (nullable = true)
|-- name: string (nullable = true)
|-- lat: double (nullable = true)
|-- long: double (nullable = true)
|-- dockcount: integer (nullable = true)
|-- landmark: string (nullable = true)
|-- installation: string (nullable = true)
joined.select(joined.start_station, joined.duration) \
    .show(2)
+--------------------+--------+
|       start_station|duration|
+--------------------+--------+
|Harry Bridges Pla...|     765|
|San Antonio Shopp...|    1036|
+--------------------+--------+
```

union, intersect, and subtract

Set operations `intersect` and `subtract` are available functions for Spark SQL DataFrames and function the same as the equivalent RDD functions described in **Hour 10, "Working the Spark API (Transformations and Actions)."** `unionAll` is available for DataFrames instead of `union`, which is available in the RDD API. Note that if you need to remove duplicates, this can be done after the `unionAll` operation using the aforementioned `distinct` or `drop_duplicates` functions.

Sorting and Ordering DataFrames

DataFrames include several standard methods for sorting or ordering.

orderBy()

Syntax:

```
DataFrame.orderBy(cols, ascending)
```

The `orderBy` method creates a new DataFrame ordered by the columns specified in the `cols` argument. `ascending` is a Boolean argument defaulting to `True`, which determines the sort order for the column. Listing 13.27 shows an example of the `orderBy` function.

LISTING 13.27   Ordering a DataFrame

```
stations = sqlContext.table("stations")
stations.orderBy([stations.name], ascending=False) \
        .select(stations.name) \
        .show(1)
+--------------------+
|                name|
+--------------------+
|Yerba Buena Cente...|
+--------------------+
```

`sort` is a function synonymous with `orderBy` in the DataFrame API.

Grouping Data in DataFrames

Grouping is a common precursor to performing aggregations on a column or columns in a DataFrame. The DataFrame API includes the `groupBy` method (which is also aliased by `groupby`), which is used to group the DataFrame on specific columns. This function returns a `pyspark.sql.GroupedData` object, which is a special type of DataFrame containing grouped data exposing common aggregate functions such as `sum` and `count`.

groupBy()

syntax:

```
DataFrame.groupBy(cols)
```

The groupBy method creates a new DataFrame containing the input DataFrame grouped by the column or columns specified in the cols argument. Listing 13.28 demonstrates the use of groupBy to average trip durations from the trips entity in our bike share dataset.

LISTING 13.28   Grouping and Aggregating Data in DataFrames

```
trips = sqlContext.table("trips")
averaged = trips.groupBy([trips.start_terminal]).avg('duration') \
                 .show(2)
+--------------+------------------+
|start_terminal|     avg(duration)|
+--------------+------------------+
|            31|2747.6333021515434|
|            32|1676.1081300813007|
+--------------+------------------+
```

Caching, Persisting, and Repartitioning DataFrames

I detailed caching, persistence and repartitioning in **Hour 12, "Advanced Spark Programming."** The DataFrame API supports similar methods to the Spark RDD API for these operations.

Methods for caching and persisting DataFrames include cache, persist, and unpersist, which behave the same as the RDD functions with the same name. Additionally, Spark SQL adds the cacheTable method, which caches a table from Spark SQL or Hive in memory. The clearCache method is used to remove the cached table from memory.

DataFrames also support the coalesce and repartition methods (which I discussed in **Hour 12, "Advanced Spark Programming"**) used to repartition DataFrames.

Saving DataFrame Output Using the DataFrameWriter

The DataFrameWriter is the interface used to write a DataFrame to external storage systems such as file systems or a database. The DataFrameWriter is accessed using DataFrame.write().

Writing Data to a Hive Table

I have demonstrated loading data into a DataFrame from a Hive table earlier. Similarly, you may often need to write data from a DataFrame to a Hive table.

saveAsTable()

Syntax:

```
DataFrame.write.saveAsTable(name,
                 format=None,
                 mode=None,
                 partitionBy=None)
```

The saveAsTable method writes the data from a DataFrame into the Hive table specified in the name argument. The format argument specifies the output format for the target table, the default is Parquet format. mode is the behavior with respect to an existing object. Valid values are append, overwrite, error, and ignore. Listing 13.29 shows an example of the saveAsTable method.

LISTING 13.29   Saving a DataFrame to a Hive Table

```
stations = sqlContext.table("stations")
stations.select([stations.station_id,stations.name]).write \
     .saveAsTable("station_names")
# load new table
station_names = sqlContext.table("station_names")
station_names.show(2)
+----------+--------------------+
|station_id|                name|
+----------+--------------------+
|         2|San Jose Diridon ...|
|         3|San Jose Civic Ce...|
+----------+--------------------+
```

There is a similar method in the DataFrame API named insertInto.

Writing Data to Parquet Files

Data from DataFrames can be written to files in any supported filesystem: local, network, or distributed. Output is written as a directory with files emitted for each partition, similar to the RDD output examples I've covered previously.

parquet()

Syntax:

```
DataFrame.write.parquet(path, mode=None, partitionBy=None)
```

The parquet method writes out the data from a DataFrame to a directory containing Parquet format files. Files are compressed according to the compression configuration settings in the current SparkContext. The mode argument specifies the behavior if the directory or files exist. Valid values for mode are append, overwrite, ignore, and error (default). partitionBy specifies the names of columns to partition the output files by (using the hash partitioner). Listing 13.30 demonstrates using parquet to save a DataFrame to a Parquet file using Snappy compression.

LISTING 13.30   Saving a DataFrame to a Parquet File or Files

```
sqlContext.setConf("spark.sql.parquet.compression.codec.", "snappy")
stations = sqlContext.table("stations")
stations.select([stations.station_id,stations.name]).write \
        .parquet("hdfs:///.../station_names", mode='overwrite')
```

ORC file can be written using the orc method, which is similar in usage. JSON files can also be written using the json method.

DataFrames can also be saved to external JDBC-compliant databases using the DataFrame.write.jdbc method.

Accessing Spark SQL

So far, I've shown examples of Spark SQL using the PySpark interactive shell that could be accessed through the command line/terminal or a notebook interface. This may not be the appropriate interface for users who are not programmers; a SQL shell or access to the Spark SQL engine from a visualization tool (such as Tableau or Excel) via ODBC may be more appropriate. I will discuss the various alternative access methods in this section.

Accessing Spark SQL Using the spark-sql Shell

Spark includes a SQL shell utility called spark-sql in the bin directory of your Spark installation. The spark-sql shell program is a lightweight REPL (read evaluate print loop) shell that can be used to access Spark SQL and Hive using your local configuration and Spark driver binaries. The shell accepts HiveQL statements, including metadata operations such as SHOW TABLES and DESCRIBE. Figure 13.6 shows an example spark-sql shell.

FIGURE 13.6
The spark-sql shell.

spark-sql is useful for testing SQL commands locally as a developer, but it is limited because it's not a SQL engine that can be accessed by other users and remote applications. This is where the Thrift JDBC/ODBC server comes into play.

Running the Thrift JDBC/ODBC server

Spark SQL can be used as a distributed query engine using a JDBC/ODBC interface. As with the spark-sql shell, the JDBC/ODBC server enables users to run SQL queries without writing Python or Scala Spark code. External applications, such as visualization tools, can connect to the server and interact directly with Spark SQL.

The JDBC/ODBC interface is implemented through a Thrift JDBC/ODBC Server. Thrift is an Apache project used for cross-language service development. The Spark SQL Thrift JDBC/ODBC server is based on the HiveServer2 project (a server interface that enables remote clients to execute queries against Hive and retrieve the results).

The Thrift JDBC/ODBC server is included with the Spark release. To run the server, execute the following command:

```
$SPARK_HOME/sbin/start-thriftserver.sh
```

All valid spark-submit command line arguments are accepted by the start-thriftserver.sh script such as --master local and so on. Additionally, you can supply Hive specific properties using the `--hiveconf` option. The Thrift JDBC/OBDC server listens on port 10000, but this can be changed using a special environment variable as shown here:

```
export HIVE_SERVER2_THRIFT_PORT=<customport>
```

You can use `beeline`, which I will discuss next, to test the JDBC/ODBC server. To stop the Thrift server, simply execute:

```
$SPARK_HOME/sbin/stop-thriftserver.sh
```

Using beeline

Beeline is a command line shell that can be used to connect to HiveServer2 or the Spark SQL JDBC/ODBC Thrift server. Beeline is a lightweight JDBC client application that is based on the SQLLine CLI project (http://sqlline.sourceforge.net/).

Beeline, like SQLLine, is a Java console-based utility for connecting to relational databases and executing SQL commands. It was designed to function similarly to other command line database access utilities such as sqlplus for Oracle, mysql for MySQL, and isql or osql for Sybase/SQL Server.

Because Beeline is a JDBC client, you can use it to test the Spark SQL JDBC Thrift server that you just started. You can use the Beeline CLI utility included with the Spark release as follows:

```
$SPARK_HOME/bin/beeline
```

At the Beeline prompt, you now need to connect to a JDBC server (the Spark SQL Thrift server we started previously). This can be done as follows:

```
beeline> !connect jdbc:hive2://localhost:10000
```

You will be prompted for a username and password to connect to the server. Figure 13.7 shows an example Beeline CLI session connecting to the Spark SQL Thrift server.

FIGURE 13.7
The Beeline Spark SQL JDBC client.

Using External Application via JDBC/ODBC

Your JDBC/ODBC server can also be connected to by other JDBC/ODBC client applications such as Tableau or Excel. This will usually require you to install the relevant JDBC/ODBC drivers on your client. You can then create a data source and connect to Spark SQL to access and process data in Hive. Consult your visualization tool vendor for more information or to obtain the specific drivers required.

TRY IT YOURSELF ▼

Accessing Spark SQL Using Beeline

In this exercise, you will start a Spark SQL Thrift server and use Beeline to connect to the server. You will then create Hive tables based upon our sample data and use Beeline and Thrift to run a SQL query against the data, executed by Spark SQL.

You will use data from the `sty-spark` S3 bucket for this exercise. If you have access to S3 (via an AWS Access Key ID and Secret Access Key), you can access the data directly as I will do in this exercise. Otherwise, you can use the https links to download the files and reference them from HDFS or your local filesystem, whichever you are more comfortable with.

1. Start your JDBC/ODBC Thrift server:

```
sudo $SPARK_HOME/sbin/start-thriftserver.sh \
--hiveconf hive.server2.thrift.port=10001 \
--hiveconf hive.server2.thrift.bind.host=10001 \
--master local
```

You can start in yarn mode as well using `--master yarn-cluster`.

2. Open a Beeline session using:

```
$SPARK_HOME/bin/beeline
```

3. At the `beeline>` prompt create a connection to your Thrift server as follows:

```
beeline> !connect jdbc:hive2://localhost:10001
Enter username for jdbc:hive2://localhost:10001: hadoop
Enter password for jdbc:hive2://localhost:10001: ******
```

You will be prompted for a `username` and `password` as shown above. The `username` provided must exist on the Thrift server and have the appropriate permissions on the filesystem.

4. After you are connected to the server, create the `trips` table from the bike-share demo by entering the following HiveQL DDL command:

```
CREATE EXTERNAL TABLE trips (
TripID int,
Duration int,
StartDate string,
StartStation string,
StartTerminal int,
EndDate string,
EndStation string,
EndTerminal int,
BikeNo int,
SubscriberType string,
ZipCode string
)
ROW FORMAT DELIMITED FIELDS TERMINATED BY ','
LOCATION 's3n://sty-spark/bike-share/trips/';
```

5. Execute the following SQL query against the table you just created:

```
SELECT StartTerminal
, StartStation
, COUNT(1) AS count
FROM trips
GROUP BY
```

```
StartTerminal, StartStation
ORDER BY count
DESC LIMIT 10;
```

6. View your Spark Application Web UI to confirm that your query executed using Spark SQL. Recall that this is accessed using port 4040 of your localhost if you are running Spark locally or the applications master host if you are using YARN (accessible from the Resource Manager UI).

Summary

In this hour, I have focused on one of the most active and exciting extensions to Spark: Spark SQL. Spark SQL evolved from Shark, a project to enable Spark evaluation of objects in Hive, to become an integral component within the Spark project. Spark SQL introduces many optimizations aimed specifically at relational-type access patterns using SQL. These optimizations include columnar storage, maintaining column and partition level statistics, and Partial DAG execution, which allows DAGs to change during processing based upon statistics and skew observed in the data.

Spark SQL also introduces the DataFrame, a structured, columnar abstraction of the Spark RDD. The DataFrame API enables many features and functions that would be familiar to most SQL developers, analysts, enthusiasts, and general users. You have explored some of the basics of the DataFrame API in this hour, including creating DataFrames from external sources and saving DataFrame output.

Finally, I covered the various methods that can be used to make Spark SQL available to users and developers including JDBC, Beeline, and the `spark-sql` shell.

Spark SQL is evolving rapidly, with new and interesting functions and capabilities being added with every minor release. In a single hour, you can only scratch the surface of the world of possibilities available using Spark SQL. But I have definitely given you enough information to be dangerous!

Q&A

Q. **Explain Partial DAG Execution (PDE) and how it optimizes processing in Spark SQL.**

A. PDE allows DAGs to be changed (and optimized) on the fly as information is discovered about the data during processing. The DAG modifications include optimization for performing joins, handling "skew" in the data, and altering the degree of parallelism used by Spark.

Q. What is the difference between the SQLContext and the HiveContext?

A. The HiveContext is an extension of the SQLContext entry point to Spark SQL. The HiveContext reads the `hive-site.xml` configuration file for information on how to connect to the Hive metastore. Using a HiveContext enables access to Hive table objects and HiveQL functions in addition to Spark SQL functions.

Q. What is the key difference between the `map` and `select` DataFrame methods?

A. The `map` DataFrame method returns an RDD, whereas `select` returns a new DataFrame.

Workshop

The workshop contains quiz questions and exercises to help you solidify your understanding of the material covered. Try to answer all questions before looking at the "Answers" section that follows.

Quiz

1. **True or false:** You are not required to supply the schema for a `DataFrame` object when it is instantiated.

2. Which `DataFrame` method is used to remove a column from the resultant DataFrame?

    A. `drop`

    B. `filter`

    C. `remove`

3. List some of the external datasources that can be used to create Spark SQL DataFrames.

4. **True or false:** A `unionAll` operation performed against two DataFrames will return a new DataFrame with de-duplicated rows from both input DataFrames.

Answers

1. **True.** The schema for a DataFrame will be inferred if it is not explicitly defined.

2. **A.**

3. Existing RDDs or DataFrames, Hive tables, text files, Parquet and ORC files, JSON objects and files, JDBC datasources.

4. **False.** `unionAll` does not remove duplicates. You would need to follow this operation with a `distinct` if you required de-duplication.

HOUR 14
Stream Processing with Spark

What You'll Learn in This Hour:

▶ What Spark Streaming is and how it works
▶ How to use discretized streams (DStreams)
▶ How to work with sliding window operations
▶ How to develop Spark Streaming applications

Real-time event processing has become a defining feature of big data systems. From sensors and network data processing to fraud detection to website monitoring and much more, the capability to consume, process, and derive insights from streaming data sources has never been more relevant. Thus far, the processing I've covered in the Spark core API and with Spark SQL has been batch-oriented. This hour is focused on stream processing and another key extension to Spark: Spark Streaming.

Introduction to Spark Streaming

Around 2008, Hadoop and associated open source big data technologies and platforms began to flourish in tech companies such as Facebook, Twitter, and others. With the proliferation of the mobile Internet, social networking, and ubiquitously well connected user populations, many of these companies recognized the value in analyzing data and providing feedback in real time.

In 2008, a company specializing in social media marketing intelligence, BackType, with a lead engineer named Nathan Marz, initiated a new project called Storm. Storm (now Apache Storm) is a distributed computation framework written predominantly in the Clojure programming language to enable distributed processing of streaming data. Storm became an early leader in open source big data real-time event processing and quickly became part of the Hadoop ecosystem. BackType and the intellectual capital behind Storm were acquired by Twitter in 2011, and Storm remains a popular integrated stream processing approach with Hadoop.

Streaming, Spark Style

The founders of Spark also realized the necessity of event/stream processing as a key component of big data platforms and looked to implement a solution within the Spark project. Although Storm delivered sub-second latency for event processing processing, there were limitations in its fault tolerance and data guarantees.

The Spark approach aimed to deliver low latency stream processing with improved fault tolerance and a guarantee that each event would be processed exactly once, even if a node failure or similar fault occurs. The Spark approach would also deliver an event processing system integrated with its RDD-based batch framework. The approach would become *Spark Streaming*.

The design goals for Spark Streaming included

 ▶ Low (second scale) latency

 ▶ One-time (and only one-time) event processing

 ▶ Linear scalability

 ▶ Integration with Spark core API

Spark Streaming Architecture

Spark Streaming introduces the concept of *discretized streams* (or *DStreams*). I will discuss these in much more detail in the next section, but DStreams are essentially batches of data stored in multiple RDDs, each batch representing a time window (typically in seconds). The resultant RDDs can then be processed using the core Spark RDD API and all of the available transformations that I've discussed at length. Figure 14.1 shows a high-level overview of Spark Streaming.

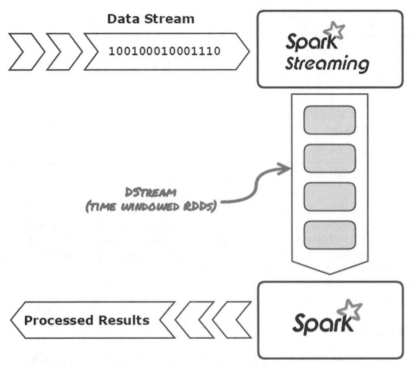

FIGURE 14.1
A high-level overview of Spark Streaming.

The StreamingContext

As with the SparkContext, SQLContext, and HiveContext program entry points I've discussed before, Spark Streaming applications have an entry point as well called the *StreamingContext*. The StreamingContext represents a connection to a Spark platform or cluster using an existing SparkContext. The StreamingContext is used to create DStreams from streaming input sources and govern streaming computation and DStream transformations.

The StreamingContext also specifies the `batchDuration` argument, which is a time interval in seconds by which streaming data will be split into batches.

After instantiating a StreamingContext, you would create a connection to a data stream and define a series of transformations to be performed. The `start` method or `ssc.start()` is used to trigger evaluation of the incoming data after a StreamingContext is established. The StreamingContext can be stopped programatically using `ssc.stop()` or `ssc.awaitTermination()`, as shown in Listing 14.1.

LISTING 14.1   Creating a StreamingContext

```
from pyspark.streaming import StreamingContext
ssc = StreamingContext(sc, 1)
...
# Initialize Data Stream
# DStream transformations
...
ssc.start()
...
# ssc.stop() or ssc.awaitTermination()
```

NOTE

Just as `sc` and `sqlContext` are common conventions for instances of the `SparkContext` and `SQLContext` or `HiveContext` respectively, `ssc` is a common convention for an instance of the StreamingContext. Unlike the former entry points, however, the StreamingContext is not automatically instantiated for you in the interactive shells `pyspark` and `spark-shell`.

Using DStreams

Discretized streams (DStreams) are the basic programming object in the Spark Streaming API. DStreams represent a continuous sequence of RDDs that are created from a continuous stream of data, with each underlying RDD representing a time window within the stream.

DStreams can be created from streaming data sources such as TCP sockets, messaging systems, streaming APIs (such as the Twitter streaming API), and more. DStreams (as an RDD abstraction) can also be created from transformations performed on existing DStreams (such as `map`, `flatMap`, and other operations).

DStreams support two types of operations:

▶ Transformations

▶ Output operations

Output operations are analogous to RDD actions. DStreams are executed lazily upon the request of an output operation, similar to lazy evaluation with Spark RDDs.

Figure 14.2 is a representation of a discretized stream, with each *t* interval representing a window of time specified by the `batchDuration` argument in the StreamingContext instantiation.

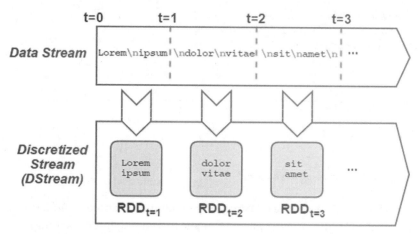

FIGURE 14.2
Spark discretized streams (DStreams).

DStream Sources

DStreams are defined within a StreamingContext for a specified input data stream, much the same way that RDDs are created for an input data source within a SparkContext. Many common streaming input sources are included in the Streaming API, such as sources to read data from a TCP socket or for reading data as it is being written to HDFS.

The basic input data sources for creating DStreams are described here:

socketTextStream()

Syntax:

```
StreamingContext.socketTextStream(hostname, port,
          storageLevel=StorageLevel(True, True, False, False, 2))
```

The socketTextStream method is used to create a DStream from an input TCP source defined by the hostname and port arguments. The data received is interpreted using UTF8 encoding, with new line termination used to define new records. The storageLevel argument that defines the storage level for the DStream defaults to MEMORY_AND_DISK_SER_2. Listing 14.2 demonstrates the use of the socketTextStream method.

LISTING 14.2   socketTextStream Method

```
from pyspark.streaming import StreamingContext
ssc = StreamingContext(sc, 1)
lines = ssc.socketTextStream('localhost', 9999)
```

```
counts = lines.flatMap(lambda line: line.split(" ")) \
            .map(lambda word: (word, 1)) \
            .reduceByKey(lambda a, b: a+b)
counts.pprint()
ssc.start()
ssc.awaitTermination()
```

textFileStream()

Syntax:

> *StreamingContext*.textFileStream(directory)

The textFileStream method is used to create a DStream by monitoring a directory from an instance of HDFS (as specified by the current system or application configuration settings). The textFileStream listens for the creation of new files in the specified directory and captures the data written as a streaming source. Listing 14.3 shows the use of the textFileStream method.

LISTING 14.3   textFileStream Method

```
from pyspark.streaming import StreamingContext
ssc = StreamingContext(sc, 1)
lines = ssc.textFileStream('hdfs:///data/incoming/')
counts = lines.flatMap(lambda line: line.split(" ")) \
            .map(lambda x: (x, 1)) \
            .reduceByKey(lambda a, b: a+b)
counts.pprint()
ssc.start()
ssc.awaitTermination()
```

There are built-in sources for common messaging platforms such as Apache Kafka, Amazon Kinesis, Apache Flume, and more. I will cover these in more detail in **Hour 20, "Using Spark with Messaging Systems."** You can also create custom streaming data sources by implementing a *custom receiver* for your desired source. At this stage, custom receivers must be written in Scala or Java.

DStream Transformations

The DStream API contains many of the transformations available through the RDD API. DStream transformations (like RDD transformations) create a new DStream by applying a function or functions to an existing DStream. Listing 14.4 and Figure 14.3 show a simplified example of DStream transformations.

LISTING 14.4   DStream Transformations

```
from pyspark.streaming import StreamingContext
ssc = StreamingContext(sc, 30)
lines = ssc.socketTextStream('localhost', 9999)
counts = lines.map(lambda word: (word, 1)) \
            .reduceByKey(lambda a, b: a+b)
counts.pprint()
ssc.start()
ssc.awaitTermination()
# output:
...
-------------------------------------------
Time: 2016-03-30 21:43:00
-------------------------------------------
(u'vitae', 1)
(u'Lorem', 1)
(u'ipsum', 1)
(u'dolor', 1)
(u'amet', 1)
(u'sit', 1)
...
```

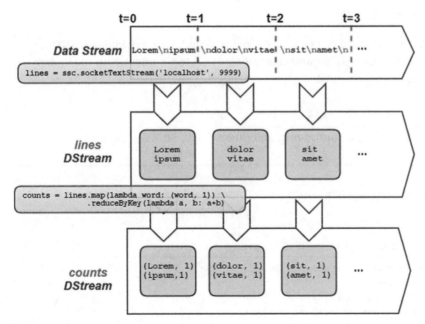

FIGURE 14.3
DStream transformations.

DStream Lineage and Checkpointing

The lineage of each DStream is maintained for fault tolerance much the same way as RDDs and DataFrames maintain their lineage. As streaming applications are long-lived applications by definition, checkpointing is often necessary. Checkpointing behaves similarly to our discussion of checkpointing RDDs in **Hour 11, "Using RDDs: Caching, Persistence, and Ouput."** The methods are slightly different, however, and to make things confusing, the methods have the same name (yet they are members of two separate classes). They are discussed next.

StreamingContext.checkpoint()

Syntax:

```
StreamingContext.checkpoint(directory)
```

The `StreamingContext.checkpoint` method enables periodic checkpointing of DStream operations for durablity and fault tolerance. The application DAG will be checkpointed at each batch interval as defined in the StreamingContext. The `directory` argument configures the directory (typically in HDFS) where the checkpoint data will be persisted.

DStream.checkpoint()

Syntax:

```
DStream.checkpoint(interval)
```

The `DStream.checkpoint` method can be used to enable periodic checkpointing of RDDs of a particular DStream. The `interval` argument is the time in seconds after which the underlying RDDs in a DStream will be checkpointed.

NOTE

The `interval` argument must be a positive multiple of the `batchDuration` set in the StreamingContext.

Listing 14.5 demonstrates the use of the functions to control checkpointing behavior in Spark Streaming.

LISTING 14.5   Checkpointing in Spark Streaming

```
from pyspark.streaming import StreamingContext
ssc = StreamingContext(sc, 30)
ssc.checkpoint('file:///opt/spark/data')
lines = ssc.socketTextStream('localhost', 9999)
counts = lines.map(lambda word: (word, 1)) \
              .reduceByKey(lambda a, b: a+b)
```

```
counts.checkpoint(30)
counts.pprint()
ssc.start()
ssc.awaitTermination()
```

Caching and Persistence with DStreams

DStreams support caching and persistence using interfaces with the same name and usage as their RDD counterparts, `cache` and `persist`. These options are especially useful for DStreams that are used more than once in downstream processing operations. Storage levels work the same with DStreams as they do with RDDs as well.

Broadcast Variables and Accumulators with Streaming Applications

Broadcast variables and accumulators are available for use in Spark Streaming applications in the same way they are implemented in native Spark applications. Broadcast variables are useful for distributing lookup or reference data that is associated with DStream RDD contents. Accumulators can be used as counters. I will discuss maintaining state specifically in the next section.

There are some limitations regarding recovery when using broadcast variables or accumulators with checkpointing enabled. If you are developing production Spark Streaming applications, you should consult the latest Spark Streaming programming guide when using broadcast variables or accumulators.

DStream Output Operations

Output operations with DStreams are similar in concept to Actions with RDDs. DStream output operations write data, results, events, or other data to a console, file system, database, or other destination. The basic DStream output operations are described here:

pprint()
Syntax:

```
DStream.pprint(num=10)
```

The `pprint` method prints the first `num` elements for each RDD in the DStream (where num is 10 by default). `pprint` is a common way to get interactive console feedback from a streaming application. I've already used `pprint` in previous streaming examples. Figure 14.4 shows the output in the console from `pprint`.

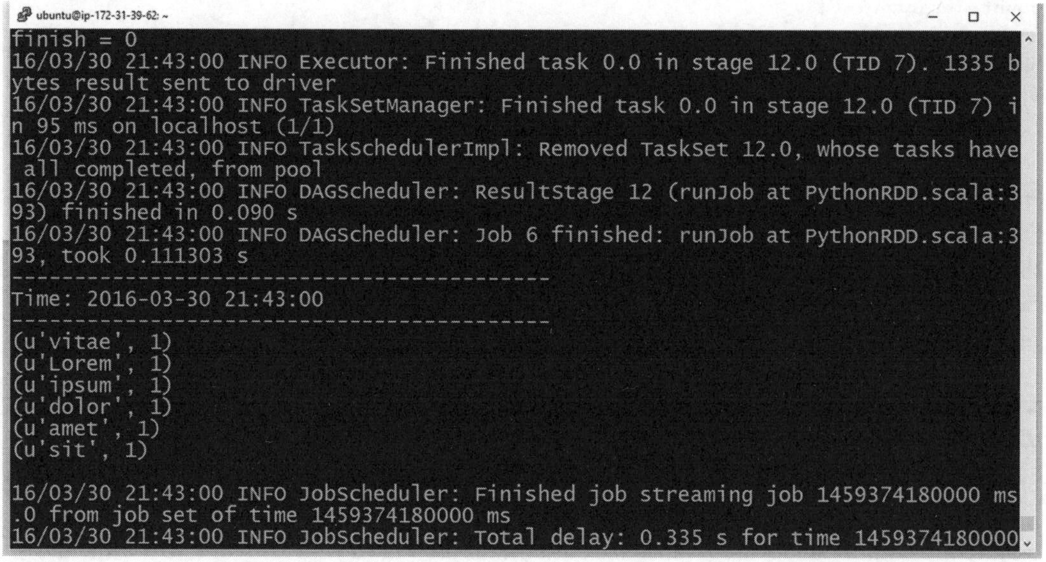

FIGURE 14.4
pprint DStream console output.

saveAsTextFiles()

Syntax:

```
DStream.saveAsTextFiles(prefix, suffix-=None)
```

The saveAsTextFiles method saves each RDD in a DStream as a text file in a target file system (local, HDFS or others). A directory of files is created with string representations of the elements contained in the DStream. Listing 14.6 shows the usage of the saveAsTextFiles method, the output directory created. An inspection of the file contents is shown in Figure 14.5.

LISTING 14.6   Saving DStream Output to Files

```python
from pyspark.streaming import StreamingContext
ssc = StreamingContext(sc, 30)
lines = ssc.socketTextStream('localhost', 9999)
counts = lines.map(lambda word: (word, 1)) \
            .reduceByKey(lambda a, b: a+b)
counts.saveAsTextFiles("file:///opt/spark/data/counts")
ssc.start()
ssc.awaitTermination()
```

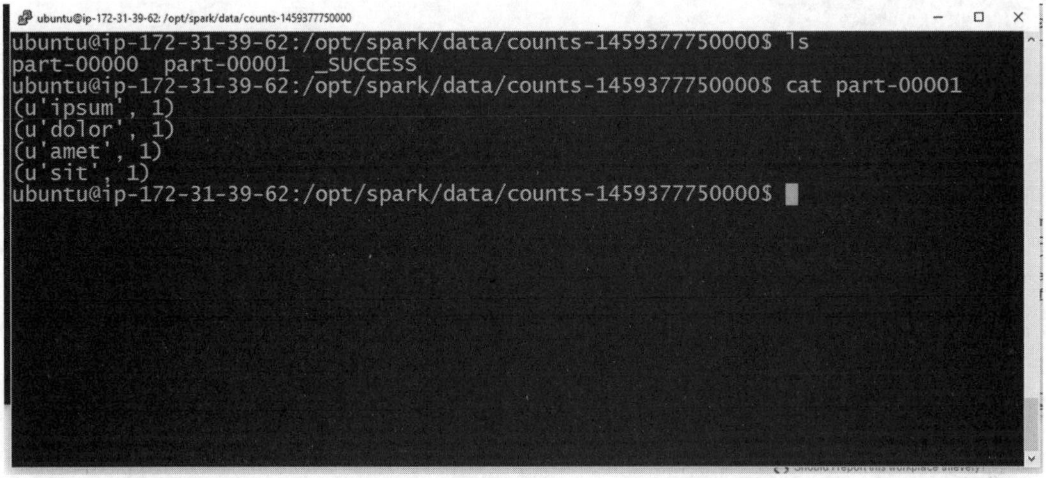

FIGURE 14.5
Text file output from saveAsTextFiles DStream method.

foreachRDD()

Syntax:

```
DStream.foreachRDD(func)
```

The foreachRDD output operation is similar to the foreach action in the Spark RDD API. It applies the function specified by the func argument to each RDD in a DStream. The foreachRDD is executed by the driver process running the streaming application and will usually force the computation of the DStream RDDs. The function used can be a named function or anonymous lambda function just as with foreach. Listing 14.7 shows a simple example of the foreachRDD method.

LISTING 14.7   Performing Functions in Each RDD in a DStream

```
from pyspark.streaming import StreamingContext
def printx(x): print("received : " + x)
ssc = StreamingContext(sc, 30)
lines = ssc.socketTextStream('localhost', 9999)
lines.foreachRDD(lambda x: x.foreach(lambda y: printx(y)))
ssc.start()
ssc.awaitTermination()
received : Lorem
received : ipsum
received : dolor
received : vitae
received : sit
received : amet
```

▼ TRY IT YOURSELF

Getting Started with Spark Streaming

In this exercise, you will stream lines from a Shakespeare text and consume the lines with the Spark Streaming application. You will then perform a "streaming word count" against the incoming data, similar to previous word count examples.

1. Copy the `shakespeare.txt` file from the Sams Teach Yourself Spark S3 bucket location to a local directory: for example, `/tmp`.

2. Open a `pyspark` shell. Note that if you are using local mode, you will need to specify at least two worker threads as shown here:

```
$ pyspark --master local[2]
```

3. Enter the following commands line by line in the `pyspark` shell:

```
import re
from pyspark.streaming import StreamingContext
ssc = StreamingContext(sc, 30)
lines = ssc.socketTextStream('localhost', 9999)
wordcounts = lines.filter(lambda line: len(line) > 0) \
              .flatMap(lambda line: re.split('\W+', line)) \
              .filter(lambda word: len(word) > 0) \
              .map(lambda word: (word.lower(), 1)) \
              .reduceByKey(lambda x, y: x + y)
wordcounts.pprint()
ssc.start()
ssc.awaitTermination()
```

Note that until you start a stream on the defined socket, you will see exceptions appear in the console output. This is normal.

4. In another terminal, using the directory containing the local `shakespeare.txt` file from Step 1 as the current directory, execute the following command:

```
while read line; do echo -e "$line\n"; sleep 1; done \
< shakespeare.txt | nc -lk 9999
```

This command reads a line from the `shakespeare.txt` file every second and send it to the netcat server.

5. You should see that every 30 seconds (the *batchInterval* set on our StreamingContext in Step 3), the lines received from the latest batch are transformed into key value pairs and counted, with output to the console similar to the output shown here:

```
-------------------------------------------
Time: 2016-03-31 20:18:00
-------------------------------------------
(u'and', 11)
(u'laugh', 1)
```

```
(u'old', 1)
(u'have', 1)
(u'trifles', 1)
(u'imitate', 1)
(u'neptune', 1)
(u'is', 2)
(u'crown', 1)
(u'changeling', 1)
...
```

State Operations

So far, my discussions of streaming applications have dealt with data statelessly, processing each batch during a batch interval independent of any other batches within a stream. Often, you want or need to maintain state across batches of data, with the state being updated as each new batch is processed. This can be accomplished using a "state" DStream.

State DStreams are created and updated using the special `updateStateByKey` transformation. This is preferred over using accumulators as shared variables in streaming applications, as `updateStateByKey` is automatically checkpointed for integrity, durability, and recoverability.

The `updateStateByKey` method is described here:

updateStateByKey()

Syntax:

```
DStream.updateStateByKey(updateFunc, numPartitions=None)
```

The `updateStateByKey` method returns a new state DStream where the state for each key is updated by applying the function specified by the `updateFunction` argument against the previous state of the key and the new values of the key.

The `updateStateBy` method expects key value pair input and returns a corresponding key value pair output, with the values updated according to the `updateFunction`.

The `numPartitions` argument can be used to repartition the output similar to other RDD methods with this argument.

NOTE

Checkpointing must be enabled in the StreamingContext using `ssc.checkpoint(directory)` to be able to use the `updateStateByKey` and create and update state DStreams.

Consider an input stream as shown here:

```
Lorem
ipsum
dolor
<pause for more than 30 seconds>
Lorem
ipsum
dolor
```

Listing 14.8 shows how you can use updateStateByKey to create and update the counts for the words received on the stream.

LISTING 14.8 State DStreams

```
from pyspark.streaming import StreamingContext
ssc = StreamingContext(sc, 30)
ssc.checkpoint("checkpoint")
def updateFunc(new_values, last_sum):
    return sum(new_values) + (last_sum or 0)
lines = ssc.socketTextStream('localhost', 9999)
wordcounts = lines.map(lambda word: (word, 1)) \
                .updateStateByKey(updateFunc)
wordcounts.pprint()
ssc.start()
ssc.awaitTermination()
# output:
...
-----------------------------------------
Time: 2016-03-31 00:02:30
-----------------------------------------
(u'Lorem', 1)
(u'ipsum', 1)
(u'dolor', 1)
...
-----------------------------------------
Time: 2016-03-31 00:03:00
-----------------------------------------
(u'Lorem', 2)
(u'ipsum', 2)
(u'dolor', 2)
...
```

Sliding Window Operations

The state operations you learned about in the previous section applied to all RDDs in the DStream. It is often useful to look at aggregations over a specific window (for instance, the last hour or last day). As this window is relative to a point in time, it's referred to as a *sliding window*.

Sliding window operations in Spark Streaming span RDDs within a DStream over a specified duration (the *window length*) and are evaluated at specific intervals (the *slide interval*). Consider Figure 14.6. If you wanted to count words seen in the last two intervals (window length) every two intervals (slide interval), you could use the reduceByKeyAndWindow function to created "windowed" RDDs.

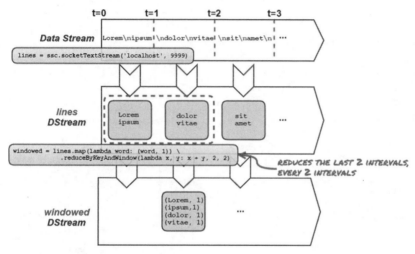

FIGURE 14.6
Sliding windows and windowed RDDs in Spark Streaming.

Sliding window functions available in the Spark Streaming API include window, countByWindow, reduceByWindow, reduceByKeyAndWindow, and countByValueAndWindow.

I will cover the two most common functions in the following sections.

window()

Syntax:

```
DStream.window(windowLength, slideInterval)
```

The window method returns a new DStream from specified batches of the input DStream. Window creates a new DStream object every interval as specified by the slideInterval argument, consisting of elements from the input DStream for the specified windowLength.

Both `slideInterval` and `windowLength` must be multiples of the `batchDuration` set in the StreamingContext. Listing 14.9 demonstrates the use of the `window` function.

LISTING 14.9   window Function

```
# send date to netcat every second:
# while sleep 1; do echo 'date'; done | nc -lk 9999
from pyspark.streaming import StreamingContext
ssc = StreamingContext(sc, 5)
dates = ssc.socketTextStream('localhost', 9999)
windowed = dates.window(10,10)
windowed.pprint()
ssc.start()
ssc.awaitTermination()
...
-------------------------------------------
Time: 2016-03-31 19:37:50
-------------------------------------------
Thu Mar 31 19:37:40 UTC 2016
Thu Mar 31 19:37:41 UTC 2016
Thu Mar 31 19:37:42 UTC 2016
Thu Mar 31 19:37:43 UTC 2016
Thu Mar 31 19:37:44 UTC 2016
Thu Mar 31 19:37:45 UTC 2016
Thu Mar 31 19:37:46 UTC 2016
Thu Mar 31 19:37:47 UTC 2016
Thu Mar 31 19:37:48 UTC 2016
Thu Mar 31 19:37:49 UTC 2016
...
-------------------------------------------
Time: 2016-03-31 19:38:00
-------------------------------------------
Thu Mar 31 19:37:50 UTC 2016
Thu Mar 31 19:37:51 UTC 2016
Thu Mar 31 19:37:52 UTC 2016
Thu Mar 31 19:37:53 UTC 2016
Thu Mar 31 19:37:54 UTC 2016
Thu Mar 31 19:37:55 UTC 2016
Thu Mar 31 19:37:56 UTC 2016
Thu Mar 31 19:37:57 UTC 2016
Thu Mar 31 19:37:58 UTC 2016
Thu Mar 31 19:37:59 UTC 2016
...
```

reduceByKeyAndWindow()

Syntax:

```
DStream.reduceByKeyAndWindow(func,
                 invFunc,
                 windowDuration,
                 slideDuration=None,
                 numPartitions=None,
                 filterFunc=None)
```

The `reduceByKeyAndWindow` method creates a new DStream by performing an associative reduce function as specified by the `func` argument to a sliding window as defined by the `windowDuration` and `slideDuration` arguments. The `invFunc` argument represents an inverse function to the `func` argument. The `invFunc` is included for efficiency to remove (or subtracts) counts from the previous window. `numPartitions` is an optional argument supported for repartitioning the output DStream. The optional `filterFunc` argument can be supplied to filter expired key value pairs—only key values pairs that satisfy the function are retained in the resultant DStream. Listing 14.10 demonstrates the use of the `reduceByKeyAndWindow` function.

LISTING 14.10   reduceByKeyAndWindow Function

```
from pyspark.streaming import StreamingContext
ssc = StreamingContext(sc, 5)
lines = ssc.socketTextStream('localhost', 9999)
windowedWordCounts = lines.map(lambda word: (word, 1)) \
                    .reduceByKeyAndWindow(lambda x, y: x + y, \
                        lambda x, y: x - y, 30, 10)
windowedWordCounts.pprint()
ssc.start()
ssc.awaitTermination()
```

NOTE

Checkpointing must be enabled when using the `reduceByKeyAndWindow` function.

Summary

In this hour, I discussed real-time data processing with Spark using Spark Streaming. Spark Streaming is a key extension to the Spark core API introducing objects and functions designed to process streams of data. One such object is the discretized stream (or DStream), which is an RDD abstraction comprised of streams of data batched into RDDs based upon time intervals.

You learned how transformation can be applied to DStreams applying functions to each underlying RDD in the DStream. I have covered state with DStreams and how this state can be accessed and updated in real time, a key capability in stream processing use cases. You also learned about sliding window operations, which operate on data "windows" (such as the last hour, last day, and so on).

I will revisit Spark Streaming and stream processing in **Hour 20, "Using Spark with Messaging Systems,"** when I introduce you to using Spark with messaging systems such as Kafka.

Q&A

Q. Why is checkpointing DStreams and their RDDs important in Spark Streaming applications?

A. Spark Streaming applications are "long lived" by definition. Lineage for DStreams and their RDDs can accumulate, which impacts fault tolerance, recovery, and performance. Periodic checkpointing is essential for Spark Streaming applications that run continuously.

Q. Why would you choose to implement a "state" DStream as opposed to using accumulators as shared variables?

A. Accumulators have limited recoverability in the event of failure, as streaming applications are long-lived. Using "state" DStreams along with checkpointing is the preferred method for maintaining state across DStream batch intervals.

Q. Explain the concept of "windowed" DStreams in Spark Streaming.

A. A windowed DStream is the result of an operation performed on a DStream over a defined time interval (window).

Workshop

The workshop contains quiz questions and exercises to help you solidify your understanding of the material covered. Try to answer all questions before looking at the "Answers" section that follows.

Quiz

1. **True or false:** The StreamingContext is the entry point for a Spark Streaming application and defines the time interval by which streams of data are discretized.

2. Which DStream output operation is used to write output to the console?

     A. print

     B. dump

     C. pprint

     D. writeToConsole

3. What are the requirements for using the `updateStateByKey` method in a Spark Streaming application?

4. What parameters are required for a "windowed" operation such as `reduceByKeyAndWindow?`

Answers

1. **True.**

2. **B.**

3. Checkpointing must be enabled in the StreamingContext and the input to the `updateStateByKey` method should be in the form of key value pairs.

4. Window length (duration of the window) and sliding interval (interval at which the window operation is performed).

Getting Started with Spark and R

What You'll Learn in This Hour:

▶ Introduction to R

▶ Introduction to SparkR

▶ Using statistical functions with SparkR

▶ Building regression models with SparkR

▶ Using SparkR with RStudio

R is a powerful programming language and software environment for statistical computing, visual analytics, and predictive modeling. For data analysts, statisticians, mathematicians, and data scientists already using R, Spark provides a scalable runtime engine for R: SparkR. For developers and analysts new to R, this hour provides a gentle introduction and shows how R can be seamlessly integrated with Spark.

Introduction to R

R is an open source language and runtime environment for statistical computing and graphics that was based upon a language called S originally developed at Bell Labs in the late 1970s. The R language is widely used among statisticians, data analysts, and data scientists as a popular alternative to SAS, IBM SPSS, and other similar commercial software packages.

Native R is primarily written in C and compiled into machine code for the targeted platform. Precompiled binary versions are available for various operating systems including Linux, MacOS, and Windows. R programs can be run from the command line as batch scripts or through the interactive shell. Additionally there are several graphical user interfaces available for R including desktop applications and web-based interfaces, which you will look at later in this chapter. R's graphical rendering capabilities combine its mathematical modeling strength with the capability to produce visual statistics and analytics, as shown in Figure 15.1.

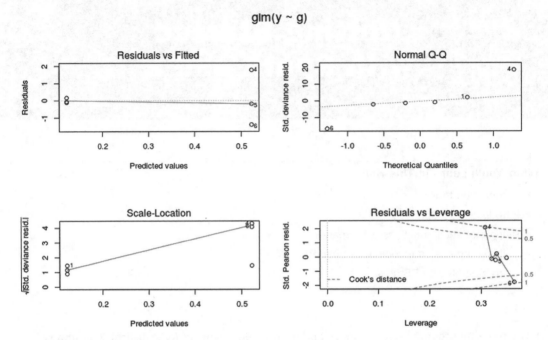

FIGURE 15.1
Visual statistics and analytics in R.

Getting Started with the R Language

R is a case-sensitive, interpreted language. R code is generally easy to spot by its non-conventional assignment operator (<-) as seen here:

```
y <- x + 2
```

Take a look at some of the building blocks of the R programming language.

R Basic Data Types

R has several basic data types used to represent data elements held within the data structures I will talk about next. The main R data types used to represent data elements are summarized in Table 15.1.

TABLE 15.1   Primary R Data Types

Type	Description	Example
Logical	Boolean value	TRUE, FALSE
Numeric	Double precision numeric value	3, 1.4, 1.1e+10
Integer	32-bit signed integer	3L, 384L
Character	String value or arbitrary length	"spark", "123", "A"

Integers can cause some confusion, especially because the L notation is used to declare them in R. R integer types are a subset of the numeric type. At the time of writing, an R integer is a 32-bit (or 4 byte) signed integer, in contrast to a *long* type in most programming languages, which is a 64-bit or 8 byte signed integer, often declared using the *nL* syntax. For conventional long numbers, you would typically use the *numeric* type in R, which is a double precision number that is capable of storing much larger numbers.

Listing 15.1 shows the use of system functions to display the maximum values for integer and numeric (double) types in R.

LISTING 15.1   Max Values for R Integer and Numeric (Double) Types

```
.Machine$integer.max
[1] 2147483647
.Machine$double.xmax
[1] 1.797693e+308
```

There are also more obscure types for complex numbers and raw byte arrays. As this is only intended to be an introduction, I won't cover these.

R Data Structures

R's data model is based upon the concept of vectors. A vector is a sequence of data elements of the same type. The members of a vector are called *components*. More complex structures are built upon vectors, such as *matrices*, which are two-dimensional data structures with data elements of the same type and *arrays*, which are multi-dimensional objects (more than two dimensions).

Importantly, R has an additional data structure called a *data frame*. Data frames in R are conceptually similar to DataFrames in Spark SQL, which I had covered in Hour 13. In fact, the Spark SQL DataFrame was inspired by the data frame construct in R. R data frames are two-dimensional data structures where columns may be of different types, but each value within a column is of the same type. Basically, this is tantamount to a table object in a relational database.

Figure 15.2 shows a representation of the basic data structures in R with sample data.

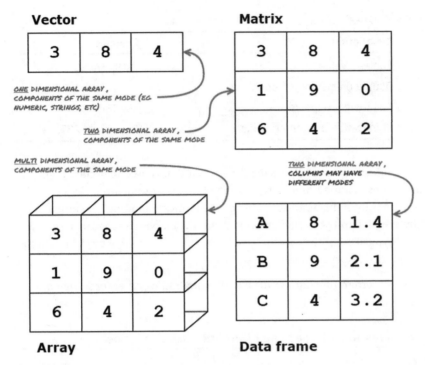

FIGURE 15.2
Data structures in R.

R has no concept of scalar values (akin to primitive types available in most common programming languages). The equivalent of a scalar variable is represented as a vector with a length of one in R. Consider Listing 15.2. If you want to create a simple variable, var, with a scalar-like assignment equal to 1, var is created as a vector with one component.

LISTING 15.2   Simple R Vector

```
> var <- 1
> var
[1] 1
```

A multi-valued vector is created using the combine or c() function, which is demonstrated in Listing 15.3.

LISTING 15.3   Combine Function to Create an R Vector

```
> vec <- c(1,2,3)
> vec
[1] 1 2 3
```

A two-dimensional matrix is created using the `matrix` command. An example of creating a 3×3 matrix using the combine function is shown in Listing 15.4. By default, elements are filled in by column. However, you can specify `byrow=TRUE` to fill in a matrix by each row.

LISTING 15.4   Creating an R Matrix

```
> mat = matrix(
+      c(1,2,3,4,5,6,7,8,9),
+      nrow=3,
+      ncol=3)
> mat
       [,1] [,2] [,3]
[1,]     1    4    7
[2,]     2    5    8
[3,]     3    6    9
```

Elements of a matrix can be accessed using subscripts and brackets. For instance, `x[i,]` is a reference to the *i*th row of the matrix, x, `x[,j]` is a reference to the *j*th column of a matrix x, and `x[i,j]` refers to the intersection of the *i*th row and *j*th column. An example of this is shown in Listing 15.5.

LISTING 15.5   Accessing Data Elements in an R Matrix

```
> mat[1,]
[1] 1 4 7
> mat[,1]
[1] 1 2 3
> mat[3,3]
[1] 9
```

R Data Frames

Arguably, the most important data structure in R is the data frame. Data frames in R can be thought of as data tables, with rows and columns where columns can be of mixed types. R data frames are the primary data structure used to interact with SparkR, as I will discuss shortly.

Data frames can be created from column vectors using the `data.frame` function as shown in Listing 15.6.

LISTING 15.6   Creating an R Data Frame from Column Vectors

```
> col1 = c("A", "B", "C")
> col2 = c(8,9,4)
> col3 = c(1.4,2.1,3.2)
> df = data.frame(col1,col2,col3)
> df
```

```
col1 col2 col3
1    A    8   1.4
2    B    9   2.1
3    C    4   3.2
```

R data frames can also be created from external sources using the `read` command. `read`
supports different sources, which are summarized in Table 15.2.

TABLE 15.2 Functions to Create an R Data Frame from an External Source

read Function	Description
read.table()	Reads a new line terminated file with fields delimited by white space in table format and creates a dataframe.
read.csv()	Same as `read.table()` using commas (,) as the field separator.
read.fwf()	Reads a table of fixed-width formatted data, a common extract format for many mainframe and other legacy systems.

There are several other SparkR specific methods for creating distributed dataframes in SparkR
from external sources, which I will discuss in the next section.

Data frames in R have several methods used to inspect and access access data from within the
data frame. Some of these are demonstrated in Listing 15.7 using the sample data frame created
in Listing 15.6.

LISTING 15.7 Accessing and Inspecting Data in R Data Frames

```
> # get element in row 1, col 2
> df[1,2]
[1] 8
> # get number of cols in the dataframe
> ncol(df)
[1] 3
> # get number of rows in the dataframe
> nrow(df)
[1] 3
> # display first row from the dataframe
> head(df, 1)
col1 col2 col3
1    A    8   1.4
```

R Functions and Packages

Most R programs involve manipulating data elements or data structures using functions. R, like
most other languages, includes many common built-in functions. A sample of the available
built-in functions is provided in Table 15.3.

TABLE 15.3   Sample Built-in R Functions

Category	Example Functions
Numeric	`abs()`, `sqrt()`, `ceiling()`, `floor()`, `log()`, `exp()`, ...
Character	`substr()`, `grep()`, `strsplit()`, `toupper()`, ...
Statistical	`mean()`, `sd()`, `median()`, `quantile()`, `sum()`, `min()`, ...
Probability	`dnorm()`, `pnorm()`, `qnorm()`, `dpois()`, `ppois()`, ...

The true power of R, however, is in libraries and packages written for R. *Packages* are collections of R functions, data, and compiled code in a well defined and described format. The directory on the system where the packages are stored is called the *library*.

R ships with a standard set of packages including several sample datasets, which I will cover shortly. Custom R packages can be also be obtained from a publicly available collection of packages contributed by an R user community called *CRAN*. You can find more information about R packages available from CRAN at **https://cran.r-project.org/**.

If you cannot find a built-in function, included package, or CRAN package to do what you need to, you can author your own package or packages as well.

Packages are installed using the R `CMD INSTALL <package>` command on the system running the R program. After a package is installed, it is loaded into the current R session using the `library(<package>)` command.

You can use the `library()` function with no arguments to view all of the packages loaded and available in the current R session as shown in Listing 15.8.

LISTING 15.8   Listing R Packages Installed and Available in an R Session

```
> library()
Packages in library '/opt/spark/R/lib':
SparkR          R frontend for Spark

Packages in library '/usr/lib/R/library':
base            The R Base Package
boot            Bootstrap Functions
class           Functions for Classification
cluster         "Finding Groups in Data": Cluster Analysis
codetools       Code Analysis Tools for R
compiler        The R Compiler Package
datasets        The R Datasets Package
...
```

As you can see from Listing 15.8, SparkR itself is an R package, which you will learn about in the next section.

Introducing SparkR

The SparkR package for R provides an interface to access Spark from R, including the implementation of distributed data frames and large-scale statistical analysis, probability, and predictive modeling operations. SparkR is included with the Spark release. The package library is available in `$SPARK_HOME/R/lib/SparkR`. SparkR provides an R programming environment that enables R programmers to use Spark as a processing engine. Specific documentation about the SparkR API is available at **https://spark.apache.org/docs/latest/api/R/index.html**.

Take a look at how to access and use SparkR now.

The SparkR Shell

The SparkR shell is the easiest way to get started with Spark and R. The command to launch the SparkR shell is `sparkR`, which is available in the `bin` directory of your Spark installation (the same directory as the other interactive shells I've mentioned, including `pyspark`, `spark-sql`, and `beeline`). SparkR starts an R session using the SparkR package with the Spark environment defaults for the specific system (such as `spark.master` and `spark.driver.memory`). Figure 15.3 shows an example of a SparkR shell.

FIGURE 15.3
The SparkR shell.

Notice that, as with `pyspark`, a SparkContext is created as `sc`. A SQLContext is also available as `sqlContext`. The SparkContext and SQLContext are required as entry points to connect your R program to a Spark cluster and to be able to use data frames.

You can also use the `sparkR` command to run R programs in batch mode. Given an R program named `helloworld.R`, Figure 15.4 demonstrates how to run the program in batch mode using sparkR.

```
ubuntu@ip-172-31-39-62:~
ubuntu@ip-172-31-39-62:~$ sparkR helloworld.R
Loading required package: methods

Attaching package: 'SparkR'

The following objects are masked from 'package:stats':

    filter, na.omit

The following objects are masked from 'package:base':

    intersect, rbind, sample, subset, summary, table, transform

[1] "Hello, world!"
ubuntu@ip-172-31-39-62:~$
```

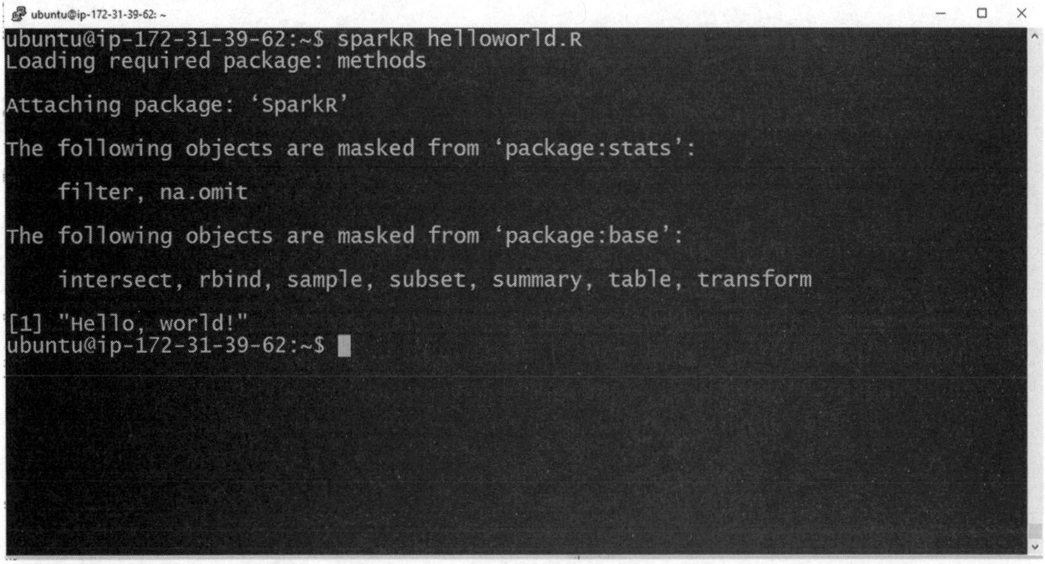

FIGURE 15.4
Running R programs in batch mode using sparkR.

Creating Data Frames in SparkR

SparkR data frames can be created in a number of ways. I will cover the most common approaches here.

Creating a SparkR Data Frame from a Local R Data Frame

Native R data frames can easily be converted into distributed data frames in SparkR. To demonstrate this, I will use the built-in R data set `mtcars`, which consists of data extracted from the 1974 issues of American magazine *Motor Trend*, including fuel consumption and 10 aspects of automobile design and performance for 32 automobiles (1973–74 models).

TIP

The R Datasets Package

One of the packages that is included with R is the `datasets` package. This package includes more than 100 diverse datasets from worldwide contributors, ranging from airline passenger numbers to air quality measurements to road casualties and violent crime rates. The datasets package also includes the famous Edgar Anderson's `Iris Data` dataset, which provides the measurements of sepal and petal length and width for 50 flowers from three species of irises—the "Hello, World" of data mining.

A complete list of the sample R data sets available in the datasets package can be viewed by entering the following in your R or sparkR interactive shell.

```
> library(help = "datasets")
```

The mtcars sample dataset is an R data frame with 32 observations on 11 variables. In Listing 15.9, using a sparkR session, the mtcars sample dataset is loaded into an R dataframe named df, and then the nrow, ncol, and head functions are used to inspect the data frame.

LISTING 15.9   mtcars Data Frame in R

```
> r_df <- mtcars
> nrow(r_df)
[1] 32
> ncol(r_df)
[1] 11
> head(r_df, 2)
              mpg cyl disp  hp drat    wt  qsec vs am gear carb
Mazda RX4      21   6  160 110  3.9 2.620 16.46  0  1    4    4
Mazda RX4 Wag  21   6  160 110  3.9 2.875 17.02  0  1    4    4
```

NOTE

Because R is a scientific and modeling language, the data terminology used to refer to elements and constructs has an experimental science and mathematical modeling context. For instance, in the sample mtcars datasets, rows are referred to as *observations* and fields within rows representing columns are referred to as *variables*.

Using the R data frame, r_df, created in Listing 15.9, Listing 15.10 demonstrates how to create a SparkR data frame using the createDataFrame SparkR API method.

LISTING 15.10   Creating a SparkR Data Frame from an R Data Frame

```
> spark_df <- createDataFrame(sqlContext, r_df)
> spark_df
DataFrame[mpg:double, cyl:double, disp:double, hp:double, drat:double,
wt:double, qsec:double, vs:double, am:double, gear:double, carb:double]
```

Creating a SparkR Data Frame from a CSV File

The simplest method for loading a SparkR data frame from a comma-separated value (CSV) file is to use the Databricks Spark CSV package. To do this, you need to launch Spark with this package included by using the `packages` argument to sparkR as shown in Listing 15.11. (Be sure to check the latest available package version, which may change.)

LISTING 15.11 Including the Databricks Spark CSV Package in SparkR

```
sparkR --packages com.databricks:spark-csv_2.10:1.3.0
```

The Spark CSV package can now be used as a source for the SparkR method `read.df`, which is a generalized function for creating a SparkR data source from an external data source. Using the `Iris Data` dataset from a CSV file stored locally (`iris.csv`), Listing 15.12 shows how to create a SparkR data frame from this file, inferring the schema from data in the file (similar concept to schema inference I spoke about with SparkSQL DataFrames in Hour 13). You can use the `schema` method to inspect the inferred schema.

LISTING 15.12 Creating a SparkR Data Frame from a CSV File

```
> iris_csv <- read.df(sqlContext, "file:///opt/spark/data/iris.csv",
+ source = "com.databricks.spark.csv",
+ header="true", inferSchema = "true")
> schema(iris_csv)
StructType
|-name = "", type = "IntegerType", nullable = TRUE
|-name = "Sepal.Length", type = "DoubleType", nullable = TRUE
|-name = "Sepal.Width", type = "DoubleType", nullable = TRUE
|-name = "Petal.Length", type = "DoubleType", nullable = TRUE
|-name = "Petal.Width", type = "DoubleType", nullable = TRUE
|-name = "Species", type = "StringType", nullable = TRUE
> ncol(iris_csv)
[1] 6
> nrow(iris_csv)
[1] 150
> head(iris_csv,2)
1:2 Sepal.Length Sepal.Width Petal.Length Petal.Width Species
1   1          5.1         3.5          1.4         0.2     setosa
2   2          4.9         3.0          1.4         0.2     setosa
```

You can also explicitly define the schema for data in a CSV file by creating a `schema` object and supplying this to the `schema` argument in the `read.df` method. This is demonstrated in Listing 15.13.

LISTING 15.13 Defining the Schema for a SparkR Data Frame

```
> iris_schema <- structType(structField("", "double"),
+     structField("Sepal.Length", "double"),
+     structField("Sepal.Width", "double"),
```

```
+    structField("Petal.Length", "double"),
+    structField("Petal.Width", "double"),
+    structField("Species", "string")
+    )
> iris_csv <- read.df(sqlContext, "file:///opt/spark/data/iris.csv",
+ source = "com.databricks.spark.csv",
+ header="true", schema=iris_schema)
```

There are also purpose-built `read` functions in the SparkR API to create SparkR data frames from other common SparkSQL external data sources, such as `read.parquet` and `read.json`.

Creating a SparkR Data Frame from a Hive Table

The SparkR interactive shell automatically instantiates a SQLContext (sqlContext) as well as a SparkContext (sc). A HiveContext, however, is currently not automatically instantiated. The SparkR API includes a method named `sparkRHive.init`, which is used to create a HiveContext. When a HiveContext is available in the SparkR session, you can use the `sql` method in the SparkR API to execute a SQL query using Spark, returning the results as a SparkR data frame object. Listing 15.14 shows an example of creating a SparkR data frame from a table in Hive.

LISTING 15.14   Creating a SparkR Data Frame from a Hive Table

```
> hiveContext <- sparkRHive.init(sc)
> iris_table <- sql(hiveContext, "SELECT * FROM iris_table")
> ncol(iris_table)
[1] 6
> nrow(iris_table)
...
[1] 150
> head(iris_table,2)
...
obs seplength sepwidth petlength petwidth species
1   5.1       3.5      1.4       0.2      setosa
2   4.9       3        1.4       0.2      setosa
3   4.7       3.2      1.3       0.2      setosa
4   4.6       3.1      1.5       0.2      setosa
5   5         3.6      1.4       0.2      setosa
```

After a SparkR data frame has been created, columns can be referenced using the `<dataframe>$<column_name>` syntax. An example of this is shown in Listing 15.15.

LISTING 15.15   Accessing Columns in a SparkR Data Frame

```
head(filter(iris_table, iris_table$petwidth > 1.0), 2)
obs seplength sepwidth petlength petwidth species
51  7         3.2      4.7       1.4      versicolor
52  6.4       3.2      4.5       1.5      versicolor
```

Using SparkR

The primary use cases for using SparkR, like R, are to perform statistical analysis of data or to build predictive models from observations and variables. In this section, I will look specifically at R's predictive modeling capabilities and how they can be used with SparkR.

Building Predictive Models with SparkR

For those of you who are data scientists, feel free to skip the next few paragraphs. For those who aren't data scientists, I won't be able to make you one in this section! Instead, I will give you a soft introduction to data science and how processes and methods used by data scientists can be extended to leverage Spark.

Introduction to Predictive Analytics

Predictive analytics at scale is one of the key functional drivers of big data platforms. Retailers want to better understand their customers and predict their buying behavior and propensity, credit providers want to assess risk involved with products and applicants, utilities companies want to predict and preempt customer churn, and so on.

Data mining is the process of discovering patterns within data that can be used in combination with each other to predict an outcome. The process of discovering the inputs to these predictions is called *predictive modeling*. Predictive modeling usually falls into one of two categories: *supervised learning* or *unsupervised learning*.

Supervised learning observations are labeled with labels such as "spam," "not spam," or "defaulted," and so on. This label is then used when observing patterns in the associated data to determine the influence these patterns have on the outcome (the label). You are "teaching" the system what a desired (or undesirable) outcome looks like, hence the name *supervised*.

In contrast, unsupervised learning does not involve classified observations. Typically, unsupervised learning involves identifying similarity between observations (or *clustering* instances).

In either case, the process of building a model typically follows the same workflow that is pictured in Figure 15.5.

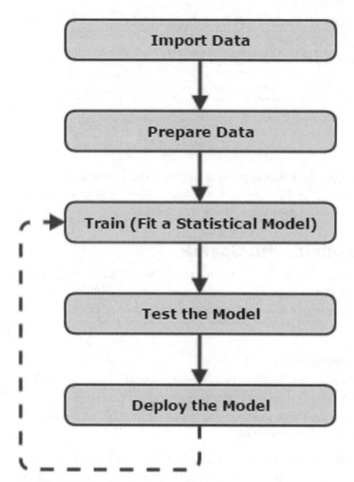

FIGURE 15.5
Steps involved in predictive modeling.

We have already looked at how to import data and have spent a considerable amount of time covering the preparation and curation of data throughout this book. The process of

▶ Fitting a statistical model to the data (or *training* the model)

▶ *Testing* the model against a known set of data not used in the training phase

▶ *Deploying* the model to predict outcomes for new data observations

is what R is exceptionally good at.

Linear Regression

Arguably one of the simplest forms of a predictive model is the *linear regression model*. Without going into the mathematics behind this, a linear regression model assigns coefficients (weights) to variables and creates a generalized linear function, the result of which is a prediction. After it is trained, tested, and deployed, the regression function is then performed against new data (observations) to predict outcomes given the known variables. The general linear model is defined as

$$y_i = \beta_0 + \beta_1 x_1 i + \dots + \beta_p x_{pi} + \varepsilon$$

where y_i is the response (or predicted outcome), β represents the coefficients or weight, and ε represents error.

R and SparkR include the function `glm()`, which is used to create a *generalized linear model*. `glm()` builds a model from observations in a data frame using an input formula in the form of

$$y \sim x_1 + x_2 \dots$$

where y is the response and x_1 and x_2 are continuous or categorical variables. Listing 15.16 shows the use of the `glm` function in SparkR to create a generalized linear model to predict sepal length from the iris dataset. The `summary` function can be used to describe the model after it has been built.

LISTING 15.16   Building a Generalized Linear Model with SparkR

```
> # prepare data frame and build model
> iris_df <- createDataFrame(sqlContext, iris)
> model <- glm(Sepal_Length ~ Sepal_Width + Species,
+ data = iris_df, family = "gaussian")
> summary(model)
$coefficients
Estimate
(Intercept)            2.2513930
Sepal_Width            0.8035609
Species__versicolor 1.4587432
Species__virginica  1.9468169
```

After you've built your model in SparkR, you can apply this to new data to make predictions using the `predict` function. This is demonstrated in Listing 15.17.

LISTING 15.17   Using a GLM to Make Predictions on New Data

```
> # predict new data
> predictions <- predict(model, new_iris_df)
> head(select(predictions, "Sepal_Length", "prediction"))
Sepal_Length prediction
```

1	5.1	5.063856
2	4.9	4.662076
3	4.7	4.822788
4	4.6	4.742432
5	5.0	5.144212
6	5.4	5.385281

Using SparkR with RStudio

So far, you've interacted with SparkR using the `sparkR` shell interface. Although this exposes all of the key functions in R for data manipulation, preparation, analysis, and modeling, it lacks the rich visualization capabilities of a desktop or browser-based interface.

RStudio is an open source IDE (Integrated Development Environment) for R. RStudio is available as a desktop application (RStudio Desktop) and as a server-based application (RStudio Server). RStudio Server enables clients to connect and interact with an R environment using their web browser. The RStudio client interface is pictured in Figure 15.6.

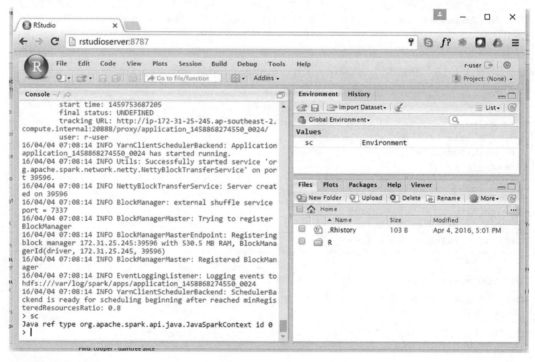

FIGURE 15.6
The RStudio web interface.

RStudio provides the full set of capabilities available from the command line interface, including built-in functions and packages as well as the capability to create and export publication-quality visual analytic outputs.

RStudio can easily be configured to use SparkR as its runtime engine for execution. Walk through this step-by-step in the Try It Yourself exercise, including creating some simple visualizations.

TRY IT YOURSELF ▼

Using RStudio with SparkR

In this exercise, you will install RStudio alongside our Spark installation and configure RStudio to use SparkR as its processign engine. For this example, I will use a Spark installation on a Red Hat/Centos system. RStudio is a compiled application with builds for various platforms. To obtain the specific build for your platform, go to www.rstudio.com/products/rstudio/download-server/.

1. From your system, download and install your specific build of RStudio. I am using Red Hat for this example, but your system may differ.

```
$ wget https://download2.rstudio.org/...x86_64.rpm
$ sudo yum install --nogpgcheck rstudio-server-rhel-....rpm
```

2. RStudio should be available on port 8787 of your server. Test this using a browser client by going to http://<yourserver>:8787/.

3. Create a new R user:

```
$ sudo useradd -d /home/r-user -m r-user
$ sudo passwd r-user
```

R users require a home directory because R automatically saves the user's "workspace" to this directory.

4. Create a home directory in HDFS (assuming you will be using Spark in `yarn-client` mode):

```
$ sudo -u hdfs hadoop fs -mkdir -p /user/r-user
$ sudo -u hdfs hadoop fs -chown r-user /user/r-user
```

5. Log in to RStudio using the r-user account created in Step 3.

6. From the Console window on the left side of the RStudio interface, at the R prompt, enter the following commands to load the SparkR package and initialize a SparkR session (SparkContext and SQLContext):

```
> library(SparkR, lib.loc = c(file.path("/opt/spark/R/lib")))
> sc <- sparkR.init()
> sqlContext <- sparkRSQL.init(sc)
```

7. Test some simple visualizations using the built-in iris dataset by entering the following at the console prompt:

```
> hist(iris$Sepal.Length,xlim=c(4,8),col="blue",freq=FALSE)
> lines(density(iris$Sepal.Length))
```

You should see the following histogram in the Plots window:

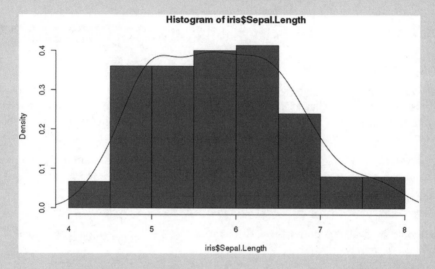

8. Try creating a SparkR data frame from one of the included R datasets. Recall that you can see information about available datasets using the following command:

```
> library(help = "datasets")
```

Then use functions from the SparkR API to manipulate, analyze, or create and test a model from the data. Documentation for the SparkR API is available at https://spark.apache.org/docs/latest/api/R/index.html.

Summary

In this hour, I introduced you to SparkR, the R package that provides access to Spark and distributed data frame operations from an R environment using the R programming language. I have also introduced the fundamental data structures available in R: vectors, matrices, arrays, and data frames.

I have covered the various methods available for creating data frames, including loading data from external sources such as flat files in a local or distributed file system or from a Hive table. You then looked at using these R data frames for distributed operations with Spark including statistical analysis and building, testing, and deploying simple linear regression models.

You learned how to access SparkR through the interactive shell included with the Spark installation. You also learned how to leverage Spark as a processing engine for the RStudio web interface.

R is continuing to grow in popularity and is finding its way from researchers at universities to business and data analysts in commercial and government organizations. As R becomes the standard for statistical analysis and modeling in many organizations, SparkR and the Spark distributed processing runtime becomes a compelling feature for analysis at scale.

Q&A

Q. What is the difference between a matrix and a data frame in the R data model?

A. Matrices are two dimensional objects consisting of vectors with components of the *same type* (or mode). Data frames, like DataFrames in Spark SQL or relational tables, are two-dimensional objects containing rows and columns, where the column types can be of *mixed of different types* or modes.

Q. What data sources can be used to create a SparkR data frame?

A. Existing R data frames, CSV files, JSON files, Parquet files, and Hive tables can all be used to create SparkR data frames.

Q. What are the typical steps involved with predictive modeling?

A. Acquire and prepare data, fit a statistical model (train a model), test the model, and deploy the model to predict responses from new data.

Workshop

The workshop contains quiz questions and exercises to help you solidify your understanding of the material covered. Try to answer all questions before looking at the "Answers" section that follows.

Quiz

1. **True or false:** SparkR is an R package included in the library located by default in $SPARK_HOME/R/lib.

2. Which type is NOT a basic data type in R?

   A. Logical

   B. Boolean

   C. Character

   D. Numeric

3. What function is used to create a SparkR data frame from an existing R data frame?

4. **True or false:** The `predict` function is used to create a generalized linear model.

Answers

1. **True.**

2. **B.** Boolean is not an R type; Boolean values are of the logical type in R.

3. `createDataFrame`

4. **False.** `glm` is used to create a generalized linear model, but `predict` is used to make predictions from new data using the model created.

HOUR 16
Machine Learning with Spark

What You'll Learn in This Hour:

▶ Machine learning and Spark MLlib
▶ Collaborative filtering using Spark MLlib
▶ Clustering using Spark MLlib
▶ Classification using Spark MLlib

Machine learning is the science of creating algorithms that are capable of learning based upon the data provided to them. Common applications of machine learning are seen every day, from recommendation engines to spam filters to fraud detection and much more. You were introduced to data mining using Spark and R in the previous chapter. Machine learning is the process of automating data mining. Spark has included a purpose-built library, MLlib, to make practical machine learning scalable, easy, and seamlessly integrated into Spark.

Introduction to Machine Learning and MLlib

In the previous hour, I introduced you to the process of creating mathematical models to predict outcomes using R. This specific implementation of predictive analytics requires an analyst, developer, or data scientist to fit (or train) a statistical model and then test and deploy the model. The behavior of the model is largely static until it is retrained.

Machine Learning Primer

Machine learning is another specific discipline within the field of predictive analytics, which refers to programs that leverage the data they collect to influence the program's future behavior. In other words, the program "learns" from the data rather than relying on explicit instructions.

Machine learning is often associated with data at scale. As more data is observed in the learning process, the higher the accuracy of the model (or the better it is at making predictions).

You can see practical examples of machine learning in everyday life including recommendation engines in ecommerce web sites, optical character recognition, facial recognition, spam filtering, fraud detection, and so on.

The three primary techniques employed in machine learning are

▶ Classification

▶ Collaborative filtering

▶ Clustering

Take a look at a high-level overview of each.

Classification

Classification is a supervised learning technique that takes a set of data with known labels and learns how to label new data based upon that information. Consider a spam filter on an email server that determines whether an incoming message should be classified as "spam" or "not spam." The classification algorithm trains itself by observing user behavior as to what they classify as spam. Learning from this observed behavior, the algorithm classifies new mail accordingly. The classification process for this example is pictured in Figure 16.1.

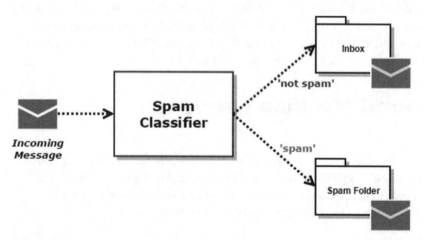

FIGURE 16.1
Classification of incoming email messages.

Classification techniques are used in a wide variety of applications across various domains ranging from oncology, where a classifier may be trained to distinguish benign tumors from malignant tumors, to credit risk analysis, where a classifier may be trained to identify a customer at risk of default on a credit product.

Collaborative Filtering

Collaborative filtering is a technique for making recommendations. It is commonly denoted by the "You might also like..." or similar sidebars or callouts on shopping websites. The algorithm processes large amounts of data observations to find entities with similar traits or characteristics and then makes recommendations or suggestions to newly observed entities based upon the previous observations.

Collaborative filtering, unlike classification, is an *un*supervised learning technique. Unlike with supervised learning, unsupervised learning algorithms can derive patterns in data without labels being supplied.

Collaborative filtering is domain-agnostic. It can be employed in a wide variety of use cases, from online retailing to streaming music and video services to travel sites to online gaming and more. Figure 16.2 depicts the process of collaborative filtering for the purpose of generating recommendations.

Products

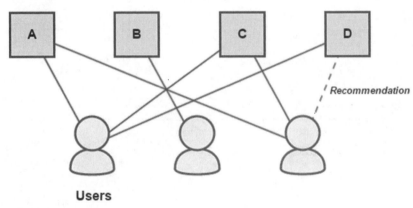

FIGURE 16.2
Collaborative filtering.

Clustering

Clustering is the process of discovering structure within collections of data observations especially where a formal structure is not obvious. Clustering algorithms discover (or "learn") what groupings naturally occur in the data provided to them.

Clustering is another example of an *un*supervised learning technique that is often used for exploratory analysis. Clusters can be determined in several ways including density, proximity, location, levels of connectivity, or size.

Some examples of clustering applications include

▶ Market or customer segmentation

▶ Finding related news articles, tweets, or blog posts

▶ Image-recognition applications where clusters of pixels cohere into discernible objects

▶ Epidemiological studies (for instance, identifying "cancer clusters")

Figure 16.3 clearly shows three clusters when you look at the relationship between sepal length and sepal width in the iris dataset. The center of each cluster is called the *centroid*. The centroid is a vector representing the mean of a variable for the observations in the cluster that can be used for approximating distances between clusters.

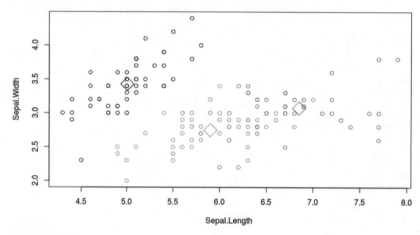

FIGURE 16.3
Clustering.

Features and Feature Extraction

In machine learning, a *feature* is a measurable attribute or characteristic of an observation. Variables for developing models are sourced from a pool of features. Examples of simple features for building a retail or financial services propensity or risk model could be annual income, total amount spent in the last 12 months in a particular category, or a three-month moving average credit card cycle balance.

Often, features don't present in the data itself. They are derived from the data, historical data, or other available data sources. Moreover, features could be aggregated or summarized from the underlying data. Creating the set of features used by an algorithm in a machine learning program is the process of *feature extraction*. Selecting and extracting an appropriate set of features is arguably as important (if not more important) as algorithm selection or tuning.

Features are often represented as numerical vectors (recall the introduction to vectors in the previous chapter). Sometimes it is necessary to represent text-based data as feature vectors. There are many established techniques for doing so including *TF-IDF* (Term Frequency-Inverse Document Frequency). TF-IDF measures the significance of an element relevant to other elements within a set. This technique is commonly used in text mining and search. For instance, you could assess how important the term "Spark" is in this book compared to all of the other books available in Amazon.

Machine Learning with Spark

Machine learning was identified early on as a key use case for Spark's memory-centric processing engine. When Spark was initially being developed, the incumbent solution for distributed machine learning in Hadoop was *Apache Mahout*. Apache Mahout was a set of machine learning libraries and functions designed to be executed against data in Hadoop using MapReduce. As Mahout was implemented using MapReduce, it was largely disk-bound. Spark, and its RDD-based architecture, provided an ideal platform for the next generation of distributed machine learning capabilities.

Spark MLlib

The Spark machine learning solution is *Spark MLlib*, a Spark subproject providing machine learning functions that can be used with RDDs. MLlib, like Spark Streaming and Spark SQL, is an integral component in the Spark program and has been included with Spark since the 0.8 release.

Spark ML

In Spark 1.2, an additional library, *Spark ML*, was introduced to extend MLlib to Spark SQL DataFrames. The APIs, algorithms, and capabilities are based upon MLlib. I will primarily focus on the foundational MLlib package in this hour because as it is an abstraction of the Spark core API. However, Spark ML may be a more natural choice if you are using Spark SQL DataFrames for data processing. The concepts and implementations are easily transferable between the two Spark machine learning APIs.

Classification Using Spark MLlib

Common approaches or algorithms used for classification in machine learning include decision trees and Naive Bayes. Both techniques learn from previous observations and make classification judgments based upon probability.

Take a look at both approaches with examples using PySpark now.

Decision Trees

Decision trees are an intuitive approach to classification where the classification process is represented as a tree. *Nodes* of the tree represent decisions that usually compare an attribute from the dataset with a constant or a label. Each decision node creates a fork in the structure until the end of the tree is reached and a classification prediction is made.

The simplest example is the "Golf (or Weather) Data Set." This simple example is often cited in data mining textbooks as a sample data set for generating a decision trees. This small data set, shown in Table 16.1, contains 14 *instances* (or observations) and 5 primary attributes—outlook, temperature, humidity, windy, and play. The temperature and humidity attributes are provided in nominal and numeric formats. The last attribute, play, is the *class attribute*, which can have a value of yes or no.

TABLE 16.1 Weather/Golf Dataset

Outlook	Numeric Temp	Nominal Temp	Numerical Humidity	Nominal Humidity	Windy	Play?
overcast	83	hot	86	high	FALSE	yes
overcast	64	cool	65	normal	TRUE	yes
overcast	72	mild	90	high	TRUE	yes
overcast	81	hot	75	normal	FALSE	yes
rainy	70	mild	96	high	FALSE	yes
rainy	68	cool	80	normal	FALSE	yes
rainy	65	cool	70	normal	TRUE	no
rainy	75	mild	80	normal	FALSE	yes
rainy	71	mild	91	high	TRUE	no
sunny	85	hot	85	high	FALSE	no
sunny	80	hot	90	high	TRUE	no
sunny	72	mild	95	high	FALSE	no
sunny	69	cool	70	normal	FALSE	yes
sunny	75	mild	70	normal	TRUE	yes

NOTE

The *weather dataset* is also included in the WEKA (Waikato Environment for Knowledge Analysis) machine learning software package, a popular free software package developed at the University of Waikato, New Zealand. Although not directly related to Spark, this package is recommended to those who wish to explore machine learning algorithms in more detail.

After using a machine learning decision tree classification algorithm against a set of input data, the model produced will evaluate each attribute and progress through the "tree" until a decision node is reached. Figure 16.4 shows the resultant decision tree for the sample weather data set using the nominal (or categorical) features.

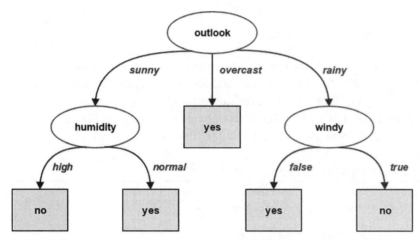

FIGURE 16.4
Decision tree for the weather data set.

Decision Trees Using Spark MLlib

Spark MLlib supports decision trees for both continuous (numerical) and categorical features. The training process parallelizes instances from a training data set and iterates over these instances to develop the resultant decision tree.

TIP
_____

Splitting Data into Training and Test Data Sets

In supervised machine learning model development, it's generally recommended that you split your input data set into two subsets: a training data set and a test data set. The training data set is used to train the model and usually comprises 60% or more of the overall input data set. The test data set is comprised of the remaining data from the input data set and is used to make predictions to validate the accuracy of the trained model.

Spark includes the `randomSplit` function to split a data set into multiple data sets for training and testing. `randomSplit` accepts an input argument *weights*, which is a list of weightings for the respective output data sets. Listing 16.1 shows an example of the `randomSplit` function.
_____

LISTING 16.1   Splitting Data into Training and Test Data Sets

```
data = sc.parallelize([1,2,3,4,5,6,7,8,9,10])
training, test = data.randomSplit([0.6, 0.4])
training.collect()
[3, 4, 5, 6, 7, 9]
test.collect()
[1, 2, 8, 10]
```

To construct an example decision tree classifier using the training data set, you first need to create an RDD consisting of LabeledPoint (pyspark.mllib.regression.LabeledPoint) objects. A LabeledPoint object contains the label (or class attribute) for an instance along with the associated instance attributes. Listing 16.2 shows an example of creating an RDD containing LabeledPoint objects. For brevity, I will use this RDD again in some of the examples.

LISTING 16.2   Creating and RDD of LabeledPoint Objects

```
from pyspark.mllib.regression import LabeledPoint
outlook = {"sunny": 0.0, "overcast": 1.0, "rainy": 2.0}
labeledpoints = [
    LabeledPoint(0.0, [outlook["sunny"],85,85,False]),
    LabeledPoint(0.0, [outlook["sunny"],80,90,True]),
    LabeledPoint(1.0, [outlook["overcast"],83,86,False]),
    LabeledPoint(1.0, [outlook["rainy"],70,96,False]),
    LabeledPoint(1.0, [outlook["rainy"],68,80,False]),
    LabeledPoint(0.0, [outlook["rainy"],65,70,True]),
    LabeledPoint(1.0, [outlook["overcast"],64,65,True]),
    LabeledPoint(0.0, [outlook["sunny"],72,95,False]),
    LabeledPoint(1.0, [outlook["sunny"],69,70,False]),
    LabeledPoint(1.0, [outlook["sunny"],75,80,False]),
    LabeledPoint(1.0, [outlook["sunny"],75,70,True]),
    LabeledPoint(1.0, [outlook["overcast"],72,90,True]),
    LabeledPoint(1.0, [outlook["overcast"],81,75,False]),
    LabeledPoint(0.0, [outlook["rainy"],71,91,True])
    ]
data = sc.parallelize(labeledpoints)
```

LabeledPoint object attributes must be float values (or objects convertible to float values—such as Boolean or int). With a categorical feature ("outlook"), you will need to create a dict or map to associate the float value used in the LabeledPoint with a categorical key.

TIP

Input Data Formats for Machine Learning in Spark

Spark's machine learning libraries support many common input formats commonly used in classification or regression modeling. An example would be the LIBSVM file format, a format from a library designed for support vector classification. Many other data structures from popular scientific and statistical packages such as `NumPy` and `SciPy` are supported within Spark's machine learning libraries as well.

Using the RDD containing LabeledPoint objects you created in Listing 16.2, you can now train a decision tree model using the `DecisionTree.trainClassifier` function in the Spark MLlib package, as shown in Listing 16.3.

LISTING 16.3   Training a Decision Tree Model with Spark MLlib

```
from pyspark.mllib.tree import DecisionTree
model = DecisionTree.trainClassifier(data=data,
        numClasses=2,
        categoricalFeaturesInfo={0: 3})
...
print(model.toDebugString())
  If (feature 2 <= 80.0)
   If (feature 1 <= 65.0)
    If (feature 1 <= 64.0)
     Predict: 1.0
    Else (feature 1 > 64.0)
     Predict: 0.0
   Else (feature 1 > 65.0)
    Predict: 1.0
  Else (feature 2 > 80.0)
   If (feature 0 in {0.0})
    Predict: 0.0
   Else (feature 0 not in {0.0})
    If (feature 1 <= 71.0)
     If (feature 1 <= 70.0)
      Predict: 1.0
     Else (feature 1 > 70.0)
      Predict: 0.0
    Else (feature 1 > 71.0)
     Predict: 1.0
```

The `DecisionTree.trainClassifier` function creates a model by training the data (a parallelized collection of `LabeledPoint` objects). The `numClasses` argument specifies how many discrete classes to predict (in this case, it is two as this example is simply predicting a binary outcome—yes/no). The `categoricalFeaturesInfo` argument is a dict or map that specifies which features are categorical and how many categorical values each of those features can take. In this case, you need to direct the `trainClassifier` method that the values representing the outlook category are discrete (for example, "sunny" or "rainy" or "overcast"). Any features not specified in the `categoricalFeaturesInfo` argument are treated as continuous.

So you have a model—what next? Now you need a method to predict the class attribute from new data that does not include the class attribute. Spark MLlib provides the `predict` function to do this. Listing 16.4 demonstrates the use of the `predict` method.

LISTING 16.4 Using a Spark MLlib Decision Tree Model to Classify New Data

```
model.predict([1.0,85,85,True])
1.0
```

As you can see from Listing 16.4, given inputs of `outlook="overcast"`, `temperature=85`, `humidity=85`, and `windy=True`, the decision to play is `1.0` (or yes). This follows the logic from the decision tree you created.

Naive Bayes

Naive Bayes is another popular technique for classification in machine learning. Naive Bayes is based upon Bayes' Theorem, a theorem describing how the conditional probability of an outcome can be evaluated from the known probabilities of its causes.

Bayes' Theorem is modeled mathematically, as shown here:

$$P\left(A|B\right) = \frac{P(B|A)P(A)}{P(B)}$$

where *A* and *B* are independent events, *P(A)* and *P(B)* are the probabilities of *A* and *B* without regard to each other. *P(A | B)* is the probability of observing event *A* given that *B* is true. *P(B | A)* is the probability of observing event *B* given that *A* is true.

Naive Bayes Classification Using Spark MLlib

Naive Bayes classfication using MLlib is implemented using the `NaiveBayes.train` method from the `pyspark.mllib.classification.NaiveBayes` package.

`NaiveBayes.train` takes an input RDD consisting of `LabeledPoint` objects (as you had used in the decision tree example) and includes an optional smoothing parameter, `lambda_`. The output is a `NaiveBayesModel` (`pyspark.mllib.classification.NaiveBayesModel`) that can be used for classification of new data using the `predict` method.

Listing 16.5 uses the weather data set to create a model using the Naive Bayes algorithm implementation in Spark MLlib and then uses this model to predict the class attribute of new data.

LISTING 16.5 Implementing a Naive Bayes Classifier Using Spark MLlib

```
from pyspark.mllib.classification import NaiveBayes, NaiveBayesModel
model = NaiveBayes.train(data=data, lambda_=1.0)
model.predict([1.0,85,85,True])
1.0
```

Collaborative Filtering Using Spark MLlib

Collaborative filtering is one of the most common applications of machine learning being used in many different domains. Spark uses the ALS (or Alternating Least Squares) technique in its collaborative filtering or recommendation module. ALS is an algorithm to perform matrix factorization. *Matrix factorization* is the process of factorization of a matrix into a product of matrices. A simple example is shown in Figure 16.5.

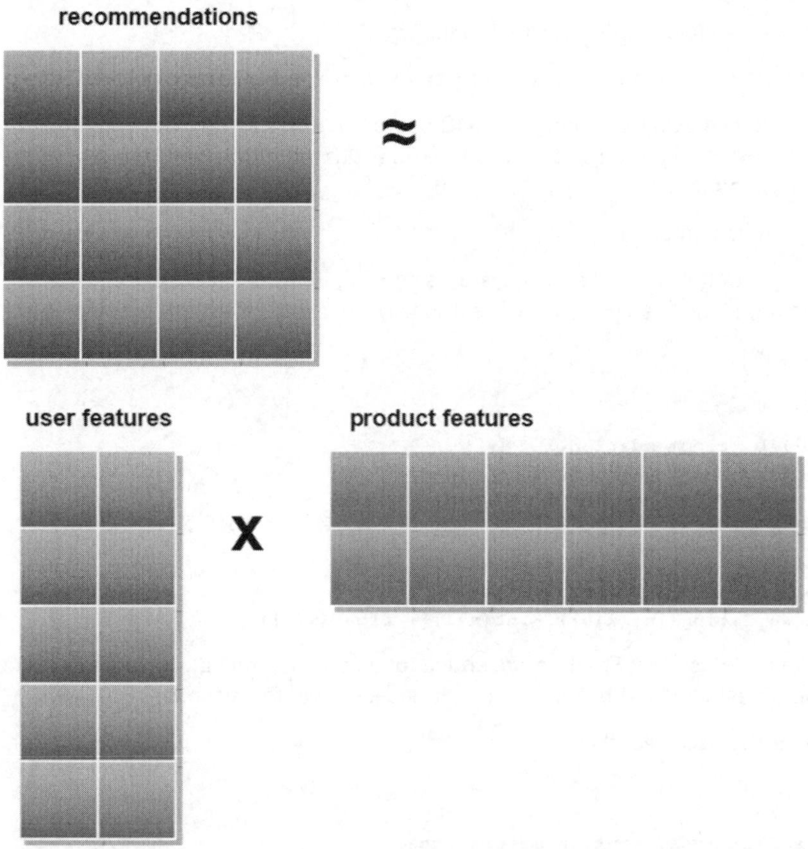

FIGURE 16.5
Matrix factorization.

A deep dive into matrix factorization and the Alternating Least Squares algorithm is beyond the scope of this book. However, ALS was selected as the preferred implementation method for machine learning in Spark because as it is a fully parallelizable algorithm.

Take a look at the implementation of a recommender using Spark MLlib and ALS in the Try It Yourself exercise here.

▼ TRY IT YOURSELF

Implementing a Recommender Using Spark MLlib

This exercise uses a subset of the Movielens dataset. The Movielens dataset was created at the University of Minnesota as a data exploration and recommendation project. The Movielens dataset captures movie ratings by user along with user and movie attributes and can be used for collaborative filtering exercises.

The website for the Movielens project is https://movielens.org/.

The subset is located at https://s3.amazonaws.com/sty-spark/movielens/movielens.dat

The subset being used contains 100,000 ratings by 943 users on 1,682 items, with each user having rated at least 20 movies. The ratings data (`movielens.dat`) is a tab-delimited, new line terminated text file with the structure

user id | item id | rating | timestamp

You can load this directly from the S3 bucket if you are using EC2, EMR, or Databricks or, alternatively, you can download the file and access it locally from your Spark environment.

1. Start a `pyspark` shell.

2. Import the required `mllib` libraries:

   ```
   from pyspark.mllib.recommendation \
   import ALS, MatrixFactorizationModel, Rating
   ```

3. Load the Movielens dataset and create an RDD containing `Rating` objects:

   ```
   data = sc.textFile("file:///opt/spark/data/movielens")
   ratings = data.map(lambda x: x.split('\t')) \
       .map(lambda x: Rating(int(x[0]), int(x[1]), float(x[2])))
   ```

   Rating is a special tuple used by Spark representing (user, product, rating). Note also that I have filtered the timestamp field because it is not necessary in this case.

4. Train a model using the ALS algorithm:

   ```
   rank = 10
   numIterations = 10
   model = ALS.train(ratings, rank, numIterations)
   ```

rank and numIterations are algorithm tuning parameters. rank is the number of latent factors in the model and numIterations is the number of iterations to run.

5. Now you can test the model, in this case, against the same dataset without the rating (you use the model to predict this attribute). You will then compare the results of the predictions with the actual ratings to determine the *mean squared error* (measuring the accuracy of the model).

```
testdata = ratings.map(lambda p: (p[0], p[1]))
predictions = model.predictAll(testdata) \
    .map(lambda r: ((r[0], r[1]), r[2]))
ratesAndPreds = ratings.map(lambda r: ((r[0], r[1]), r[2])) \
    .join(predictions)
MSE = ratesAndPreds.map(lambda r: (r[1][0] - r[1][1])**2) \
    .mean()
print("Mean Squared Error = " + str(MSE))
Mean Squared Error = 0.485872124844
```

As I've discussed, a good practice is to divide your input dataset into two discrete sets (one for training and another for testing). This can help avoid *overfitting* your model.

6. To save the model to be used for new recommendations, use the model.save function as shown here:

```
model.save(sc, "file:///opt/spark/data/ratings_model")
```

7. To reload the model in a new session (for instance, to deploy the model against real time data from a Spark DStream), use the MatrixFactorizationModel.load function as shown here:

```
from pyspark.mllib.recommendation \
    import MatrixFactorizationModel
reloaded_model = MatrixFactorizationModel.load \
            (sc, "file:///opt/spark/data/ratings_model")
```

Clustering Using Spark MLlib

As discussed, clustering algorithms discover groups or clusters of associated instances within a collection of data. A common approach to clustering is the *k-means* technique.

k-means Clustering

k-means clustering is an iterative algorithm used in machine learning and graph analysis (I will cover graph processing specifically in **Hour 18, "Graph Processing with Spark"**).

Consider a set of data in a plane (this could represent a variable and an independent variable on an x, y axis for simplicity). The objective of the k-means algorithm is to find the center of each cluster presented in the data as pictured in Figure 16.6.

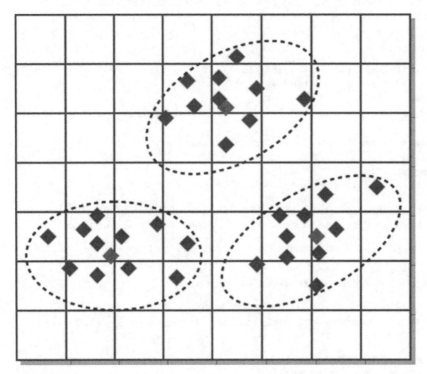

FIGURE 16.6
k-means clustering.

The k-means approach works as follows:

▶ Select K random points as starting center points (centroids).

▶ For each point, find the closest K and allocate the point to the cluster associated with K.

▶ Calculate the mean (center) of each cluster by averaging all of the points in that cluster.

▶ Iterate until no points are reassigned to new clusters.

As you can see, this is a brute force, parallelizable, iterative routine, which makes it very well suited to Spark.

k-means Clustering Using Spark MLlib

k-means is implemented in Spark using the `pyspark.mllib.clustering.KMeans` package. Listing 16.6 demonstrates how to train a k-means clustering machine learning model using the sample `kmeans_data` dataset provided as part of the Spark release.

LISTING 16.6   Training a k-means Clustering Model Using Spark MLlib

```
from pyspark.mllib.clustering import KMeans, KMeansModel
from numpy import array
from math import sqrt
# Load and parse the data
data = sc.textFile("file:///opt/spark/data/mllib/kmeans_data.txt")
parsedData = data.map(lambda line: array( \
                [float(x) for x in line.split(' ')]))
# Build the model (cluster the data)
clusters = KMeans.train(parsedData, 2, maxIterations=10,
                runs=10, initializationMode="random")
```

Notice that this example uses the NumPy library. This is a special Python mathematical library automatically available when using PySpark. After you have a k-means clustering model, you can evaluate the error rate within each cluster as shown in Listing 16.7.

LISTING 16.7   Evaluating a k-means Clustering Model

```
# Evaluate clustering by computing Within Set Sum of Squared Errors
def error(point):
    center = clusters.centers[clusters.predict(point)]
    return sqrt(sum([x**2 for x in (point - center)]))

WSSSE = parsedData.map(lambda point: error(point)) \
    .reduce(lambda x, y: x + y)
print("Within Set Sum of Squared Error = " + str(WSSSE))
Within Set Sum of Squared Error = 0.692820323028
```

As with the collaborative filtering and classification models, you typically need to persist the model so that it can be loaded in a new session to evaluate new data. Listing 16.8 demonstrates the use of the `save` and `load` functions to accomplish this.

LISTING 16.8   Saving and Reloading a Clustering Model

```
# Save and load model
clusters.save(sc, "hdfs:///.../kmeans_model")
reloaded_model = KMeansModel.load(sc, "hdfs:///.../kmeans_model")
```

Summary

Machine learning is an exciting area of computer science. As more storage and computing capabilities are available at a lower cost, we can harness the true power of machine learning to help us make better decisions.

In this hour, I introduced you to MLlib—Spark's machine learning library. The MLlib sub project and API are built upon the RDD model. MLlib includes many common machine learning algorithms and utilities to perform data preparation, feature extraction, model training, and testing. MLlib is designed to be a succinct, user-friendly yet functionally rich, powerful, and scalable machine learning abstraction on top of Spark.

I have covered the three primary techniques used in machine learning: classification, collaborative filtering, and clustering. I have discussed their specific applications and common uses and their implementations using Spark MLlib.

I also briefly discussed the Spark ML library, which is Spark's machine learning abstraction built on top of Spark SQL DataFrames. The APIs, algorithms, and capabilities are quite similar to MLlib (as they are predominantly based on this library). However, Spark ML may be a more natural choice if you are using Spark SQL DataFrames for preprocessing.

I can only provide you with a high-level introduction to machine learning and Spark MLlib in the one hour allotted to this topic. However, hopefully I've inspired you to dive deeply into this area within Spark.

Q&A

Q. **What are the three primary techniques employed in machine learning? Give an example of each.**

A. Clustering (identifying epidemiological clusters—such as cancer clusters), classification (a spam filter in an email system), collaborative filtering (a recommendation engine on an ecommerce website).

Q. **What is a *feature* and what is the process of *feature extraction*?**

A. In machine learning, a feature is a measurable attribute or characteristic of an observation. Variables for developing models are sourced from a pool of features. *Feature extraction* is the process of deriving the set of features used by a machine learning algorithm.

Q. **What is the difference between the Spark MLlib and Spark ML machine learning packages?**

A. Spark MLlib is a machine learning abstraction built on top of Spark RDDs. This is Spark's original machine learning sub project. Spark ML, which was a later addition to the Spark family, is Spark's machine learning library built on top of Spark SQL DataFrames. Both packages include a similar set of machine learning algorithms and utilities.

Workshop

The workshop contains quiz questions and exercises to help you solidify your understanding of the material covered. Try to answer all questions before looking at the "Answers" section that follows.

Quiz

1. Image recognition, finding related news articles, and customer segmentation are common use cases for what machine learning technique?

2. Which technique is used to determine relevance of terms within a document with respect to other documents?

3. Which function would you use to randomly split a data set into a training and test data set to build a classification model?

4. Naive Bayes and decision trees are algorithms commonly used for which category of machine learning?

Answers

1. Clustering.

2. TF-IDF (Term Frequency—Inverse Document Frequency).

3. `randomSplit()`

4. Classification.

HOUR 17

Introducing Sparkling Water (H2O and Spark)

What You'll Learn in This Hour:

▶ Introduction to H2O

▶ Using the H2O Flow Interface

▶ Using Sparkling Water (H2O on Spark)

In the past two hours, I have covered statistical analysis and predictive modeling using R and Spark and machine learning with Spark MLlib. In this hour, I will introduce you to another popular open source machine learning application and in-memory prediction engine, H2O. H2O provides "deep learning" capabilities, combining a powerful set of algorithms with intuitive interfaces. Sparkling Water is the convergence of Spark and H2O, enabling H2O to leverage the distributed processing platform.

Introduction to H2O

The H2O project started in 2011 to help developers and data scientists easily leverage powerful machine learning algorithms in their applications. H2O was developed by experts in statistical and mathematical computing and machine learning and was designed for both scale and usability.

H2O can efficiently trial thousands of potential models as part of discovering patterns in a data set. H2O includes capabilities such as grid search to discover the best parameters for a model, the facility to deal with missing features, and low latency scoring.

H2O Deep Learning

Along with common machine learning algorithms and techniques (such as those discussed in the previous chapter), H2O includes its *deep learning* implementation. Deep learning is an extension of neural networks machine learning algorithms. In machine leaning, neural networks represent a family of algorithms inspired by biological neural networks such as those in the central nervous systems of animals. These algorithms are used to estimate or approximate functions that can depend on a large number of inputs.

H2O's deep learning algorithms are distributed, iterative, and adaptive and include features such as

▶ Automatic adaptive learning rate

▶ Grid search for parameter optimization and model selection

▶ Model checkpointing for reduced run times and model tuning

▶ Automatic imputation of missing values

▶ Automatic tuning of communication versus computation for best performance

H2O Flow

Many machine learning utilities require a deep understanding of algorithms and tuning parameters. In contrast, H2O provides an intuitive web interface (see H2O Flow pictured in Figure 17.1), along with a set of REST APIs as well as seamless integration into many other common data science and analytics tools.

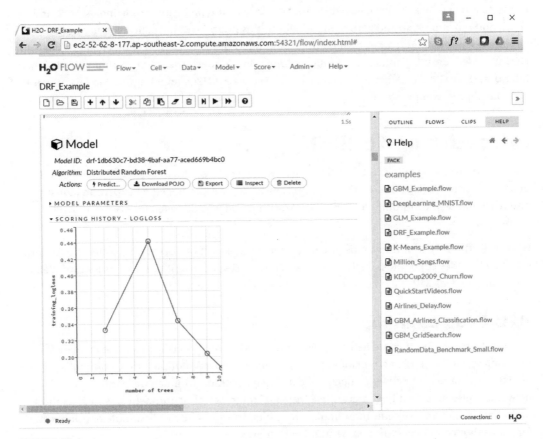

FIGURE 17.1
H2O Flow.

H2O Flow provides a web-based interactive environment enabling users to combine code execution, text, mathematics, plots, Markdown, and more within a notebook application (similar to the Zeppelin and Jupyter notebook applications I covered previously).

As with the other notebook applications I've covered, H2O Flow enables you to import data and build, test, and profile different models using a sequence of executable cells. H2O's data preparation and machine learning functions are exposed through its own DSL (Domain Specific Language). H2O also includes interactive help and example flows to get you started.

For power users, H_2O Flow also exposes options for fine-grained control of the learning process.

H2O Architecture

H2O is written in Java, Python, and R and is able to use data from cloud data sources such as S3 and other object storage platforms or distributed file systems such as HDFS. The H2O engine exposes an API with interfaces to R, Scala, and Python including notebook applications such as Jupyter/IPython, Microsoft Excel, Tableau, and more, in addition to the H2O Flow API and web interface.

H2O's in-memory model building and scoring engine supports most common machine learning algorithms, including those introduced in the previous chapter. H2O can be run on Hadoop (YARN), which I demonstrate in the next Try It Yourself exercise. It can also be run in standalone mode and using Spark, which I will cover shortly.

A high-level overview of H2O, its interfaces, and execution platform is shown in Figure 17.2.

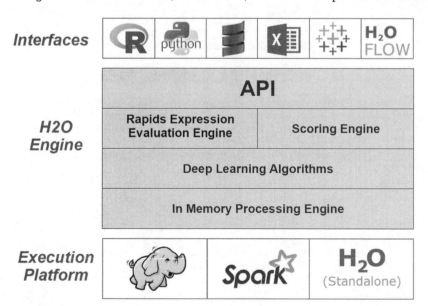

FIGURE 17.2
High-level overview of H2O.

Delving deeper, the H2O engine itself is implemented in several layers, which include the following:

▶ In-memory distributed (not-persistent) key value (KV) store layer

▶ Light-weight MapReduce layer (based upon the MapReduce concepts discussed in **Hour 7, "Understanding MapReduce Concepts"**)

▶ "Pre-baked" algorithms layer (H2O implementations of common machine learning and deep learning algorithms)

▶ API layer (including REST, JSON, R, Python, Excel, and REPL)

All of the layers are orchestrated in a distributed processing framework known as a H2O Cloud. There is much more detailed information about the H2O architecture available from the H2O website at **www.h2o.ai/**.

Running H2O on Hadoop

H2O can be deployed using Hadoop, scheduled by YARN (Yet Another Resource Negotiator)—Hadoop's resource management platform. Using this deployment method, H2O is deployed as a Hadoop Map Reduce driver, and the H2O engine runs inside a Map task (or tasks) running on one or more nodes in the Hadoop cluster. The containers hosting the H2O processes are then managed by YARN, as pictured in the YARN Resource Manager UI in Figure 17.3.

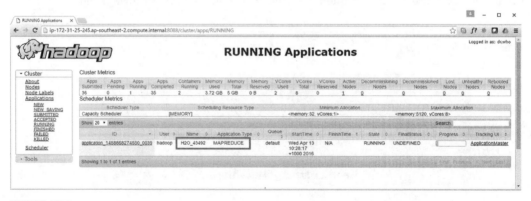

FIGURE 17.3
H2O on Hadoop.

Running H2O in Hadoop (YARN)

For this exercise, you will need a Hadoop installation. You can use an Amazon Web Services (AWS) Elastic MapReduce cluster (as discussed in **Hour 5, "Deploying Spark in the Cloud,"**). I will use EMR in this example.

1. Locate the latest instructions for installing H2O on Hadoop from www.h2o.ai/download/ h2o/hadoop.

2. Choose the appropriate download link for your specific distribution of Hadoop. There are prebuilt releases for Cloudera, Hortonworks, and MapR. For EMR, you can use the latest Cloudera (CDH) release. Download the release from a host with access to the Hadoop cluster (I use the EMR master node in this case):

```
wget <download_link> -O h2o-<release>.zip
```

3. Unzip the release and navigate into the release directory:

```
unzip h2o-3.8.2.2-*.zip
cd h2o-3.8.2.2-*
```

4. Submit the H2O driver program as a Hadoop job using the `hadoop jar` command:

```
hadoop jar h2odriver.jar \
    -libjars h2odriver.jar \
    -nodes 1 \
    -mapperXmx 2g \
    -output h2o_dir
```

You should see the terminal output shown in Figure 17.4, which includes the H2O Flow UI address.

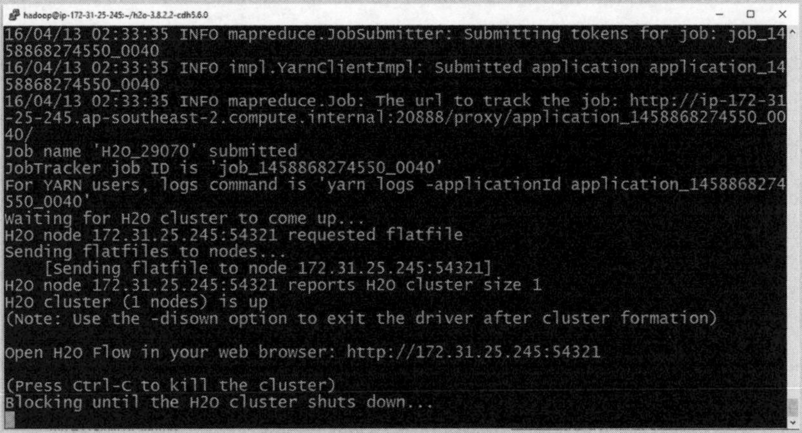

FIGURE 17.4
H2O Hadoop driver terminal output.

The driver is run in "blocking mode" and can be shut down either by using Ctrl+C in the terminal or by using the Hadoop tools to kill running applications (such as `yarn application -kill`).

5. Use a browser to navigate to the H2O Flow Web UI (by default, this runs on port 54321) (see Figure 17.5).

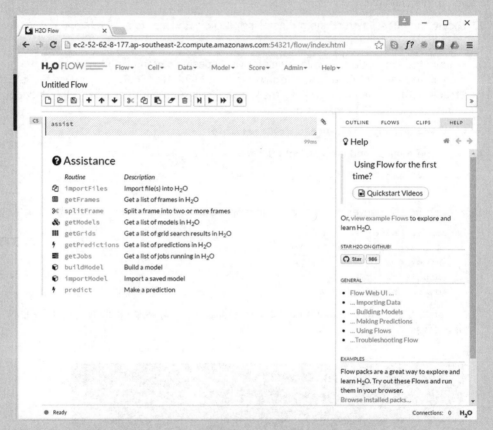

FIGURE 17.5
The H2O Flow UI.

6. In the right pane, locate and click the View Example Flows link. H2O Flow includes several example flows with sample data to illustrate the usage of H2O and the Flow interface. Select one such as `DeepLearning_MNIST.flow`, which is a database of handwritten digits commonly used for training image processing and character recognition systems. After you have loaded a sample flow as a H2O notebook, select **Flow → Run All Cells** from the top menu.

7. Explore the output from a sample flow. This shows you the series of steps taken to train and test a model along with model validation and performance statistics.

Sparkling Water—H2O on Spark

Sparkling Water combines H2O's machine learning, deep learning, and scoring capabilities with Spark's distributed, in-memory, RDD-based transformation platform. Sparkling Water can be accessed from R, Scala, Python, or through the Flow interface I showed you in the previous section.

Spark is especially good at data profiling, data preparation, and feature extraction using either the RDD API or the more abstract DataFrame API. These are the common precursory steps to predictive modeling. Sparkling Water enables a single data pipeline combining data preparation and advanced machine learning techniques using H2O. Figure 17.6 shows an example of a Sparkling Water data processing, modeling, and scoring/classification pipeline.

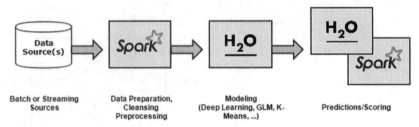

FIGURE 17.6
A Spark and H2O processing pipeline.

Furthermore, Spark's stream processing capability using DStreams in the Spark Streaming library enables Sparkling Water pipelines to perform feature extraction from real-time incoming data and then leverage H2O's prediction and low latency scoring engine to deploy models. Additionally, Spark SQL enables seamless query access and visualization from data within the Sparkling Water processing pipeline.

Sparkling Water Architecture

Sparkling Water is implemented as a Spark application running on a Spark cluster. The Sparkling Water Spark application, which includes all of the H2O libraries and modules, is submitted using spark-submit or initialized using one of the interactive REPL shells. Then the H2O processes described in the previous section (distributed key value store, pre-baked algorithms, lightweight map reduce framework, and so on) are instantiated with executor JVM's running on workers in the Spark cluster—similar to the way H2O running on Hadoop worked in the previous Try It Yourself exercise. Now, however, you are using the Spark runtime processing framework (including the RDD and DataFrame APIs) instead of the Hadoop MapReduce framework.

Figure 17.7 shows an example of submitting a Sparkling Water application using spark-submit (by including the Sparkling Water library via the --jars or --packages option).

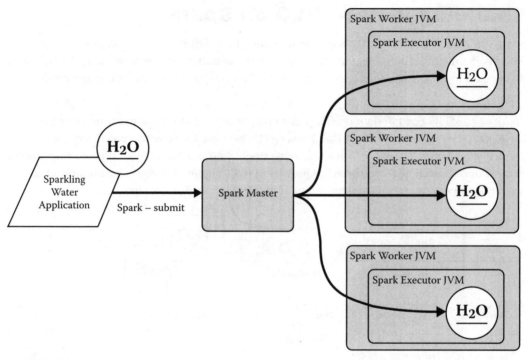

FIGURE 17.7
Sparkling Water.

To run Sparkling Water interactively, you can use the following options:

- ▶ `sparkling-shell` (pre-configured Sparkling Water shell application)

- ▶ `spark-shell` or `pyspark` (including the Sparkling Water library via the `--jars` or `--packages` option)

- ▶ PySparkling (implemented as a preconfigured Python shell— `pysparkling`—or as a module callable from within a Python application submitted using `spark-submit`)

PySparkling Water

As this book is focused on using Spark via the Python API, I will focus my Sparkling Water examples on the `pysparkling` shell and Python module specifically. PySparkling uses the SparkContext to create a *H2OContext*, the entry point for a Sparkling Water application.

The `H2OContext` creates a H2O cloud within executors in the Spark cluster. The PySparkling package then exposes all H2O functions from the Python API, implementing calls to the H2O cloud (cluster) using the REST API. Listing 17.1 shows an example of creating a `H2OContext` from a `pysparkling` session.

LISTING 17.1   Creating a PySparkling H2OContext Object

```
from pysparkling import *
hc = H2OContext(sc).start()
import h2o
```

The H2OContext `start()` method creates a H2O cloud on the Spark Cluster. You can see the H2O cloud information, including the H2O Flow connection details from the terminal output in Spark, as shown in Figure 17.8.

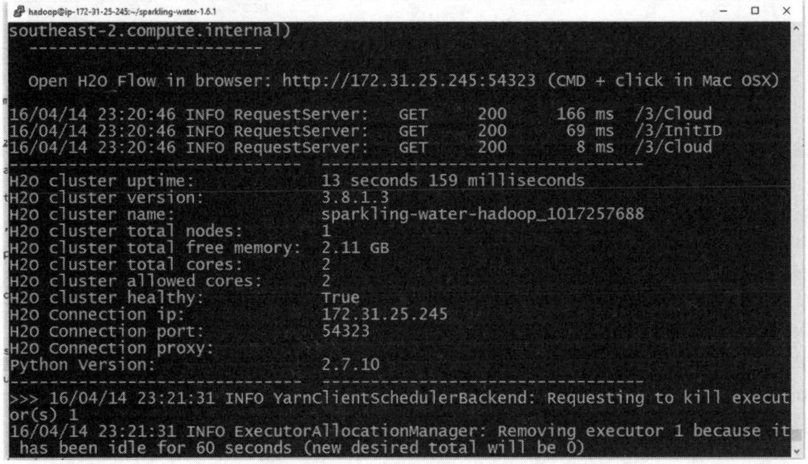

FIGURE 17.8
H2O cloud running in Spark.

You can use the `dir()` function to view available functions in the H2O Python module as shown in Listing 17.2.

LISTING 17.2   Listing Functions in the H_2O Python Module

```
dir(h2o)
[...,'H2ODeepLearningEstimator', 'H2OEstimator', 'H2OFrame', ...]
```

As well as the API functions available directly in the Python shell via the h2o module, you can also use the Flow UI. Selecting Admin → Cluster Status from the Flow menu displays information similar to the shell output. This is pictured in Figure 17.9.

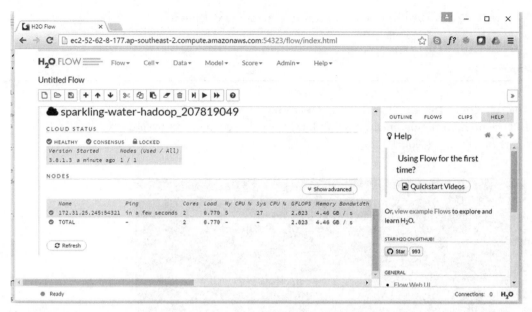

FIGURE 17.9
Sparkling Water cluster status using the Flow UI.

Using PySparkling, developers can exchange objects freely between Spark's native data structures (RDDs and DataFrames) and H2O's data structures, specifically the H2OFrame.

H2OFrame

A H2OFrame object is similar to a Spark SQL, Pandas, or R DataFrame object. It is a tabular structure consisting of rows and columns with a defined schema and column- and row-based accessors. H2OFrames can be loaded from files in a filesystem (local, HDFS, S3, or others) or from data in native python data structures (for example, lists or tuples).

Listing 17.3 shows how to create a H2OFrame from a Python object (in this case, a list of tuple objects) within a `pysparkling` shell.

LISTING 17.3   **Creating a H2OFrame from a Python Object**

```
testdata = [(1, 'a', 0.1), (2, 'b', 0.2), (3, 'c', 0.3)]
h2oframe = h2o.H2OFrame(testdata)
h2oframe
C1   C2      C3
----  ----   ----
1    a       0.1
2    b       0.2
3    c       0.3
```

The import_file method in the h2o module enables you to create a H2OFrame object directly from a file. Using this approach, you can also declare a schema using the col_types argument. Column names are inferred from a header line in the CSV file if one exists. Listing 17.4 shows an example of this.

LISTING 17.4 Creating a H2OFrame from a File

```
column_type = ['String','Numeric','Numeric','Numeric','Numeric'...]
data = h2o.import_file(path ="../airport.csv",
                col_types = column_type)
Date          TmaxF    TminF    TmeanF    PrcpIn    SnowIn    ...
---------    -------  -------  --------  --------  --------

1/1/2005        41       25       33        0.31      0
1/2/2005        54       33       43.5      0.08      0
1/3/2005        36       32       34        0.36      0
1/4/2005        35       30       32.5      0.05      1.2
1/5/2005        31       26       28.5      0.38      6.2
1/6/2005        27       12       19.5      0.19      2.4
...
```

As mentioned, an H2OFrame can also be created from a parallelized collection of objects (an RDD, in this case). This can be done in PySparkling using a connected H2OContext object (hc in our case). Listing 17.5 provides an example of creating a H2OFrame from an RDD. The RDD could have been loaded from any of the methods I've detailed in this book (for example, sc.textFile), or the RDD could have been the result of a Spark transformation performed against another RDD or RDDs.

LISTING 17.5 Creating a H2OFrame from a Spark RDD

```
rdd = sc.parallelize([(1, 'a', 0.1), (2, 'b', 0.2), (3, 'c', 0.3)])
H2OFrame = hc.as_h2o_frame(rdd)
_1  _2      _3
----  ----   ----
1   a       0.1
2   b       0.2
3   c       0.3

[3 rows x 3 columns]
```

H2OFrame objects are easily converted back to Spark SQL DataFrames using the as_spark_frame method of the H2OContext object. Listing 17.6 demonstrates converting the H2OFrame created in the previous code listing into a Spark SQL DataFrame.

LISTING 17.6   Converting a H2OFrame to a Spark SQL DataFrame

```
df = hc.as_spark_frame(H2OFrame)
df.show()
+---+---+---+
| _1| _2| _3|
+---+---+---+
|  1|  a|0.1|
|  2|  b|0.2|
|  3|  c|0.3|
+---+---+---+
```

After you have an H2OFrame and a running H2OContext running in Spark, there are several functions available to you, including frame-level operations such as show, head, and tail, as well as column-level functions such as numerical functions including cos, sqrt, log, min, max, and more, string functions such as substring, strsplit, tolower, and timestamp functions such as day, week, year, and more.

There are also summary functions available on H2OFrame objects such as the summary function, which provides column level statistics for data contained in a H2OFrame. Listing 17.7 demonstrates the H2OFrame summary method.

LISTING 17.7   H2OFrame summary Function

```
H2OFrame.summary()
           _1      _2      _3
-------   ----  ------   ----
type      int   string   real
mins      1.0   NaN      0.1
mean      2.0   NaN      0.2
maxs      3.0   NaN      0.3
sigma     1.0   NaN      0.1
zeros     0     0        0
missing   0     0        0
0         1.0   a        0.1
1         2.0   b        0.2
2         3.0   c        0.3
```

There is also a more verbose describe method that provides the column-level statistics from the summary method as well as providing information about the physical distribution of the data within the H2O cloud (running on the Spark cluster). Listing 17.8 demonstrates the describe method.

LISTING 17.8   Detailed H2OFrame Information Using the describe Method

```
H2OFrame.describe()
Rows:3 Cols:3
Chunk compression summary:
chunk_type      chunk_name           count    count_percentage      size    ...
------------    -----------------    -------  ------------------    ------
C0L             Constant Integers    3        25                    240  B
C0D             Constant Reals       6        50                    480  B
CStr            String               3        25                    237  B
Frame distribution summary:
size          number_of_rows      number_of_chunks_per_column    number_of_chunks
------------------    ------    ----------------    -------------------------
172.31.25.245:54321   957  B    3                      4
mean                  957  B    3                      4
min                   957  B    3                      4
max                   957  B    3                      4
stddev                  0  B    0                      0
total                 957  B    3                      4
_1      _2        _3
-------  ----  -------  ----
type     int    string  real
mins     1.0    NaN     0.1
mean     2.0    NaN     0.2
maxs     3.0    NaN     0.3
sigma    1.0    NaN     0.1
zeros    0      0       0
missing  0      0       0
0        1.0    a       0.1
1        2.0    b       0.2
2        3.0    c       0.3
```

Most importantly, you can now use any of the machine learning and deep learning modeling methods and prediction functions exposed through the h2o Python API. All of these methods are designed to operate against H2OFrame objects.

TRY IT YOURSELF ▼

Getting Started with Sparkling Water

In this exercise, you will get a H2O cloud up and running on Spark using PySparkling Water.

1. Go to the H2O website and locate the download link for Sparkling Water:
   http://www.h2o.ai/download/sparkling-water/spark16

   Download the zip package from a client or node in your Spark cluster, using wget for example:

   ```
   wget http://h2o-release.../sparkling-water-1.6.1.zip
   ```

2. Unpack the Sparkling Water package and change directories to the `sparkling-water-*` directory:

```
unzip sparkling-water-1.6.1.zip
cd sparkling-water-1.6.1
```

3. Install the prerequisite Python modules for PySparkling using `pip`:

```
sudo pip install tabulate
sudo pip install future
```

4. Set the required environment variables. These could also be set using the `spark-env.sh` file:

```
export SPARK_HOME=/opt/spark
export HADOOP_CONF_DIR=/etc/hadoop/conf
export SPARKLING_HOME=/.../sparkling-water-1.6.1
```

5. Start an interactive PySparking session by entering the following command:

```
bin/pysparkling
```

6. Start your H2O cloud in Spark using the following commands in the `pysparking` shell:

```
from pysparkling import *
hc = H2OContext(sc).start()
import h2o
```

7. Try creating a sample H2OFrame using some of the functions demonstrated. Explore the `h2o` Python API at https://h2o-release.s3.amazonaws.com/h2o/rel-turan/4/docs-website/h2o-py/docs/intro.html

8. Exit the `pysparking` shell by pressing Ctrl+D.

9. Download the sample PySparkling Water script—`ChicagoCrimeDemo.py`—from the Sams Teach Yourself Spark S3 Bucket: https://s3.amazonaws.com/sty-spark/scripts/ch17/ChicagoCrimeDemo.py

10. From the directory where you downloaded the `ChicagoCrimeDemo.py` file, execute the following command (you may need to ensure the environment variables set in Step 4 are still available):

```
export TOPDIR=$SPARKLING_HOME
source $SPARKLING_HOME/bin/sparkling-env.sh
SCRIPT_H2O_SYS_OPS=${H2O_SYS_OPS:-""}
$SPARK_HOME/bin/spark-submit \
--jars $SPARKLING_HOME/assembly/build/libs/$FAT_JAR \
--master local[*] \
--driver-memory 2g \
--driver-java-options "$SCRIPT_H2O_SYS_OPS" \
--driver-class-path $SPARKLING_HOME/assembly/build/libs/$FAT_JAR \
--py-files $PY_EGG_FILE \
--conf spark.driver.extraJavaOptions="-XX:MaxPermSize=384m" \
ChicagoCrimeDemo.py
```

This demo will build a deep learning predictive model to determine the probability of arrest for a specific crime given a set of attributes such as the season, day of the week, location, and temperature. After the deep learning modeling process, you should see output similar to this:

```
Model Details
=============
H2ODeepLearningEstimator :  Deep Learning
Model Key:  DeepLearning_model_python_1460701846006_1
Status of Neuron Layers: predicting Arrest, 2-class ...
...
ModelMetricsBinomial: deeplearning
** Reported on train data. **
MSE: 0.0843697875364
R^2: 0.594764520868
LogLoss: 0.277477070413
AUC: 0.935812731128
Gini: 0.871625462256
Confusion Matrix (Act/Pred) for max f1 @ threshold = ...
false     true     Error    Rate
-----    -------   ------   -------   --------------
false   5255       394     0.0697    (394.0/5649.0)
true     534      1836     0.2253    (534.0/2370.0)
Total   5789      2230     0.1157    (928.0/8019.0)
```

The next steps are to save your model and use it to predict class attributes of new data instances.

Saving H2O Models

Models created with H2O can be exported to a native H2O format using the `save_model` function. The saved model can then be reloaded using the `load_model` function. Listing 17.9 shows an example of this.

LISTING 17.9 Saving and Loading H2O Models in Native Format

```
h2o.save_model(dl_model,"<my_path>")
# Creates the file:
# DeepLearning_model_python_1460705514417_1
...
reloaded_model = h2o.load_model(".../DeepLearning_model_...")
...
```

POJO

H2O also allows you to save models in POJO format (or Plain Old Java Object format). POJO can easily be deployed within Java applications, including web service-based applications. POJO models are a convenient deployment vector for REST-based scoring APIs, commonly implemented as a scoring service (for credit risk scoring, as an example). Listing 17.10 shows an example of exporting a model as a POJO.

LISTING 17.10   Saving a H2O Model in POJO Format

```
h2o.download_pojo(reloaded_model)
# POJO Output Excerpt
...
// The class representing column Domestic
class DeepLearning_model_python_1460707006286_1_ColInfo_3 implements java.
io.Serializable {
  public static final String[] VALUES = new String[2];
  static {
    DeepLearning_model_python_1460707006286_1_ColInfo_3_0.fill(VALUES);
  }
  static final class DeepLearning_model_python_1460707006286_1_ColInfo_3_0
  implements java.io.Serializable {
    static final void fill(String[] sa) {
      sa[0] = "false";
      sa[1] = "true";
    }
  }
}
...
```

CAUTION

POJO Size Is Limited

Some models can get exceptionally large. POJOs are not supported for source files larger than 1GB in size.

Summary

In this hour, I rounded off the discussion of machine learning on Spark by introducing H2O—an open source, scalable in memory machine learning application—and its integration with Spark, Sparkling Water.

Along with its support for most common machine learning algorithms such as k-means clustering, generalized linear modeling, and regression techniques, Naive Bayes, and others, H2O enables Deep Learning capabilities—a branch of machine learning extending neural networks algorithms. Deep learning is especially adept at pattern recognition.

Sparkling Water is executed as a Spark application with seamless access to both Spark RDD and DataFrame API objects and methods and H2O data structures and functions.

H2O is growing in popularity in the data science and analyst community as a powerful open source alternative to other commercial and non-commercial machine learning, scoring platforms, and visual statistics and analytics packages. Sparkling Water combines Spark's rich data transformations and stream processing capabilities with H2O's ability to perform deep learning and low latency scoring.

Much more information about H2O and Sparkling Water is available from the H2O website at www.h2o.ai/.

Q&A

Q. What are some of the advantages of using H2O for machine learning?

A. H2O uses a high performance, in-memory engine for modeling and low latency scoring operations. H2O includes most common machine learning algorithms along with its deep learning extensions and also supplies interfaces to many common data science and analytics tools. H2O is designed for distributed machine learning with data at scale.

Q. What interfaces are available for H2O?

A. H2O Flow (notebook-style web-based user interface and API), R and Python APIs, and Sparkling Water (H2O on Spark).

Q. How does H2O integrate with Spark?

A. Sparkling Water is H2O's integration with Spark. Sparkling Water runs as a Spark application launched in a Spark executor. Data can be used interchangeably between H2O and Spark using H2OFrame objects. Spark can be used to provide data preprocessing and stream processing services, with H2O used to provide its powerful machine learning and scoring services.

Workshop

The workshop contains quiz questions and exercises to help you solidify your understanding of the material covered. Try to answer all questions before looking at the "Answers" section that follows.

Quiz

1. Automatic handling of missing values, automatic adaptive learning rates, and performance tuning and grid-search for parameters and models are features of which H_2O machine learning technique?

2. What is the integration of Python with Sparkling Water called?

3. What is the class name of the context for a Sparkling Water application?

4. **True or false:** H2OFrames can be used as input for MLlib algorithms.

Answers

1. Deep learning.

2. PySparkling Water.

3. `H2OContext`.

4. **True**.

Graph Processing with Spark

What You'll Learn in This Hour:

▶ Overview of graphs, graph theory, and graph processing

▶ Introduction to graph processing in Spark using GraphX

▶ Introduction to GraphFrames

▶ Performing PageRank in Spark

The world is increasingly more interconnected. Many of today's problems and challenges require the modeling of the relationships between different entities or discrete data items. Graph processing provides a framework-based approach to evaluating these relationships. Spark provides a full set of graph data abstractions, transformations, and algorithms to meet these challenges at scale. In this hour, I discuss graphs, "graph-able" problems, and Spark's approach to graph processing—GraphX and GraphFrames.

Introduction to Graphs

A *graph* is a set of *vertices* (or nodes) that are connected to each other via *edges* (or lines). Graphs can be of different types or have different defining characteristics, including the following:

▶ Directed: All the edges are directed from one vertex to another

▶ Undirected: All the edges are bidirectional (or have no defined direction)

▶ Cyclic: Containing at least one graph cycle

▶ Acyclic: Containing no graph cycles (sometimes referred to as a "tree")

▶ Weighted: Weights are assigned to edges or vertices

▶ Unweighted: All edges and vertices have no weights

I've covered directed acyclic graphs (DAGs) at length in this book with respect to Spark's execution planning. DAGs are common in scheduling and modeling dependencies.

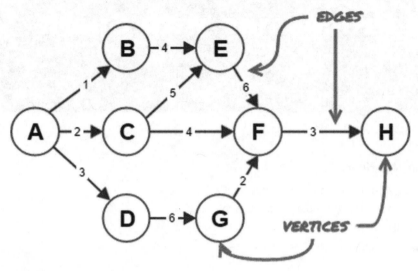

FIGURE 18.1
A directed acyclic graph.

In a directed graph, as in Figure 18.1, vertices can have indegrees and/or outdegrees. The *indegree* of a vertex is the number of inbound edges to a vertex. The *outdegree* of a vertex is the number of outbound edges from a vertex. For example, vertex *E* has an indegree of 2 and an outdegree of 1.

Graph problems are seen in many domains from the Internet, including web content and social networks to epidemiology to counter-terrorism to road, rail, and air transportation and much more. With some imagination, many traditional data problems can be modeled as a graph. Graph problem solving requirements can include the following:

▶ Finding the shortest path between vertices or nodes in a graph

   Example: routing traffic in a network

▶ Determining the maximum flow within a network

   Example: scheduling airline flights

▶ Determining the *minimum spanning tree* within a graph

   Example: rolling out a fiber optic network using the minimum amount of fiber

▶ Identifying *strongly connected components* within a graph

▶ Example: identifying the spread of epidemics

Graph processing often involves traversing a graph and performing computations at each vertex. Because graph processing is focused upon the relationships between elements, parallelization can be challenging. The first challenge is often extracting relationships between elements and representing the data in a parallelizable format. After you have identified the relationships, one such format for parallelization is the *adjacency list*.

An adjacency list represents the relationships between vertices in a graph as a list of edges. Conceptually, it's usually easier to start with an *adjacency matrix*—which represents the relationships between vertices in a sparse matrix—and then create a list from the matrix.

Consider the example of the weighted DAG in Figure 18.1. It starts by building a matrix consisting of each vertex on each axis. If a vertex is directly connected to another vertex, the value for the intersection in the matrix is the weight (in this case, this could be the "*cost*") assigned to the relationship. If there is no connection between vertices, the value at the intersection is zero (including the intersection between a vertex and itself). A sample adjacency matrix for the sample graph is shown in Figure 18.2.

	A	B	C	D	E	F	G	H
A	0	1	2	3	0	0	0	0
B	0	0	0	0	4	0	0	0
C	0	0	0	0	5	4	0	0
D	0	0	0	0	0	0	6	0
E	0	0	0	0	0	6	0	0
F	0	0	0	0	0	0	0	3
G	0	0	0	0	0	2	0	0
H	0	0	0	0	0	0	0	0

FIGURE 18.2
An adjacency matrix.

An adjacency matrix is quite sparse. A more efficient structure is the adjacency list, which takes the adjacency matrix and turns it into a list, eliminating the zeros. The following is an adjacency list representation of the preceding adjacency matrix where the connected vertex and weight is represented as a tuple.

```
A, [(B,1),(C,2)(D,3)]
B, [(E,4)]
C, [(E,5),(F,4)]
D, [(G,6)]
E, [(F,6)]
F, [(H,3)]
G, [(F,2)]
```

This structure can be further flattened into a list of *triplets*, a structure to define an edge by source, destination, and relationship. The flattened list is shown here:

```
(A,B,1)
(A,C,2)
(A,D,3)
(B,E,4)
(C,E,5)
(C,F,4)
(D,G,6)
(E,F,6)
(F,H,3)
(G,F,2)
```

This flattened list represents the edges in a graph and can be used along with a list of vertices and their attributes to perform the graph computations mentioned. Spark (including the RDD and DataFrame APIs and all others) can be used to prepare the data, and then Spark's graph processing extensions (which I will discuss next) can be used to process the data.

Graph Processing in Spark

Graph theory has been in existence since the 18th century and many graph algorithms pre-date modern computing. However, with the birth and exponential expansion of the Internet and related search engine processing, the scale of the problem outstripped existing capabilities and approaches. The search engine providers revolutionized graph processing, introducing a new set of parallel processing approaches to graph computation.

Google, Pregel, and PageRank

In the early days, Google's "secret sauce" and major differentiator was its search engine algorithms. Google was able to traverse vast amounts of web content and determine relevance and connectedness for search engine query response. One such algorithm was *PageRank*, which was actually named after one of Google's founders, Larry Page. PageRank traverses a graph where web pages are the vertices and inbound and outbound links are edges. PageRank is used to determine search engine weightings, web page relevance, and query results based upon the quality and quantity of inbound links to a particular web page. PageRank has since been generalized and adapted as an algorithm to evaluate relationships in many other domains, industries, and applications.

In addition to Google's work on parallel algorithms to process graph data, Google had also developed their own graph processing framework and systems. In 2010, Google released a whitepaper (yes, another one!) that described their graph processing system called *Pregel*. The whitepaper was titled "Pregel: A System for Large-Scale Graph Processing."

The Pregel paper outlined Google's approach to large-scale graph computing. Google's Pregel system could scale to billions of vertices and edges and was capable of implementing the PageRank algorithm in a succinct and efficient manner.

GraphX: Spark's Graph Processing System

The initiators of Spark at the UC Berkeley AMPLab were inspired by the Pregel whitepaper and project and appreciated the need to provide parallel graph processing capabilities to the Spark project. The first iteration of these capabilities was *Bagel*. Bagel was Spark's implementation of Google's Pregel graph processing framework.

In release 0.9 of Spark, Bagel was superseded by Spark's new graph processing framework and API, *GraphX*. The GraphX Spark subproject was formally introduced and outlined in the AMPLab research paper titled "GraphX: A Resilient Distributed Graph System on Spark."

As quoted from the abstract from the whitepaper: "GraphX provides powerful new operations to simplify graph construction and transformation." GraphX was designed to leverage Spark's RDD constructs and distributed memory-centric architecture and provide the fault tolerance and support for interactive data mining that was lacking in many of the existing frameworks.

At the time of writing, GraphX supports only the Scala and Java APIs. However, the Python bindings for GraphX are expected to be released soon in the pygraphx module. Note that Python graph processing functions are currently supported in the GraphFrames package, which I will discuss in the next section.

I will provide a brief overview here of the GraphX API using the design documentation for the Python implementation (pygraphx).

VertexRDDs, EdgeRDDs, and GraphRDDs

The GraphX API includes several RDD abstractions to maintain data within graph structures and components. These abstractions expose functions and algorithms used in graph processing.

VertexRDD Objects

The *VertexRDD* is an unordered set of vertex tuples. The first element in the tuple is the VertexID, which must only occur once in a VertexRDD. The value element in the vertex tuple contains properties and attributes of the vertex. Listing 18.1 demonstrates the construction of a VertexRDD.

LISTING 18.1 VertexRDDs

```
rdd = sc.parallelize([(1,('Alice','manager")),(2,('Bob','engineer'))])
vertices = VertexRDD(rdd)
vertices.count()
2
```

NOTE

The pygraphx library is not yet released, so these examples are subject to change. These code listings are provided to demonstrate GraphX concepts only using Python.

The VertexRDD exposes several methods optimized for graph processing, which include `filter`, `mapValues`, `leftJoin`, and `innerJoin` and set comparison operations `diff` and `minus`.

EdgeRDD Objects

The `EdgeRDD` is an optimized object containing an unordered indexed RDD of edge tuples, which consist of source vertex IDs, destination vertex IDs, and a relationship attribute. The `EdgeRDD` is distributed with a specified `PartitionStrategy`. Within each partition, edge attributes and adjacency structure are stored separately, enabling maximum reuse when changing attribute values. Listing 18.2 demonstrates the `EdgeRDD`.

LISTING 18.2 EdgeRDD

```
rdd0 = sc.parallelize([(1,3,('worksWith')),
                       (2,3,('knows')),
                       (3,1,('likes'))])
edges = EdgeRDD(rdd0)
edges.count()
3
```

EdgeRDD objects expose methods optimized and useful for graph construction, processing, and analysis including `filter`, `mapValues`, `leftJoin`, and `innerJoin`.

GraphRDD Objects

The `GraphRDD` object provides an atomic processing unit consisting of a VertexRDD and EdgeRDD. The GraphRDD object inherits data types from the underlying vertex and edge RDDs. Listing 18.3 demonstrates the VertexRDD.

LISTING 18.3   VertexRDD

```
graph = GraphRDD(vertices, edges)
```

Graphing Algorithms in GraphX

Several common parallel graph processing algorithms are available as methods that operate on GraphRDD objects. Listing 18.4 shows a sample PageRank operation performed against a GraphRDD.

LISTING 18.4   pageRank Algorithm

```
ranks = graph.pageRank(0.0001).vertices
```

The *connected components* algorithm is used to approximate clusters. Listing 18.5 demonstrates the `connectedComponents` algorithm performed against a GraphRDD.

LISTING 18.5   connectedComponents Algorithm

```
cc = graph.connectedComponents().vertices
```

Triangle count is another common graph algorithm used to measure the number of triangles in the graph, a common method of identifying clusters within a graph or network. Listing 18.6 demonstrates the `triangleCount` function performed on a `GraphRDD` object.

LISTING 18.6   `triangleCount` Algorithm

```
triCounts = graph.triangleCount().vertices
```

Next, I will cover the DataFrame abstraction for graph processing: GraphFrames.

Introduction to GraphFrames

GraphFrames are a special graph representation or abstraction of the Spark SQL DataFrames discussed in detail in **Hour 13, "Using SQL with Spark."** GraphFrames are constructed from separate DataFrames containing vertices and edges and their associated attributes. GraphFrames expose graph functions such as `degrees`, `edges`, and `vertices` and graph algorithm implementations such as `bfs` (breadth-first search), `shortestPaths`, and `pageRank`. GraphFrames are similar to the GraphX project discussed in the previous section. However, GraphX and GraphRDDs are built on the RDD API instead.

Accessing the GraphFrames Library

At the time of writing, GraphFrames are available as a Spark package and can be downloaded as source code or as a pre-built release from the following location:

http://spark-packages.org/package/graphframes/graphframes

You can access Python and Scala API documentation for GraphFrames from this site as well.

TIP

Spark Packages

Spark Packages is a community-contributed collection of packages for Apache Spark. More than 200 packages are available, ranging from connectors for various data sources, specialized packages for Spark streaming, graph manipulation and machine learning, tools and utilities, and more. You can find a list of all packages available at http://spark-packages.org/.

To access the GraphFrames package, simply supply the package in your `pyspark`, `spark-submit`, or `spark-shell` command using the `--packages` argument, as shown in Listing 18.7. The version and release of the package specified will be automatically downloaded from the `spark-packages` maven repository and made available to your Spark application or interactive session.

LISTING 18.7   GraphFrames Package

```
$SPARK_HOME/bin/pyspark \
            --packages graphframes:graphframes:0.1.0-spark1.6
```

Inside your program, you will need to import the graphframes Python module as shown in Listing 18.8.

LISTING 18.8   Importing the graphframes Python module

```
from graphframes import *
```

Creating a GraphFrame

To create a GraphFrame, you first need to create DataFrames for your graph vertices and edges. The vertices DataFrame needs to include a named id, which represents a unique ID for the vertex. Listing 18.9 demonstrates the creation of a vertex DataFrame.

LISTING 18.9   Creating a Vertex DataFrame

```
vertices = sqlContext.createDataFrame([
                ("1", "Jeff", 46),
                ("2", "Paul", 43),
                ("3", "Doug", 45)
                ], ["id", "name", "age"])
```

The vertex DataFrame often contains other significant attributes or features for each entity depending upon your specific application. The only caveat is the unique *id* column.

Next, you need an edge DataFrame to represent the relationships of the vertices. The edge DataFrame needs to include src and dst named columns representing the source and destination vertices respectively. In the example in Listing 18.10, I've also included a "relationship" attribute to describe the relationship between the vertices.

LISTING 18.10   Creating an Edge DataFrame

```
edges = sqlContext.createDataFrame([
                ("1", "2", "friend"),
                ("2", "3", "follow"),
                ("3", "2", "follow")
                ], ["src", "dst", "relationship"])
```

Having created DataFrames for the vertices and edges of your graph, you are now ready to create a GraphFrame. This is done by using the GraphFrame object constructor, supplying the vertices and edges DataFrame objects, as shown in Listing 18.11.

LISTING 18.11   Creating a GraphFrame

```
graph = GraphFrame(vertices, edges)
```

GraphFrame Operations

GraphFrame objects have several innate properties, which are available through the GraphFrames API. These properties are accessible via methods including the vertices and edges methods, which return DataFrame objects consisting of the vertices and edges that make up the graph. Listing 18.12 demonstrates these methods.

LISTING 18.12 vertices and edges Methods

```
# vertices
graph.vertices.show()
+---+------+---+
| id|  name|age|
+---+------+---+
|  1|  Jeff| 46|
|  2|  Paul| 43|
|  3|  Doug| 45|
+---+------+---+
graph.vertices.count()
3


# edges
graph.edges.show()
+---+---+------------+
|src|dst|relationship|
+---+---+------------+
|  1|  2|      friend|
|  2|  3|      follow|
|  3|  2|      follow|
+---+---+------------+
graph.edges.count()
3
```

As the return values from these methods are DataFrames, all available DataFrame methods (such as join, union, intersection, and others) are accessible.

There are also methods that return information about the degrees of each vertex, that is, the number of inbound and outbound edges to each vertex. There are also specific methods for inDegrees and outDegrees. These methods are demonstrated in Listing 18.13.

LISTING 18.13   degrees, inDegrees, and outDegrees Methods

```
graph.degrees.show()
+---+------+
| id|degree|
+---+------+
|  1|     1|
|  2|     3|
|  3|     2|
+---+------+
```

```
graph.inDegrees.show()
+---+--------+
| id|inDegree|
+---+--------+
|  2|       2|
|  3|       1|
+---+--------+
graph.outDegrees.show()
+---+---------+
| id|outDegree|
+---+---------+
|  1|        1|
|  2|        1|
|  3|        1|
+---+---------+
```

Motifs

A *motif* represents specific structural patterns in a graph. It is implemented using domain-specific language (DSL). You can think of this in terms similar to a regular expression in text processing. Motifs are discovered using the find method against a `GraphFrame` object. The DSL is in the general form of $(vertex_n)\text{-}[e]\text{->}(vertex_m)$, where $vertex_m$ and $vertex_n$ are arbitrary column names for vertices in the graph and e is an arbitrary column name given to the resultant edge. You can supply multiple expressions to the find method by using the semicolon (;) separator, for instance, to find multiple connections. Listing 18.14 is a simple demonstration of motifs.

LISTING 18.14 Motifs

```
motifs = graph.find("(1)-[edge]->(2)")
motifs.show()
+-------------+-------------+-------------+
|         edge|            1|            2|
+-------------+-------------+-------------+
| [1,2,friend]|  [1,Jeff,46]|  [2,Paul,43]|
| [3,2,follow]|  [3,Doug,45]|  [2,Paul,43]|
| [2,3,follow]|  [2,Paul,43]|  [3,Doug,45]|
+-------------+-------------+-------------+
motifs.printSchema()
root
|-- edge: struct (nullable = false)
|    |-- src: string (nullable = true)
|    |-- dst: string (nullable = true)
|    |-- relationship: string (nullable = true)
```

```
|-- 1: struct (nullable = false)
|    |-- id: string (nullable = true)
|    |-- name: string (nullable = true)
|    |-- age: long (nullable = true)
|-- 2: struct (nullable = false)
|    |-- id: string (nullable = true)
|    |-- name: string (nullable = true)
|    |-- age: long (nullable = true)
```

Note the output from the printSchema method of the motifs object. Each column is a struct (a tuple with named columns), the edge struct is a triplet, and the vertex columns (1 and 2) are structs representing the input vertices to the graph. As all of the GraphFrame methods return DataFrame objects, you can access nested values using standard DataFrame operators as shown in Listing 18.15.

LISTING 18.15   Accessing Struct Values in Motifs

```
motifs.select("edge.relationship").show()
+------------+
|relationship|
+------------+
|      friend|
|      follow|
|      follow|
+------------+
```

Subgraphs

A *subgraph* is a subset of of a graph created from a filtered set of vertices and/or edges from a source graph. Subgraphs can have many applications, from epidemiology to social network analysis. Listing 18.16 demonstrates creating a simple subgraph by filtering the vertices and edges of our original GraphFrame.

LISTING 18.16   Creating a Subgraph

```
v2 = graph.vertices.filter("age > 43")
e2 = graph.edges.filter("relationship = 'friend'")
subgraph = GraphFrame(v2, e2)
```

Subgraphs can also be created by combining find expressions (motifs) and filter expressions.

Using Graphing Algorithms with GraphFrames

The power of GraphFrames is the graph parallel processing algorithms available in the API that operate directly on these structures. The GraphFrames API includes methods such as bfs (breadth-first search), shortestPaths, connectedComponents, stronglyConnected-Components, triangleCount, pageRank, and more. I will give an example of the pageRank method in the Try It Yourself exercise.

TRY IT YOURSELF ▼

Implementing PageRank with GraphFrames

In this exercise, you will perform several common graph evaluation processes against the Bay Area Bike Share dataset. You will use inDegrees and outDegrees functions and the PageRank algorithm to identify the most significant terminals.

1. Download the stations and trips CSV files from the Sams Teach Yourself Spark S3 bucket (if you have not done so in a previous exercise):

   https://s3.amazonaws.com/sty-spark/bike-share/stations/stations.csv

   https://s3.amazonaws.com/sty-spark/bike-share/trips/trips.csv

2. Launch pyspark using the GraphFrames package:

```
$SPARK_HOME/bin/pyspark \
        --packages graphframes:graphframes:0.1.0-spark1.6 \
        --master local
```

3. Import all methods from the graphframes module:

```
from graphframes import *
```

4. Load the stations dataset into an RDD and create a vertices DataFrame:

```
stations = sc.textFile('s3://sty-spark/bike-share/stations') \
            .map(lambda x: x.split(',')) \
            .map(lambda x: (int(x[0]), str(x[1])))
vertices = sqlContext.createDataFrame(stations, \
            ['id', 'station_name'])
vertices.show(3)
+---+--------------------+
| id|        station_name|
+---+--------------------+
|  2|San Jose Diridon ...|
|  3|San Jose Civic Ce...|
|  4|Santa Clara at Al...|
+---+--------------------+
```

5. Load the `trips` dataset into an RDD and create an `edges` DataFrame:

```
trips = sc.textFile('s3://sty-spark/bike-share/trips') \
            .map(lambda x: x.split(',')) \
            .map(lambda x: (int(x[4]), int(x[7])))
edges = sqlContext.createDataFrame(trips, \
            ['src', 'dst'])
edges.show(3)
+---+---+
|src|dst|
+---+---+
| 50| 70|
| 31| 27|
| 47| 64|
+---+---+
```

6. Create a GraphFrame, `graph`, from the `vertices` and `edges` DataFrames:

```
graph = GraphFrame(vertices, edges)
```

7. Use the `inDegrees` and `outDegrees` methods to determine which terminals have the most inbound and outbound trips respectively:

```
graph.inDegrees \
        .sort('inDegree', ascending=False) \
        .show(3)
+---+--------+
| id|inDegree|
+---+--------+
| 70|   34810|
| 69|   22523|
| 50|   17810|
+---+--------+
graph.outDegrees \
        .sort('outDegree', ascending=False) \
        .show(3)
+---+---------+
| id|outDegree|
+---+---------+
| 70|    26304|
| 69|    21758|
| 50|    17255|
+---+---------+
```

8. Use the `pageRank` method against the station graph and return a list of the top five most significant stations.

```
results = graph.pageRank(resetProbability=0.15, maxIter=10)
results.vertices \
        .sort('pagerank', ascending=False) \
        .show(3)
+---+-------------------+-------------------+
| id|       station_name|           pagerank|
+---+-------------------+-------------------+
|  2|San Jose Diridon ...|3.2111761175492375|
| 70|San Francisco Cal...|2.7337555447149966|
| 28|Mountain View Cal...|1.9744749683770122|
+---+-------------------+-------------------+
```

The `resetProbability` argument is the probability of resetting to a random vertex, whereas the `maxIter` argument specifies the fixed number of iterations for the algorithm to run.

Summary

Graphs are everywhere, from social networks to epidemiology to counter-terrorism to road, rail, and air transportation and to the Internet itself. Representing data as a graph enables a new set of programming algorithms and functions that can evaluate relationships between nodes in a graph.

The rapid expansion of graph processing has tracked the proliferation of the Internet, social networks, and the subsequent emergence of big data processing technologies. Although graph theory as a set of mathematical and practical concepts can be traced back nearly 300 years, the capability to efficiently (and economically) store and process vast amounts of related data is relatively new.

As many graph problems can be parallelized and often require recursion, Spark is an ideal platform for graph evaluation. Spark includes native graph processing capabilities through the GraphX project, which provides optimized graph computation on Spark's parallel in-memory processing platform.

In this hour, I introduced the different types of graphs, covered the concepts of edges and vertices, and looked at solving various problems using a graphing approach such as shortest distance, breadth-first search, and PageRank. You were introduced to the GraphX library in the Java and Scala APIs (and soon to be available in the Python API) and the `GraphFrame` object available using the `graphframes` package and used GraphFrames and the graph functions in Spark to demonstrate various graphing concepts.

Although graph processing applications are rapidly expanding, GraphX in Spark is still relatively nascent and emerging. If this specific discipline is relevant or of particular interest to you, I would recommend staying current with the new features, functions, and interfaces that will be introduced in the project.

Q&A

Q. What are GraphFrames and how are they created?

A. A GraphFrame is an abstraction of the Spark SQL DataFrame designed to represent graphs and graph `relationships`. GraphFrames are constructed from separate DataFrames containing vertices and edges and their associated attributes. GraphFrames expose graph functions such as `degrees`, `edges`, and `vertices` and graph algorithm implementations such as `bfs`, `shortestPaths`, and `pageRank`.

Q. What is a motif in Spark GraphFrames?

A. A *motif* represents specific structural patterns in a graph. It is implemented using domain-specific language (DSL). You can think of this in terms similar to a regular expression in text processing. For example, to find and return all edges [e] connecting vertices a and b, you could express this as a motif:

```
motif = gframe.find("(a)-[e]->(b)")
```

Q. Explain PageRank and giveits background.

A. PageRank is an algorithm developed by Google (and named after one of its founders, Larry Page). PageRank was originally developed by Google to measure relative importance of web pages for Google search results, but has since been adapted to many other domains and applications. PageRank traverses a graph to determine the number and weighting of all inbound edges to a vertex. Nodes or vertices with more higher quality inbound links are likely to be more relevant or significant.

Workshop

The workshop contains quiz questions and exercises to help you solidify your understanding of the material covered. Try to answer all questions before looking at the "Answers" section that follows.

Quiz

1. True or false: A graph is a set of vertices connected by edges.

2. Which of the following is not a characteristic or type of graph?

   A. Directed, undirected

   B. Cyclic, acyclic

   C. Circular, uncircular

   D. Weighted, unweighted

3. What is a *triplet* in the context of graph processing? Give an example in a social networking context.

4. Combining a set of filtered edges and/or filtered vertices from a graph creates what resultant structure?

Answers

1. **True.**

2. **C.**

3. A triplet is a structure (for example, a tuple or struct) typically in the form [`source`, `destination`, `relationship`] used to describe an edge's relationships in a graph. For instance, to represent "jeff" following "doug" in a social network, the following triplet could be used: *["Jeff", "Doug", "follow"].*

4. A subgraph.

HOUR 19
Using Spark with NoSQL Systems

What You'll Learn in This Hour:

▶ Introduction to NoSQL concepts and systems
▶ Using Spark with HBase
▶ Using Spark with Cassandra
▶ Using Spark with DynamoDB and Other NoSQL Platforms

Moore's law and the birth and explosion of mobile ubiquitous computing have permanently altered the data and computing (and database) landscape. That is not to say that the relational database is dead—far from it—but there are now new sets of problems and increasingly aggressive nonfunctional, nonrelational requirements that necessitate alternative approaches to data storage, management, and processing. This new data paradigm requires us to look at data in terms of *cells* rather than just the relational paradigm of tables, rows, and columns. Enter NoSQL, offering a completely new set of tools and capabilities designed to meet the demands of today's and tomorrows data requirements. In this hour, I will introduce you to NoSQL systems and methodologies and look at their integration with Spark processing workflows.

Introduction to NoSQL

Sparks ascension closely follows the ascension and proliferation of NoSQL systems. Before I discuss Spark integration with NoSQL, I will take a step back and give you a background and overview of NoSQL.

Bigtable: The Beginnings of the NoSQL Movement

In 2006, Google released a whitepaper that would outline a new paradigm for databases and data storage. The paper was titled "Bigtable: A Distributed Storage System for Structured Data."

Bigtable was the distributed storage system for managing structured data at Google. However, unlike existing RDBMS platforms, Bigtable was designed to reliably scale to the petabytes of data and thousands of machines that Google's application workload demanded.

At the time, Bigtable was used by several Google products including Google Analytics, Google Finance, and Google Earth.

Bigtable introduced some new concepts such as column families, uninterpreted column types, and runtime column definitions and sparsity, while extending some core massively parallel processing (MPP) database concepts such as shared nothing and distributed primary indexes.

Bigtable paved the way for several Apache projects, including HBase, Cassandra, and Accumulo. I will discuss HBase and Cassandra, two direct descendants of Bigtable, in the coming sections, but Google's work and the Bigtable paper inspired a new generation of thinking in data structure and storage. It ultimately paved the way for other popular data stores today, including MongoDB and others.

NoSQL is an integral product of the big data movement, and the Google Bigtable paper was a major catalyst for the movement.

NoSQL System Characteristics

There is some friendly disagreement about what NoSQL means, from *not SQL* to *not only SQL* to other interpretations or definitions. Regardless of the ambiguity around the nomenclature, NoSQL systems come in different variants, which I will describe in further detail shortly. All of the variants share some common properties, specifically:

▶ They are schemaless at design time and "schema-on-read" at run time: This means they do not have predefined columns, but columns are created with each PUT (INSERT) operation, and each record, document, or data instance can have a different schema than the previous instance.

▶ Data has no predefined relationship to any other object: This means there is no concept of foreign keys or referential integrity (declarative or otherwise). Relationships may exist between data objects or instances, but they are discovered or leveraged at runtime rather than prescribed at design time.

▶ Joins are typically avoided: In most NoSQL implementations, joins are kept to an absolute minimum—if not avoided altogether. This is typically accomplished by denormalizing data, often with a trade-off of storing duplicate data. However, with most NoSQL implementations leveraging cost efficient commodity or cloud infrastructure, the material cost is offset by the computation cost reduction of not having to perform excessive joins when the data is accessed.

In all cases, there is no logical or physical model that dictates how data is structured, unlike a third normal form data warehouse or online transaction processing system.

Moreover, NoSQL systems are typically distributed (like Apache Cassandra or HBase) and are structured for fast lookups. Write operations are typically faster as well, as many of the overheads of traditional relational database systems are not used (like datatype or domain checks, atomic/blocking transactions, or management of transaction isolation levels).

NoSQL systems, in the majority of cases, are built for scale and scalability (from petabytes of storage to queries bounded in terabytes), performance, and low friction (or having the ability to adapt to changes). NoSQL systems are often more analytically friendly as they often provide a denormalized structure, which is conducive to feature extraction, machine learning, and scoring.

Types of NoSQL Systems

As mentioned, NoSQL systems come in several variants or categories, which are *key value stores*, *document stores*, and *graph stores*, each of which is described in further detail with examples.

Key Value Stores

Key value stores contain a set or sets of indexed keys and associated values. Values are typically uninterpreted byte arrays, but can represent complex objects (such as nested maps, structs, or lists). The schema is not defined at design time; however, some storage properties such as column families (which are effectively storage containers for values) and compression attributes can be defined at table design time. Examples of key value stores include HBase, Cassandra, and DynamoDB.

Document Stores

Document stores or document databases store complex objects, documents, such as JSON or BSON objects or other complex, nested objects. The documents are assigned a key or document ID, and the contents would be the semi-structured document data. Examples of document stores include MongoDB and CouchDB.

Graph Stores

Graph stores are based upon the graph theory and processing concepts discussed in the previous hour (**Hour 18, "Graph Processing with Spark"**). Examples of graph stores include Neo4J and GraphBase.

With that introduction, in the remaining sections, you will look at some examples of popular NoSQL systems and their integrations with Spark.

Using Spark with HBase

HBase is perhaps the closest descendant (and purest implementation) of Bigtable. HBase was a Hadoop ecosystem project designed to deliver a distributed, massively scalable key value store on top of HDFS.

HBase Data Model and Shell

HBase stores data as a sparse, multidimensional, sorted map. The map is indexed by its key (the row key), and values are stored in cells (consisting of a column key and column value). The row key and column keys are strings and the column value is an uninterpreted byte array (which could represent any primitive or complex data type). HBase is multidimensional, as each cell is versioned with a time stamp.

At table design time, one or more *column families* is defined. Column families will be used as physical storage groups for columns. Different column families may have different physical storage characteristics such as block size, compression settings, or the number of cell versions to retain.

Although there are projects such as Hive and Phoenix to provide SQL access read and write data in HBase, the natural methods to access and update data in HBase are essentially `get`, `put` and `scan` and `delete`. HBase includes a shell program as well as programmatic interfaces for multiple languages. The HBase shell is an interactive Ruby REPL shell with access to HBase API functions to create and modify tables and read and write data. The shell application can be accessed by entering `hbase shell` on a system with the HBase client binaries available (see Figure 19.1).

FIGURE 19.1
HBase shell.

Listing 19.1 demonstrates the use of the `hbase shell` to create a table and to insert data into the table.

LISTING 19.1   Creating a Table and Inserting Data in HBase

```
hbase> create 'my-hbase-table', \
hbase* {NAME => 'cf1', COMPRESSION => 'SNAPPY'}, \
hbase* {NAME => 'cf2'}
```

```
=> Hbase::Table - my-hbase-table

hbase> put 'my-hbase-table', 'rowkey1', 'cf1:fname', 'John'
hbase> put 'my-hbase-table', 'rowkey1', 'cf1:lname', 'Doe'
hbase> put 'my-hbase-table', 'rowkey2', 'cf1:fname', 'Jeffrey'
hbase> put 'my-hbase-table', 'rowkey2', 'cf1:lname', 'Aven'
hbase> put 'my-hbase-table', 'rowkey2', 'cf1:city', 'Hayward'
hbase> put 'my-hbase-table', 'rowkey2', 'cf2:photo', '<image>'
```

The `create` statement creates a new HBase table with two column families (*cf1* and *cf2*). One column family is configured to use compression and the other is not. The subsequent `put` statements insert data into a cell as defined by the row key (*rowkey1* or *rowkey2*, in this case) and a column specified in the format '*<column_family>:<column_name>*'. Unlike a traditional database, the columns are not defined at table design time and are not typed (recall all data is an uninterpreted array of bytes). A scan command of the new table is shown in Listing 19.2.

LISTING 19.2   Scanning Our HBase Table

```
hbase> scan 'my-hbase-table'
ROW            COLUMN+CELL
 rowkey1       column=cf1:fname, timestamp=1461234568799, value=John
 rowkey1       column=cf1:lname, timestamp=1461234568877, value=Doe
 rowkey2       column=cf1:city, timestamp=1461234569032, value=Hayward
 rowkey2       column=cf1:fname, timestamp=1461234568923, value=Jeffrey
 rowkey2       column=cf1:lname, timestamp=1461234568960, value=Aven
 rowkey2       column=cf2:photo, timestamp=1461234570769, value=<image>
```

Figure 19.2 depicts the conceptual view of the data inserted.

Row Key	Column Family "cf1"	Column Family "cf2"
rowkey1	fname: John, lname: Doe	
rowkey2	fname: Jeffrey, lname: Aven, city: Hayward	photo: *<image>*

FIGURE 19.2
HBase data.

As you can see from Figure 19.2, HBase supports *sparsity*. Not every column needs to exist in each row in a table and nulls are not stored.

Although HBase data is stored on HDFS (an immutable file system), HBase allows in place updates to cells within HBase tables. It does this by creating a new version of the cell with a new time stamp if the column key already existed, and then a background *compaction* process collapses multiple files into a smaller number of larger files.

Listing 19.3 demonstrates an update to an existing cell and the resultant new version.

LISTING 19.3   Updating a Cell in HBase

```
hbase> # update a cell
hbase* put 'my-hbase-table', 'rowkey2', 'cf1:city', 'Melbourne'

hbase> # get the latest version of a cell
hbase* get 'my-hbase-table', 'rowkey2', {COLUMNS => ['cf1:city']}
COLUMN          CELL
 cf1:city       timestamp=1461276401653, value=Melbourne

hbase> # get multiple versions of a cell
hbase* get 'my-hbase-table', 'rowkey2', {COLUMNS => ['cf1:city'], VERSIONS => 2}
COLUMN          CELL
 cf1:city       timestamp=1461276401653, value=Melbourne
 cf1:city       timestamp=1461276230733, value=Hayward
```

Data Distribution in HBase

HBase data is stored in `HFile` objects in HDFS. `HFile` objects are the intersection of a column family (storage group) and a sorted range of row keys. Ranges of sorted row keys are referred to as *regions* (also known as *tablets* in Bigtable). Regions are assigned to a *region server* by HBase (see Figure 19.3). Regions are used to provide fast row key lookups, as the regions (and row keys they contain) are known by HBase. HBase splits and compacts regions as necessary as part of its normal operation. Non-row key-based lookups, such as looking for a column key and value satisfying a criteria, are slower. However, HBase uses *bloom filters* to help expedite the search.

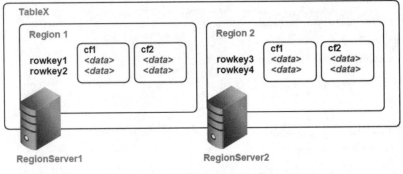

FIGURE 19.3
HBase regions.

HBase and Spark

Because HBase is a closely associated and dependent project to Hadoop, there are purpose-built Hadoop MapReduce InputFormat and OutputFormat classes to read from and write to HBase from Hadoop MapReduce applications. These InputFormats and OutputFormats in general form can be used by other projects, such as Spark.

HBase read access is supported through Spark using the HadoopRDD or newAPIHadoopRDD method (the preferred method). The newAPIHadoopRDD enables you to specify the InputFormat to read data. In this case, you would use the org.apache.hadoop.hbase.mapreduce. TableInputFormat InputFormat.

To write data out to HBase from a Spark RDD, you would use the saveAsNewAPIHadoopDataset method with the necessary configuration to connect to your HBase instance.

I will demonstrate the process of reading and writing to and from HBase using Spark in the following Try It Yourself exercise.

TRY IT YOURSELF

Reading and Writing HBase Data Using Spark

Setting up HBase is beyond the scope of this book. However, HBase is a normal inclusion in many Hadoop vendor's distributions (such as Cloudera or Hortonworks), including the sandbox VM environments provided by these vendors. You can also provision HBase as an additional application in AWS Elastic MapReduce (EMR). For this exercise, you will need a system with Hadoop, HBase, and Spark installed and running.

1. Open HBase shell:

```
$ hbase shell
```

2. From the hbase shell prompt, create a table people with a single column family cf1 (with the default storage options):

```
hbase> create 'people', 'cf1'
```

3. Create several cells in two records in the table using the put method:

```
hbase> put 'people', 'userid1', 'cf1:fname', 'John'
hbase> put 'people', 'userid1', 'cf1:lname', 'Doe'
hbase> put 'people', 'userid1', 'cf1:age', '41'
hbase> put 'people', 'userid2', 'cf1:fname', 'Jeffrey'
hbase> put 'people', 'userid2', 'cf1:lname', 'Aven'
hbase> put 'people', 'userid2', 'cf1:age', '46'
hbase> put 'people', 'userid2', 'cf1:city', 'Hayward'
```

4. View the data in the table using the `scan` method as follows:

```
hbase> scan 'people'
ROW       COLUMN+CELL
userid1  column=cf1:age, timestamp=1461296454933, value=41
...
```

5. Open another terminal session and launch `pyspark` using the arguments shown here:

```
pyspark \
--master local \
--driver-class-path \
"/usr/lib/hbase/*:/usr/lib/hbase/lib/*:../spark-examples.jar"
```

You can also use `yarn-client` mode instead; the paths to the HBase libraries may vary depending upon your platform. The `spark-examples.jar` file is located in `$SPARK_HOME/lib`.

6. Read the data from the people table using Spark:

```
conf = {"hbase.zookeeper.quorum": "localhost", \
 "hbase.mapreduce.inputtable": "people"}
keyConv = \
 "org.apache.spark.examples.pythonconverters.
 ImmutableBytesWritableToStringConverter"
valueConv = \
 "org.apache.spark.examples.pythonconverters.HBaseResultToStringConverter"

hbase_rdd = sc.newAPIHadoopRDD(
 "org.apache.hadoop.hbase.mapreduce.TableInputFormat",
 "org.apache.hadoop.hbase.io.ImmutableBytesWritable",
 "org.apache.hadoop.hbase.client.Result",
 keyConverter=keyConv,
 valueConverter=valueConv,
 conf=conf)
hbase_rdd.collect()
```

The output should resemble

```
[(u'userid1', u'{"qualifier" : "age", "timestamp" : ...)..]
```

7. Within your `pyspark` shell, create a new parallelized collection of users and save the contents of the Spark RDD to the `people` table in HBase:

```
conf2 = {"hbase.zookeeper.quorum": "localhost",
 "hbase.mapred.outputtable": "people",
 "mapreduce.outputformat.class": "org.apache.hadoop.hbase.mapreduce.
 TableOutputFormat",
 "mapreduce.job.output.key.class": "org.apache.hadoop.hbase.
 io.ImmutableBytesWritable",
```

```
    "mapreduce.job.output.value.class": "org.apache.hadoop.io.Writable"}
keyConv2 = \
 "org.apache.spark.examples.pythonconverters.
 StringToImmutableBytesWritableConverter"
valueConv2 = \
 "org.apache.spark.examples.pythonconverters.StringListToPutConverter"

newpeople = sc.parallelize([('userid3', ['userid3', 'cf1', 'fname',
'NewUser'])])
newpeople.saveAsNewAPIHadoopDataset(
 conf=conf2,
 keyConverter=keyConv2,
 valueConverter=valueConv2)
```

8. In your `hbase shell`, run the `scan` method again to confirm the new user from the Spark RDD in Step 7 exists in the HBase `people` table:

```
hbase> scan 'people'
ROW          COLUMN+CELL
userid1 column=cf1:age, timestamp=1461296454933, value=41
...
userid3 column=cf1:fname, timestamp=146..., value=NewUser
```

Although this book is based on Python, there are other Spark HBase connector projects available designed for the Scala API such as the `spark-hbase-connector` at **https://github.com/ nerdammer/spark-hbase-connector**. If you will be using Spark with HBase, I would encourage you to look at the available projects for Spark HBase connectivity.

Using Spark with Cassandra

Another notable project emanating from the Bigtable paper was *Apache Cassandra*. Cassandra was initially developed at Facebook and later released as an open source project under the Apache software licensing scheme.

DataStax, the commercial entity often associated with the Cassandra project, was formed in 2010 by ex-employees of Rackspace to provide an enterprise distribution and support for the open source project (in a similar vein to Cloudera's and Hortonwork's relationships with the Hadoop project).

Conceptually Cassandra is similar to HBase in its application of the core NoSQL principles, such as not requiring a predefined schema (although Cassandra lets you define one), no referential integrity, and so on. However, there are some differences in its physical implementation, predominantly in the fact that HBase has many Hadoop ecosystem dependencies (such as HDFS, ZooKeeper, and more), whereas Cassandra is more monolithic in its implementation (having fewer external dependencies). They also have some differences in their cluster architecture—where

HBase is a master-slave architecture, Cassandra is a symmetric architecture using a "gossip" protocol to pass messages and govern cluster processes. There are many other differences, including the way each system manages consistency, but for the purposes of this discussion, I'll leave it there.

Cassandra Data Model

Similar to HBase, Cassandra is a multidimensional, distributed map. Cassandra tables are called *keyspaces* and contain row keys and column families (referred to as *tables*). Columns exist within column families, but are not defined at table design time. Data is located at the intersection of a row key, column family, and column key.

In addition to row keys, Cassandra also supports *primary keys*, which can also contain a *partition key* and a *clustering key* in the case of composite primary keys. These directives are used for storage and distribution of data and service fast lookups by key.

Unlike HBase, Cassandra enables (and even encourages) you to define structure (a schema) to your data and assign data types. Cassandra supports *collections* within a table used to store nested or complex data structures such as sets, lists, and maps. Furthermore, Cassandra enables you to define secondary indexes to expedite lookups based upon non-key values.

Cassandra Query Language (CQL)

The *Cassandra Query Language (CQL)* is a SQL-like language for interacting with Cassandra. CQL supports the full set of DDL and DML operations for creating, reading, updating, and deleting objects in Cassandra. Because CQL is a SQL-like language, it supports ODBC and JDBC interfaces, enabling access from common SQL and visualization utilities. CQL is also available from an interactive shell environment, cqlsh.

Listing 19.4 demonstrates creating a keyspace and table in Cassandra using the cqlsh utility.

LISTING 19.4 Creating a Keyspace and Table in Cassandra Using cqlsh

```
cqlsh> CREATE KEYSPACE mykeyspace
       WITH REPLICATION = { 'class' : 'SimpleStrategy', 'replication_factor' : 1 };

cqlsh> USE mykeyspace;

cqlsh> CREATE TABLE users (
       user_id int PRIMARY KEY,
       fname text,
       lname text
       );
```

```
cqlsh> INSERT INTO users (user_id,  fname, lname)
       VALUES (1745, 'john', 'smith');
cqlsh> INSERT INTO users (user_id,  fname, lname)
       VALUES (1744, 'john', 'doe');
cqlsh> INSERT INTO users (user_id,  fname, lname)
       VALUES (1746, 'jane', 'smith');

cqlsh> SELECT * FROM users;
 user_id | fname | lname
---------+-------+-------
    1745 |  john | smith
    1744 |  john |   doe
    1746 |  jane | smith
```

This should look very familiar to you if you come from a background that includes relational databases such as SQL Server, Oracle, or Teradata.

Accessing Cassandra Using Spark

As the Cassandra and Spark movements are closely linked in their ties back to the big data/open source software community, there are several projects and libraries available to enable read/write access to Cassandra from Spark programs. Some of the projects providing this support include

https://github.com/datastax/spark-cassandra-connector

http://tuplejump.github.io/calliope/pyspark.html

https://github.com/TargetHolding/pyspark-cassandra

Furthermore, many of the available projects have been built and provisioned as Spark Packages (available at https://spark-packages.org/).

I will use the `TargetHolding pyspark-cassandra` package for these demonstrations, but you are encouraged to investigate all of the possible connectivity options available (or write your own!).

NOTE

With many projects, classes, scripts, examples, or artifacts in the open source world, you will often find system, library, or class dependencies you need to satisfy. For instance, in the subsequent example, I needed to download and supply the latest `guava-*.jar` file in order to satisfy a dependency. Resourcefulness is a necessity when working with open source software!

For the following examples, run the `pyspark` command provided in Listing 19.5 first, note the `config` option required to configure the Cassandra connection.

LISTING 19.5   pyspark Command with pyspark-cassandra Package

```
$SPARK_HOME/bin/pyspark --master local \
--packages TargetHolding:pyspark-cassandra:0.3.5 \
--driver-class-path /usr/share/cassandra/lib/guava-17.0.jar \
--conf spark.cassandra.connection.host=127.0.0.1
```

Listing 19.6 shows how to load the contents of the users table created in Listing 19.4 into an RDD.

LISTING 19.6   Reading Cassandra Data into a Spark RDD

```
import pyspark_cassandra
sc.cassandraTable("mykeyspace", "users").collect()
...
[Row(fname=u'john', lname=u'smith', user_id=1745),
 Row(fname=u'john', lname=u'doe', user_id=1744),
 Row(fname=u'jane', lname=u'smith', user_id=1746)]
```

Writing Spark data out to a Cassandra table is demonstrated in Listing 19.7.

LISTING 19.7   Updating Data in a Cassandra Table Using Spark

```
import pyspark_cassandra
rdd = sc.parallelize([{
"user_id": 1747,
"fname": "Jeffrey",
"lname": "Aven"
}])

rdd.saveToCassandra(
"mykeyspace",
"users",
)
```

Running a SELECT * FROM users command in cqlsh, you can see the results of the insert from Listing 19.7 in Listing 19.8.

LISTING 19.8   Cassandra Insert Results

```
cqlsh> USE mykeyspace;
cqlsh:mykeyspace> SELECT * FROM users;
 user_id | fname   | lname
---------+---------+-------
 1745    |   john  | smith
 1747    | Jeffrey | Aven
```

```
1744      |   john  |   doe
1746      |   john  |  smith
(4 rows)
```

Using Spark with DynamoDB and More

Following the Bigtable paper, multiple NoSQL project initiatives were underway. Apache HBase was being championed by Yahoo!, and Facebook was developing Cassandra. Other open source initiatives such as Accumulo (developed by the National Security Agency (NSA) to provide cell-level security to HBase) were progressing as well. Meanwhile, Amazon was working on its own NoSQL solution, DynamoDB.

Amazon DynamoDB

In 2007, Amazon released their own whitepaper entitled "Dynamo: Amazon's Highly Available Key-Value Store." At this stage, the AWS was still in its infancy, and the technology was mainly designed to meet Amazon's internal operational requirements. Later DynamoDB, would become a generally available NoSQL PaaS (Platform-as-a-Service) offering in AWS.

DynamoDB's data model is composed of *tables* containing items, which are composed of one or more *attributes*. Like Cassandra, Dynamo tables have a *primary key* that is used for storage and fast retrieval. Dynamo also supports secondary indexes. DynamoDB is both a key value store and a document store, as objects could be treated as documents.

Because DynamoDB was designed as a web service, it has rich integration with many other language bindings and SDKs. DDL and DML statements are implemented using Dynamo's API endpoints and JSON-based DSL.

In 2007, Amazon released their own whitepaper entitled "Dynamo: Amazon's Highly Available Key-Value Store." At this stage, the AWS was still in its infancy, and the technology was mainly designed to meet Amazon's internal operational requirements. Later, DynamoDB would become a generally available NoSQL PaaS (Platform-as-a-Service) offering in AWS.

Reading and writing data to and from DynamoDB using Spark is peformed using the `newAPIHadoopRDD` and/or `saveAsNewAPIHadoopDataset` methods referencing the `DynamoInputFormat` and `DynamoDBOutputFormat` classes, which are available from Amazon. Listing 19.9 demonstrates accessing DynamoDB from Spark.

NOTE

You will need to supply the DynamoDB connector libraries as arguments to `spark-submit` or `pyspark`, for example:

```
$ pyspark --jars /usr/share/aws/emr/ddb/lib/emr-ddb-hadoop.jar
```

LISTING 19.9   Accesing Amazon DynamoDB from Spark

```
conf = {"dynamodb.servicename": "dynamodb", \
  "dynamodb.input.tableName": "myDynamoDBTable", \
  "dynamodb.endpoint": "dynamodb.us-east-1.amazonaws.com", \
  "dynamodb.regionid": "us-east-1"}
dynamo_rdd = sc.newAPIHadoopRDD(
  "org.apache.hadoop.dynamodb.read.DynamoDBInputFormat",
  "org.apache.hadoop.io.Text",
  "org.apache.hadoop.dynamodb.DynamoDBItemWritable",
  conf=conf)
dynamo_rdd.collect()
```

Other NoSQL Implementations

Other common or popular NoSQL platforms include document stores such as MongoDB and CouchDB, key value stores such as Couchbase and Riak, and memory-centric key value stores such as Memcached and Redis. There are also the full text search and indexing platforms that have been adapted to become general-purpose NoSQL platforms. These include Apache Solr and ElasticSearch, which were both based upon the Lucene early search engine processing project.

Many of these have available InputFormat and OutputFormat classes in Hadoop that enable them to be used to read and write RDD data in Spark. Check the project or vendor's website or GitHub for your selected NoSQL platform's integration. If an integration does not exist, you could always develop your own. Documentation on building your own custom Hadoop input and output format classes is available at http://hadoop.apache.org/.

The Future for NoSQL

As you can see, NoSQL is a fast-moving area. There are new market entrants all the time, from novel solutions to evolution and adaptations of existing solutions. Even the established vendors such as Microsoft, Oracle, and Teradata, traditionally the proponents of conventional relational database technologies, are expanding into this area.

NoSQL platforms provide the unique combination of massive scalability and fine-grained, as well as coarse-grained, accessibility, servicing both low-latency operational patterns as well as batch analytic patterns. These characteristics make NoSQL an ideal companion to Spark.

Summary

Since the Google Bigtable whitepaper in 2006, the database landscape has been irrevocably altered. NoSQL databases have become a viable alternative to traditional SQL systems, offering Internet scale storage capabilities and query boundaries, as well as fast read and write access to support distributed device and mobile application interactions. NoSQL concepts and implementations have emerged in parallel to Spark because these concepts both emanated from early Google and Yahoo! work.

In this hour, I introduced you to NoSQL concepts and looked at some practical applications of key value and document stores—Apache HBase, Apache Cassandra, and Amazon DynamoDB. I also discussed the high-level cluster architecture as well as the conceptual and physical data models of each platform.

Additionally, I have demonstrated how Spark could interact with various NoSQL platforms as both a consumer and provider of data. Hopefully, I've inspired you to explore this area further. Happy NoSQL-ing!

Q&A

Q. **What are the key functional characteristics of a NoSQL database?**

A. NoSQL systems are schemaless at design time and schema-on-read at run time, meaning they do not have predefined columns. Columns are created with each PUT (INSERT) operation, and each record, document, or data instance can have a different schema than the previous instance. Also, data typically have no predefined relationship to any other object, meaning there is no concept of foreign keys or referential integrity, and joins are not natively implemented.

Q. **What are the different types of NoSQL stores?**

A. Key value stores, document stores, and graph stores.

Q. **What are the primary differences between HBase and Cassandra's implementation of Bigtable?**

A. HBase relies on many other independent Hadoop ecosystem components such as HDFS and Zookeeper, whereas Cassandra has a monolithic implementation. HBase clusters implement a master-slave architecture, whereas Cassandra has a peer-to-peer symmetric distributed architecture. HBase data is entirely untyped (uninterpreted array of bytes), whereas Cassandra supports schemas and data type definitions as an option.

Workshop

The workshop contains quiz questions and exercises to help you solidify your understanding of the material covered. Try to answer all questions before looking at the "Answers" section that follows.

Quiz

1. Which method is used to save RDD data to a table is HBase?

2. The `put` method in HBase is used to do which of the following?

    A. Insert a new row key along with a data cell into a table

    B. Insert a new cell (column key and value) into an existing row

    C. Update the value for an existing cell

    D. All of the above

3. What Cassandra data construct is used to represent complex objects such as sets, lists, or maps?

4. What are the basic components in the DynamoDB data model?

Answers

1. `saveAsNewAPIHadoopDataset`.

2. **D.**

3. A collection.

4. Tables, items, and attributes.

Using Spark with Messaging Systems

Message queues have traditionally been an integral component for enabling communication between disparate systems. In recent times, with the rise of ubiquitous mobile computing and the Internet of Things (IoT), messaging platforms have moved beyond middleware or brokerage systems to systems servicing low latency, high throughput communication requirements, often feeding into real-time stream processing engines (like Spark!). In this hour, I will cover some common messaging systems and their integration into Spark.

Overview of Messaging Systems

Messaging systems were originally formed to provide middleware functionality—more specifically, *message oriented middleware* (MOM). This area saw rapid expansion in the 80s to integrate legacy systems with newer systems (such as mainframe to early distributed systems). Notable companies such as TIBCO (The Information Bus Company) made these technologies an integral part of mainstream computing. Later in the 90s, as mailbox, user messaging, and group communication platforms emerged and evolved, messaging system technologies adapted to these emerging usages.

Today messaging systems and platforms provide much more functionality than just simple integration. They are critical part of the mobile computing and Internet of Things (IoT) landscape. Projects such as JMS (Java Message Service), Kafka, ActiveMQ, ZeroMQ (ØMQ), RabbitMQ, Amazon SQS (Simple Queue Service), Kinesis, and more have added to the existing landscape of more established commercial solutions such as TIBCO EMS (Enterprise Message Service), IBM WebSphere MQ, and Microsoft Message Queuing (MSMQ).

Messaging systems are traditionally asynchronous in their operation and are used to exchange control and event messages or to buffer or queue data, which is what I will focus on in this chapter.

Pub-Sub Messaging Exchange Pattern

There are several types of exchange patterns in use in messaging systems, but we will focus on the most common pattern—*publish-subscribe* (or *pub-sub*).

In a pub-sub model, the message *consumer* (the client or subscriber), is decoupled from the message *producer* (or publisher)—meaning the publisher and subscriber do not communicate directly with each other. The messaging platform acts as a broker to intermediate messages between the publisher and subscriber. Figure 20.1 illustrates the pub-sub model.

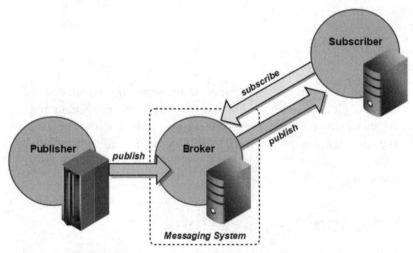

FIGURE 20.1
Pub-sub messaging system.

Message Filtering

Subscribers in a pub-sub messaging model usually consume messages selectively. There are two primary methods for filtering messages not intended for certain subscribers: *topic filtering* and *content filtering*.

With topic filtering, messages are published to named *topics*. Topics manage messages belonging to a particular category. Subscribers to a topic will receive messages for that specific topic. This enables a messaging system to multiplex several topics to many subscribers on a single message bus. Publishers are responsible for defining the topics to which a subscriber can subscribe. Subscribers will receive all messages for a topic to which they have subscribed.

Content filtering filters messages based upon conditions or filters defined by the subscriber. Only messages satisfying the content filter criteria are delivered to the subscriber.

Many current messaging systems implement both filtering methods, enabling subscribers to subscribe to a topic and to define content-based filters.

Message Buffering and Queuing

Because messaging systems typically operate in an asynchronous manner, the publisher and subscriber will often read to and write from the message queue at different times. This means the messages must be buffered and queued for subscribers to consume. The queue typically has limits for the number of messages retained or for the TTL (time-to-live) for a given message.

Moreover, different messaging systems will have different characteristics, such as the capability to replay messages from a previous offset as opposed to messaging systems that only allow subscribers to consume new messages from the time they subscribe. This makes some messaging systems more conducive to data exchange (such as Apache Kafka) versus other messaging platforms better-suited to serving control or event messages that do not require the capability to replay messages.

Now let's take a look at some messaging systems commonly used with big data and Spark implementations.

Using Spark with Apache Kafka

Apache Kafka, originally developed at LinkedIn, is a popular open source project written in Scala designed for message brokering and queuing between various Hadoop ecosystem projects. Here I will briefly cover Kafka's architecture and messaging model.

Kafka Overview

Kafka is a distributed, reliable, low latency, pub-sub messaging platform. Conceptually, Kafka acts as a *write ahead log (WAL)* for messages, much the same way a transaction log or journal functions in an ACID data store. This log-based design provides durability, consistency, and the capability for subscribers to replay messages if required.

Publishers are called *producers*, and producers write data to *topics*. Subscribers, called *consumers*, read messages from specified topics. Figure 20.2 summarizes the relationships among producers, topics, and consumers. Messages themselves are uninterpreted byte arrays that can represent any object or primitive data type. Common message content formats include JSON and Avro (an open source Hadoop ecosystem data serialization project).

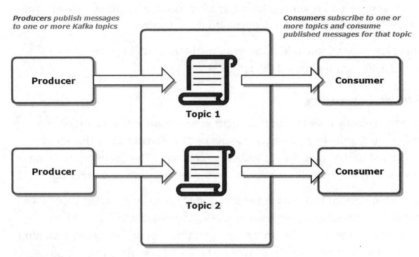

Producers *publish messages to one or more Kafka topics*

Consumers *subscribe to one or more topics and consume published messages for that topic*

FIGURE 20.2
Kafka producers, consumers, and topics.

Kafka Cluster Architecture

Kafka is a distributed system consisting of one or more *brokers*, typically on separate nodes of a cluster. Brokers manage *partitions*, which are ordered, immutable sequences of messages for a particular topic. Partitions are replicated across multiple nodes in a cluster to provide fault tolerance. Topics may have many partitions.

Each topic in Kafka is treated as a *log* (an ordered collection of messages) with a unique *offset* assigned to each message. Consumers can access messages from a topic based upon these offsets (allowing a consumer to replay previous messages).

NOTE
Kafka only retains messages for a specified period of time. After the specified retention period, messages will be purged and access to these messages (for replay or otherwise) will no longer be possible for consumers.

Kakfa uses Apache Zookeeper to maintain state between brokers. Zookeeper is an open source distributed configuration and synchronization service used by many other Hadoop ecosystem projects including HBase. Zookeeper is typically implemented in a cluster configuration called an *ensemble*, typically deployed in odd numbers (such as three or five).

Figure 20.3 presents the Kafka cluster architecture.

A majority of nodes, or a *quorum* of nodes, successfully performing an action (such as updating a state) is required. A quorum is required to "elect" a leader. A *leader* in a Kafka cluster is the node responsible for all reads and writes for a specific partition—every partition has a leader.

Other nodes are considered *followers*. Followers consume messages and update their partitions. If the leader is unavailable, a new leader will be elected by Kafka.

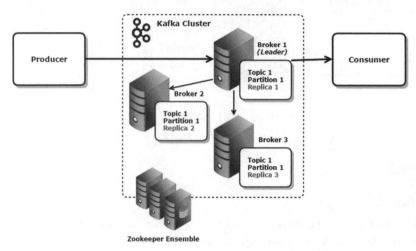

FIGURE 20.3
Kafka cluster architecture.

More detailed information about Kafka is available at http://kafka.apache.org/.

Spark and Kafka

Spark's support for Kafka is closely aligned with the Spark Streaming project. Kafka's performance and durability make it a platform well-suited to servicing Spark Streaming processes.

Common usage scenarios for Kafka and Spark include Spark Streaming processes reading data from a Kafka topic and performing event processing on the data stream or a Spark process serving as a producer and writing output to a Kafka topic.

There are two approaches for consuming messages from a Kafka topic using Spark: using receivers or accessing messages directly from a broker.

Receivers

Receivers are processes that run within Spark executors. Each receiver is responsible for an input DStream created from messages from a Kafka topic. Receivers query the Zookeeper quorum for information about brokers, topics, partitions, and offsets. Additionally, receivers implement a separate write ahead log (WAL)—typically stored in HDFS—for durability and consistency. Messages and offsets are committed to the WAL, and then receipt of the message is acknowledged by updating the consumed offset in Zookeeper. This ensures messages can be processed "once and only once" across multiple receivers if this guarantee is required. The WAL implementation ensures durability and crash consistency in the event of receiver failure. Figure 20.4 summarizes Spark Streaming Kafka receivers.

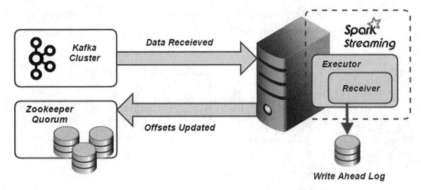

FIGURE 20.4
Spark Streaming Kafka receivers.

Direct Stream Access

Although the receiver method for reading messages from Kafka provides durability and "once and only once processing," the blocking WAL write operations result in a performance impact. A newer, alternative approach to stream consumption from Kafka is the *direct* approach. The direct approach does not use receivers (or write ahead logging). Instead the Spark driver queries Kafka for updates to offsets for each topic and directs application executors to consume specified offsets in topic partitions directly from Kafka brokers.

The direct approach uses the SimpleConsumer Kafka API as opposed to the high-level ConsumerConnector API used with the receiver approach. The direct method provides durability, recoverability, and enabling "once and only once" (transactional) processing semantics equivalent to the receiver approach without incurring the WAL overhead. Figure 20.5 summarizes the Spark Streaming Kafka Direct API.

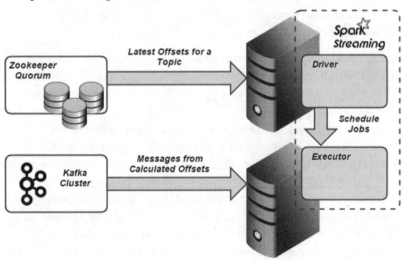

FIGURE 20.5
Spark Streaming Kafka Direct API.

KafkaUtils

In both the receiver and direct approach to stream acquisition from a Kafka topic, the KafkaUtils package is used with the Scala, Java, or Python API. To use KafkaUtils you need to download or compile the `spark-streaming-kafka-assembly` jar file. You will do this in the Try It Yourself exercise. Listing 20.1 shows an example of starting a `pyspark` session including the `spark-streaming-kafka-assembly` jar file. The same process applies for `spark-shell` or `spark-submit`.

LISTING 20.1 Using Spark KafkaUtils

```
$SPARK_HOME/bin/pyspark \
        --jars spark-streaming-kafka-assembly_2.10-1.6.1.jar
```

With the `spark-streaming-kafka-assembly` jar file included in a Spark session and a `StreamingContext` available, you can now access methods from the KafkaUtils class, including methods to create a stream using the receiver or direct approach. Take a look at these methods now.

createDirectStream()

Syntax:

```
KafkaUtils.createDirectStream(ssc,
                topics,
                kafkaParams,
                fromOffsets=None,
                keyDecoder=utf8_decoder,
                valueDecoder=utf8_decoder,
                messageHandler=None)
```

The `createDirectStream` method is used to create a Spark Streaming DStream object from a Kafka topic (or topics). The DStream consists of key value pairs, where the key is the message key and the value is the message itself. The `ssc` argument is a `StreamingContext` (as discussed in **Hour 14, "Stream Processing with Spark"**). The `topics` argument is a list of one or more Kafka topics to consume. The `kafkaParams` argument is used to pass additional parameters to Kafka (such as a list of Kafka brokers to communicate with). The `fromOffsets` argument specifies the starting point for the stream to start reading from. If this is not supplied, the stream will be consumed from the either the smallest or largest offset available in Kafka (controlled by `auto.offset.reset` setting in the `kafkaParams` argument). The optional `keyDecoder` and `valueDecoder` arguments are used to decode message key and value objects, defaulting to decoding these objects using UTF8. The `messageHandler` argument is an optional argument to supply a function to access message meta data. Listing 20.2 demonstrates the use of the `createDirectStream` method.

LISTING 20.2   KafkaUtils.createDirectStream Method

```
from pyspark.streaming import StreamingContext
from pyspark.streaming.kafka import KafkaUtils
ssc = StreamingContext(sc, 30)
stream = KafkaUtils.createDirectStream \
    (ssc, ["my_kafka_topic"], {"metadata.broker.list": "localhost:9092"})
```

There is also a similar direct method in the KafkaUtils package named createRDD, which is designed for batch access from a Kafka buffer, specifying a start and end offset for a topic and partition.

The receiver method is accessed using the createStream function of the KafkaUtils package, which is described here:

createStream()

Syntax:

```
KafkaUtils.createStream(ssc,
                zkQuorum,
                groupId,
                topics,
                kafkaParams=None,
                storageLevel=StorageLevel(True,
                True, False, False, 2),
                keyDecoder=utf8_decoder,
                valueDecoder=utf8_decoder)
```

The createStream method is used to create a Spark Streaming DStream object from a Kafka topic (or topics) using a high-level Kafka consumer API and receiver (including a WAL). The ssc argument is a StreamingContext. The zkQuorum argument specifies a list of Zookeeper nodes for the receiver to interact with. The groupId argument specifies the group ID for the consumer. The topics argument is a dict consisting of the topic name to consume and number of partitions to create; each partition is consumed using a separate thread. The kafkaParams argument specifies additional parameters to pass to Kafka. The storageLevel argument is the storage level to use for the WAL (the default equates to MEMORY_AND_DISK_SER_2). The keyDecoder and valueDecoder arguments are used to specify functions to decode message keys and values respectively. Both default to the utf8_decoder function. Listing 20.3 demonstrates the use of the createStream method.

LISTING 20.3   KafkaUtils.createStream (Receiver) Method

```
from pyspark.streaming import StreamingContext
from pyspark.streaming.kafka import KafkaUtils
ssc = StreamingContext(sc, 1)
stream = KafkaUtils.createStream(ssc, \
        "localhost:2181", \
        "spark-streaming-consumer", \
        {"my_kafka_topic": 1})
```

Using Spark with Kafka

In this exercise, you will install a single-node Kafka system. You will use this platform to create messages through a producer and consume these messages as a DStream in a Spark Streaming application.

This exercise requires an installation of Zookeeper. Zookeeper is a requirement for installing HBase, so if you have an installation of HBase (like the one used in the Try It Yourself exercise in the previous chapter), you can use this. Otherwise, a release of Zookeeper along with startup scripts and configuration is included in the Kafka release tarball. More information about Zookeeper is available at https://zookeeper.apache.org/.

You will also need to download the `spark-streaming-kafka-assembly` jar. You can download the release targeting your Spark version from the following location:

http://mvnrepository.com/artifact/org.apache.spark/spark-streaming-kafka-assembly_2.10

1. Download the latest Kafka release from http://kafka.apache.org/downloads.html.

2. Unpack tar.gz archive and create a Kafka home:

    ```
    $ tar -xvf kafka_2.11-0.9.0.1.tgz
    $ sudo mv kafka_2.11-0.9.0.1/ /opt/kafka/
    $ export KAFKA_HOME=/opt/kafka
    ```

3. Start the Kafka server:

    ```
    $KAFKA_HOME/bin/kafka-server-start.sh \
     $KAFKA_HOME/config/server.properties
    ```

4. Create a test topic:

    ```
    $KAFKA_HOME/bin/kafka-topics.sh \
      --create \
      --zookeeper localhost:2181 \
      --replication-factor 1 \
      --partitions 1 \
      --topic my_kafka_topic
    ```

5. List available topics:

    ```
    $KAFKA_HOME/bin/kafka-topics.sh \
      --list \
      --zookeeper localhost:2181
    ```

    This should return the `my_kafka_topic` topic created in Step 4.

6. Open a second terminal ("terminal 2"), and start a consumer:

    ```
    $KAFKA_HOME/bin/kafka-console-consumer.sh \
      --zookeeper localhost:2181 \
      --topic my_kafka_topic \
      --from-beginning
    ```

7. Open a third terminal ("terminal 3"), and create a test message in the `my_kafka_topic` topic:

```
$KAFKA_HOME/bin/kafka-console-producer.sh \
   --broker-list localhost:9092 \
   --topic my_kafka_topic
```

This opens a console. Enter a test message like *this is a test message* in the console. Exit the producer console using Ctrl+C.

8. You should see the test message entered by the producer process in Step 7 in your consumer console process started in Step 6. This confirms that Kafka is up and running.

9. Close the consumer process started in Step 6 using Ctrl+C.

10. In the same terminal the consumer was running in (terminal 2), start a `pyspark` session using the `spark-streaming-kafka-assembly` jar downloaded as a prerequisite:

```
$SPARK_HOME/bin/pyspark \
   --jars spark-streaming-kafka-assembly_2.10-1.6.1.jar
```

11. In the `pyspark` session, enter the following statements:

```
from pyspark.streaming import StreamingContext
from pyspark.streaming.kafka import KafkaUtils
ssc = StreamingContext(sc, 30)
brokers = "localhost:9092"
topic = "shakespeare"
stream = KafkaUtils.createDirectStream \
(ssc, [topic], {"metadata.broker.list": brokers})
lines = stream.map(lambda x: x[1])
counts = lines.flatMap(lambda line: line.split(" ")) \
             .map(lambda word: (word, 1)) \
             .reduceByKey(lambda a, b: a+b)
counts.pprint()
ssc.start()
ssc.awaitTermination()
```

Note that the `topic` needs to exist before running the code in this step otherwise you will get errors.

12. In terminal 3, create a new `shakespeare` topic:

```
$KAFKA_HOME/bin/kafka-topics.sh \
   --create \
   --zookeeper localhost:2181 \
   --replication-factor 1 \
   --partitions 1 \
   --topic shakespeare
```

13. In terminal 3, pipe the output of your `shakespeare.txt` file into a producer console session:

```
$KAFKA_HOME/bin/kafka-console-producer.sh \
  --broker-list localhost:9092 \
  --topic shakespeare < shakespeare.txt
```

14. You should see the results of our streaming word count reading from the Kafka topic in terminal 2:

```
-------------------------------------------
Time: 2016-04-25 04:41:00
-------------------------------------------
(u'fawn', 12)
(u'mustachio', 1)
(u'Debts', 1)
(u'woods', 10)
(u'spiders', 3)
(u'hanging', 33)
(u'offendeth', 1)
(u'beadsmen', 1)
(u'scold', 8)
...
```

Spark, MQTT, and the Internet of Things

IoT (or the *"Internet of Things"*) is a popular term encompassing the universe of connected devices (such as sensors, monitors, components, RFID tags, smart devices, and more) communicating with each other, control systems, and monitoring systems over the Internet. From concepts such as smart homes and smart cities to asset tracking, air quality monitors, and wearables, the advancements in low power wireless technology, the seemingly infinite IPv6 address space and the ubiquitous Internet have enabled countless IoT device applications and billions of devices.

IoT devices can have unique characteristics, such as requiring authentication, acknowledgement of messages sent and received, and predefined behavior in the event of a disconnection. This requires the establishment of standard protocols to manage the M2M (machine to machine) transport of events and signals. One such protocol is *MQTT (MQ Telemetry Transport)*.

MQTT Overview

MQTT is a lightweight M2M IoT TCP-based communication protocol originally invented by IBM in 1999 and is now an open standard. MQTT is implemented using pub/sub messaging systems involving a broker, not entirely dissimilar to Kafka's implementation. However, MQTT is a protocol as opposed to a platform; MQTT brokers are available in platforms such as HiveMQ, Mosquitto, and the AWS IoT PaaS offering.

MQTT Transport Protocol

MQTT packets are transported between publishers, brokers, and subscribers (see Figure 20.6) using TCP port 1883 and 8883, as designated by the Internet Assigned Numbers Authority (IANA) (www.iana.org). Port 8883 is reserved for encrypted communication over SSL.

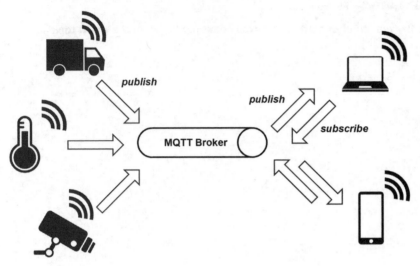

FIGURE 20.6
MQTT pub-sub architecture.

MQTT clients and servers communicate using various control packets, which include connection and disconnection events, subscribe and unsubscribe requests, message publishing and acknowledgements, and more. Because the MQTT protocol is designed for limited bandwidth networks with potentially intermittent connectivity, control packets are kept as succinct as possible. However, the data payload can scale up to 256MB if required. Furthermore, The MQTT protocol defines a quality of service (QoS) for each message. The QoS level determines guarantees around message delivery and the potential to receive duplicate messages.

MQTT defines the behavior in the event of an abnormal or unexpected disconnection of a client from a server. This is done by defining a "last will and testament" (LWT). As with the real-life equivalent the LWT gives the server instructions about what actions to take (notifications, and so on) in the event of a deceased client.

MQTT provides support for authentication using a user name and password with an MQTT packet as well as support for wire encryption using SSL. An additional secret key or private key encryption can be implemented by the developer.

Message Structure

MQTT messages are published to a broker that is typically a TCP endpoint such as `tcp://broker.myhost.com:1883`. Messages are published to a topic (as they are in the Kafka model), topics in an MQTT broker have a hierarchical naming scheme such as the following:

`devices/components/temperature`

Wildcards can be used by subscribers to subscribe to multiple topics, as in, for example, `devices/components/+`. The data itself included in the message (the *payload*) is uninterpreted and as such can represent strings (using any encoding), maps (including JSON), and even binary data.

MQTT Clients

MQTT clients are available for a variety of popular languages such as Java and Python, as well as for low-level languages such as C and C++.

More detailed information about the MQTT protocol, specification, and clients can be found at http://mqtt.org/.

Using Spark with MQTT

MQTT messaging is supported in Spark Streaming using the `MQTTUtils` package (`pyspark.streaming.mqtt.MQTTUtils`). `MQTTUtils` allows a DStream to be created from messages pulled from an MQTT broker. This is accomplished using the `createStream` method, which is described here:

createStream()
Syntax:

```
MQTTUtils.createStream(ssc,
               brokerUrl,
               topic,
               storageLevel=StorageLevel(True, True, False, False, 2))
               )
```

The `createStream` method is used to create a Spark Streaming DStream object from messages from an MQTT broker. The `brokerUrl` argument is the MQTT broker URI (for example, `tcp://iot.eclipse.org:1883`). The topic argument is the hierarchical topic name (for example, `sensors/temperature`). The `storageLevel` argument represents the storage level used by the WAL implemented by the `createStream` method, defaulting to `MEMORY_AND_DISK_SER_2`.

Listing 20.4 demonstrates a simple variation of the word count application to count events by type by reading messages from an MQTT broker.

LISTING 20.4 Spark Streaming Using MQTTUtils

```
from pyspark.streaming import StreamingContext
from pyspark.streaming.mqtt import MQTTUtils
ssc = StreamingContext(sc, 30)
brokerUrl = "tcp://iot.eclipse.org:1883"
topic = "sensors/temperature"
events = MQTTUtils.createStream(ssc, brokerUrl, topic)
counts = events.map(lambda event: (event, 1)) \
             .reduceByKey(lambda a, b: a+b)
counts.pprint()
ssc.start()
ssc.awaitTermination()
```

NOTE

MQTT support will be moved to Spark Packages (https://spark-packages.org/) as of the 2.0 release of Spark: https://issues.apache.org/jira/browse/SPARK-13843

Using Spark with Amazon Kinesis

Amazon Kinesis is Amazon Web Services' fully managed distributed messaging platform inspired by (or at least very similar to) Apache Kafka. Kinesis is AWS's next-generation message queue service, introducing real-time stream processing at scale as an additional messaging alternative to their original Simple Queue Service (SQS) offering.

The AWS Kinesis product family includes Amazon Kinesis Analytics, which enables SQL queries against streaming data, and Amazon Kinesis Firehose, which enables the capability to capture and load streaming data directly into Amazon S3, Amazon Redshift (an AWS cloud-based data warehouse platform), and other AWS services. The Kinesis component I will discuss specifically in this section is *Amazon Kinesis Streams*.

Kinesis Streams

A Kinesis Streams application involves producers and consumers in the same way as other messaging platforms discussed. Producers and consumers can be mobile applications or other systems within AWS or otherwise.

A Kinesis *stream* is an ordered sequence of data records, with each record given a sequence number and assigned to a *shard* (similar to a partition) based upon a *partition key*. Shards are distributed across multiple instances in the AWS environment. Producers put data into shards and consumers get data from shards (see Figure 20.7).

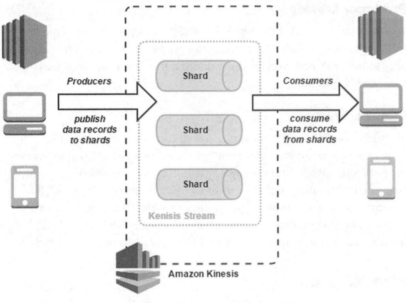

FIGURE 20.7
Amazon Kinesis streams.

Streams can be created using the AWS console, CLI, or the Streams API. Figure 20.8 demonstrates creating a stream using the AWS Management Console.

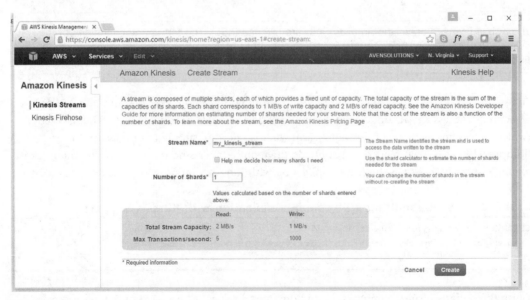

FIGURE 20.8
Creating a Kinesis stream using the AWS Management Console.

Amazon Kinesis Producer Library

The Amazon Kinesis Producer Library (KPL) is the set of API objects and methods used for producers to egest records to a Kinesis stream. The KPL enables producers to put records into Kinesis with the capability to buffer records, receive the result of a put as an asynchronous callback, write to multiple shards, and more.

Amazon Kinesis Client Library

The Amazon Kinesis Client Library (KCL) is the consumer API to connect to a stream and consume data records. The KCL is typically an entry point for record processing (such as event stream processing using Spark Streaming) from a Kinesis stream. The KCL also performs important functions (such as checkpointing processed records) using Amazon's DynamoDB key value store to maintain a durable copy of the Stream applications state—this table is created automatically in the same region as your Streams application using your AWS credentials. The KCL is available in various common languages including Java, Node.js, Ruby, and Python.

Using Spark with Kinesis

Access to Kinesis Streams from a Spark Streaming application is provided via the `KinesisUtils` package (`pyspark.streaming.kinesis.KinesisUtils`) using the `createStream` method. The `createStream` method creates a receiver using the Kinesis Client Library (KCL), returning a DStream object.

> NOTE
>
> The KCL is licensed under the Amazon Software License (ASL). The terms and conditions of the ASL scheme vary somewhat from the Apache, GPL, and other open source licensing frameworks. You can find more information at https://aws.amazon.com/asl/.

To use the `KinesisUtils.createStream` function, you need an AWS account and API access credentials (Access Key ID and Secret Access Key); you will also need to create a Kinesis Stream (which is beyond the scope of this book). You will also need to supply the necessary Kinesis libraries which can be provided by supplying the required jar using the `--jars` argument. An example showing how to submit an application with Kinesis support is provided in Listing 20.5.

LISTING 20.5   Submitting a Streaming Application with Kinesis Support

```
$SPARK_HOME/bin/spark-submit \
--jars /usr/lib/spark/extras/lib/spark-streaming-kinesis-asl.jar
...
```

Given these prerequisites, a description and an example (see Listing 20.5) of the `KinesisUtils.createStream` is provided here.

`createStream()`

Syntax:

```
KinesisUtils.createStream(ssc,
                kinesisAppName,
                streamName,
                endpointUrl,
                regionName,
                initialPositionInStream,
                checkpointInterval,
                storageLevel=StorageLevel(True, True, False, True, 2),
                awsAccessKeyId=None,
                awsSecretKey=None,
                decoder=utf8_decoder)
```

The `createStream` method creates an input stream that pulls messages from a Kinesis stream using the Kinesis Client Library (KCL) and returns a DStream object. The `ssc` argument is an instantiated Spark Streaming Context. The `kinesisAppName` argument is a unique name used by the Kinesis Client Library (KCL) to update state in the DynamoDB backing table. The `streamName` is the Kinesis stream name assigned when the stream was created. The `endpointUrl` and `regionName` arguments are references to the AWS Kinesis service and region (for example, **https://kinesis.us-east-1.amazonaws.com** and us-east-1 respectively). The `initialPositionInStream` is the initial starting position for messages in the stream; if checkpointing information is available, this is not used. The `checkpointInterval` is the interval for Kinesis checkpointing. The `storageLevel` argument is the RDD Storage level to use for storing received objects (defaulting to `StorageLevel.MEMORY_AND_DISK_2`). The `awsAccessKeyId` and `awsSecretKey` arguments are your AWS API credentials. The `decoder` is the function used to decode message byte arrays (defaulting to `utf8_decoder`).

LISTING 20.6   Spark Streaming Using Amazon Kinesis

```
from pyspark.streaming import StreamingContext
from pyspark.streaming.kinesis import KinesisUtils
from pyspark.streaming.kinesis import InitialPositionInStream

ssc = StreamingContext(sc, 30)
appName = "KinesisCountApplication"
streamName = "WordStream"
endpointUrl = "https://kinesis.us-east-1.amazonaws.com"
regionName = "us-east-1"
awsAccessKeyId = "AKIAIUZXXXXXXXXN"
awsSecretKey = "5BKpURtLXhHfqhobtUXXXXXXXX"
```

```
# connect to Kinesis Stream
lines = KinesisUtils.createStream(
        ssc, appName, streamName, endpointUrl, regionName,
        InitialPositionInStream.LATEST, 2,
        StorageLevel.MEMORY_AND_DISK_2,
        awsAccessKeyId, awsSecretKey)
counts = lines.flatMap(lambda line: line.split(" ")) \
            .map(lambda word: (word, 1)) \
            .reduceByKey(lambda a, b: a+b)
counts.pprint()
ssc.start()
ssc.awaitTermination()
```

Much more information about Kinesis is available at https://aws.amazon.com/kinesis/.

Summary

In this hour, you learned about messaging systems. Although middleware platforms have existed for decades, the emergence of open source software (OSS), ubiquitous mobile computing, and the Internet of Things (IoT) has resulted in a rapid resurgence and expansion of these systems.

Messaging systems (also known as message queues or message brokers) enable disparate systems to exchange messages (control messages or event messages) in an asynchronous yet reliable manner. Messaging systems such as Apache Kafka and Amazon Kinesis have become integral components of the big data open source and cloud computing landscape, whereas lightweight message transport protocols such as MQTT have become central to IoT and device messaging.

In this hour, I have provided you with a high level overview of Kafka, Kinesis, and MQTT and their integration with Spark Streaming. Spark provides out of the box support for Kafka, Kinesis, MQTT brokers, and other messaging platforms. Using the messaging platform consumer libraries and utilities provided with the Spark Streaming sub project, Spark Streaming applications can connect to message brokers and consume messages into DStream objects. Messaging systems are common data sources in complex event-processing pipelines powered by Spark applications. As the universe of connected devices continues to expand and M2M (machine-to-machine) data exchange proliferates, Spark Streaming and Messaging will become even more important.

Q&A

Q. What are the types of filtering performed in pub-sub messaging systems?

A. Topic filtering, in which publishers define topics and subscribers subscribe to topics and receive messages only for those particular topics. Content filtering, in which subscribers define content filter criteria that determine which messages they receive.

Q. What is the difference between the "receiver" and "direct" approaches to consuming messages from a Kafka topic in a Spark Streaming application?

A. The receiver approach creates a long-running process within a Spark executor that receives messages from Kafka for a defined topic and maintains offsets received using a combination of a write ahead log (WAL) and a Zookeeper quorum. In contrast, in the direct approach the Spark driver calculates offsets and instructs executors to consume messages directly from their partitions on Kafka brokers. Both approaches guarantee delivery and the ability to guarantee "once-only processing." The latter approach does not incur the overhead of write ahead logging.

Q. What key characteristics are incorporated into the MQTT protocol to benefit IoT applications?

A. The MQTT defines lightweight control packets to handle connection and disconnection events, subscribe and unsubscribe requests, message publishing and acknowledgements, and more. The MQTT protocol also defines a quality of service (QoS) for each message, providing various levels of delivery guarantee for a range of different devices and applications. MQTT defines the behavior in the event of an abnormal or unexpected disconnection of a client from a server. This is done by defining a "last will and testament" (LWT), giving the server instructions on what actions to take (notifications, and so on) in the event of a disconnected client. MQTT also provides support for authentication using a user name and password as well as support for wire encryption using SSL.

Workshop

The workshop contains quiz questions and exercises to help you solidify your understanding of the material covered. Try to answer all questions before looking at the "Answers" section that follows.

Quiz

1. What are publishers and subscribers referred to in Apache Kafka?

2. Which `KafkaUtils` method is used to consume messages using a *receiver*?

    A. `createDirectStream`

    B. `createStream`

    C. `createReceiver`

    D. `createRDD`

3. Which TCP ports are reserved with the IANA for the MQTT transport protocol?

4. True or false: The `KinesisUtils.createStream` method creates a receiver using the Kinesis Client Library (KCL), returning a DStream object.

Answers

1. Producers and consumers.

2. B.

3. 1883 and 8883.

4. **True.**

HOUR 21
Administering Spark

What You'll Learn in This Hour:

▶ Spark configuration, defaults, and precedence
▶ Administering a Spark standalone cluster
▶ Administration considerations for running Spark on YARN
▶ Spark application and job scheduling

Throughout most of this book I have focused predominantly on application development, data processing, and analytics using Spark. In this hour, I will cover some basic concepts and practices involved with administering Spark clusters or Spark applications running on YARN clusters.

Spark Configuration

Recall from our previous chapters that there are several different Spark cluster deployment methods (or cluster managers) available. These include the following:

▶ Standalone
▶ YARN
▶ Mesos

I will discuss standalone and YARN specifically for the purposes of this chapter. In **Hour 3, "Installing Spark,"** I discussed deploying Spark in Standalone mode, which involved starting Spark masters and Spark slaves.

In **Hour 2, "Understanding Hadoop,"** I discussed Hadoop (HDFS and YARN) clusters, which can be used to deploy Spark processing clusters. Installing and configuring Hadoop is typically the job of a Hadoop administrator.

Using either the standalone or YARN cluster manager deployment options, there are several environment variables and configuration settings you should be familiar with as they will affect the behavior, capacity, and performance of Spark.

Spark Environment Variables

Spark environment variables are set by the `spark-env.sh` script located in the `$SPARK_HOME/conf` directory. The variables are used to set Spark daemon behavior and configuration and to set environment-level application configuration settings (such as which Spark master an application should use). The `spark-env.sh` script is read by

- Spark standalone master and worker daemons upon startup.

- Spark applications using `spark-submit`.

An excerpt of a typical `spark-env.sh` file is shown in Listing 21.1. You can set environment variables in a similar fashion in your shell environment if you are using `pyspark` or `spark-shell`.

LISTING 21.1   Spark Environment Variables Set in the spark-env.sh FIle

```
export SPARK_HOME=${SPARK_HOME:-/usr/lib/spark}
export SPARK_LOG_DIR=${SPARK_LOG_DIR:-/var/log/spark}
export HADOOP_HOME=${HADOOP_HOME:-/usr/lib/hadoop}
export HADOOP_CONF_DIR=${HADOOP_CONF_DIR:-/etc/hadoop/conf}
export HIVE_CONF_DIR=${HIVE_CONF_DIR:-/etc/hive/conf}

export STANDALONE_SPARK_MASTER_HOST=sparkmaster.local
export SPARK_MASTER_PORT=7077
export SPARK_MASTER_IP=$STANDALONE_SPARK_MASTER_HOST
export SPARK_MASTER_WEBUI_PORT=8080

export SPARK_WORKER_DIR=${SPARK_WORKER_DIR:-/var/run/spark/work}
export SPARK_WORKER_PORT=7078
export SPARK_WORKER_WEBUI_PORT=8081

export SPARK_DAEMON_JAVA_OPTS="-XX:OnOutOfMemoryError='kill -9 %p'"
```

Take a look at some of the most common Spark environment variables and their use.

Cluster Manager Independent Variables

These environment variables include the following:

- `SPARK_HOME`—Root of the Spark installation directory (such as, for example, `/opt/spark` or `/usr/lib/spark`, and so on.).

TIP

Always Set the SPARK_HOME Variable

Make sure you set this variable, especially if you have multiple versions of Spark installed on the system. Failing to set this variable is a common cause of issues when running Spark applications.

▶ `JAVA_HOME`—Location where Java is installed.

▶ `PYSPARK_PYTHON`—Python binary executable to use for PySpark in both driver and workers. If this is not specified, the default Python installation will be used (resolved by `which python`). This should definitely be set if you have more than one version of Python on any driver or worker instances.

▶ `PYSPARK_DRIVER_PYTHON`—Python binary executable to use for PySpark in driver only (defaults to the value defined for `PYSPARK_PYTHON`).

▶ `SPARKR_DRIVER_R`—R binary executable to use for SparkR shell (default is `R`).

Hadoop-Related Environment Variables

These variables are required for Spark applications requiring access to HDFS (from any deployment mode), YARN (if running in yarn-client or yarn-cluster mode), and objects in HCatalog or Hive.

▶ `HADOOP_CONF_DIR`, `YARN_CONF_DIR`—Location of the Hadoop configuration files (typically `/etc/hadoop/conf`). This is used by Spark to locate the default filesystem (usually the URI of the HDFS NameNode) and the address of the YARN ResourceManager. Either environment variable can be set, but typically, setting `HADOOP_CONF_DIR` is preferred.

▶ `HADOOP_HOME`—Location where Hadoop is installed. This is used by Spark to locate the Hadoop configuration files.

▶ `HIVE_CONF_DIR`—Location of the Hive configuration files. This is used by Spark to locate the Hive metastore and other Hive properties when instantiating a HiveContext object.

There are also environment variables specific to HiveServer2, such as `HIVE_SERVER2_THRIFT_BIND_HOST` and `HIVE_SERVER2_THRIFT_PORT`. Typically, just setting `HADOOP_CONF_DIR` is sufficient because Spark can infer the other properties relative to this.

Spark Standalone Daemon Environment Variables

These environment variables are read by daemons (masters and workers) in a Spark standalone cluster.

▶ `SPARK_MASTER_IP`—Hostname or IP address of the host running the Spark master process. This should be set on all nodes of the Spark cluster and on any client hosts that will be submitting applications.

▶ `SPARK_MASTER_PORT`/`SPARK_MASTER_WEBUI_PORT`—Ports used for IPC communication and the master web UI respectively. If these are not specified, the defaults of 7077 and 8080 are used.

▶ SPARK_MASTER_OPTS/SPARK_WORKER_OPTS—Additional Java opts supplied to the JVM hosting the Spark master or Spark worker processes. If this is used, the value should be in the standard form -Dx=y. Alternatively, you can set the SPARK_DAEMON_JAVA_OPTS environment variable, which will apply to all Spark daemons running on the system.

▶ SPARK_DAEMON_MEMORY—Amount of memory to allocate to the master, worker and HistoryServer processes (defaults to 1 GB).

▶ SPARK_WORKER_INSTANCES—Sets the number of worker processes per slave node (defaults to 1).

▶ SPARK_WORKER_CORES—Sets the number of CPU cores for the Spark worker process to be used by executors on the system.

▶ SPARK_WORKER_MEMORY—Sets how much total memory workers have to grant to executors.

▶ SPARK_WORKER_PORT/SPARK_WORKER_WEBUI_PORT—Ports used for IPC communication and the worker web UI respectively. If these are not specified, the defaults of 8081 for the web UI and a random port for the worker port are used.

▶ SPARK_WORKER_DIR—Sets the working directory for worker processes.

Spark on YARN Environment Variables

These environment variables are specific to Spark applications running on a YARN cluster (either in cluster or client deployment mode).

▶ SPARK_EXECUTOR_INSTANCES—Specifies the number of executor processes to start in the YARN cluster (defaults to 2).

▶ SPARK_EXECUTOR_CORES—Number of CPU cores allocated to each executor (defaults to 1).

▶ SPARK_EXECUTOR_MEMORY—Memory allocated to each executor (defaults to 1 GB).

▶ SPARK_DRIVER_MEMORY—Amount of memory allocated to Driver processes when running in cluster deploy mode (defaults to 1 GB).

▶ SPARK_YARN_APP_NAME—The name of your application. This displays in the YARN ResourceManager UI (defaults to Spark).

▶ SPARK_YARN_QUEUE—The named YARN queue to which applications are submitted by default (defaults to default). Can also be set by a spark-submit argument. This determines allocation of resources and scheduling priority. (I will discuss scheduling later in this chapter.)

▶ SPARK_YARN_DIST_FILES/SPARK_YARN_DIST_ARCHIVES—Comma-separated list of files of archives to be distributed with the job. These files can then be referenced by executors at runtime.

NOTE

As previously mentioned, the `HADOOP_CONF_DIR` environment variable must be set when deploying a Spark application on YARN.

Cluster Application Deployment Environment Variables

These variables are used for applications submitted in cluster mode, that is, applications using the standalone or YARN cluster managers submitted with the `--deploy-mode cluster` option to `spark-submit`. In the case of YARN, this property can be combined with the `master` argument as `--master yarn-cluster`. These variables are read by executors and drivers running on worker nodes of the cluster (Spark workers or YARN NodeManagers).

Options read by executors and drivers running inside the cluster include the following:

▶ `SPARK_LOCAL_IP`—Sets the IP address of the machine to bind Spark processes to.

▶ `SPARK_PUBLIC_DNS`—The hostname the Spark driver uses to advertise to other hosts.

▶ `SPARK_CLASSPATH`—Sets the default classpath for Spark. This is important if you are importing additional classes not packaged with Spark that you will refer to at runtime.

▶ `SPARK_LOCAL_DIRS`—Configures the directories to use on the system for RDD storage and shuffled data.

When running an interactive Spark session (`pyspark` or `spark-shell`), `spark-env.sh` is not read and the environment variables in the current users environment (if set) are used.

Many Spark environment variables have an equivalent configuration property that can be set in a number of additional ways, which I will discuss next.

Spark Configuration

Spark configuration parameters are typically set on a node (such as a master or worker node) or an application (by the driver host submitting the application). They often have a more restricted scope (such as for the life of an application) than their equivalent environment variables, and take higher precedence than these.

There are numerous Spark configuration properties related to many different operational aspects; I will cover some of the most common properties now.

▶ `spark.master`—Address of the Spark master (such as, for example, `spark://master:7077` for a standalone cluster). If the value is `yarn`, then the Hadoop configuration files will be read to locate the YARN ResourceManager (there is no default value for this property).

▶ `spark.driver.memory`—Configures the amount of memory allocated to the driver (defaults to 1 GB).

▶ `spark.executor.memory`—Configures the amount of memory to use per executor process (defaults to 1 GB).

▶ `spark.executor.cores`—Configures the number of cores to use on each executor. In standalone mode, this property defaults to using all available cores on the worker node. Setting this property to a value less than the available number of cores enables multiple concurrent executor processes to be spawned. In YARN mode, this property defaults to 1 (core per executor).

▶ `spark.driver.extraJavaOptions`, `spark.executor.extraJavaOptions`—Additional Java opts supplied to the JVM hosting the Spark driver or executor processes. If this is used, the value should be in the standard form, `-Dx=y`.

▶ `spark.driver.extraClassPath`, `spark.executor.extraClassPath`—Additional classpath entries for the driver and executor processes if you require additional classes to be imported that are not packaged with Spark.

▶ `spark.dynamicAllocation.enabled`, `spark.shuffle.service.enabled`—Used together to modify the default scheduling behavior in Spark. (I will come back to these shortly when I discuss dynamic allocation.)

Setting Spark Configuration Properties

Spark configuration properties can be set through the `$SPARK_HOME/conf/spark-defaults.conf` file, which is read by Spark applications and daemons upon startup. An excerpt from a typical `spark-defaults.conf` file is shown in Listing 21.2.

LISTING 21.2 Spark Configuration Properties in the spark-defaults.conf File

```
spark.master                    yarn
spark.eventLog.enabled          true
spark.eventLog.dir              hdfs:///var/log/spark/apps
spark.history.fs.logDirectory   hdfs:///var/log/spark/apps
spark.executor.memory           2176M
spark.executor.cores            4
```

Spark configuration properties can also be set programmatically in your driver code using the `SparkConf` object; an example of this is shown in Listing 21.3.

LISTING 21.3 Setting Spark Configuration Properties Programmatically

```
from pyspark.context import SparkContext
from pyspark.conf import SparkConf
conf = SparkConf()
conf.set("spark.executor.memory","3g")
sc = SparkContext(conf=conf)
```

There are also several `SparkConf` methods to set specific common properties. These methods are shown in Listing 21.4.

LISTING 21.4   Spark Configuration Object Methods

```
from pyspark.context import SparkContext
from pyspark.conf import SparkConf
conf = SparkConf()
conf.setAppName("MySparkApp")
conf.setMaster("yarn")
conf.setSparkHome("/usr/lib/spark")
```

In most cases, setting Spark configuration properties using arguments to `spark-submit`, `pyspark`, and `spark-submit` is recommended, as setting configuration properties programmatically requires code changes or rebuilding (in the case of Scala or Java applications).

NOTE

Prior to Spark version 1.0, this was the only way to set Spark configuration properties, so you can still find numerous examples of this on the Internet.

Setting configuration properties as arguments to `spark-submit`, `pyspark`, and `spark-submit` can be done using specific named arguments (for common properties such as `--executor-memory`). Properties not exposed as named arguments can be provided using `--conf PROP=VALUE` (to set an arbitrary Spark configuration property) or `--properties-file FILE` (to load additional arguments from a configuration file). Examples of both methods are shown in Listing 21.5.

LISTING 21.5   Passing Spark Configuration Properties to spark-submit

```
# setting config properties using arguments
$SPARK_HOME/bin/spark-submit --executor-memory 1g \
--conf spark.dynamicAllocation.enabled=true \
myapp.py

# setting config properties using a conf file
$SPARK_HOME/bin/spark-submit \
--properties-file test.conf \
myapp.py
```

You can use the `SparkConf.toDebugString()` method to print out the current configuration for a Spark application, as demonstrated in Listing 21.6.

LISTING 21.6 Showing the Current Spark Configuration

```
from pyspark.context import SparkContext
from pyspark.conf import SparkConf
conf = SparkConf()
print(conf.toDebugString())
. . .
spark.app.name=PySparkShell
spark.master=yarn-client
spark.submit.deployMode=client
spark.yarn.isPython=true
. . .
```

As you can see, there are several ways to pass the same configuration parameter, including as an environment variable, as a spark default configuration property, or as a command line argument. Table 21.1 shows some of the various ways to set the same property in Spark.

TABLE 21.1 Configuration Options

Argument	Configuration Property	Environment Variable
--master	spark.master	SPARK_MASTER_IP/
		SPARK_MASTER_PORT
--name	spark.app.name	SPARK_YARN_APP_NAME
--executor-memory	spark.executor.memory	SPARK_EXECUTOR_MEMORY
--executor-cores	spark.executor.cores	SPARK_EXECUTOR_CORES
--queue	spark.yarn.queue	SPARK_YARN_QUEUE

These are just a few. Many other properties have analogous settings.

TIP

Defaults for Environment Variables and Configuration Properties

You may notice, by looking at the conf directory of a fresh Spark deployment, that by default the spark-defaults.conf and spark-env.sh files are not implemented. Instead, templates are provided (spark-defaults.conf.template and spark-env.sh.template). You are encouraged to copy these templates and rename them without the .template extension and make the appropriate modifications for your environment.

Configuration Precedence

Configuration properties set directly within an application using a SparkConf object take the highest precedence, followed by arguments passed to spark-submit, pyspark, or spark-shell, followed by options set in the spark-defaults.conf file. Many configuration properties have system default values that are used in the absence of properties explicitly set otherwise through the other means discussed. Figure 21.1 depicts the order of precedence for Spark configuration properties.

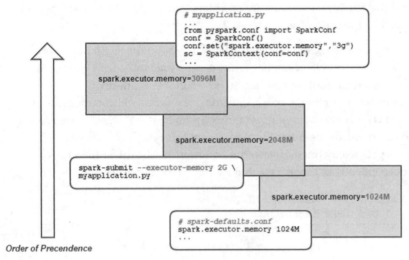

Order of Precendence

FIGURE 21.1
Spark configuration precedence.

Configuration Management

Managing configuration is one of the biggest challenges involved in administering a Spark cluster (or any cluster for that matter). Often, configuration settings need to be consistent across different hosts (for example, different worker nodes in a Spark cluster). Configuration management and deployment tools such as Puppet and Chef can be useful for managing Spark deployments and their configurations. If you are deploying and managing Spark as a part of a Hadoop deployment using a commercial Hadoop distribution, Spark configuration can be managed using the Hadoop vendor's management interface (such as, for instance, Cloudera Manager for Cloudera installations or Ambari for Hortonworks installations).

Administering Spark Standalone

Deploying Spark using the standalone cluster manager is often the easiest method to get a Spark environment up and running (because there are no requirements on an external cluster manager such as YARN or Mesos). Spark releases include all of the necessary libraries, binaries, and scripts to deploy a Spark standalone cluster in a local environment or an AWS EC2 environment using the ec2 scripts discussed in **Hour 5, "Deploying Spark in the Cloud."**

Let's quickly revisit the Spark standalone cluster manager because it has been a while since I introduced this subject.

Spark Standalone Revisited

Spark standalone clusters consist of masters and slaves. The Spark master is responsible for negotiating and allocating resources to run on Spark slaves (instances running one or more Spark worker processes). The resources allocated are executors that are capable of running tasks at the request of a Spark driver program (see Figure 21.2).

Spark applications running on a Spark standalone cluster can be submitted with one of two deploy modes: `client` or `cluster`. When applications are submitted in `client` mode, the driver runs on the client. This requires the client host to have suitable connectivity to the cluster (specifically to executors running on workers), because the driver will communicate bidirectionally with the executors allocated to its program. By contrast, `cluster` mode is often referred to as "fire and forget" mode, because the driver (recall this is the program running the `SparkContext`) is dispatched by the master to run on a worker. The driver then runs asynchronously and independently of the process that submitted the application.

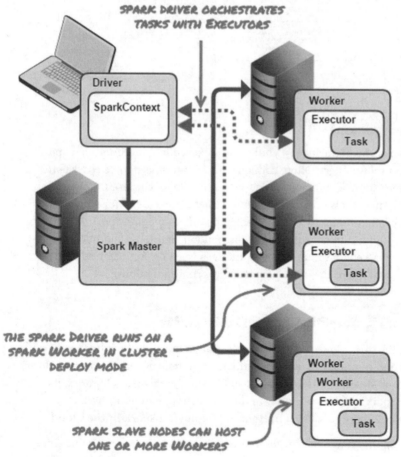

FIGURE 21.2
Spark standalone cluster.

Deploying Spark Standalone Clusters

As I had covered in **Hour 3**, deploying a Spark standalone cluster involves starting a Spark master, or two Spark masters in a HA (high availability) configuration, and one of more Spark slave instances.

Spark master instances are started using the `$SPARK_HOME/sbin/start-master.sh` script, which creates an instance of the `org.apache.spark.deploy.master.Master` class. Spark slaves are started using the `$SPARK_HOME/sbin/start-slave.sh` script, which creates one or more instances of the `org.apache.spark.deploy.worker.Worker` class (by default, one instance will be created but a single slave node can host multiple worker instances).

There is also a `$SPARK_HOME/sbin/start-all.sh` script which starts the master and all workers.

Resource Allocation for Spark Standalone Applications

Executors are allotted compute and memory resources when they are instantiated. The amount of memory assigned to an executor is configurable using the `spark.executor.memory` configuration property discussed previously. If this is not set, the default value of 1GB is used.

By default, Spark allocates one executor per worker. This executor uses all available cores on the worker. If the `spark.executor.cores` configuration value is set, Spark will determine how many executors to allocate based upon the number of cores on a worker divided by the `spark.executor.cores` value.

Exploring the Spark Master and Spark Slave UIs

After you have deployed a Spark standalone cluster, you can use the Spark master and worker UIs to view the status of components of the cluster and manage applications running on the cluster. The Spark master UI is served on port 8080 of the master node instance, as shown in Figure 21.3.

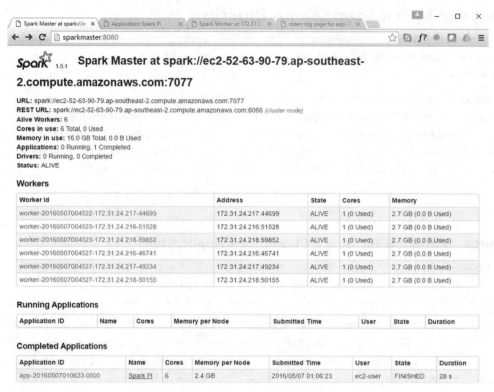

FIGURE 21.3
Spark master UI.

You can see the worker nodes in a standalone cluster from the master UI and click through the links to redirect to the respective spark worker UI. The Spark worker UI is served on port 8081 (by default) on each worker node instance, as shown in Figure 21.4.

FIGURE 21.4
Spark worker UI.

From the worker UI, you can see high-level information about the worker (including the memory and CPU cores allocated to the worker). You can also view the status of executors running on the worker. The `stdout` and `stderr` links can be used to view the output and errors from the executor process, as shown in Figure 21.5.

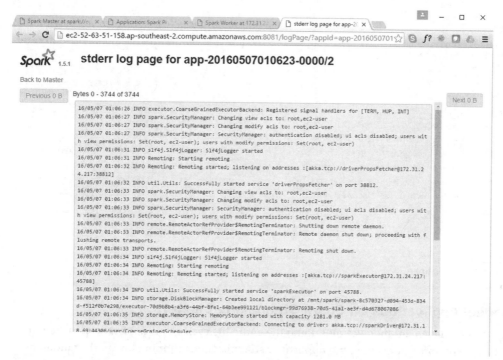

FIGURE 21.5
Spark executor logs.

Clicking the Application ID link from the Running Applications section of the master UI takes you to an application summary including a list of all of the executors allocated to the application and direct links to the workers hosting the executors and executor logs (see Figure 21.6).

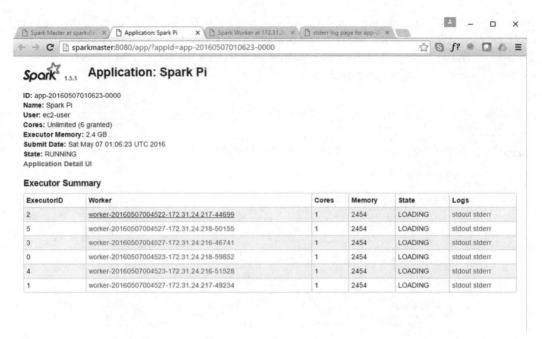

FIGURE 21.6
Spark application summary.

Managing Applications on Spark Standalone Clusters

Application management involves managing the entire life cycle of an application, including submitting, monitoring, and stopping applications. Applications running on Spark standalone clusters can be viewed and managed in several ways.

One approach to managing applications running on a Spark standalone cluster is to use the Spark master web UI discussed previously. You can not only view the status and get executor logs from running applications, as you have seen, but you can also stop running applications by using the Kill link associated with a running application, as shown in Figure 21.7.

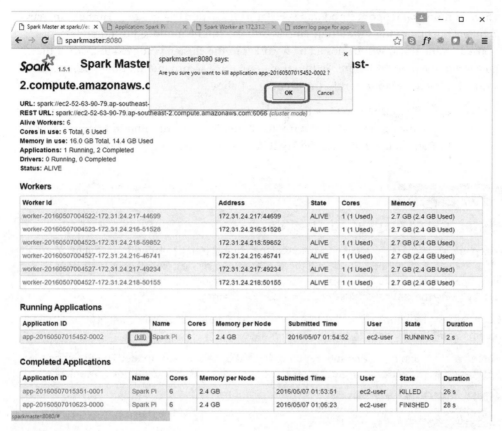

FIGURE 21.7
The Kill link.

The information in the master web UI is available programmatically using the REST API exposed by the master process. An example of obtaining a list of applications is shown in Listing 21.7.

LISTING 21.7   Viewing Applications Using the REST API

```
$ curl sparkmaster:8080/api/v1/applications
[ {
"id" : "app-20160507015452-0002",
"name" : "Spark Pi",
"attempts" : [ {
"startTime" : "2016-05-07T01:54:52.694GMT",
"endTime" : "2016-05-07T01:55:20.542GMT",
"sparkUser" : "ec2-user",
"completed" : true
} ]
}, ...
]
```

Applications running on a Spark standalone cluster using `--deploy-mode cluster` (thereby running independently of the submitting process or host) can be managed using `spark-submit`. Because the driver will be hosted by a worker in the cluster, you need to instruct the driver how to handle a driver failure. Setting the `--supervise` argument of the `spark-submit` script configures the driver to restart in the event of a failure.

You can also use `spark-submit` to view the status of a running Spark application in `cluster` deploy mode and use the `spark-submit` script to kill applications running in `cluster` mode using the `--kill` flag. You will do this the Try It Yourself exercise.

▼ TRY IT YOURSELF

Submitting and Managing Applications in Cluster Deployment Mode

In this exercise, you will use a multi-node standalone cluster (refer to **Hour 3, "Installing Spark"** regarding installing a multi-node Spark cluster in standalone mode). Recall also from **Hour 5, "Deploying Spark in the Cloud,"** that you can deploy a standalone cluster in AWS using EC2 instances by using the `$SPARK_HOME/ec2/spark-ec2` script.

1. Open an SSH terminal connected to a node in the Spark standalone cluster (it is generally recommended to connect to the master instance).

2. Submit a long running Spark application in `cluster` deployment mode. The Pi estimator application (`org.apache.spark.examples.SparkPi`) can be used for convenience.

```
$SPARK_HOME/bin/spark-submit \
--master spark://<sparkmaster>:6066 \
--deploy-mode cluster \
--class org.apache.spark.examples.SparkPi \
$SPARK_HOME/lib/spark-examples-*.jar 1000
```

Notice that that the Spark Master REST URL using port 6066 is used for `cluster` mode submission and management. You should see a response similar to that shown in the following. Note the `submissionId` returned.

```
{
"action" : "CreateSubmissionResponse",
"message" : "Driver successfully submitted as ...",
"serverSparkVersion" : "1.5.1",
"submissionId" : "driver-20160507024853-0003",
"success" : true
}
```

3. Use the `spark-submit --status` argument with the `submissionId` returned from Step 2 to view the status of the running application.

```
$SPARK_HOME/bin/spark-submit \
--master spark://<sparkmaster>:6066 \
--status driver-20160507024853-0003
```

You should see a response similar to the following:

```
{
"action" : "SubmissionStatusResponse",
"driverState" : "RUNNING",
"serverSparkVersion" : "1.5.1",
"submissionId" : "driver-20160507024853-0003",
"success" : true,
"workerHostPort" : "172.31.24.218:59852",
"workerId" : "worker-20160507004523-172.31.24.218-59852"
}
```

Note that you can see the worker that the driver is running on.

4. Open the master web UI. You can see the applications running in `cluster` deployment mode in the Running Drivers section. You will also see the Submission ID (`driver-...`) in the UI.

5. Use the `spark-submit --kill` argument to stop the running application.

```
$SPARK_HOME/bin/spark-submit \
--master spark://<sparkmaster>:6066 \
--kill driver-20160507024853-0003
```

You should see a response similar to the following:

```
{
"action" : "KillSubmissionResponse",
"message" : "Kill request for driver-... submitted",
"serverSparkVersion" : "1.5.1",
"submissionId" : "driver-20160507024853-0003",
"success" : true
}
```

6. Note the application in the master web UI, and note the application in the Completed Drivers section. The application should show the state "KILLED."

Scheduling with Spark Standalone

There are two levels of scheduling involved with Spark applications, applicable to all cluster managers:

▶ Scheduling and prioritization between different applications

▶ Scheduling within a single application

Scheduling Multiple Concurrent Spark Applications

Scheduling between applications is governed by the cluster manager, which determines which applications get access to what proportion of resources within a finite pool of memory and CPU resources in the cluster. In standalone mode, concurrent applications are scheduled on a "first in first out" (FIFO) basis, with each application consuming all available resources and holding these resources for the life of the application.

This inter-application scheduling behavior can be influenced by limiting the resources available to an application using the `spark.cores.max` and `spark.executor.memory` configuration properties. Configuring these properties allows other applications to use available resources and run concurrently. This configuration needs to be done by the client submitting the application within the driver code or in the `spark-defaults.conf` file.

Scheduling Multiple Jobs within a Spark Application

Scheduling within a single application is required when an application includes more than one action (called a *job*). By default, Spark schedules multiple jobs within an application in FIFO order. An alternative to the default FIFO scheduler is the FairScheduler, which is designed to ensure the cluster is utilized as efficiently as possible and to share resources proportionally across different jobs.

Using the FairScheduler, each action can be run independently as its own DAG, and if sufficient resources are available to the application, the actions can be run concurrently because they may have no direct dependency upon one another.

Using the FairScheduler determines the share of resources across pools (which are defined in the application and in the driver's configuration). Pools in the FairScheduler are assigned an equal share of resources allocated to the application. Pools are assigned a `weight` that determines the share of resources allocated. For instance, a `weight` of 2 gets the equivalent share of two applications. Pools can also be configured with a `minShare`, which specifies that the application must be allocated a predefined share of resources assigned to the application. This setting is used for high SLA operations that must take precedence over lower priority jobs within the same application.

The scheduler configuration is located in an XML file. A template for this file can be found at `$SPARK_HOME/conf/fairscheduler.xml.template`; the contents of this file are shown in Listing 21.8.

LISTING 21.8   Example Scheduler XML File

```
<?xml version="1.0"?>
<allocations>
  <pool name="production">
    <schedulingMode>FAIR</schedulingMode>
    <weight>1</weight>
    <minShare>2</minShare>
  </pool>
  <pool name="test">
    <schedulingMode>FIFO</schedulingMode>
```

```
    <weight>2</weight>
    <minShare>3</minShare>
  </pool>
</allocations>
```

As seen from Listing 21.8, pools can use the FIFO scheduler (as they would by default) or the FAIR scheduler.

The scheduler configuration is referenced by the `spark.scheduler.allocation.file` property set in your `SparkConf` object within your driver code. An example of setting this property is shown in Listing 21.9.

LISTING 21.9   Setting the spark.scheduler.allocation.file Property

```
from pyspark.context import SparkContext
from pyspark.conf import SparkConf
conf = SparkConf()
conf.set("spark.scheduler.allocation.file", \
  "/opt/spark/conf/scheduler.xml")
sc = SparkContext(conf=conf)
```

Applications must specify the pool their jobs should run in using the `spark.scheduler.pool` local property of the `SparkContext`. This is demonstrated in Listing 21.10.

LISTING 21.10   Configuring the Pool for a Spark Application

```
sc.setLocalProperty("spark.scheduler.pool", "production")
```

Jobs within your application will now be scheduled according to the policy assigned to the "production" pool, in this case.

Administering Spark on YARN

YARN is a popular cluster manager for scheduling Spark and is often available when Spark co-resides with Hadoop for the purposes of using HDFS. Administering YARN is typically the job of the Hadoop administrator, but there are some general administrative considerations you should be aware of as a Spark developer or engineer using Spark on YARN.

Spark on YARN Revisited

YARN clusters consist of master nodes (running the ResourceManager process) and slave nodes (running the NodeManager process). The ResourceManager performs a function similar to the Spark master in standalone mode. However, the ResourceManager allocates YARN containers for applications. One of the containers is called the ApplicationsMaster. In `cluster` application deployment mode, the ApplicationsMaster hosts the Spark driver process.

The ApplicationsMaster requests YARN containers on NodeManagers in the cluster to host Spark executor processes. These executors then communicate and coordinate with the Spark driver for the application. Figure 21.8 recaps a Spark on YARN deployment.

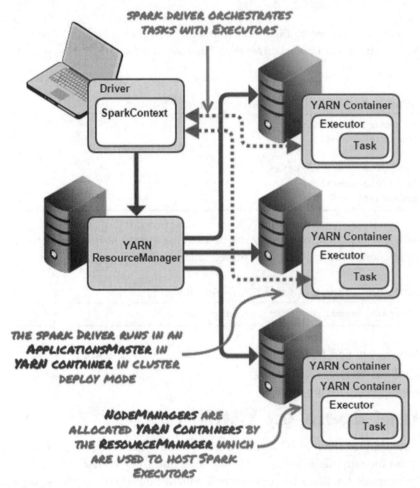

FIGURE 21.8
Spark on YARN.

Deploying Spark on YARN

Deploying Spark on a YARN cluster is very straightforward. You simply need to set the `HADOOP_CONF_DIR` or `YARN_CONF_DIR` environment variable (so Spark can locate the YARN ResourceManager), submit your application using `spark-submit`, or run an interactive shell such as `pyspark` with the `--master yarn` argument.

You also should specify the `--deploy-mode` argument to either `client` or `cluster` for non-interactive applications submitted using `spark-submit` or just specify `client` for interactive applications.

NOTE

You need to ensure the release of Spark you are using was compiled with support for Hadoop. The releases built for Hadoop can be easily identified by the hadoop name (such as `spark-1.6.1-bin-hadoop2.6.tgz`).

A recap of submitting an application to a YARN cluster is shown in Listing 21.11. Several additional arguments are specific to YARN applications submission, including the following:

▶ `--driver-cores`

The number of CPU cores allocated to the driver process (running in the ApplicationsMaster process on a NodeManager).

▶ `--num-executors`

The number of executors required for the application (each executor is allocated to a YARN container).

▶ `--queue`

The YARN queue; these will be defined by the YARN scheduler (typically the CapacityScheduler or the FairScheduler in YARN) as configured by the Hadoop administrator.

LISTING 21.11   Submitting a Spark Application to a YARN Cluster

```
$SPARK_HOME/bin/spark-submit \
--master yarn \
--deploy-mode cluster \
--driver-cores 2 \
--num-executors 4 \
--queue batch_queue \
--class org.apache.spark.examples.SparkPi \
$SPARK_HOME/lib/spark-examples-*.jar 1000
```

Managing Spark Applications Running on YARN

The ResourceManager UI is often your best staring point when managing Spark applications running on YARN. The ResourceManager UI is exposed on port 8080 of the YARN resource manager instance.

The UI can be used to view the status of a running, failed, or completed Spark job; to view YARN container logs for a job; or to redirect to the Spark application UI. You can use the ApplicationsMaster link to access the Spark application UI (served on port 4040 by default of the instance running the ApplicationsMaster process for the Spark application) as shown in Figures 21.9 and 21.10.

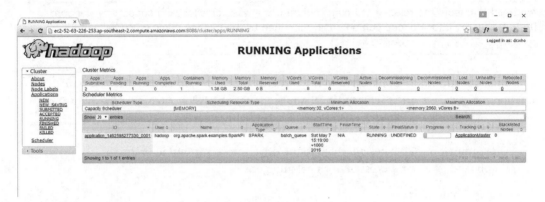

FIGURE 21.9
YARN ResourceManager UI.

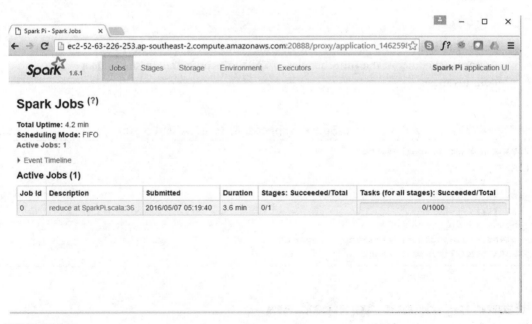

FIGURE 21.10
Spark application UI through the YARN ApplicationsMaster.

YARN provides a CLI utility (`yarn`) that can be used to view the status of a job or all jobs running on a YARN cluster. An example of this is shown in Listing 21.12.

LISTING 21.12   Using the yarn Command

```
$ yarn application -list
Application-Id                     Application-Name Application-Type ...
application_1462598277330_0001     SparkPi          SPARK            ...
application_1462598277330_0002     SparkPi          SPARK            ...
```

You can see all of the available command line options for the `yarn` command using `yarn --help`.

Just as with an application running in `cluster` deploy mode on a standalone cluster, Spark applications running on a YARN cluster in cluster mode cannot be killed simply by exiting the invoking process. The `yarn` command can be used to kill a running Spark job, as shown in Listing 21.13.

LISTING 21.13   Using the yarn Command to Kill a Running Spark Application

```
$ yarn application -kill application_1462598277330_0001
...
Killing application application_1462598277330_0001
...
```

YARN Scheduling

YARN provides the capability to schedule multiple concurrent applications and to allocate resources appropriately. YARN has several scheduling approaches available that can be used across different applications and within a single application. Options include the FairScheduler (which is analogous to the FairScheduler available in standalone cluster mode), the CapacityScheduler (which provides limits on application resource use based upon users and queues to ensure fairness and stability of the cluster), and the FIFOScheduler.

The particular allocation allotted to an application is determined by the user that submitted the application and the queue the application was submitted to. The queue is configured using the `--queue` argument of the `spark-submit`, `pyspark`, or `spark-shell` commands as shown previously or the `SPARK_YARN_QUEUE` environment variable.

Configuring the YARN scheduler, queues, and allocations is typically the role of the Hadoop administrator because these are global settings affecting all users and applications. However, using the Scheduler link of the ResourceManager UI, you can view scheduler configuration and the current state of the available queues, as shown in Figure 21.11.

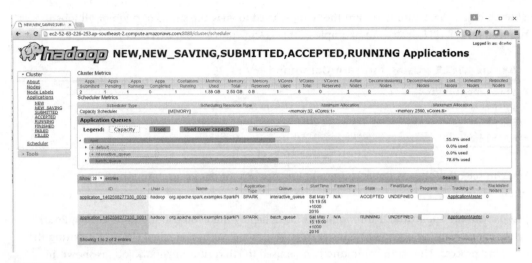

FIGURE 21.11
Viewing YARN scheduler status and queues.

Dynamic Resource Allocation

By default, Spark requests YARN containers on NodeManagers to host the executors requested by the developer or analyst in their configuration or command line arguments, and these executors and their host containers will be consumed for the life of the application (whether they are required for processing or not). This is often not optimal, especially for long-lived applications such as `pyspark` or `spark-shell` interactive environments. A better solution is to use is *Dynamic Resource Allocation*.

Dynamic Resource Allocation is designed to let applications scale their resource allocation up and down as required. Spark applications configured to use Dynamic Resource Allocation can not only request additional resources (executors) when they are needed but release resources that are no longer required back to the cluster resource pool.

To enable Dynamic Resource Allocation, you need to set the `spark.dynamicAllocation.enabled` and `spark.shuffle.service.enabled` settings to `true`. This can be set in the `spark-defaults.conf`, in the`-conf` or `--properties-file` command line arguments, or in the `SparkConf` object.

Scheduling within a single Spark application works the same as in the Spark standalone cluster manager. By default, this is the FIFO scheduler, but the FairScheduler option and configuration (as discussed in the previous section) can be used as an alternative.

Summary

In this hour, you have explored some of the concepts and activities involved in administering a Spark cluster. Specifically, you have explored administering Spark in standalone cluster mode or Spark running on a YARN cluster, although Mesos is an alternative cluster manager that is available as well. Regardless of the cluster manager used, configuration deployment and management is one of the key challenges involved in administration of any system. This is especially challenging in a distributed environment where configuration parameters need to be changed across multiple systems. Tools such as Puppet, Chef, and Ansible can be used to deploy and manage configurations, as can cluster management tools such as Cloudera Manager and Ambari, where Spark is deployed using a Hadoop vendor's distribution.

I have discussed specific common Spark environment variables and configuration parameters and looked at the order of precedence in applying Spark configuration. You looked at the specific management tasks involved with managing Spark applications and clusters running in standalone and YARN modes, such as checking the status of or killing running applications and managing application and job scheduling with Spark.

In the next hour, I will extend the discussion to another common administration activity—monitoring and logging.

Q&A

Q. What is the best approach to setting Spark configuration properties and why?

A. In most cases, setting Spark configuration properties using arguments to `spark-submit`, `pyspark`, and `spark-submit` is recommended, because setting configuration properties programmatically requires code changes or rebuilding (in the case of Scala or Java applications).

Q. What are the goals of the FairScheduler?

A. The FairScheduler is designed to ensure the cluster is utilized as efficiently as possible, enabling short running jobs to coexist with long running jobs and to share resources proportionally.

Q. How does Spark determine the number of executors available to a cluster?

A. In standalone mode, Spark allocates one executor per worker (by default) or the number of cores on a worker divided by the `spark.executor.cores` configuration value, if set. In YARN mode, the `--num-executors` argument is used to determine the number of executors available.

Workshop

The workshop contains quiz questions and exercises to help you solidify your understanding of the material covered. Try to answer all questions before looking at the "Answers" section that follows.

Quiz

1. True or false: The `SPARK_HOME` variable should always be set, especially if you have multiple versions of Spark installed.

2. Which method of setting Spark configuration properties has the highest precedence?

    A. Setting environment variables using `spark-env.sh`

    B. Setting configuration properties using `spark-defaults.conf`

    C. Supplying configurations as arguments to `spark-submit`

    D. Setting configuration properties in your code using a `SparkConf` object

3. Which `spark-submit` argument is used to stop a running Spark application in cluster deploy mode on a Spark standalone cluster?

4. **True or false:** A given slave node can host only one Spark worker process.

Answers

1. **True.**

2. **D.**

3. `--kill`.

4. **False.** A slave node can host multiple workers. By default, one worker is deployed per slave node. However, you can change the value of the `SPARK_WORKER_INSTANCES` environment variable to spawn more than one worker process on a slave node.

Monitoring Spark

What You'll Learn in This Hour:

▶ Monitoring applications using the Spark application UI

▶ Using the Spark History Server

▶ Collecting Spark metrics

▶ Logging in Spark

Continuing on the theme of Spark administration, other common requirements involved with managing Spark include monitoring processes and tasks. This chapter covers monitoring and logging in Spark, which is required for the troubleshooting of failed or underperforming applications and tasks as well as for system capacity planning.

Exploring the Spark Application UI

As you have seen, each Spark application serves an application web UI on port 4040 (by default) on the driver host. If the driver host is running more than one application, each subsequent application will be served on successive ports (such as 4041, 4042, and so on).

If you are using YARN as your cluster manager, YARN will provide a proxy address to the application UI. This is accessible using the ApplicationsMaster link from the YARN ResourceManager UI (as discussed in **Hour 21, "Administering Spark"**).

The application UI provides key information about the behavior and performance of your Spark application and includes several tabs that you will need to be familiar with. They are described in more detail here.

Consider the Spark routine in Listing 22.1, which is running in a single `pyspark` session (you can try this yourself!).

LISTING 22.1 Example Spark Routine

```python
import re

# load data
shakespeare = sc.textFile('s3://sty-spark/shakespeare')
stopwords = sc.textFile('s3://sty-spark/stopwords') \
            .flatMap(lambda line: re.split('\W+', line))

words = shakespeare.filter(lambda line: len(line) > 0) \
                .flatMap(lambda line: re.split('\W+', line)) \
                .filter(lambda word: len(word) > 1) \
                .map(lambda x: x.lower())
significant_words = words.subtract(stopwords) \
                        .map(lambda x: (x,1))
counts = significant_words.reduceByKey(lambda x, y: x + y)

# first action:
# show top 10 most frequently occurring words
counts.takeOrdered(5, key=lambda x: -x[1])
[(u'thou', 5443), (u'thy', 3812), (u'shall', 3608),
(u'thee', 3104), (u'good', 2888)]

# second action:
# sum length of all words
totallen = counts.map(lambda x: len(x[0])) \
                .reduce(lambda x, y: x + y)

# third action:
# compute average word length
print("Average length for non stop words is: " + \
        str(totallen/counts.count()))
Average length for non stop words is: 7

counts.persist(StorageLevel.MEMORY_AND_DISK_SER_2)
# fourth action:
# used to force RDD persistence
counts.take(5)
```

Jobs

A job in the Jobs tab of the application UI represents the series of tasks and stages as a result of performing a Spark action or multiple actions. For example, the code in Listing 22.1 included four discrete actions, so there are four completed jobs listed, along with summary information about each job, as you can see in the Jobs tab of the Spark application UI shown in Figure 22.1.

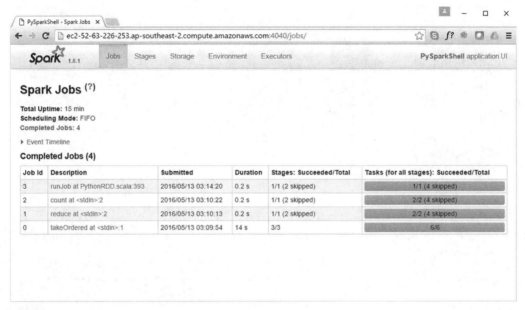

FIGURE 22.1
Spark application UI—Jobs tab (summary).

Note that the summary view also shows you the Scheduling Mode (as I discussed in the previous chapter).

Clicking on a job takes you to a detailed view of that particular job. The detailed view enables you to visualize the job DAG using the DAG Visualization link, as shown in Listing 22.2. You can view a time series chronology of events using the Event Timeline link.

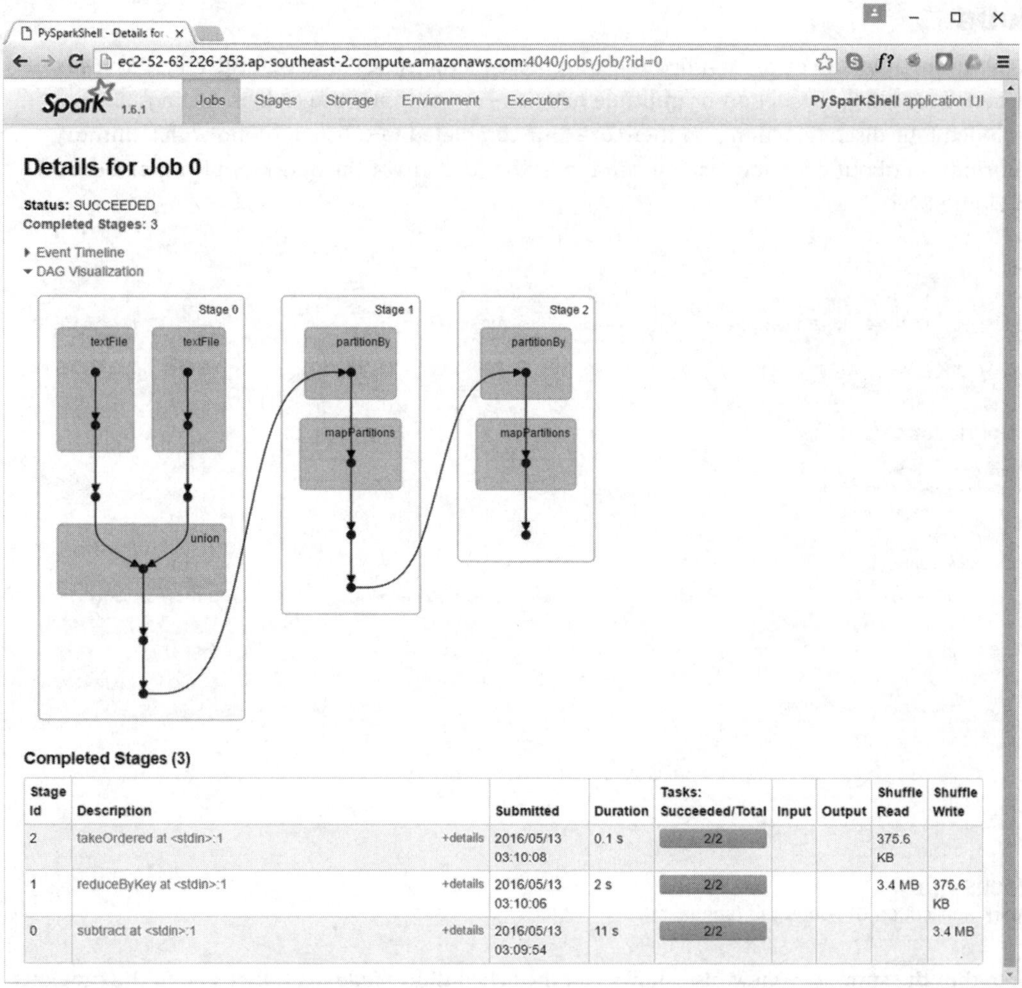

FIGURE 22.2
Spark application UI—Jobs tab (details).

Stages

Jobs are executed in *stages* (which are groups of tasks that can be performed in parallel) as I have discussed previously. The Stages tab of the Spark application UI is used to provide further information about each stage involved with each job. The default view summarizes all stages for all jobs, as shown in Figure 22.3.

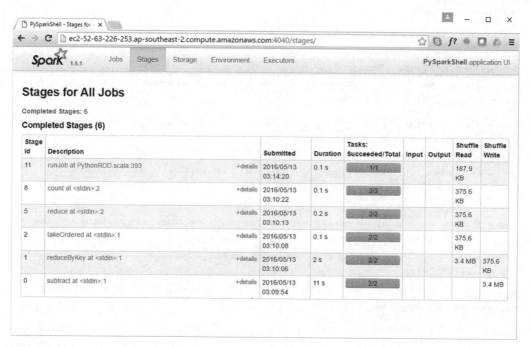

FIGURE 22.3
Spark application UI—Stages tab (summary).

Clicking one of the stage links takes you to the Stage Detail view, which provides metrics and detailed stage information at a task level and an executor level. The Stage Detail view for one of the stages in the routine is shown in Figure 22.4.

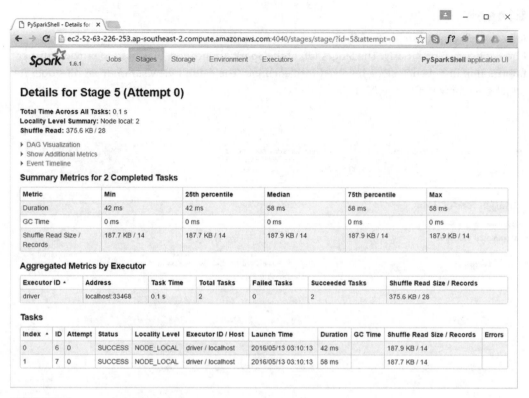

FIGURE 22.4
Spark application UI—Stages tab (details).

Storage

The Storage tab of the Spark application UI shows information about RDDs that have been cached or persisted (refer back to **Hour 11**, **"Using RDDs: Caching, Persistence, and Output,"** in which I discussed caching and persistence). Cached or persisted RDDs within your application are listed in the summary view of the Stages tab, as shown in Figure 22.5.

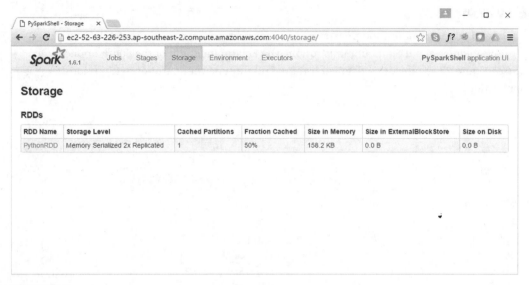

FIGURE 22.5
Spark application UI—Storage tab (summary).

The summary view shows high-level information about the stored object, including the amount of memory or disk used, the storage level, and the number of partitions. For more detail on any one stored object, click on the link for the RDD, which redirects you to the RDD Storage Detail view, as shown in Figure 22.6. This detailed view gives you specific information about the distribution of the object (namely, which executors are storing which partitions for the RDD).

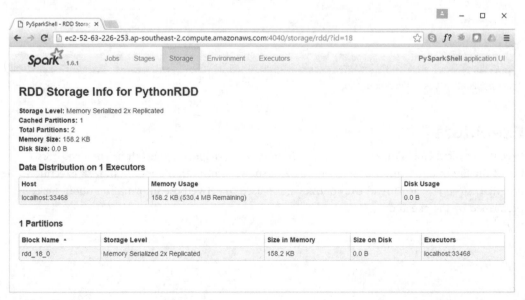

FIGURE 22.6
Spark application UI—Storage tab (details).

Environment

I discussed Spark configuration properties and environment information in detail in the previous chapter about Spark administration. The Environment tab of the Spark application UI (see Figure 22.7) provides a detailed listing of all runtime configuration settings for the application.

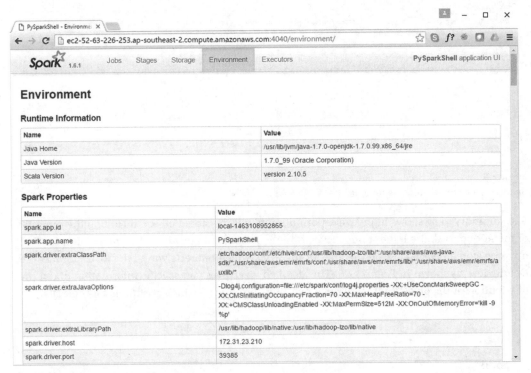

FIGURE 22.7
Spark application UI—Environment tab.

Executors

Executors execute tasks and store RDD partition data for a Spark application. The Executors tab of the Spark application UI (see Figure 22.8) shows information about both task execution and RDD storage. The Thread Dump link can be used to get verbose information about tasks performed by the executor.

FIGURE 22.8
Spark application UI—Executors tab.

If you use a `SQLContext` to perform Spark DataFrame operations, you will also see an additional SQL tab, with information specific to Spark SQL. Furthermore, if you initiate a `StreamingContext`, you will see a Streaming tab with information specific to Spark Streaming.

Viewing the Status of All Running Applications

The application UI only includes information about the one specific application. To view high-level information about all applications running on the cluster, you need to use the master UI provided by the respective cluster manager in use, such as, for instance, the Spark master UI for a Spark Standalone cluster or the YARN ResourceManager UI for a YARN cluster, as discussed in the previous chapter. From the cluster manager UI, you are able to redirect to the application UI for a specified running application.

As discussed in the previous chapter, there are also APIs and command line tools (like the `yarn` CLI) that enable you to view the status of all applications running on the cluster.

The application UI is only available for the life of the application. To view the status of and obtain information and metrics about completed applications, you need to use the Spark History Server, which I will discuss in more detail in the next section.

Spark History Server

As you have seen, both Spark through the application UI served on port 4040 of the driver host and the ResourceManager UI when running on YARN provide great visibility into running applications. However, the Spark application UI is terminated when the driver terminates, which does not provide you with the capability to profile completed jobs.

Instead, Spark provides a separate service for aggregating status and metrics for completed applications, the *Spark History Server*.

Deploying the Spark History Server

The Spark History Server is started using the `$SPARK_HOME/sbin/start-history-server.sh` script, which spawns an instance of the `org.apache.spark.deploy.history.HistoryServer` class. The History Server web UI is served on port 18080 (by default) on the host running the `HistoryServer` process.

Configuring the Spark History Server

Each application specifies a `spark.eventLog.dir` or`spark.history.fs.logDirectory` configuration property. If this property points to a shared or distributed filesystem such as HDFS, application logs can be accessed by a History Server running on another host.

The History Server UI is updated on an interval determined by the `spark.history.fs.update.interval` configuration property on the instance running the `HistoryServer` daemon. The History Server retains the last 50 applications by default (configurable by the `spark.history.retainedApplications` configuration parameter).

Exploring the Spark History Server UI

The History Server shows a list of completed applications, as shown in Figure 22.9. Clicking the link for a specific application displays an application UI with the same tabs and information available in the application UI covered in the last section. The only difference is that the History Server allows access to this information for applications that are completed (successfully or otherwise).

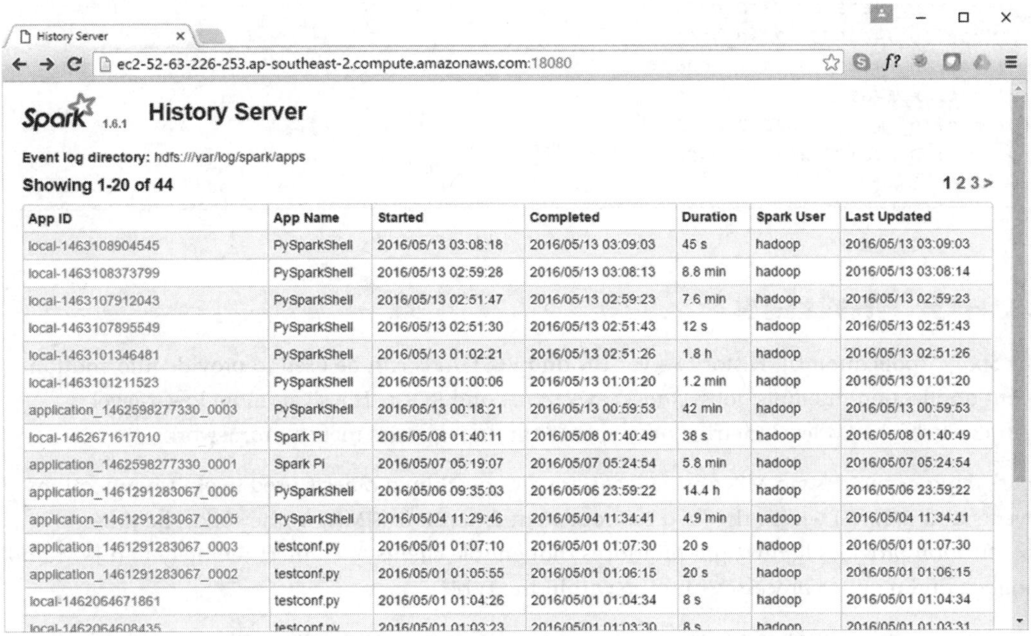

FIGURE 22.9
Spark History Server UI.

Spark History Server API Access

In addition to the web UI, the History Server provides API access to all of the metrics and information it collects and maintains. The API is served from the http://<server-url>:18080/api/v1 endpoint. There are numerous API methods to get a list of completed applications or to drill into jobs, executors, stages, storage, or other properties of a completed application. A full list of endpoints can be found in the Spark documentation (obtainable from https://spark.apache.org).

The API can be accessed using curl (a command line utility), postman (a browser-based REST client) or programmatically (such as by using the requests library in Python, as demonstrated in Listing 22.2).

LISTING 22.2   Accessing the History Sever REST API

```python
import requests
all_apps = requests.get('http://localhost:18080/api/v1/applications') \
                    .json()
len(all_apps)
47
for app in all_apps:
    print(app["id"])
```

```
application_1462598277330_0003
application_1462598277330_0001
application_1461291283067_0006
application_1461291283067_0005
application_1461291283067_0003
application_1461291283067_0002
...
```

Spark Metrics

The Spark application UI, History Server UIs and REST APIs can be used to provide information about application attempts, jobs, stages, executors, and RDDs. However, more lower-level metrics, such as JVM level metrics, are exposed through Spark's metrics framework.

Spark exposes metrics via MBeans. *MBeans* are managed Java objects used to emit notifications (events and metrics) within the Java Management Extensions (JMX) framework. The JMX specification provides lightweight interfaces that enable clients to connect remotely to a JVM and manage and monitor processes running within the JVM.

MBeans can emit metrics via broadcast messages (*JMX broadcasts*), which can be accessed through *JMX Ports* for JMX monitoring solutions such as JConsole, Nagios, or Zabbix.

Spark metrics can also be integrated as *metrics sinks*, exposing data that can be integrated into common cluster monitoring solutions and metrics visualization platforms such as Ganglia and Graphite.

Some of the metrics sinks options available in the `org.apache.spark.metrics.sink` package include

- ▶ `CsvSink`—Saves Spark metrics to CSV files.
- ▶ `ConsoleSink`—Outputs metrics to the console.
- ▶ `JmxSink`—Allows Spark metrics to be viewed in a JMX console.
- ▶ `GangliaSink`—Sends Spark metrics to Ganglia.
- ▶ `GraphiteSink`—Sends Spark metrics to Graphite.

Spark metrics configuration (including sink specification and configuration) is read from a `metrics.properties` file, usually located in the `$SPARK_HOME/conf` directory. A template `metrics.properties` file is included in the vanilla Spark build as `$SPARK_HOME/conf/metrics.properties.template`. This file can be copied and edited as required.

Spark metrics are exposed through *sources* such as the `org.apache.spark.metrics.source.JvmSource`, which collects JVM statistics from Spark executor and driver processes including memory usage, thread counts, and garbage collection information.

Configure a `metrics.properties` file and explore capturing Spark metrics in the Try It Yourself exercise now.

 TRY IT YOURSELF

Collecting Spark Metrics

In this exercise, you will set up a simple CSVSink to capture metrics for a Spark application. This exercise can be performed using your Spark standalone cluster.

1. Create a new `metrics` folder under your `$SPARK_HOME` directory on the driver instance of your cluster and assign ownership to the user you will be running your programs with (in this case, the `ubuntu` user).

```
$ sudo mkdir $SPARK_HOME/metrics
$ sudo chown ubuntu:ubuntu $SPARK_HOME/metrics/
```

2. On your driver instance, create a new `metrics.properties` file in the `$SPARK_HOME/conf` directory.

```
$ cd $SPARK_HOME/conf; vi metrics.properties
```

3. Add the following configuration to the empty `metrics.properties` file created in Step 2.

```
# Enable CsvSink for all instances
*.sink.csv.class=org.apache.spark.metrics.sink.CsvSink

# Polling period for CsvSink
*.sink.csv.period=1
*.sink.csv.unit=seconds

# Polling directory for CsvSink
*.sink.csv.directory=/opt/spark/metrics

# Worker instance overlap polling period
worker.sink.csv.period=1
worker.sink.csv.unit=seconds

# Enable jvm source for instance master, worker, driver and executor
master.source.jvm.class=org.apache.spark.metrics.source.JvmSource
worker.source.jvm.class=org.apache.spark.metrics.source.JvmSource
driver.source.jvm.class=org.apache.spark.metrics.source.JvmSource
executor.source.jvm.class=org.apache.spark.metrics.source.JvmSource
```

Note that you need to specify the path explicitly for the directory `*.sink.csv.directory` because environment variables will not be expanded. Save the file and exit your text editor.

4. Run an example program specifying the `metrics.properties` file.

```
$SPARK_HOME/bin/spark-submit  \
--class org.apache.spark.examples.SparkPi \
--master spark://sparkmaster:7077 \
--files=$SPARK_HOME/conf/metrics.properties \
--conf spark.metrics.conf=$SPARK_HOME/conf/metrics.properties \
$SPARK_HOME/lib/spark-examples-*.jar 100
```

5. List the files in the `$SPARK_HOME/metrics` directory on your driver instance.

```
$ ls $SPARK_HOME/metrics
```

Several CSV files are created, such as:

```
app-2016....driver.BlockManager.disk.diskSpaceUsed_MB.csv
app-2016....driver.BlockManager.memory.maxMem_MB.csv
app-2016....driver.BlockManager.memory.memUsed_MB.csv
app-2016....driver.BlockManager.memory.remainingMem_MB.csv
app-2016....driver.jvm.heap.committed.csv
app-2016....driver.jvm.heap.init.csv
...
```

6. Inspect one of the CSV files:

```
$ cat $SPARK_HOME/metrics/*.driver.jvm.heap.committed.csv
```

You should see comma-separated values that include a timestamp (a long value such as 1463307101) and a value representing the metric reading at that time.

You should also explore some of the other monitoring tools and built-in metrics sinks available for Spark (including Ganglia and Graphite).

Logging in Spark

Developers often require detailed information about applications or processes. This is necessary to troubleshoot failed processes as well as to analyze performance. A common approach is to add `print` statements to your code, although this is not very scalable and is difficult to implement when running in a distributed system (print to where?). A better, more extensible, and more scalable alternative is *logging*. Logging provides the application developer with more control and granularity over what gets logged and how it gets logged.

Log4j

Spark uses Log4j as its logging framework. Log4j is a Java-based logging library commonly used by Java applications, processes, and daemons. Log4j enables developers to implement *loggers* (objects that represent a log file output) and to log various events according to specific criteria and severity levels.

Severity levels defined in the Log4j specification are summarized in Table 22.1 ordered by their verbosity (from the least verbose to the most).

TABLE 22.1 Log4j Severity Levels

Log Level	Description
OFF	Used to turn off all logging.
FATAL	Severe errors that typically cause premature termination of the application.
ERROR	Runtime errors. These are often followed by a Java stack trace.
WARN	Warnings. Typically these are not necessarily errors, but they may lead to issues (such as the use of deprecated APIs).
INFO	Informational and status messages implemented by the developer.
DEBUG	Include additional detailed information about the process or application as implemented by the developer.
TRACE	More detailed logging level than DEBUG, including lower-level process information.
ALL	Log everything (TRACE through to FATAL).

Log4j also includes log management capability with its *appenders* (classes that manage where log events are sent to and how logs are stored, rotated, and managed). Some of the common Log4j appenders available are listed in Table 22.2.

TABLE 22.2 Log4j Appenders

Log4j Appender	Description
ConsoleAppender	Logs events to the console stderr (by default).
FileAppender	Logs events to a file.
RollingFileAppender	Extends FileAppender to back up the log files when they reach a certain size.
SyslogAppender	Logs events to a remote syslog daemon.
JDBCAppender	Logs events to a database via JDBC.

There are also appenders available for popular messaging platforms such as Kafka, JMS (Java Message Service), and ZeroMQ.

The log4j.properties File

The log4j.properties file is used to specify the default logging configuration for applications and processes using Log4j. In the case of Spark, this file is located in the $SPARK_HOME/conf directory. For other applications, it is typically located with their configuration files (for Hadoop, it's located in /etc/hadoop/conf by convention).

Spark releases do not include a `log4j.properties` file. Instead, they include a template file (`log4j.properties.template`) that can be copied, renamed to `log4j.properties`, and modified with the desired log configuration. Listing 22.3 shows an example excerpt from a `log4j.properties` file.

LISTING 22.3   The log4j.properties File

```
. . .
# Set everything to be logged to the console
log4j.rootCategory=INFO,console
log4j.appender.console=org.apache.log4j.ConsoleAppender
log4j.appender.console.target=System.err
log4j.appender.console.layout=org.apache.log4j.PatternLayout
log4j.appender.console.layout.ConversionPattern=%d{yy/MM/dd HH:mm:ss} %p %c{1}:
%m%n
. . .
```

As you can see from Listing 22.3, the `log4j.properties` file sets the default configuration for what gets logged (in this case, `INFO` messages and above), how it gets logged (the log file *layout*), where it gets logged, and how logs are managed (using the `ConsoleAppender`, in this case). Example log events using this configuration are shown in Listing 22.4.

LISTING 22.4   Example Log Events

```
16/05/14 07:01:34 INFO SparkContext: Running Spark version 1.6.1
16/05/14 07:01:36 INFO SecurityManager: Changing view acls to: hadoop
16/05/14 07:01:36 INFO SecurityManager: Changing modify acls to: hadoop
16/05/14 07:01:37 INFO Utils: Successfully started service 'sparkDriver' on port
40806.
16/05/14 07:01:38 INFO Slf4jLogger: Slf4jLogger started
16/05/14 07:01:38 INFO Remoting: Starting remoting
16/05/14 07:01:39 INFO SparkEnv: Registering MapOutputTracker
16/05/14 07:01:39 INFO SparkEnv: Registering BlockManagerMaster
16/05/14 07:01:39 INFO SparkEnv: Registering OutputCommitCoordinator
16/05/14 07:01:39 INFO Utils: Successfully started service 'SparkUI'
16/05/14 07:01:39 INFO HttpServer: Starting HTTP Server
. . .
```

If the `log4j.properties` file is not available in the `$SPARK_HOME/conf` directory, Spark will use the first `log4j.properties` file found in the Java classpath for the respective process. You can also specify the `log4j.properties` file by specifying a JVM option using the `-D` option within the `--driver-java-options` argument of `spark-submit`, `pyspark`, or `spark-shell`, as shown in Listing 22.5 (using this method the file does not even need to be named `log4j.properties`).

LISTING 22.5   Specifying the log4j.properties File Using JVM Options

```
$SPARK_HOME/bin/spark-submit  \
--class org.apache.spark.examples.SparkPi \
--master local \
--driver-java-options \
  "-Dlog4j.configuration=log4j.properties.erroronly" \
$SPARK_HOME/lib/spark-examples-*.jar 1000
```

Much more information about Log4j configuration settings can be found at http://logging.apache.org/log4j.

Spark Daemon Logging

Spark daemons (such as the Spark master and Spark worker in standalone mode or the Spark History Server) write their log files to `$SPARK_HOME/logs`. The `$SPARK_HOME/logs` directory will be created if it does not exist. The log directory and log level can be changed using the `log4j.properties` file in the `$SPARK_HOME/conf` directory.

TIP

Check the Daemon Logs to Troubleshoot Failed Master or Worker Processes

Checking the daemon log files (such as `$SPARK_HOME/logs/spark-root-org.apache.spark.deploy.worker.Worker-1-sparkworker.out`) should be your first step in troubleshooting Spark daemons that terminate unexpectedly or fail to start.

Spark Executor Logs

In standalone mode, workers write their executor log files out to a work directory on each slave node (`$SPARK_HOME/work` by default). This is configurable using the `$SPARK_HOME/conf/log4j.properties` file as well. Because locating and reading these files from the local executor instance can be challenging in a distributed environment, it is often easier to view the application executor logs using the Spark worker UI in standalone mode, as shown in Figure 22.10.

FIGURE 22.10
Locating executor logs in standalone mode using the Spark worker UI.

Clicking the `stderr` link shown in Figure 22.10 displays the log events shown in Figure 22.11.

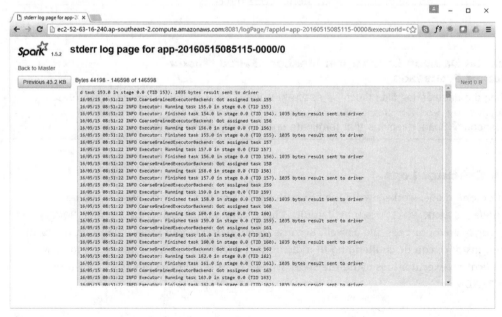

FIGURE 22.11
Executor log events shown in the worker UI.

In YARN mode, the executor logs are stored with the YARN container logs. These can be located using the YARN ResourceManager UI, clicking through to the ApplicationsMaster or History (if the application has completed) link in the UI. You will see a Logs link for each application attempt, as shown in Figure 22.12. Clicking this link redirects you to the container logs for the particular process.

FIGURE 22.12
YARN container logs.

YARN also performs regular *log aggregation*, aggregating logs from NodeManagers local directories into HDFS, providing secure, durable long-term storage and making these files easily accessible.

Logging within an Application

Although log levels can be set in the log4j.properties file, as you have seen, this often does not provide the flexibility needed during the application development process. A better solution is to set the log level within your program. This can be done using the setLogLevel method of the SparkContext object, as shown in Listing 22.6.

LISTING 22.6   Setting Log Levels within an Application

```
...
sc.setLogLevel('ERROR')
...
```

You can also log events programmatically within an application by creating a "logger" object using the `org.apache.log4j.LogManager.getLogger` method and then calling the `info`, `error`, `warn`, `debug` or `trace` methods of the logger object created, as shown in Listing 22.7.

LISTING 22.7   Logging Events within Your Spark Program

```
log4jLogger = sc._jvm.org.apache.log4j
LOGGER = log4jLogger.LogManager.getLogger(__name__)
LOGGER.info("pyspark script logger initialized")
16/05/15 08:27:35 INFO __main__: pyspark script logger initialized
```

Summary

Spark provides multiple insights into cluster health as well as application performance through various interfaces. In this hour, I have covered the interfaces available, which include the application web UI, the Spark History Server UI and REST APIs, the Spark metrics framework, as well as application and executor log files.

The application UI provides detailed information about running applications, including information about jobs (discrete actions within an application), stages (groups of tasks which can be performed in parallel) and executors (the host processes running tasks). In addition, you can get runtime information about the application configuration and details specific to SparkSQL or Spark Streaming applications.

The Spark History Server collects information from completed applications, successful or otherwise. The History Server is a valuable source of information for troubleshooting failed applications or profiling performance of successful applications. The History Server also serves its data via a REST API by which the data can be accessed and manipulated programmatically.

Spark also exposes key low-level metrics, such as JVM metrics, to its metrics framework. Spark metrics can be read by common metrics collection platforms such as Ganglia and Graphite, enabling them to be easily visualized and tracked over time.

With any application, log files are usually the best source of information as to what has happened or is happening in an application, and Spark is no exception. Spark uses Log4J to manage its log files, daemons, and application process write events, messages, and exceptions to log files according to the defined log levels.

All of these tools can be used to profile, monitor, and troubleshoot applications running on your Spark cluster. You will use these monitoring techniques again in **Hour 24, "Improving Spark Performance."**

Q&A

Q. Explain the various tabs available in the Spark application UI and their purpose.

A. The Spark application UI includes a Jobs tab, which provides information about individual DAGs within the application or interactive session; a Stages tab, which includes stage information including tasks and shuffle operations; a Storage tab, which includes information about cached or persisted RDD objects; an Environment tab, which lists the runtime configuration for the application; and an Executors tab, which includes storage and task execution information for each executor involved in the application.

Q. What is the purpose of a metrics sink and what sinks are available natively for Spark metrics?

A. A metrics sink is used to define how to collect metrics emitted from a metrics source. Sinks available in the Spark metrics framework include `CsvSink`, `ConsoleSink`, `JmxSink`, `GangliaSink`, and `GraphiteSink`.

Q. What function do Log4j appenders perform, and what types of appenders are available?

A. Log4j appenders are used to redirect log output. There are appenders available to write log events to the console, files, JDBC data sources, or message queues. Appenders are also used to manage log files. For instance, the `RollingFileAppender` rotates and backs up log files based upon a specified size or time interval.

Workshop

The workshop contains quiz questions and exercises to help you solidify your understanding of the material covered. Try to answer all questions before looking at the "Answers" section that follows.

Quiz

1. True or false: A *job,* as shown in the application UI Jobs tab, is the result of a Spark transformation.

2. List the options available for Spark metrics collection, summarizing and reporting.

3. What are the levels available with the Log4J logging framework? (Order these by their respective verbosity in descending order—that is, from most verbose to least verbose—if possible.)

4. True or false: The Spark History Server can be used to view the status of a running Spark application.

Answers

1. **False.** A *job* is the result of a Spark *action*.

2. `JmxSink, GangliaSink, GraphiteSink, ConsoleSink, CsvSink`.

3. `ALL, TRACE, DEBUG, INFO, WARN, ERROR, FATAL, OFF`.

4. **False.** The Spark History server collects status and metrics from completed Spark applications.

HOUR 23
Extending and Securing Spark

What You'll Learn in This Hour:

- ▶ Perimeter security and network isolation for Spark
- ▶ Securing Spark communication
- ▶ Authentication and authorization for Spark
- ▶ Securing Spark using Kerberos

The Spark platform provides a feature and function-rich, powerful distributed processing environment typically provided with liberal access to a vast amount of data. However, this power and extensibility comes with some important security considerations. In this hour, I introduce you to some key security concepts and look at ways to secure the Spark platform to address security considerations.

Isolating Spark

Big data platforms (including Hadoop and Spark) provide low friction access to high fidelity data and extensive history. They originated in start-ups, social networking, search companies, and research laboratories, far from the mainstream enterprises such as banking institutions, retailers, and telecommunications companies in which this technology is proliferating today.

Security was not the primary consideration (if it was any real consideration at all) from the early beginnings of the big data and open source software movement. As the technology was increasingly used to process more valuable and sensitive information, the need for security and solutions for information security and governance started to emerge.

NOTE

It is important to note that Spark security is still very much evolving (even more so than Hadoop, which is further along in its assimilation into the enterprise). It is worth staying up to date with new security features as they become available in new releases of Spark.

Before I talk specifically about securing Spark, I first need to discuss some general security concepts involved with securing big data environments.

Perimeter Security

The first security model to be introduced into big data platforms such as Hadoop was *perimeter security*. Perimeter security is the practice of placing storage and processing assets in a private network that is not directly addressable from outside networks such as enterprise networks or the public Internet.

Specific user access and management interfaces are exposed through an *edge node* (which is placed on the perimeter with access to both the private and public networks). Open ports are minimized on the edge node to expose only required services.

These techniques effectively reduce the attack surface area of the system and provide a control point that can also act as a kill switch, if required (isolating the cluster from any external access). This approach can be used with on-premise bare metal systems or virtualized private or public clouds with software defined networks (such as AWS). Figure 23.1 depicts a high level architecture employing perimeter security.

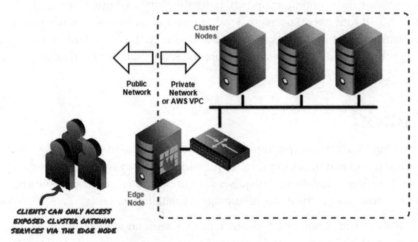

FIGURE 23.1
Perimeter security.

Often, the edge node is used to create an SSH Tunnel, which can then be used to proxy applications and interfaces (such as the Spark application UI and YARN Resource Manager UI) that may not be routable from the outside network. In such cases, access to the edge node via SSH is typically limited to administrators and support personnel.

Perimeter security remains the most common and best practice approach to security for big data systems, although it is typically used in combination with other techniques, as I will discuss later in this chapter.

Gateway Services

Gateway services typically run on instances that have access to both the public networks (where the users reside) and private networks (where the storage, compute, application, or management services reside). They often run on edge nodes or the equivalent thereof.

You have seen some examples of gateway services throughout this book. These include the Zeppelin, Jupyter, JDBC Thrift Server, and HiveServer2, which provide user access allowing users to run interactive notebook or SQL applications. Message brokers and APIs are also common gateway services to an isolated application processing platform such as Spark.

There are also projects that expose "Spark as a Service" interfaces, such as the spark-jobserver project created at Ooyala and the Livy project created by Cloudera. These projects expose a REST API for submitting Spark jobs and interacting with a Spark back end. Livy is incorporated with the Cloudera HUE (Hadoop User Environment) project, a web-based user interface to access Hadoop and Hadoop ecosystem components.

Management services and interfaces (such as the management web UIs for Hadoop and Spark you have seen in this book) also provide gateway services. These are often served via reverse proxies (such as NGINX or HAProxy) from an edge node in the environment.

The Apache Knox project provides a secure API gateway for accessing files in HDFS as part of a perimeter security implementation for Hadoop.

Authentication and Authorization

Authentication is the process of confirming the identity of a user or host (a *principal*), this is typically done by checking credentials such as a user name and password.

Authorization is the process of determining whether a principal is allowed to perform an action (such as reading a file or writing to a directory). This is typically accomplished by checking an *access control list (ACL)*. ACLs for HDFS, for example, determine what access levels the owner of an object, members of a group, and other users have to an object in the filesystem (directory or file).

Policies are similar to ACLs and are used for resource authorization. However, policies tend to be more fine-grained or involve a series of actions that often require the implementation of multiple ACLs. Policies are often more granular than users and groups and are applied to *roles*. Roles tend to be more functional, such as "reporting user" or "support engineer," and users may enter and leave groups routinely as their job requirements dictate. This approach to authorization is known as *role-based access control (RBAC)*.

Ranger and Sentry are two separate Apache projects that are used to create, administer, and enforce policies on Hadoop platforms that can be extended to Spark. If you are interested in pursuing this subject beyond this introduction, try visiting these projects' websites, **http://ranger.apache.org/** and **http://sentry.apache.org/**, for more detailed information about policies and RBAC.

I will discuss authentication again later in this chapter when I introduce Kerberos.

Securing Spark Communication

As you have seen, participants in a Spark cluster frequently need to communicate with one another. For instance, the users need to submit jobs and drivers need to communicate with executors. The master needs to communicate with workers, executors need to exchange data with one another, and so on. The simplest method to authenticate participants in a Spark cluster is to use a shared secret.

Spark Authentication Using a Shared Secret

Basic authentication for inter-process communication and user access can be achieved by creating a shared secret. A *shared secret* is a token known to all of the participants and users of the cluster. This token must be supplied as part of the daemon configuration for Spark daemons such as masters and workers, and must be supplied in application configuration when submitting Spark applications or requesting actions in interactive Spark shells.

Shared secret authentication is enabled by setting the `spark.authenticate` configuration property equal to `true`. For background processes (such as daemons), you would normally set this using the `spark-defaults.conf` file. For application submission, you could use any of the means discussed previously to set runtime configuration (`spark-defaults.conf`, command line arguments, the `SparkConf` object, and so on).

When it's enabled, you would create a secret using the `spark.authenticate.secret` configuration parameter set in the same way as the previous parameter. This shared secret must be the same for all participants; otherwise, they will not be able to communicate.

NOTE
_____

When running Spark on YARN, you only need to set the `spark.authenticate` property. The shared secret will be automatically generated and disseminated to executors at submission time and will be unique for each application.
_____

Try this now with the Spark standalone multi-node cluster.

Securing a Spark Standalone Cluster Using a Shared Secret

In this exercise, you will secure a multinode Spark standalone cluster by setting a shared secret.

1. Stop the Spark master:

```
$ sudo $SPARK_HOME/sbin/stop-master.sh
```

2. Stop the Spark worker (or workers) running on the Spark slave node(s):

```
$ sudo $SPARK_HOME/sbin/stop-slave.sh
```

3. On the Spark master node and all slave nodes, update the `spark-defaults.conf` to add the shared secret configuration. Use a shared secret of *"mysecret."* This can be done using a text editor (such as `vi` or `vim`) or using the Linux `sed` commands given here:

```
$ sudo sed -i "\$aspark.authenticate\ttrue" \
$SPARK_HOME/conf/spark-defaults.conf
```

```
$ sudo sed -i "\$aspark.authenticate.secret\tmysecret" \
$SPARK_HOME/conf/spark-defaults.conf
```

For other platforms, you can make these configuration changes using your preferred text editor.

4. Start the Spark master:

```
$ sudo $SPARK_HOME/sbin/start-master.sh
```

5. Start the Spark worker instances on the slave node(s):

```
$ sudo $SPARK_HOME/sbin/start-slave.sh \
spark://sparkmaster:7077
```

6. From another host on the network with Spark installed and with access to the master and worker(s), run the following command:

```
$SPARK_HOME/bin/spark-submit \
--class org.apache.spark.examples.SparkPi \
--master spark://sparkmaster:7077 \
$SPARK_HOME/lib/spark-examples*.jar 10
```

You should see some very nasty messages! You should see some equally nasty exceptions supplying an incorrect shared secret by using the following command:

```
$SPARK_HOME/bin/spark-submit \
--class org.apache.spark.examples.SparkPi \
--master spark://sparkmaster:7077 \
--conf spark.authenticate=true \
--conf spark.authenticate.secret=wrongsecret \
$SPARK_HOME/lib/spark-examples*.jar 10
```

7. From the same host used in step 6, submit the following command supplying the correct shared secret:

```
$SPARK_HOME/bin/spark-submit \
--class org.apache.spark.examples.SparkPi \
--master spark://sparkmaster:7077 \
--conf spark.authenticate=true \
--conf spark.authenticate.secret=mysecret \
$SPARK_HOME/lib/spark-examples*.jar 10
```

You should see that using the correct shared secret, all Spark processes can communicate with each other, and the application completes successfully!

Encrypting Spark Communication

Spark processes frequently need to communicate with one another. This communication could be of a control nature (such as drivers issuing instructions to executors) or a data exchange operation (such as a shuffle operation or data being returned to a driver). In either case, the data in transit can be secured with encryption (particularly if the communication happens over a public network).

Spark provides native support for encrypting inter-process communication (IPC) using Secure Sockets Layer (SSL), the same wire encryption protocol you're familiar with when accessing secure websites using `https`. Spark also provides support for encrypting data transferred during shuffle operations using SASL (Simple Authentication and Security Layer).

NOTE

Currently, Spark does not support encryption for data at rest (including RDD data persisted to disk on executors). If at rest encryption is required, consider using an encrypted file system on the relevant volumes of the executor hosts.

Configuring SSL for Spark Communication

SSL can be configured independently for Spark's internal messaging system (inter-process communication or IPC) as well as for HTTP for broadcast and file server communication. The steps required to implement SSL for Spark IPC traffic on a standalone cluster using a self-signed certificate are as follows:

1. Generate a key pair on a server in the cluster.

2. Import the key pair to each participant in the cluster (master and all slaves hosting workers).

3. Enable and configure SSL in the `spark-defaults.conf` on each node of the cluster.

4. Restart the master and workers.

Try it now on our Spark standalone cluster.

Encrypting IPC in a Spark Standalone Cluster

In this exercise, you will configure SSL for all IPC traffic between the master, workers, and drivers in a Spark standalone cluster.

1. From the master node in your Spark cluster, generate a key pair using `keytool`, a utility provided with the Java Development Kit (JDK) to create and manage certificates.

```
$ keytool -genkeypair \
-alias standalone_ssl \
-keyalg RSA \
-keysize 2048 \
-keypass mykeypassword \
-keystore mykeystore \
-dname "CN=J Aven, OU=Big Data Solutions,
O=Aven Solutions,
L=Melbourne,
S=Victoria,
C=Australia"
```

When prompted for a keystore password, enter **mykeystorepassword**.

2. Export the certificate using the `keytool` utility:

```
$ keytool -exportcert \
-alias standalone_ssl \
-file ssl_cert.Cer \
-keystore mykeystore
```

Enter the keystore password from above when prompted.

3. Import the certificate into a trust store using the `keytool` utility, as shown here:

```
$ keytool -importcert \
-trustcacerts \
-alias standalone_ssl \
-file ssl_cert.Cer \
-keystore mytruststore \
-keypass mykeypassword \
-noprompt
```

You are prompted to create a new password for the truststore. Enter **mytruststorepassword**.

You should now have files named `mykeystore` and `mytruststore` in your current directory.

4. Make a `keys` directory on all nodes (master, worker(s) and your driver instance):

   ```
   $ sudo mkdir $SPARK_HOME/keys
   ```

5. Copy the `mykeystore` and `mytruststore` files in your current directory to the `$SPARK_HOME/keys` directory on all nodes (you can use a utility like `scp` to accomplish this).

6. Modify the `spark-defaults.conf` on all nodes to include the following encryption configuration (you can do this on one node and `scp` the file to the other nodes).

   ```
   spark.ssl.enabled true
   spark.ssl.enabledAlgorithms TLS_RSA_WITH_AES_128_CBC_SHA, TLS_RSA_WITH_
   AES_256_CBC_SHA
   spark.ssl.protocol TLSv1.2
   spark.ssl.keyPassword mykeypassword
   spark.ssl.keyStore /opt/spark/keys/mykeystore
   spark.ssl.keyStorePassword mykeystorepassword
   spark.ssl.trustStore /opt/spark/keys/mytruststore
   spark.ssl.trustStorePassword mytruststorepassword
   ```

   Note that environment variables are not expanded in the `spark-defaults.conf` file, so you will need to reference the absolute path on the Spark node — driver, master and worker(s).

7. Create a `log4j.properties` file (if you have not done this already) in the `$SPARK_HOME/conf` directory on the master and/or worker nodes of the cluster (you can do this by copying the `log4j.properties.template` file to a file named `log4j.properties`). Modify this file to configure the log level to DEBUG:

   ```
   # change this line...
   # log4j.rootCategory=INFO, console
   # to this...
   log4j.rootCategory=DEBUG, console
   ```

   You will use this to validate that encryption has been configured correctly and is active.

8. Stop the master:

   ```
   $ sudo $SPARK_HOME/sbin/stop-master.sh
   ```

9. Stop all workers on all slave nodes:

   ```
   $ sudo $SPARK_HOME/sbin/stop-slave.sh
   ```

10. Start the master:

    ```
    $ sudo $SPARK_HOME/sbin/start-master.sh
    ```

11. Start the worker(s):

    ```
    $ sudo $SPARK_HOME/sbin/start-slave.sh \
    spark://sparkmaster:7077
    ```

12. Inspect the log file on either the master or a worker:

```
$ cat $SPARK_HOME/logs/*.out
```

You should find entries similar to the following to validate that encryption is working correctly:

```
...
16/05/20 04:49:53 DEBUG SecurityManager: SSLConfiguration for file server:
SSLOptions{enabled=true, keyStore=Some(/opt/spark/keys/mykeystore),
keyStorePassword=Some(xxx), trustStore=Some(/opt/spark/keys/
mytruststore), trustStorePassword=Some(xxx), protocol=Some(TLSv1.2),
enabledAlgorithms=Set(TLS_RSA_WITH_AES_128_CBC_SHA, TLS_RSA_WITH_AES_256_CBC_
SHA)}
16/05/20 04:49:53 DEBUG SecurityManager: SSLConfiguration for Akka:
SSLOptions{enabled=true, keyStore=Some(/opt/spark/keys/mykeystore),
keyStorePassword=Some(xxx), trustStore=Some(/opt/spark/keys/
mytruststore), trustStorePassword=Some(xxx), protocol=Some(TLSv1.2),
enabledAlgorithms=Set(TLS_RSA_WITH_AES_128_CBC_SHA, TLS_RSA_WITH_AES_256_CBC_
SHA)}
...
```

13. Run a test job from a driver instance used in Steps 4, 5, and 6:

```
$SPARK_HOME/bin/spark-submit \
--class org.apache.spark.examples.SparkPi \
--master spark://sparkmaster:7077 \
--conf spark.authenticate=true \
--conf spark.authenticate.secret=mysecret \
$SPARK_HOME/lib/spark-examples*.jar 10
```

All Spark IPC communication is now encrypted!

You can also supply encryption options including secret keys and keystore locations using JVM options supplied using the SPARK_MASTER_OPTS, SPARK_WORKER_OPTS, or SPARK_DAEMON_JAVA_OPTS environment variables.

SASL encryption can be configured for block transfer (shuffle) traffic between nodes by setting the spark.authenticate.enableSaslEncryption property to true as shown in Listing 23.1.

LISTING 23.1 Configuring SASL Encryption for Block Transfer Services

```
$SPARK_HOME/bin/spark-submit \
--class org.apache.spark.examples.SparkPi \
--master spark://172.31.12.5:7077 \
--conf spark.authenticate=true \
--conf spark.authenticate.secret=mysecret \
--conf spark.authenticate.enableSaslEncryption=true \
$SPARK_HOME/lib/spark-examples*.jar 10
```

NOTE

SSL support for the encrypting client/server traffic to and from the Spark Web UIs is targeted for release in Spark version 2.0.

Securing the Spark Web UI

The web UIs provided by the Spark processes including the driver, master/worker in a standalone cluster and the Spark History Server are extremely useful for Spark analysts, developers, data scientists, or administrators. However, in their vanilla configuration, these web UIs provide no security (by means of authentication or authorization). The current method available to secure these interfaces is Java Servlet Filters.

Java Servlet Filters

Authentication and authorization can be provided for the Spark UIs (master, worker, and application) using Java Servlet Filters. *Java Servlet Filters* are custom code modules that are used to filter access to resources within a web application. Although writing servlets is beyond the scope of this book, you can find numerous examples and tutorials about this topic on the web.

Authentication

Servlets can be used to enforce a requirement that a user enter credentials before a web page (such as one of the various Spark UIs) is served to the client. Suppose you built a Java servlet in a class named `BasicAuthenticationFilter` and packaged this in a jar called `basicauth.jar`. You then created an interactive Spark session using the code in Listing 23.2.

LISTING 23.2   Basic Authentication for the Spark UI Using Java Servlets

```
$SPARK_HOME/bin/pyspark \
--master spark://sparkmaster:7077 \
--conf spark.ui.filters=BasicAuthenticationFilter \
--jars basicauth.jar
```

The `spark.ui.filters` property will now use the `BasicAuthenticationFilter` servlet from the `basicauth.jar` package to perform basic authentication to the Spark application UI as shown in Figure 23.2.

FIGURE 23.2
Basic authentication for the Spark application UI.

Authorization

Servlets can also be used to provide rudimentary role-based access control for the Spark application UI. This feature is enabled by setting the `spark.acls.enable` configuration property to `true`. If this property is set, the filter that was used to authenticate the user can now determine what access that user has to the user interface based upon their role. The configuration properties used to control access are listed in Table 23.1.

TABLE 23.1   Spark UI Authorization Configuration Properties

Property	Description
`spark.admin.acls`	Comma-separated list of users/administrators that have view and modify access to all Spark jobs.
`spark.modify.acls`	Comma-separated list of users that have modify access to the Spark job (who can kill a Spark job through the UI, for example).
`spark.ui.view.acls`	Comma-separated list of users that have view access to the Spark UI.

An example of submitting a Spark application implementing access control for the UI using a servlet class called `RoleBasedAccessFilter` in a package named `rolebasedfilter.jar` is shown in Listing 23.3.

LISTING 23.3   Implementing ACLs for the Spark UI

```
$SPARK_HOME/bin/spark-submit \
--master spark://sparkmaster:7077 \
--conf spark.ui.filters=RoleBasedAccessFilter \
--conf spark.ui.view.acls=user1,user2 \
--conf spark.ui.modify.acls=support-user \
--conf spark.ui.admin.acls=spark-admin \
--jars rolebasedfilter.jar \
my-production-job.py
```

Securing Spark with Kerberos

Kerberos is a network authentication protocol that has become the de facto standard for authentication in distributed computing environments. It is the principal authentication mechanism for secure Hadoop clusters (which often host Spark as well).

Kerberos Overview

Kerberos involves negotiations between several independent participants that coordinate with one another to authenticate and authorize a host or user (known as a *principal*).

Kerberos requires messages to be exchanged between three parties. Kerberos message exchange participants include

- ▶ The client (requesting a service)
- ▶ The server (providing the request service)
- ▶ A Kerberos Key Distribution Center (KDC)

The KDC is responsible for authenticating and authorizing a client. The KDC is an independent component (not provided by Spark or Hadoop). Most Linux distributions include the MIT KDC. For Windows systems, a KDC is provided by the Active Directory Domain Controller(s).

The three-way exchange between the client, KDC, and service is pictured in Figure 23.3.

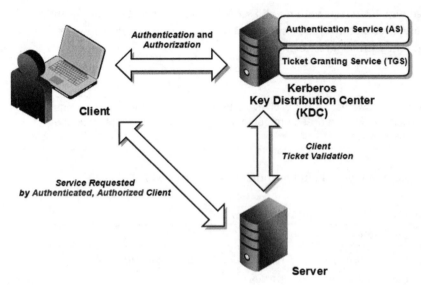

FIGURE 23.3
Kerberos exchange participants.

Some Kerberos concepts and terminology you should be familiar with include

▶ Principal—A unique entity that can be authenticated (a host or a user). In a secure, "Kerberized" cluster, all host, user, and service accounts must have a Kerberos principal.

▶ Keytab file—A file storing Kerberos principals and their associated keys. Keytab files enable service accounts and batch users or other noninteractive processes to be authenticated by Kerberos.

▶ Realm—A group of users and hosts participating in a Kerberos secured network, analogous to a domain in Microsoft Active Directory parlance.

▶ Authentication service (AS)—A service that accepts user access credentials and verifies these with the KDC database. If the credentials are verified, the KDC issues a Ticket Granting Ticket (TGT) to the client.

▶ Ticket Granting Ticket (TGT)—A ticket used to request a service ticket from the Ticket Granting Server. Ticket Granting Tickets are issued as part of the logon process with an expiry time.

▶ Service ticket—A ticket that validates that a principal can access a service.

▶ Ticket Granting Service (TGS)—A service that issues a service ticket to an authenticated and authorized principal.

After it's authenticated and authorized with a valid service ticket, the client can access the desired service. Credentials do not need to be submitted with each subsequent request because the authenticated status of a principal is cached.

NOTE

It is important to note that passwords are not exchanged between participants. Instead, passwords are used to compute encryption keys in a Kerberos authentication system. Encryption is used extensively in the Kerberos protocol.

A few Kerberos client commands you should be familiar with are listed in Table 23.2.

TABLE 23.2   Kerberos Client Commands

Command	Description
Kinit	Used to request a TGT (often as part of the logon process)
Klist	Used to list your current tickets
Kdestroy	Used to delete your tickets

Kerberos with Hadoop

Most Hadoop vendors recommend implementing Kerberos to secure a Hadoop cluster. Some general steps to "Kerberize" a Hadoop cluster include

- ▶ Install and configure a Kerberos KDC.

- ▶ Install Kerberos client libraries on all cluster nodes.

- ▶ Synchronize clocks across all cluster nodes (timestamps are integral to Kerberos)—using NTP is recommended.

- ▶ Ensure reverse domain name lookups work correctly.

- ▶ Create keytab files for all service principals (such as `hdfs`, `yarn`).

- ▶ Make necessary configuration changes to Hadoop configuration files.

- ▶ Restart Hadoop services.

Kerberos is an "all in" protocol. After you implement Kerberos, *all* components in the cluster must be Kerberos-aware, Kerberos-enabled, and configured correctly for your Kerberos environment.

NOTE

Kerberos is a highly specialized topic. If you are responsible for installing, configuring, and managing Kerberos, you should refer to the security guides provided for your Linux or Hadoop distribution.

Kerberos Configuration with Spark

Kerberos is not supported for authentication on a Spark standalone cluster. You will need to used the methods discussed in the previous section to provide inter-process authentication. Moreover, a standalone Spark cluster will not be able to directly access a Kerberized HDFS cluster. In this case, you would need to use a gateway service such as Knox to access HDFS.

Kerberos is supported when running Spark on YARN, which is often used when processing data stored in HDFS. Kerberos authenticates clients, allowing them to submit applications and launch interactive sessions on Spark.

Listing 23.4 demonstrates how to create a `spark` batch user, a Kerberos service principal and keytab file, and how to submit a Spark job on a Kerberized YARN cluster.

LISTING 23.4   Using Spark on a Kerberized Hadoop Cluster

```
# create a spark user in the hadoop group
# ensure this user is created on all nodes of the cluster
$ sudo useradd spark -g hadoop

# create a Kerberos service principal
$ sudo kadmin.local -q "addprinc -randkey spark/name@REALM.COM"

# create a keytab file for the principal
$ sudo kadmin.local -q "xst -k /etc/security/keytabs/spark.keytab spark/name@REALM
.COM"

# change ownership and permissions for the keytab file
$ sudo chown spark:hadoop /etc/security/keytabs/spark.keytab
$ sudo chmod 400 /etc/security/keytabs/spark.keytab

# obtain TGT for spark principal
$ sudo su spark;kinit -kt \
/etc/security/keytabs/spark.keytab spark/name@REALM.COM

# submit your Spark application
$ /opt/spark/bin/spark-submit \
--class org.apache.spark.examples.SparkPi \
--master yarn-cluster \
/opt/spark/lib/spark-examples*.jar 10
```

The principal and keytab file can also be explictily supplied as arguments to pyspark, spark-shell, or spark-submit when running in yarn mode. The Kerberos-related arguments to these utilities are described in Table 23.3.

TABLE 23.3 Kerberos Arguments to spark-submit, pyspark, and spark-shell

Agrument	Description
--principal	Kerberos principal used to authenticate to the KDC.
--keytab	Full path to the keytab file for the principal specified using the --principal argument. The keytab file will be copied to the application master node and used to renew login tickets periodically.

Also, when running Spark against a Kerberized Hadoop cluster, the Spark History Server process will require a Kerberos principal and keytab file.

Summary

In this hour, I have introduced security concepts such as isolation, authentication, and authorization. I discussed how isolation can be achieved for Hadoop and Spark systems by employing perimeter security and how specific user access and management interfaces can be exposed in this architecture.

I also covered how to secure communication between participants in a Spark cluster (drivers, workers, master) using SSL by setting the spark.authenticate property and how to control access to the Spark UIs using Java servlet filters.

Finally, you were introduced to Kerberos. Kerberos provides an authentication service by exchanging messages (keys or tokens) between parties in a distributed system (the client, a key distribution center or KDC, and a service). Kerberos is the de facto standard for strong authentication in distributed systems (generally accepted as the recommended authentication service for Hadoop).

Security in Spark is a fluid and emerging area. You should expect to see many more security-related improvements in future releases of Spark and commercial Hadoop distributions, so stay tuned!

Q&A

Q. What is *perimeter security* and why is it a best practice security principle for big data systems (including Spark)?

A. Perimeter security is the practice of isolating storage and processing assets within a private network, exposing necessary gateway user and management services only through an edge node or bastion host. By limiting host and port access to the core platform, the "attack surface area" of the system is effectively limited. This not only limits exposure to outside threats but creates a control point (or "kill switch") for the system.

Q. Perimeter security aside, what options are available for securing the various Spark user interfaces?

A. Spark UIs can use javax servlet filters to provide authentication and authorization (providing role-based access control to various UI components). Furthermore, transport security between the client and server using SSL will be released in the next major version of Spark.

Q. What are the independent parties involved in Kerberos authentication and what are their respective roles?

A. Kerberos exchange participants involved in the authentication process include the *client*, who requests access to a service; the *Kerberos Key Distribution Center* or *KDC*, which authenticates and authorizes the client to access the service; and the *server*, which provides the requested service.

Workshop

The workshop contains quiz questions and exercises to help you solidify your understanding of the material covered. Try to answer all questions before looking at the "Answers" section that follows.

Quiz

1. **True or false:** *Authentication* is the process of determining which resources a user can access.

2. Which project is used to provide a secure gateway to access HDFS?

   A. Apache Ranger

   B. Apache Knox

   C. Apache Sentry

3. List the steps involved in enabling shared secret authentication between Spark cluster participants.

4. **True or false:** Passwords are sent across the network when using Kerberos.

Answers

1. **False.** Authentication is the process of identifying a user or host (principal). *Authorization* is the process of determining which resources an authenticated user can access.

2. **B.** Apache Ranger and Apache Sentry provide authorization and enforce polices and role-based access control (RBAC) for Hadoop and other ecosystem components.

3. Set the `spark.authenticate` configuration property equal to `true` for each Spark cluster host or process, and then create a secret using the `spark.authenticate.secret` configuration parameter for all participants (the last step is not required when using Spark on YARN).

4. **False.** Passwords are not exchanged between participants. Instead, passwords are used to compute encryption keys in a Kerberos authentication system.

Improving Spark Performance

What You'll Learn in This Hour:

▶ Performance benchmarks available for Spark systems
▶ Application development best practices
▶ Identifying processing bottlenecks in Spark applications
▶ Optimizing Spark applications

Managing the performance of distributed systems (such as Spark) is a complex challenge. Many factors can influence performance and throughput of the system. The administrator's challenge is to establish and maintain a performance baseline for the system. The developer's or analyst's challenge is to identify, minimize, and mitigate processing bottlenecks in Spark routines. In this hour, I will cover Spark performance management concepts and practices that apply to both administrators and developers.

Benchmarking Spark

As an administrator of a system, before you can begin the task of tuning and optimizing your platform, you must first establish a performance baseline. Without one, you have no empirical way to assess whether any changes you have made to the system had a positive effect on overall performance. In this section, I will cover some methods that provide this baseline and ongoing measurement.

Benchmarks

Benchmarks are a common approach to establishing a baseline and assessing performance relative to the baseline at future points in time, either on a recurring basis (once a month, once a year, and so on), or after any significant changes to the processing environment (when a new node or nodes are added to the cluster, for instance).

Benchmarks are typically designed to perform workloads similar to that which would occur under normal operations. Additionally, benchmarks are designed not to be influenced by factors such as statistics or caching. This makes the benchmark results more meaningful as they cannot be biased or influenced by any specific system optimizations.

Much of the basis for data processing benchmarks stems from database and business intelligence (BI) vendors requiring a tool or framework by which to measure themselves against their competitors (for example, Oracle database versus SQL Server database query performance).

Transaction Processing Performance Council and TPC-DS

The Transaction Processing Performance Council (TPC) is an organization founded in the late 1980s to establish industry standards for database performance benchmarks. The TPC has published several benchmark standards for various database workloads including *TPC-C*, which is a benchmarking standard of OLTP (online transaction processing) systems, and *TPC-H*, which is a standard for DSS (decision support systems).

The TPC has recently introduced new benchmarks to include the emergent big data platforms in addition to their established set of benchmarks for relational database systems. New standards that have emerged include the following:

▶ **TPC-DS**—A recent standard established for benchmarking big data SQL engines (such as Impala and SparkSQL)

▶ **TPCx-HS**—The first published standard for benchmarking Hadoop systems

The TPC-DS standard is used by Databricks to benchmark performance in Spark 2.0 against previous releases and other available big data SQL engines. The TPC-DS queries used in these benchmarks are available in the `spark-sql-perf` project on GitHub: https://github.com/databricks/spark-sql-perf

Terasort

Terasort is a long-standing Hadoop benchmark. Terasort exercises the MapReduce framework in Hadoop and provides a meaningful benchmark for the system. Terasort, as it is colloquially known, is actually comprised of three components:

▶ **Teragen**—Generates a terabyte (or another configurable amount of random data)

▶ **Terasort**—Sorts the random data set generated by the Teragen utility

▶ **Teravalidate**—Validates that the resultant dataset from the Terasort utility has been correctly sorted

Because the Terasort suite of utilities generates random data, each successive test cannot be influenced, coerced, or advantaged in any way.

Terasort in its Hadoop MapReduce implementation is commonly run to benchmark Hadoop clusters testing HDFS, YARN, and MapReduce. There are many derivatives of Terasort that have been independently developed, including variants that use Spark (map and sortByKey or reduceByKey) instead of MapReduce.

There are many more benchmarks available specifically targeting HFDS including TestDFSIO, NNBench, MRBench, and others. These utilities are typically included with each Hadoop release.

spark-perf

spark-perf is a Databricks project available on GitHub that can be used to run tests and benchmarks against Spark systems (using any of the available cluster managers).

spark-perf includes specific tests for MLlib, Spark Streaming, and the Spark core API. You will run one of the Spark core tests in the next Try It Yourself exercise. A list of core tests available and usage for running the spark-perf Spark core tests is shown in Listing 24.1.

LISTING 24.1   spark-perf Core Tests

```
# list tests
$SPARK_HOME/bin/spark-submit --master local core_tests.py --list
AggregateByKey
AggregateByKeyInt
AggregateByKeyNaive
BroadcastWithBytes
BroadcastWithSet
Count
CountWithFilter
SchedulerThroughputTest
SortByKey
SortByKeyInt

# show usage
$SPARK_HOME/bin/spark-submit --master local core_tests.py --help
Usage: core_tests.py [options] test_names
Options:
-h, --help              show this help message and exit
--num-trials=NUM_TRIALS
--num-tasks=NUM_TASKS
--reduce-tasks=REDUCE_TASKS
--num-records=NUM_RECORDS
--inter-trial-wait=INTER_TRIAL_WAIT
--unique-keys=UNIQUE_KEYS
--key-length=KEY_LENGTH
--unique-values=UNIQUE_VALUES
--value-length=VALUE_LENGTH
--num-partitions=NUM_PARTITIONS
```

```
--broadcast-size=BROADCAST_SIZE
--random-seed=RANDOM_SEED
--storage-location=STORAGE_LOCATION
--persistent-type=PERSISTENT_TYPE
--wait-for-exit
-l, --list          list all tests
-a, --all           run all tests
```

`spark-perf` also includes specific tests for Spark MLlib and Spark Streaming as well.

Figure 24.1 and Figure 24.2 show an example of running a `spark-perf` benchmark using a Zeppelin notebook, summarizing the test results and visualizing the results of each test instance.

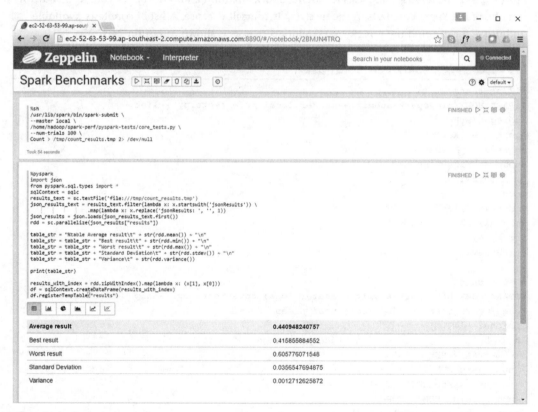

FIGURE 24.1
Running a Spark benchmark using Zeppelin.

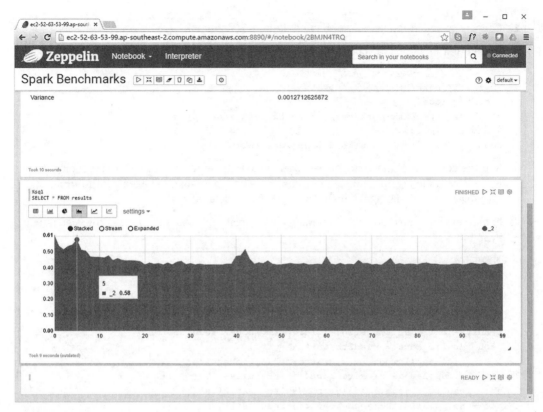

FIGURE 24.2
Visualizing Spark benchmark results using Zeppelin.

In the next exercise, you can run a sample benchmark using `spark-perf`.

TRY IT YOURSELF ▼

Running Benchmark Tests on Spark

In this exercise, you will use the `spark-perf` project along with the Zeppelin notebook interface to perform a benchmark against a Spark system. You will need a Zeppelin server available with access to your Spark cluster for this exercise if you want to visualize the test results (otherwise, you can just return the results as text to the console).

1. Clone the `spark-perf` GitHub repository from the host you will be submitting Spark applications from

   ```
   $ git clone https://github.com/databricks/spark-perf.git
   ```

   Note the directory to which you cloned this repository. In my case, it's `/home/hadoop`.

2. Connect to your Zeppelin server and create a new notebook.

3. In your first input cell in your notebook, enter the following:

```
%sh
/usr/lib/spark/bin/spark-submit \
--master local \
/home/hadoop/spark-perf/pyspark-tests/core_tests.py \
--num-trials 100 \
Count > /tmp/count_results.tmp 2> /dev/null
```

Run the contents of the cell. This will execute 100 trials for the Count test, sending the stdout to a file (/tmp/count_results.tmp) and ignoring messages sent to stderr. If you want to run this again, make sure this file is deleted first.

4. In the next input cell, enter the following code, which will load and process the results using PySpark:

```
%pyspark
import json
from pyspark.sql.types import *

sqlContext = sqlc
results_text = sc.textFile('file:///tmp/count_results.tmp')
json_results_text = results_text \
        .filter(lambda x: x.startswith('jsonResults')) \
        .map(lambda x: x.replace('jsonResults: ', '', 1))
json_results = json.loads(json_results_text.first())
rdd = sc.parallelize(json_results["results"])

table_str = "%table Average result\t" + \
                str(rdd.mean()) + "\n"
table_str = table_str + "Best result\t" + \
                str(rdd.min()) + "\n"
table_str = table_str + "Worst result\t" + \
                str(rdd.max()) + "\n"
table_str = table_str + "Standard Deviation\t" + \
                str(rdd.stdev()) + "\n"
table_str = table_str + "Variance\t" + str(rdd.variance())
print(table_str)

results_with_index = rdd \
        .zipWithIndex().map(lambda x: (x[1], x[0]))
df = sqlContext.createDataFrame(results_with_index)
df.registerTempTable("results")
```

Note the tabular test results displayed.

5. In the next input cell in your notebook, enter the following SQL statement:

```
%sql
SELECT * FROM results
```

6. Use the visualization tools to create a scatter plot, line chart, or area chart to plot the test results as shown in Figure 24.2.

This is just a sample approach to benchmarking Spark performance. As discussed, there are many other benchmarks available, or you can develop your own!

Canary Queries

Benchmarks can be quite pervasive and have an impact on normal operations, so for that reason they are typically scheduled infrequently (for example, once a month or upon a significant change to the system). An alternative or supplementary approach to system performance monitoring is to schedule more regular *canary queries*.

Canary queries are sample queries that you run frequently to measure system responsiveness and throughput. You then look for outlier results from these queries (abnormally long elapsed times) as an indication that the system may be under stress or there may be an issue (such as nodes becoming unavailable).

The term "canary query" stems from the practice of taking canaries into coal mines. If the canaries died, miners were alerted to the build-up of dangerous gases. Canary queries are common on data warehouse platforms. Although there is no strict guidance on what a canary query should consist of, it is generally accepted that you should make the query something succinct and that itself does not put a load on the system.

Performance Monitoring Solutions

Monitoring solutions (such as Ganglia) can be used to capture canary query results, enabling you to visualize results over time. There are also cloud-based monitoring solutions such as Datadog (www.datadoghq.com/) that enable you to collect and send metrics remotely and build dashboards and alerts (if a metric is outside a specific range, for instance).

Datadog has a library of community contributed "integrations" that capture specific data for popular open source projects such as HDFS, YARN, Kafka, Cassandra, and other popular big data projects.

Importantly, Datadog has an integration for Spark (http://docs.datadoghq.com/integrations/spark/) that collects metrics about Spark tasks, jobs, and stages. A sample Datadog dashboard using Spark metrics collected by Datadog is shown in Figure 24.3.

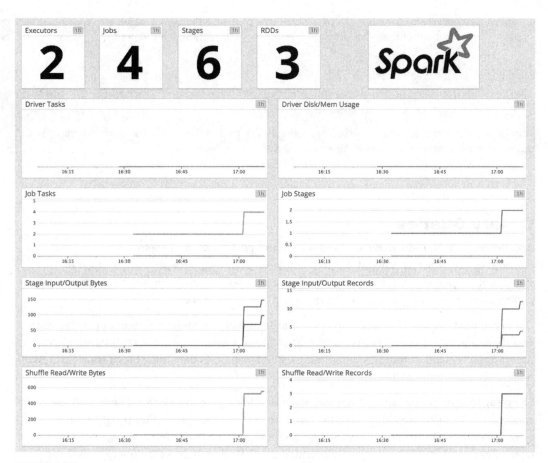

FIGURE 24.3
DataDog Spark integration.

Application Development Best Practices

In this section, I will run through some tips, techniques, and considerations to optimize your Spark applications. I have already introduced you to some of these concepts throughout the course of this book, but they are worth revisiting.

Application Development Optimizations

The Spark runtime framework will generally do its best to optimize stages and tasks within a Spark application. However, as a developer, there are many optimizations you can do that may make a significant performance difference. I discuss some of these in the following sections.

Filter Early, Filter Often

It sounds obvious, but filtering nonrequired records or fields early in your application can have a significant impact on performance. Big data (particularly event data, log data, or sensor data) is often characterized by a low "signal-to-noise" ratio. Filtering out "noise" early saves processing cycles, IO, and storage in subsequent stages. `filter` transformations can be used to remove unneeded records, whereas `map` transformations can be used to project only required fields in an RDD. These operations should be performed before operations that may invoke a shuffle such as `reduceByKey` or `groupByKey`. They should also be used before and after a `join` operation. These small changes can make the difference between hours and minutes or minutes and seconds.

Performing Associative Operations

Associative operations such as sum and count are common requirements when programming in Spark, you have seen numerous examples of these operations throughout this book. Oftentimes, on distributed, partitioned datasets, these associative key value operations may involve a shuffle. Typically, the `join`, `cogroup`, and transformations that have the *By* or *ByKey* in their name (such as `groupByKey` or `reduceByKey`) can involve a shuffle. This is not necessarily a bad thing because it is often required. However, if you need to perform a shuffle with the ultimate objective of performing an associative operation (counting occurrences of a key for instance), there are different approaches that can provide very different performance outcomes.

The best example of this is the difference between using `groupByKey` versus using `reduceByKey` to perform a `sum` or `count` operation. Both operations can be used to achieve the same result. However, if you are grouping by a key on a partitioned or distributed dataset solely for the purposes of aggregating values for each key, `reduceByKey` will generally be a better approach.

`reduceByKey` will combine values for each key prior to any required shuffle operation, thereby reducing the amount of data sent over the network and reducing the computation and memory requirements for tasks in the next stage. Consider the two code examples shown in Listing 24.2. Both will provide the same result.

LISTING 24.2   Associative Operations in Spark

```python
rdd.map(lambda x: (x[0],1)) \
  .groupByKey() \
  .mapValues(lambda x: sum(x)) \
  .collect()

# preferred method
rdd.map(lambda x: (x[0],1)) \
  .reduceByKey(lambda x, y: x + y) \
  .collect()
```

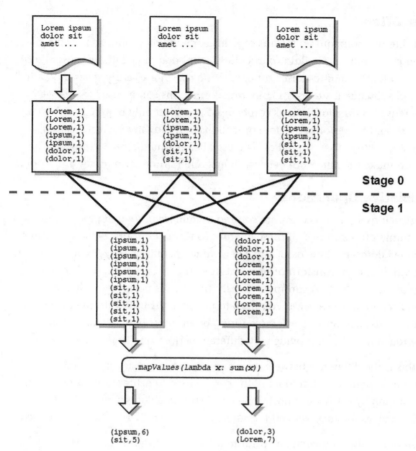

FIGURE 24.4
groupByKey for an associative operation.

Figure 24.4 depicts the groupByKey implementation. Contrast this with Figure 24.5, which shows the functionally equivalent reduceByKey implementation.

As you can see from the preceding figures, reduceByKey performs a local combine before shuffling the data.

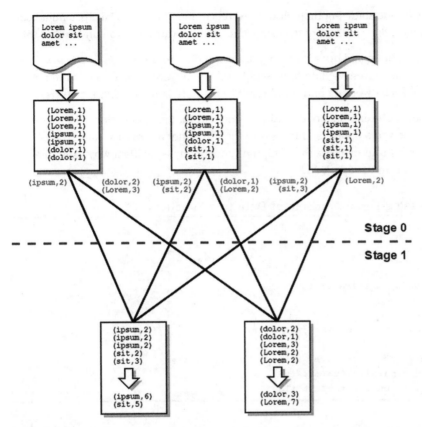

FIGURE 24.5
reduceByKey for an associative operation.

Some other alternatives to groupByKey are combineByKey, which can be used if the inputs and outputs to your reduce function are different, and foldByKey, which will perform an associative operation providing a zero value. Additional functions to consider include treeReduce, treeAggregate, and aggregateByKey. You can find more information and examples of these transformations in the Spark API documentation.

Functions and Closures

Recall our discussions on functions and closures in **Hour 8, "Getting Started with Scala"** and **Hour 9, "Functional Programming with Python"** regarding Scala and Python respectively. Functions are sent to executors in a Spark cluster enclosing all bound and free variables.

This is an enabler of efficient, shared-nothing distributed processing. It can also be a potential issue that impacts performance (and stability) at the same time. It's important that you understand this.

A key example of issues that could arise is passing too much data to a function in a Spark application. This will cause excessive data to be sent to the application executors at runtime, which will result in excess network IO and could result in memory issues on Spark workers.

Listing 24.3 shows a fictitious example of declaring a function that encloses a large object and then passing that function to a Spark map transformation. A better alternative shown is to parallelize the large object and then use the data in a functionally equivalent way using the available transformations in the Spark API.

LISTING 24.3   Passing Large Amounts of Data to a Function

```
. . .

massive_list = [...]
def big_fn(x):
    # function enclosing massive_list
    . . .
. . .
rdd.map(lambda x: big_fn(x)).saveAsTextFile...

# parallelize data which would have otherwise been enclosed
massive_list_rdd = sc.parallelize(massive_list)
rdd.join(massive_list_rdd).saveAsTextFile...
```

Similarly, a better approach for smaller objects may be to use the `broadcast` method to create a broadcast variable as I had discussed in **Hour 12, "Advanced Spark Programming"** (recall that broadcast variables are distributed using an efficient peer-to-peer sharing protocol based on BitTorrent).

Collecting Data

`collect` and `take` are useful functions in Spark. Recall that these are actions that will trigger evaluation of your RDD, including its entire lineage. When executing `collect`, ALL resultant records from the RDD will be returned to the driver from the executors on which the final tasks in the lineage are executed. For large datasets, this can be in gigabytes or terabytes orders of magnitude. This can not only create unnecessary network IO, but in many cases, can result in exceptions if there is insufficient memory on the driver host to store the collected objects.

`take(n)` or `takeSample` are better options if you just need to inspect the output data. If the transformation is part of an ETL routine, the best practice would be to save the dataset to a filesystem (such as HDFS) or a database (such as Teradata, Cassandra, and so on).

The key point here is not to bring too much data back to the driver if it's not absolutely required.

Serialization and Spark Performance

I first introduced serialization for RDDs in **Hour 11, "Using RDDs: Caching, Persistence, and Output."** Recall that serialization is the process of packaging an object into a "wire transfer" format so the object can be sent across the network or read in by a process. Serialization makes subsequent reading of the object more efficient. Deserialization is the inverse process.

Serialization for persisted objects can save memory, reduce bandwidth, and improve read operations. There is, of course, a trade-off when using serialization for RDD storage because writing serialized objects will typically take longer than nonserialized objects, but the trade-off may pay dividends. Serialized RDD storage can be achieved using the `persist(storageLevel=StorageLevel.MEMORY_ONLY_SER)` or the `cache` methods. `MEMORY_ONLY_SER` is actually the default for PySpark `cache` and `persist` methods. Recall that this does not take effect until the first action is performed against the RDD.

If you are using the Scala or Java APIs with Spark, you may also benefit by using *Kryo* serialization as opposed to the default Java serialization used by Spark, which is typically slower than alternative serialization libraries. Note that this may have minimal impact in PySpark applications, but may be worth trying. Listing 24.4 shows you how to enable Kryo serialization.

LISTING 24.4 Using Kryo Serialization

```
conf.set("spark.serializer", "org.apache.spark.serializer.KryoSerializer")
```

System, Configuration, or Job Submission Optimizations

In addition to application development optimizations, there are also some system-wide or platform changes that can also provide substantial increases to performance and throughput.

Optimizing Parallelism

I will discuss parallelism and its relation to distributed input data as well as Spark partitions in the next section, "**Optimizing Partitions**." However, a configuration parameter that could be beneficial to set at an application level or using `spark-defaults.conf` is the `spark.default.parallelism` setting.

`spark.default.parallelism` specifies the default number of RDD partitions returned by transformations such as `reduceByKey`, `join`, and `parallelize` where the `numPartitions` argument is not supplied.

Dynamic Allocation

Spark's default runtime behavior is that the executors requested or provisioned for an application are retained for the life of the application. If the application is *long lived* (such as a `pyspark` session or Spark Streaming application), this may not be optimal, particularly if the executors are idle for long periods of time and other applications are unable to get the resources they require.

Dynamic allocation is a property available for Spark applications, where executors can be released back to the cluster resource pool if they are idle for a specified period of time. Dynamic allocation is typically implemented as a system setting to help maximize use of system resources.

LISTING 24.5   Enabling Spark Dynamic Allocation

```
spark.dynamicAllocation.enabled=true
# enables Dynamic Allocation, which is disabled by default
spark.dynamicAllocation.minExecutors=n
# lower bound for the number of executors
spark.dynamicAllocation.maxExecutors=n
# upper bound for the number of executors
spark.dynamicAllocation.executorIdleTimeout=ns
# the time at which an executor will be removed if it has been idle
# defaults to 60s
```

PyPy

PyPy is an alternative Python interpreter and **just-in-time** (JIT) compiler that I had introduced you to in **Hour 9, "Functional Programming with Python."** PyPy's JIT compiler enables Python functions to be run closer to lower-level machine code, making them more efficient and more performant.

PyPy can be used as the Python interpreter for PySpark by designating the pypy binary using the PYSPARK_PYTHON and PYSPARK_DRIVER_PYTHON environment variables, as shown in Listing 24.6.

LISTING 24.6   Using PyPy with PySpark

```
export PYSPARK_PYTHON=/path_to_pypy/pypy
export PYSPARK_DRIVER_PYTHON=/path_to_pypy/pypy
pyspark ...
```

As seen in Figure 24.6, PySpark is now using PyPy as the interpreter.

FIGURE 24.6
PySpark using PyPy.

PyPy is not typically installed by default on most systems, so you will need to download and install this separately, which is beyond the scope of this book. More information is available at http://pypy.org/.

Project Tungsten

A recent adjunct project to Spark named Project Tungsten was announced in 2015. Project Tungsten is designed to implement just-in-time (JIT) compilation for Spark methods and routines, making more efficient use of system resources and lessening the runtime reliance on Java or the Java Virtual Machine (JVM). This in itself eliminates many operations related to the JVM such as Garbage Collection (GC), byte code compilation, and serialization.

Project Tungsten will improve memory and system cache management and exploit the performance features of today's CPUs, GPUs, and compilers. Project Tungsten is an ongoing initiative that will be progressively introduced into the Spark core and Spark SQL engines. Some of this integration had started as far back as version 1.4, but you will see much more incorporation of the improvements enabled by Project Tungsten in versions 2.0 and later of Spark. So watch this space!

Optimizing Partitions

Recall from the discussion in **Hour 12, "Advanced Spark Programming"** that partitioning can have a significant impact on performance, negatively or positively. Here, I revisit partitioning, looking at the detrimental effects of inefficient partitioning and how to avoid these issues.

Inefficient Partitioning

Inefficient partitioning is one of the major contributors to sub-optimal performance in a distributed Spark processing environment. Take a closer look at some of the common causes.

Too Many Small Partitions

Small partitions (or partitions containing a small amount of data) are inefficient as this will result in many small tasks. Often, the overhead of spawning these tasks is greater than the processing required to execute the tasks.

A `filter` operation on a partitioned RDD may result in some partitions being much smaller than others. The solution to this problem is to follow the filter operation with a `repartition` or `coalesce` function (specifying a number less than the input RDD), which will combine small partitions into a fewer number of more appropriately sized partitions.

Recall that the difference between `repartition` and `coalesce` is that `repartition` will always shuffle records if required, whereas `coalesce` accepts a `shuffle` argument that can be set to `False`, avoiding a shuffle. `coalesce` can only be used to reduce the number of partitions, whereas `repartition` can be used to increase or reduce the number of partitions.

Also working with small files in a distributed filesystem will result in small, inefficient partitions as well. This is especially true for filesystems such as HDFS, where blocks form the natural boundary for Spark RDD partitions created from a `textFile` operation, for example. In such cases a block can only be associated with one file object, so a small file results in a small block resulting in a small RDD partition. One option for addressing this issue is to specify the `numPartitions` argument of the `textFile` function, which will specify how many RDD partitions to create from the input data. This is pictured in Figure 24.7.

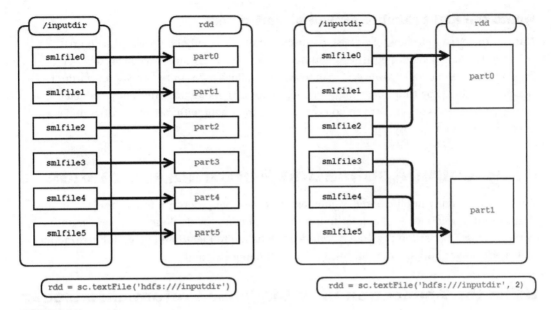

FIGURE 24.7
Optimizing partitions loaded from small files.

The `spark.default.parallelism` configuration property mentioned in the previous section can also be used to designate the desired number of partitions for an RDD.

Large Partitions

Exceptionally large partitions can also cause performance issues. A common cause for large partitions is loading an RDD from one or more large compressed files, compressed using an unsplittable compression format (such as gzip).

Because unsplittable compressed files are not indexed and cannot be split (by definition), the entire file must be processed by one executor. If the uncompressed data size exceeds the memory available to the executor, the partition may be spilled to disk, causing performance issues.

Solutions to this problem include the following:

▶ Avoid using unsplittable compression if possible

▶ Uncompress each file locally (for example, to /tmp) before loading the file into an RDD

▶ `repartition` immediately after the first transformation against the RDD

Moreover, large partitions can also be a result of a shuffle operation using a custom partitioner (such as a month partitioner for a corpus of log data where one month is disproportionately larger than the others). In this case, the solution would be to `repartition` or `coalesce` after the reduce operation using a HashPartitioner.

Whats the Right Number or Size of Partitions?

This is a rhetorical question, or at best, a question that could only be answered with an "it depends." As a general heuristic, if you have fewer partitions than executors, some of the executors will be idle. However, the optimal or "Goldilocks" number or size for partitions is often only found by trial and error. A good practice is to make this an input parameter (or parameters) to your program so you can easily experiment with different values and see what works best for your system or your application.

Diagnosing Application Performance Issues

You have seen many application development practices and programming techniques, in this chapter and throughout the book for that matter, that can provide significant performance improvement. This section provides a simple introduction to identifying potential performance bottlenecks in your application that will help you to address them.

Using the Application UI to Diagnose Performance Issues

The Spark application UI that you have seen throughout this book is probably the most valuable source of information about application performance. The application UI contains detailed information and metrics about tasks, stages, scheduling, storage, and more that can help you in diagnosing performance issues. Recall from our discussions that the application UI is served on port 4040 (or successive ports, if more than one application is running) of the host running the driver for the application. For YARN clusters, the application UI is available via the ApplicationsMaster link in the YARN ResourceManager UI. Take a further look at how you can identify various performance issues using the application UI.

Shuffle and Task Execution Performance

Recall that an *application* consists of one or more *jobs* (as a result of an action such as `saveAsTextFile`, `collect`, or `count`). A job consists of one or more *stages* which consist of one or more *tasks*. Tasks operate against an RDD partition. The first place to look when diagnosing performance issues is to look at the stage summary (from the Stages tab of the application UI). From this tab, you can see the duration of each stage and see the amount of data shuffled (as shown in Figure 24.8).

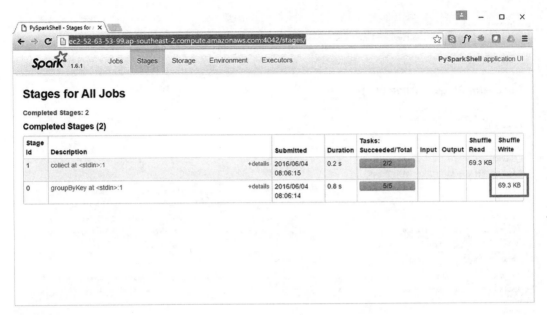

FIGURE 24.8
Spark application UI stage summary.

By clicking on a stage (from the Description column of the Completed Stages table), you can see details for that stage, including the Duration and Write Time for each task in the stage. This is where you may see disparity in the durations or write times of different tasks as shown in Figure 24.9.

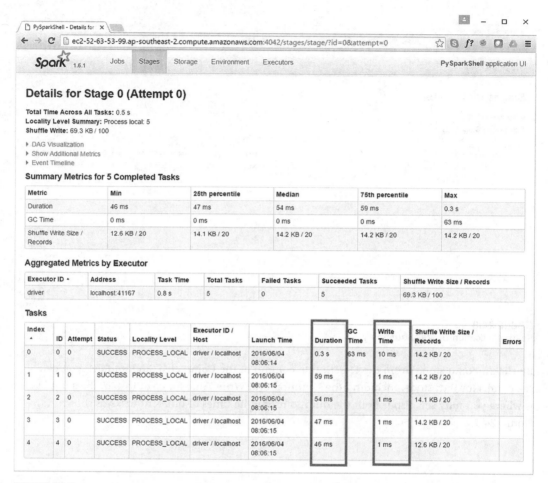

FIGURE 24.9
Spark application UI stage detail—shuffle and task execution information.

The difference in task durations or write times may be an indication of inefficient partitioning, as discussed in the previous section.

Collection Performance

By clicking on the collect stage (Stage 1 as shown in Figure 24.8), you can see metrics related to the collection process, including the records and data size collected, as well as the duration of collection tasks as shown in Figure 24.10.

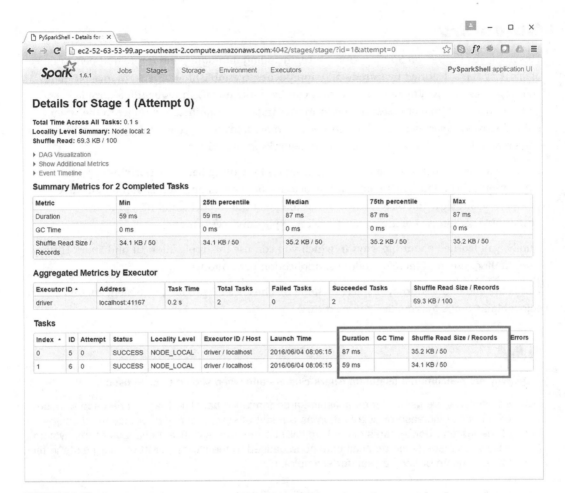

FIGURE 24.10
Spark application UI stage detail—collection information.

Using the Spark History UI to Diagnose Performance Issues

Recall that the application UI is only available during an application's lifetime (which makes it useful for diagnosing issues with running applications). It's useful and sometimes necessary to profile performance of completed applications (completed successfully or otherwise) as well. Recall our introduction to the Spark History Server in **Hour 22, "Monitoring Spark."** The Spark History Server provides us with the same information as the application UI for completed applications. Moreover, you can often use completed application information in the Spark History Server as an indicative benchmark for the same applications currently running.

Summary

This hour was focused on Spark performance, including managing and improving performance of Spark systems. I started by introducing approaches to establishing a performance baseline. You were then exposed to benchmarks that can be run relatively infrequently to profile performance over time or assess the performance impact of significant changes to the system. I also discussed *canary queries*, which can be run more frequently. These queries can indicate that there may be performance issues with or bottlenecks in the cluster.

I discussed several best practice tips and techniques for writing better (performing) Spark applications, including how to optimize associative operations and implement an effective partitioning strategy. You also learned about the potential impact small files or large unsplittable compressed archives can have on application performance.

Finally, you learned about the ways in which you can use the application UI and Spark History Sever to diagnose, and therefore address, application performance issues.

This is the end of our journey! I sincerely hope this has been a productive, beneficial, and enjoyable 24 hours for you. See you next time.

Q&A

Q. Why are benchmarks useful for Spark clusters and when should they be used?

A. Benchmarks are useful for establishing a performance baseline that can be used to assess performance increase or degradation as a result of system changes or increased usage of the system. Benchmarks should typically be run after significant changes to the system have been made (such as additional nodes added to the cluster) or at regular points in time (once a month or once a year, for example).

Q. What are some common causes for small, inefficient partitions and how could you address this?

A. A `filter` operation on a partitioned RDD may result in some partitions being much smaller than others. Also, working with small files in a distributed filesystem will result in small, inefficient partitions as well. An approach to optimizing partitions (and thus optimizing the tasks that will run against these partitions) would be to follow the RDD load or `filter` operation with a `repartition` or `coalesce` operation into a smaller, more optimal number of partitions.

Q. What considerations are there when passing functions (which include other objects or data) to `map` transformations in a Spark application? What are some alternative approaches to consider?

A. Functions passed to `map` transformations will enclose the free and bound variables associated with the function. If these variables involve a large amount of data, this data will be passed from the driver to each executor involved in the application. This could result in excessive network IO and could cause memory issues on the executors. Alternative approaches could be to parallelize the data associated with the function and use RDD transformations, which can take advantage of the parallelized data. Another approach may be to use a broadcast variable, which will transfer the object more efficiently.

Workshop

The workshop contains quiz questions and exercises to help you solidify your understanding of the material covered. Try to answer all questions before looking at the "Answers" section that follows.

Quiz

1. **True or false:** Comprehensive benchmark tests for Spark should be run infrequently, whereas simple canary queries can be run more frequently.

2. What environment variables need to be modified to use PyPy as the Python interpreter for PySpark?

3. What can the `repartition` function be used for that `coalesce` function cannot?

4. **True or false:** The Spark application and Spark History Server user interfaces provide useful information in identifying performance issues.

Answers

1. **True.**

2. `PYSPARK_PYTHON` and `PYSPARK_DRIVER_PYTHON`.

3. `repartition` can be used to increase or reduce the number of partitions. `coalesce` can only be used to reduce the number of partitions.

4. **True.**

Index

Symbols

<- (assignment operator) in R, 344

A

ABC programming language, 166

abstraction, Spark as, 2

access control lists (ACLs), 503

accumulator() method, 266

accumulators, 265–266

  accumulator() method, 266

  custom accumulators, 267

  in DStreams, 331, 340

  usage example, 268–270

  value() method, 266

  warning about, 268

ACLs (access control lists), 503

actions

  aggregate actions, 209

    fold(), 210

    reduce(), 209

  collect(), 207

  count(), 206

  defined, 47, 206

  first(), 208–209

  foreach(), 210–211

    map() transformation versus, 233

  lazy evaluation, 107–108

  on RDDs, 92

  saveAsHadoopFile(), 251–252

  saveAsNewAPIHadoopFile(), 253

  saveAsSequenceFile(), 250

  saveAsTextFile(), 93, 248

  spark-ec2 shell script, 65

  take(), 207–208

  takeSample(), 199

  top(), 208

adjacency lists, 400–401

adjacency matrix, 401–402

aggregation, 209

  fold() method, 210

  foldByKey() method, 217

  groupBy() method, 202, 313–314

  groupByKey() method, 215–216, 233

  reduce() method, 209

P

U

PEARSON